Refugee Workers in
the Indochina Exodus,
1975–1982

ALSO BY LARRY CLINTON THOMPSON

*William Scott Ament and the Boxer Rebellion:
Heroism, Hubris and the "Ideal Missionary"*
(McFarland, 2009)

Refugee Workers in the Indochina Exodus, 1975–1982

Larry Clinton Thompson

McFarland & Company, Inc., Publishers
Jefferson, North Carolina, and London

LIBRARY OF CONGRESS CATALOGUING-IN-PUBLICATION DATA

Thompson, Larry Clinton, 1941–
    Refugee workers in the Indochina exodus, 1975–1982 / Larry Clinton Thompson.
        p.   cm.
    Includes bibliographical references and index.

    ISBN 978-0-7864-4529-5
    softcover : 50# alkaline paper ∞

    1. Refugees — Indochina. 2. Refugees — Government policy — United States. 3. Refugees — Service for — United States. 4. Indochinese — United States — History — 20th century. I. Title.
HV640.5.I5T56   2010
959.704'3086914 — dc22   2010008490

British Library cataloguing data are available

©2010 Larry Clinton Thompson. All rights reserved

No part of this book may be reproduced or transmitted in any form or by any means, electronic or mechanical, including photocopying or recording, or by any information storage and retrieval system, without permission in writing from the publisher.

Cover image: Cambodian woman and children (photograph by Berta Romero); background ©2010 Shutterstock

Manufactured in the United States of America

McFarland & Company, Inc., Publishers
  Box 611, Jefferson, North Carolina 28640
    www.mcfarlandpub.com

For Amy and Chuck
Good Children

Table of Contents

Introduction   1

1. The Dominos Begin to Fall   5
2. Saigon: April 1975   16
3. Cambodia: April 1975   32
4. The Hmong Escape Laos   47
5. Guam: Halfway to America   62
6. Resettlement   75
7. Indochinese Refugees in America   91
8. Leftover Refugees in Thailand   103
9. Before the Deluge   120
10. Cambodia: Holocaust Denial   130
11. Indochina: The Perpetual War   139
12. The Boat People Come Ashore   150
13. Solving the Boat People Crisis   161
14. The Push Back at Preah Vihear   171
15. Sa Kaeo and Khao I Dang Holding Centers   182
16. The Land Bridge and Cambodian Famine   200
17. Being a Refugee   217
18. The End of the Beginning   234

Chapter Notes   249
Bibliography   263
Index   269

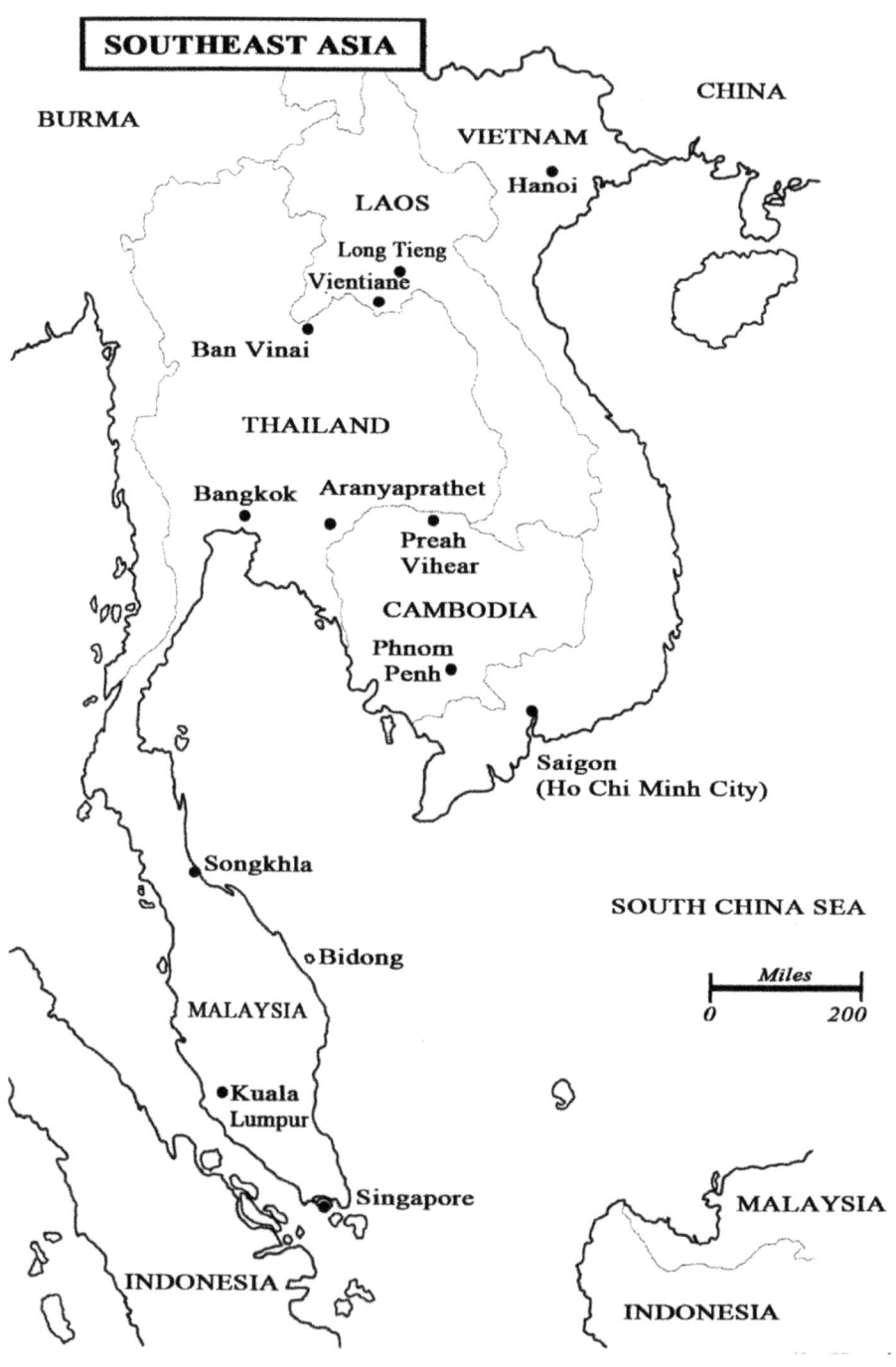

Map adapted from "Emergency Refugee Health Care," US HHS 4, by Kathryn Kelly-Hensley.

INTRODUCTION

The Vietnam War was the most divisive event in American history since the Civil War. The war shattered the faith of many Americans in the honesty of their government and the idealism of their society. The fall of the three Indochinese countries—Vietnam, Cambodia, and Laos—to communist armies in 1975 was the low point of American fortunes during the Cold War. Within a handful of years those fortunes would dramatically change as America emerged reborn and communism sank like a stone.

Not least of the reasons for the rebound of the United States was the sense of national purpose engendered by Indochinese refugees whose flight and rescue not only confirmed in American minds the inherent goodness of their society; but also assuaged their guilt about leaving friends and allies behind when they lost their long, brutal war in Indochina. Imperfectly, and with qualms and controversies, the United States took in 1.3 million Indochinese refugees as new residents in the 25 years following the war, one-half of them during the seven years covered by this book.[1] Few would now dispute that the Indochinese have enriched American life with their intelligence, ambition, and accomplishments.

This is the story of a few people, mostly Americans, who took on the lonely task of helping the people left behind in the aftermath of the Vietnam War. These few kept the nation's interest and sense of obligation to the Indochinese alive while many Americans longed to lapse into amnesia. The refugee workers were mostly irreverent young men and women who found in refugees a labor of love that satisfied their restless idealism. Without their passionate dedication, far fewer Indochinese would be living today in the United States and other countries around the world — or, in fact, living at all. Their work was a life or death endeavor.

Lionel Rosenblatt, one of the main characters of this book, compares the refugee workers in Southeast Asia in the late 1970s to the barnstorming pilots of the early twentieth century. The barnstormers blazed the trail for the aviation industry — but when that industry became established they were relegated to the sidelines. So it was with the pioneering refugee workers. They were individualistic advocates rather than analysts, doers rather than observers, and they led with their hearts. They came from both ends of the political spectrum. Some were die-hard anti-communists who came to refugee work through their experiences with the military, CIA, and State Department; others were leftist peaceniks, longhaired hippies, anti-military, and anti-establishment. They worked together in the monumental endeavor of ensuring the survival of Indochinese refugees. Most of the refugee workers did not achieve fortune or fame, but few would trade their experiences.

The most eloquent comment about the United States and the resettlement of Indochinese refugees was by diplomat Alan Carter, evacuated from the American Embassy in Saigon in April 1975: "It must indeed be the most infrequent of all happenings in the U.S. government to undertake a program with clear-cut goals.... The sense of commitment was unparalleled and the scope of reward unequaled. All the frustration, all the problems, all the dissention and all the bureaucratic warfare were, in the final analysis, over-ridden by purpose, energy, and dedication.... In the end it was the human spirit and not the classic bureaucracy which set the tone and the pace and ensured the ultimate success of the program."[2]

* * *

What we Americans usually call the "Vietnam War" would more accurately be called the "Indochinese War" as it extended to all three Indochinese countries in the 1960s and 1970s. However, I bow to convention in often referring to it as the Vietnam War. What was called the Khmer Republic and Kampuchea, I call by the more familiar name of Cambodia, and I call the people Cambodians. The exception is the Khmer Rouge, as that is the common name for the fanatic and genocidal agrarian communists who ruled Cambodia from 1975 to 1979. The people I call the Hmong were usually called the Meo — a derogatory term — in the 1970s. Hmong is the name by which they are now known and it is their name for themselves. What is today Ho Chi Minh City I have referred to by its old name of Saigon.

The word "Indochinese" itself is a convenient fiction. The three countries making up Indochina share a history of Buddhism, cultural influences from either or both India and China, and French rule from the late 19th century until 1954. All three have tropical monsoon climates with distinct wet and dry seasons, rugged and forested mountains rising to 9,000 feet elevations, and cultivate rice as their main crop and dietary staple. By 1975, all three had been ravaged by war between communism and capitalism — to put the Vietnam War in its simplest ideological terms. The people of the three Indochinese countries, however, speak different languages, write them with different scripts, and have few ties of kinship or affection. In particular, there is a long history of animosity between Vietnam and Cambodia. Moreover, within the boundaries of all three countries are numerous ethnic minorities, diverse in language and culture, similar in the antipathy generally shown them, and returned in kind, by the dominant ethnic group of their respective countries.

Introduction

In 1975, the three Indochinese countries had a geographic area slightly larger than Texas and a population of 56 million. Vietnam, North and South, had 46 million people, Cambodia seven to eight million, and Laos probably less than three million. Vietnam was heavily populated in persons per square mile; Laos and Cambodia were more lightly populated. All three countries were poor and the mass of people depended upon agriculture for a living, although French investment, Chinese commerce, and American military spending had enriched a fortunate minority of the population, especially in Vietnam.

I apologize to the hundreds of dedicated people whose names and accomplishments are recorded only briefly here or not at all. A thorough history of the Indochinese refugee program would easily be three or four times the length of this book. My intention was to write an account of interest to the general reader and highlight the work of key individuals and major events in Southeast Asia and the United States. I am not aware of any other book that has attempted the same. I have relied mostly on the memories of refugees and refugee workers in compiling this story. Their memories sometimes differ in fact and substance, but mistakes and misinterpretations are of course my responsibility. I would like to extend a personal word of thanks to Mac Thompson (no relation) who read and suggested many improvements to the manuscript.

My sources include a dozen large boxes heavy with papers given or loaned me by a large number of people. These consist of government memorandums and reports, State Department telegrams, and other miscellaneous documents, mostly unpublished, that I found in dusty boxes in the basements or attics of former refugee workers. In footnotes I have identified these documents by title and date (if possible) and "author's files" to indicate that they are in my possession. In due course, in cooperation with their owners, I plan to donate these documents to an interested library or archive.

1

THE DOMINOS BEGIN TO FALL

The conquest of South Vietnam was terrible and swift. The first domino, Phuoc Binh, a provincial capital 75 miles from Saigon, fell on January 7, 1975. The small city was of little strategic or tactical importance. What was important for the North Vietnamese Army (NVA) attacking Phuoc Binh and the South Vietnamese defending the city was the reaction of the Americans. In the face of a massive North Vietnamese violation of the 1973 Paris Peace Accords, South Vietnam hoped that the United States would assist in turning back the North. For their part the North Vietnamese dipped a toe in the water to evaluate how boldly they could press their offensive without retaliation from the Americans.

The North Vietnamese attack inflicted heavy casualties on South Vietnam forces and about 3,000 civilians of the 30,000 in Phuoc Binh fled, thus becoming the first refugees of the communist offensive.[1] Many of the escapees were Montagnards—the highland peoples of Vietnam. That thousands of Montagnards had been abandoned in Phuoc Binh to the mercies of the NVA caused little comment, concern, or remorse among higher authorities, American or Vietnamese. A sentiment in both Washington and Saigon was that the Montagnards and the mountainous spine of South Vietnam — one third of the country — were of little strategic importance.

The United States did not come to the rescue of Phuoc Binh. President Gerald Ford stated the American position on January 21. A reporter asked, "Mr. President, are there circumstances in which the U.S. might actively re-enter the Vietnam War?" Ford replied, "I cannot foresee any at the moment."[2]

Phuoc Binh, however, set off an alarm bell for Lionel Rosenblatt, a 31-year-old Foreign Service officer at the Department of State in Washington. Lionel had formerly served in Vietnam. He called a meeting of interested officers to begin contingency planning for evacuating Vietnamese vulnerable to persecution if the North Vietnamese continued their advance. The meeting in January 1975 attracted, among others, Frank Wisner, the most senior of the group and Ken Quinn, a Cambodian expert assigned to the National Security Council. A group of a dozen coalesced around Lionel and met frequently in the State

Department cafeteria. Most of the members of the "lunch group," or "bad boys" as Wisner called them, had served in Vietnam and spoke Vietnamese.[3] Several had Vietnamese wives. They urged their bosses to plan for an evacuation of allies and friends if North Vietnam conquered the South. To stimulate evacuation planning and shake up the establishment, the lunch group circulated a memo with an estimate of one million potential Vietnamese evacuees. Jim Bullington, the Vietnam Desk officer, compiled the estimate. His rationale was that the United States had 17,600 employees on its payroll in South Vietnam.[4] The majority of them would wish to be evacuated. The extended families of Vietnamese numbered about ten for each employee. Employees and families totaled 17,600 multiplied by ten for a total of 176,000 potential evacuees.

Then, there were 93,000 additional Vietnamese who had worked for the United States in the past. Many of them would find it prudent to leave South Vietnam. Ten family members times 93,000 ex-employees is 930,000. Add that to 176,000 for the families of present employees and the total of potential evacuees came to 1.1 million.[5] Thus, the lunch group projected a scenario of one million people wishing to leave Vietnam for their own safety. Even if that estimate proved inflated, the number of evacuees would be large enough to require massive deployment of U.S. resources for transportation and protection. While the lunch group hoped some evacuees would find a home in other countries, the assumption of the group was that most of them would be brought to the United States.

The memo from the lunch group disappeared as if falling into a black hole. Although Washington officials often predicted a bloodbath as a consequence of a North Vietnamese victory, they neglected to focus on the South Vietnamese who would be threatened by the communists and should, from a sense of honor and decency, be helped to leave the country. Later, the lunch group proposed to the Embassy in Saigon that Rosenblatt and others journey out to Saigon to assist in the evacuation. Wisner recalled the response from the Embassy as "thanks, but no thanks."[6] Ambassador Graham Martin in Saigon, a martinet of iron will, would brook no interference from Washington with the management of his Embassy.

* * *

A decade earlier an assistant secretary of defense had written a confidential memorandum quantifying U.S. objectives in South Vietnam: "70 percent — to avoid a humiliating U.S. defeat (to our reputation as a guarantor). 20 percent — to keep SVN (and the adjacent territory) from Chinese hands. 10 percent — to permit the people of SVN to enjoy a better, freer way of life."[7] The admission at this early date that the dominant American objective in the Vietnam War was to avoid a "humiliating defeat" is extraordinary. More than 50,000 Americans would die trying to achieve that objective. The U.S. sought peace with honor for years, with enormous bloodshed, before declaring mission

1. The Dominos Begin to Fall

accomplished on January 27, 1973. On that date, the United States, its ally the Republic of South Vietnam, and North Vietnam and its ally, the Provisional Revolutionary Government of South Vietnam (the Viet Cong), signed a peace accord in Paris. The main points of the agreement were a ceasefire, an end to the U.S. combat role in Vietnam, and the return of prisoners of war (POWs). By that time the return of American POWs had become the driving force of U.S. policy.

The United States complied with the accord by withdrawing all American military personnel — except Marine guards, attaches, and a military assistance group — from South Vietnam, and ceased providing air support to its South Vietnamese allies. North Vietnam returned 591 American POWs. About 25 percent of South Vietnam, mostly lightly populated areas in the Central Highlands, remained under communist control and fighting between North and South continued unabated over large areas of contested land. North Vietnam benefited most from the agreement. South Vietnam gained nothing except promises from President Richard Nixon and Secretary of State Henry Kissinger of continued economic and military assistance and American intervention should North Vietnam break the accord. The other two Indochinese countries, Laos and Cambodia, were also embroiled in the war, but did not participate in the negotiations.

With the POWs returned, the flagging American resolve to continue propping up South Vietnam with military force evaporated. What Nixon and Kissinger hoped to achieve was breathing space to enable the government of South Vietnam to survive. But Nixon's presidency was destroyed by the Watergate scandal and Vice President Gerald M. Ford replaced him. Congress passed laws to limit the president's war-making powers and cut back the administration's aid requests for Vietnam.

After signing the peace accord, the North Vietnamese spent nearly two years preparing for a renewed war. In December 1974, they were ready and launched their dry-season offensive against Phuoc Binh. This coincided with a decision by the Khmer Rouge communists in Cambodia to intensify their attacks against the American-supported government of Lon Nol. The third Indochinese country, Laos, was relatively peaceful at the end of 1974, but the events in Vietnam and Cambodia would soon re-ignite the war between the communist Pathet Lao and their North Vietnamese allies against the faltering Royal Lao government.

The debacle at Phuoc Binh was followed by two months of preparation and positioning by North Vietnam. On March 10, 1975, three divisions of the NVA struck at the highland city of Ban Me Thout. The city fell the next day. Other locations in the Central Highlands also came under attack. On March 14, President Thieu made the decision to abandon not only Ban Me Thout Province but also the highland provinces of Kontum and Pleiku. Thieu's thinking was that by abandoning the highlands the South Vietnamese could reinforce their garrisons in coastal cities such as Danang and Hue. The decision to withdraw was kept secret and not shared with the Montagnard allies of South Vietnam. The Montagnards were abandoned.

The withdrawal of the South Vietnamese army from the highlands was a rout that acquired the name "Convoy of Tears." "Panic set in," said Colonel David Hackworth, America's most decorated soldier in Vietnam. "The worst thing that can happen to an army is fear takes over.... That's what happened here. We had this raging inferno of fear that just got the generals, the colonels, the majors, the sergeants, the privates—everybody was running. It was just chaos...."[8] Many South Vietnamese officers gathered their families and flew away in helicopters, leaving the soldiers without leaders. The soldiers deserted and civilians fled in panic joining the soldiers on an old highway road leading out of Pleiku and going south and east toward the coast to what the refugees hoped would be safety. "Those fleeing the communists in Vietnam resorted to each and every kind of conveyance: buses, tanks, trucks, armored personnel carriers, private cars.... The vehicles were jammed with soldiers and overloaded with family members—from babes in arms to aged grandparents—packed on top or clinging to the side. Many of those who fell off were crushed by the vehicle behind." Thousands more fled on foot. The NVA kept the defenseless mob under attack for 15 days.[9] Tens of thousands died.

Vietnamese were accustomed to leaving their homes behind and fleeing for safety. By 1973, about 10 million people—one half the population of South Vietnam—had been displaced by war since 1954.[10] Saigon had swelled from a population of one to three million due to an influx of refugees. Vietnamese learned from hard experience to run for their lives. "We are all experts at escaping," said one Vietnamese woman.[11]

With the conquest of the highlands complete, the NVA's focus shifted to the heavily populated coast. The panic and retreat continued. On March 25, Hue, the ancient capital of Vietnam, fell without resistance and the same day North Vietnamese shelled Danang, South Vietnam's second largest city. So rapid was the NVA's advance that Dan Oderdorfer, a reporter for *The Washington Post*, shouted over the phone to an editor seeking clarification of the situation, "Hell, we're losing provinces between editions."[12]

On March 25 American Consul Albert Francis in Danang ordered the evacuation of Consulate dependents, non-essential personnel, and other Americans living in the city. Within two or three days the Vietnamese residents and the remnants of the South Vietnamese army were clamoring to flee. The Consulate staff assisted Vietnamese employees and associates to leave, at first by plane on Air America to Cam Ranh Bay and Saigon. The U.S. Navy sent five tugboats towing six barges and several civilian transports to assist as the NVA closed in on the city. The owners of hundreds of Vietnamese vessels took matters into their own hands and steamed and sailed out of the bay heading south or out to sea where the transport vessels waited to take them to Saigon and other cities.

1. The Dominos Begin to Fall

One of the last flights out of Danang was an Air America C-47. Air America was the CIA–owned airline that flew ancient planes to every corner of Southeast Asia. Consul Francis was badly beaten trying to keep it from being mobbed by soldiers. The sea evacuation was equally brutal and chaotic. The plan was to load up the barges with American and Vietnamese evacuees and tow them to the transport vessels waiting offshore. The biggest barge, *Big Blue*, had at least 7,500 people aboard. "People were getting out to the barges on basket boats, rowboats, sampans. People were shot trying to board the barges and thrown into the sea."[13] The people on the barges waited for days before they were finally towed out to sea and loaded onto the waiting ships. In the meantime they suffered from hunger, thirst, robbery, and outright murder by Vietnamese soldiers aboard. Russell Mott, an American official, counted 75 bodies on the *Big Blue*, mostly women with small children.[14] Nobody knows how many people died in Danang but about 70,000 Vietnamese were evacuated. Most of them went to Cam Ranh, the huge but now mostly abandoned U.S. air and naval base.

Panic spread south down the coast from Danang. At Nha Trang the Vietnamese general and his senior officers left their posts and boarded a helicopter to Saigon on April 1, leaving behind a leaderless mob of soldiers. The Embassy ordered the evacuation of the American Consulate that same afternoon. The Americans got out safely in unseemly haste, leaving more than 100 of their Vietnamese employees behind. Two days later, the South Vietnamese army abandoned Cam Ranh in the now-typical pattern: the senior officers fled their posts. A young Vietnamese captain told of the stirring speech by a general to his officers begging them to resist the advance of the communists. "You men have to stay in this spot to fight the communists. United to fight! Don't divide; don't separate! ... Don't run! Fight! Use your weapons! Fight until your last drop of blood!"[15] Then, the general abandoned his officers and men — to end up a refugee in America. Evacuees from Danang who thought they had found safety in Cam Ranh were on the run again. This time most headed for Saigon.

Most of the American diplomats and other Embassy personnel in Vietnam were courageous and inventive, but they were a handful, not nearly enough to deal with a large evacuation even if the planning and execution had been of the highest order. To have organized an effective evacuation in Danang, Nha Trang, or later Saigon, would have required a well-planned military operation with thousands of U.S. military personnel on the ground and hundreds of aircraft and boats. Such a massive effort was unacceptable to the United States, its people and government exhausted by the long, losing effort in Vietnam. Washington was in denial. The U.S civilians and military on the ground in Vietnam did the best they could without reinforcements other than a few additional Marines called in to provide security. So cautious was the U.S. that naval ships to assist in the evacuation remained 40 miles offshore. The U.S. feared that to advance any closer would spark combat.

Despite the chaos in the north, at the end of March Saigon was still "astonishingly normal. Not a shot had been fired; everything was functioning. The restaurants were going; the schools were going. The Embassy club was operating normally. You could still get fantastic meals for relatively little money. Excellent French wines. The international airlines were flying in and out ... the American Embassy has a two hour lunch period."[16] Ambassador Martin still believed, as did Secretary Kissinger, that the situation might be salvaged by a deal with North Vietnam for the creation of a coalition government in the South and that South Vietnam could continue to exist as a country truncated by the loss of the highlands and the northern half of its territory. However, North Vietnam, after a war of 30 years, was not going to be deterred; it called its blitzkrieg the "Ho Chi Minh Campaign" and adopted the slogan, "Lightning speed, daring, and more daring." It declared it would celebrate victory over South Vietnam by the May 19 birth date of Ho Chi Minh.[17] It didn't take that long.

The most perceptive — and pessimistic — analysis was by the lunch group's Ken Quinn who, after a visit to Vietnam, wrote that South Vietnam "may be totally defeated in as little as three weeks.... The morale of the army and civilian population is critically low and bordering on national despair. Fear of the communists is widespread, and people from all walks of life are now searching for a way to flee the country. Panic is seemingly just below the surface."[18] Quinn was dead on. South Vietnam was defeated in three weeks and four days. Quinn, who was married to a Vietnamese, told his in-laws to leave Vietnam as soon as possible. He set up an informal evacuation program with political officer Lacey Wright and CIA analyst Frank Snepp. The three compiled lists of Vietnamese who should be offered the opportunity to evacuate.[19]

The experiences in Danang and Nha Trang frightened the Americans. "One overriding lesson ... was that the element most to be feared was panic," said Ambassador Graham Martin. "Panic could be the killer, the destroyer, the paralyzing agent which had to be avoided at all costs.... Closely allied was the concern that we did not so conduct ourselves that our allies, feeling abandoned, would turn on the American presence in our last days. A great deal of coolness was imperative."[20] Cool Martin was—to the point of indifference to the concern of some Embassy officers and the lunch group in Washington who worried that the evacuation would be too little and too late to get vulnerable Vietnamese out of the country.

Martin's coolness in Saigon was echoed by failure to conceive of a refugee crisis in Washington. That Washington had not focused on the potential number of evacuees from Vietnam was brought home at Congressional hearings on April 8 and 9, 1975. One half of Vietnam had been lost by that time and hundreds of thousands of people had fled the communist advance. But, testifying before Congress, John Thomas, the director of the Intergovernmental Committee on European Migration (ICEM), discounted the notion that a large number of Vietnamese would be evacuated. "I have seen figures, 100,000, 200,000 — I do not think it is going to be anything like that at all...."

"Do you have a figure in mind?" asked Congressman Hamilton Fish.

"Well, I would say for starters if you had something about in the neighborhood of possibility of ... something in the neighborhood of 10,000 to 15,000."[21]

Washington refused to look at the realities of the situation until April 14 when Assistant Secretary of State Phillip C. Habib ventured an estimate that Vietnamese evacuees could "get up to a figure of 150,000."[22] Congress, the administration, and the American people finally confronted the reality that a military disaster and refugee crisis was at hand. Under Secretary of State Lawrence Eagleburger asked Clay McManaway to set up a task force for the evacuation of Vietnam. McManaway established his headquarters in the windowless seventh-floor Operations Center and virtually lived there for the next two months.[23] On April 18, President Ford announced the creation of an Interagency Task Force (IATF) to "coordinate all activities concerning evacuation of U.S. citizens, Vietnamese citizens, and third country nationals from Vietnam and refugee and resettlement problems relating to the Vietnam conflict." McManaway became the operations officer of the IATF. The members of Rosenblatt's lunch group were folded into its operations.[24]

* * *

President Thieu's decision to abandon the highlands isolated nearly one million Montagnards. The Montagnards, or Dega, were not a single people. Rather, they belonged to about 30 tribes— ethnic groups— speaking languages from two language families: Mon-Khmer, related to Cambodian, and Austronesian, widely spoken all over the Pacific. The Montagnards comprised only five percent of the population of South Vietnam but they were spread over nearly one half of the land area. They lived in the rugged beauty of the Central Highlands, which rose to elevations of more than 8,000 feet and sloped down to meet the sea near the narrow waist of the country. The ethnic Vietnamese lived on the narrow strips of flat land along the coast and in the broad swampy Mekong delta south of Saigon. Relations between the Vietnamese lowlanders and the Montagnard highlanders were never good. The Vietnamese were Buddhist and Catholic, merchants, urban dwellers and farmers of irrigated paddy rice. The Montagnards practiced shifting cultivation and were traditionally animists, although many became Protestant Christians. The lowland Vietnamese called the Montagnards "Moi," which translates as "savage," or "nguoi sac toc," "colored people."

Like the French before them, many Americans serving in Vietnam discovered a bond with the Montagnards. An American missionary would say of them, "They're completely different from the Vietnamese in both language and culture. With the Bru [a Montagnard ethnic group] I feel completely at home. They are generally open and straightforward. They say exactly what they think and feel. But I've always felt the Vietnamese operate on two levels. The Bru say of them, 'The Vietnamese have two gall bladders.'"[25]

The bond between the Montagnards and the U.S. Special Forces, the famous Green Berets, was strong. "These Americans did more than just unload a bunch of antique firearms on the tribesmen, they came to stay and to lead and live with the people in the villages. They patrolled with them, lived with them, died with them. They learned to speak Jarai and Rhade and all the other languages. They were initiated into tribal brotherhood, formally and informally. In the highlands in the '60s you could see American soldiers with half a dozen tribal bracelets on a wrist, each signifying a personal alliance and commitment to a tribe."[26]

By 1975 the Green Berets had long been withdrawn from the highlands; the Montagnards were left high and dry and neither the government of South Vietnam nor the United States gave them any further consideration. Strategists argued that the highlands were unimportant for the survival of South Vietnam. That the U.S.'s staunchest allies in Vietnam lived in the highlands seemed never to have entered their calculations.

On April 4, six Montagnard leaders met with three American Embassy officers, including Colonel George D. Jacobson, special assistant to the ambassador for field operations, and described their plight. In the previous 20 days all their traditional lands had been lost, said the Montagnards, and only 6,000 of them were still in areas controlled by South Vietnam. One thousand of those escapees had worked with the Americans and were targeted for execution. Because of reports that Montagnards had helped the NVA, "both sides are now out to kill the Montagnards and now we ask for the protection of the U.S. government."

The delegation asked the Embassy to evacuate the one thousand targeted Montagnards who could "carry on the fight outside the country to attract the attention of the United Nations and the World to the genocide of the Montagnard race." The Montagnards offered to continue the fight against the North Vietnamese with U.S. assistance. "The Montagnard people are not afraid to die. They will fight to regain their lands but they do not want to be killed senselessly like animals. If the GVN [Government of Vietnam] intends to take back the highlands we will fight, if they let us, but if they don't hold ... we want your protection so that the seed of the Montagnard will not disappear."[27]

Jacobson, overburdened by the rapid march of events, asked that minutes of the meeting be prepared "for his study" and said that he "would need time to consider" the issues before responding. When the dust settled, the number of Montagnards evacuated from Vietnam in 1975 was a handful—probably fewer than one hundred. In a time of crisis, it was all too easy to forget the small, quiet people of the highlands.

* * *

While the conquests of the NVA brought Vietnam back onto the front pages of newspapers, Americans were mostly indifferent to events in Vietnam. On April 11, *The Washington Post* reported that 70 percent of Americans believed that the fall of Cambodia and Vietnam to the communists was inevitable, but 82 percent opposed further military aid to Vietnam and only 44 percent favored humanitarian aid.[28] Americans did not want to remember the divisive war that had brought their country closer to anarchy than it had been at any time since the Civil War. *Time* magazine in its April 28, 1975, edition — published while the conquest of Saigon was underway — featured tennis player Jimmy Connors on its cover.

Americans working in Vietnam felt a profound sense of shame and embarrassment. This was coupled with a sinking spirit, verging on superstition, that the United States of America was jinxed at every turn, condemned to failure, and fast sinking into mediocrity. In Washington, Lionel Rosenblatt became increasingly restive as it became obvious that the government of South Vietnam would soon be no more. Lionel was a State Department veteran of Vietnam, assigned there in 1967 fresh out of Harvard and a bored year at Stanford Law School. He worked in what became the controversial anti-insurgency Phoenix program in the highlands. Lionel was a far cry in character from the stereotypical analytical, careful-to-a-fault diplomat. Swarthy, crowned by bushy black hair and sporting a formidable mustache, Lionel had charm, easy confidence, an ability to make things happen, and a rashness that often got him into trouble. Trouble came soon. Assigned to a provincial town, he worked with Vietnamese police and military officers to investigate corruption by a Vietnamese colonel, but the young American learned that struggle against the pervasive corruption in the South Vietnamese government had unpleasant consequences. One night, an intruder with explosives strapped around his waist was shot and killed outside the fenced compound where Lionel and his Vietnamese colleagues lived. Rosenblatt, the likely target, was quickly evacuated by helicopter to Saigon. He attributed his survival to loyal Vietnamese guards and he vowed that he would help protect the men who had saved him.

Lionel was highly regarded in the State Department for his quick intelligence and formidable powers of persuasion. In mid–April 1975, however, with the end of South Vietnam in sight, he took the unconventional decision to return to Saigon and pay back the debt he had incurred to the Vietnamese who saved his life in 1967. He would find his friends and former colleagues and offer them the opportunity to leave the country before the North Vietnamese took over. Another Foreign Service officer, Craig Johnstone, a veteran of five years in Vietnam, joined him. Craig later told a *Washington Post* reporter that his Vietnamese friends were "honorable decent men who deserve to be saved.... They were good friends and they worked with us. To leave them and not express the slightest concern was repugnant to us.... We knew Saigon, we spoke Vietnamese, and we felt we could do something."[29]

Rosenblatt and Johnstone were alarmed at the paucity of planning in the U.S. government for an evacuation of vulnerable Vietnamese. Telegrams between Secretary of State Henry Kissinger and Ambassador Graham Martin in Saigon showed that the priorities of the United States government rested with preventing panic, projecting American steadfastness, and hoping for a last minute avoidance of defeat. A top secret telegram from Kissinger to Martin on April 17 described the Washington mood: "You should know that at the WSAG [Washington Special Action Group] meeting today there was almost no support for the evacuation of Vietnamese, and for the use of American force to help protect any evacuation. The sentiment of our military, DOD [Department of Defense] civilians and CIA colleagues was to get out fast and now.

"In addition ... the Congressional situation is fast getting out of hand. Our task — yours and mine — is to prevent panic both in Saigon and Washington...."[30]

On that same day, April 17, Kissinger instructed Ambassador Martin to speed up the draw down of non-essential American personnel. Not until April 22 did the Department of Justice announce that it would waive immigration requirements to "parole" 130,000 Vietnamese refugees into the U.S.[31] With this authority, a team of Embassy personnel working at Tan Son Nhut airport speeded up their already-established evacuation procedures. April 22 was also the date on which the last major battle of the war between North and South ended at Xuan Loc, 40 miles north of Saigon. The NVA won and the road to Saigon was open. At this point the NVA halted its advance to refit and catch its breath before the final push on Saigon. The halt may also have been to permit the Americans time to evacuate the capital. North Vietnam was careful not to risk bringing the Americans back into the war. Thus, prudence dictated that causing American casualties was to be avoided. The NVA pause for a few days allowed the evacuation to swing into high gear in Saigon.

On April 23, transport aircraft began arriving in Saigon from U.S. bases in the Philippines at the rate of two per hour and evacuees over the next week totaled 7,000 per day. That same day, President Ford himself put the denouement on the American presence in Vietnam. Kissinger and Martin were still maneuvering to prevent an abject defeat. Ford, however, had given up. He told his aide Robert Hartmann that he wanted to tell Americans that it was time to "think about the future" rather than the past. "Why don't you just say that?" Hartman asked.

"Ford's first reaction was to worry if Kissinger would agree.... On Ford's staff, however, the feeling was growing that Kissinger's advice reflected more concern for his own reputation than the President's." Ford instructed Hartmann come up with a few lines to insert into the text of a speech at the very last moment.[32]

Ford made his speech at the field house of Tulane University in New Orleans. After introductory remarks, he turned to the war in Vietnam.

"Today, America can regain the sense of pride that existed before Vietnam. But it cannot be achieved by fighting a war that is finished as far as America is concerned." Thunderous applause from the audience of students followed those lines.

He continued. "We, of course, are saddened indeed by the events in Indochina. But these events, tragic as they are, portend neither the end of the world nor of America's leadership in the world.... Let us resolve tonight to rediscover the old virtues of confidence and self-reliance and capability that distinguished our forefathers two centuries ago."[33]

Ford told the American people it was time to heal the internal wounds the United States had suffered in the long agony of the Vietnam War. Meanwhile, Lionel and Craig, fearing that their Vietnamese friends would be left behind in the evacuation and taking matters into their own hands—defying a prohibition of unauthorized travel to Vietnam by the State Department—had flown to Saigon.

2

SAIGON: APRIL 1975

Lionel Rosenblatt and Craig Johnstone arrived in Saigon on April 22, 1975, on one of the last scheduled Pan American flights to the city, now coming under siege by the North Vietnamese Army. A flight attendant told Lionel that she had drawn up her will before the flight and that 200 Pan Am pilots and attendants had turned down the dubious honor of flying to Saigon. Only 58 passengers were on the giant 747, most en route, as were Lionel and Craig, to rescue Vietnamese friends, wives, mistresses, or children. Three Vietnamese women, wives of Americans, were going back in a desperate bid to get their families out of the country. Lionel's advice to them was "guard your American passports with your lives, because those passports are all that will distinguish you from a horde of Vietnamese trying to escape the country." He would always wonder whether any of the women succeeded or were trapped when the North Vietnamese captured the city.[1]

Lionel and Craig calculated that they could sneak into Saigon for a few days, put Vietnamese friends and colleagues on evacuation flights, and nobody in the State Department would be the wiser. On arriving, Lionel first contacted Nguyen Thi Hue.* Hue was Catholic and spoke English. Her family had fled twice from the communists. Hue worked for the American Embassy, helping Vietnamese displaced by the war. She was smart, experienced, and vulnerable, but not at all certain that she wanted to leave Vietnam. The Embassy had told her that parents and children were eligible for evacuation along with the employee, but Hue was unmarried, had no children and her parents were dead. However, she had three sisters and three brothers and their children, whom she was unwilling to leave behind. The family had tried to leave Vietnam a few days earlier. A brother had purchased a boat, but as they were preparing to set out to sea, the government confiscated the boat. Now they were stuck and Hue was agonizing over whether she should leave Vietnam or stay with her family. The call from Lionel resolved her doubts. She agreed to help him and he agreed to get all her family out of Vietnam.[2]

*Vietnamese names consist of the family, middle, and given name in that order. Usually a person is referred to by his given name. Some Vietnamese reverse their names to Anglicize them.

2. Saigon

Rosenblatt and Johnstone next telephoned a friend in the Embassy, political officer Joe McBride, to get help and advice. McBride responded with astonishment, "What are you doing here?" Only hours earlier an angry deputy chief of mission had scoured the political section looking for anyone who had had contact with Rosenblatt and Johnstone. They were ordered to report "personally to the DCM," McBride's boss, when the two appeared. Rosenblatt and Johnstone if found, McBride believed, would be bundled onto the next airplane and sent home.

Now alerted that they were fugitives from their own government, Lionel and Craig went underground. McBride advised them to contact Jim Eckes at Continental Airlines, which had been ferrying American soldiers and government officials to and from Vietnam for years.[3] Eckes was accommodating. He saw that the end was near. He gave them shoeboxes full of soon-to-be-worthless Vietnamese currency and a Volkswagen van for transportation. He also assigned to them an employee, a female driver named Huu. In a country of delicate, graceful, and gracious women Huu was an anomaly. She was built like a linebacker, and was frank, outspoken, and a fearless and aggressive driver — just the person they needed for their desperate enterprise. Huu extracted from them a promise of seats on an evacuation plane for her brother and herself.

With secrecy advisable, Lionel took the heart-wrenching step of shaving off his bushy mustache in an attempt at disguise. Johnstone and he then telephoned Vietnamese friends they wanted to help evacuate and arranged meetings in the downtown Catholic cathedral. The two Americans quickly briefed the Vietnamese. "You should consider leaving as you may be in danger when the North Vietnamese conquer Saigon. We'll help you if you want to go. You have five minutes to make up your mind." The Americans could not promise the Vietnamese that they would go to the United States, only that they would be flown out of the country. "We did not attempt to persuade the Vietnamese to leave," said Rosenblatt. "We emphasized it was their decision. What we tried to do was give them a realistic picture of their options."[4]

Some of the Vietnamese were still optimistic. "There's plenty of time," they said. "Can we decide later? Perhaps in a couple of months?" Rosenblatt and Johnstone told them that Saigon would be overrun in days.

One father, a policeman, wanted to go but was frightened. "People going to America are rich and speak English. I have no money; I am uneducated. What's going to happen to us? My family and I might starve." Lionel took a twenty-dollar bill out of his pocket, gave it to the man and told him, "I can't tell you that life will be easy for you if you leave Vietnam. I don't know what will happen to you. But I will give you my personal guarantee that you won't starve. Take this money — and if you're ever hungry I'll send you more." The father took the twenty and nodded that they would leave.

Once a family decided in favor of evacuation, Lionel and Craig told them to pack a single bag each and arranged a rendezvous. Huu crammed as many evacuees as possible into the VW van and one of the two Americans rode along to Tan San Nhut airport. They anticipated problems getting through the gates guarded by Vietnamese soldiers. A white face, even in those last days, might still be an asset. At the gates of the airport, discipline was breaking down. Many soldiers were drunk or frantic as they realized the Americans and many of their countrymen were leaving while they were left behind to defend a collapsing country. Rosenblatt, Johnstone, Huu, and their charges cajoled their way past the guards with false ID cards and handfuls of money.

Their next step was the paperwork to permit the Vietnamese to board the U.S. military aircraft now leaving the airport regularly. The Embassy had set up an evacuation center called "Dodge City" in a gymnasium at Tan Son Nhut. Embassy officers such as Ken Moorefield worked in the gymnasium, interviewing and processing evacuees—both Americans (more than 5,000 American civilians lived in Saigon) and Vietnamese. Vietnamese had to establish their bona fides. If their names were not on one of the lists of eligible evacuees, they were interviewed. Senior South Vietnamese officials and their families were almost automatically eligible; employees and former employees of the United States and their families were eligible; employees of American companies or institutions closely associated with the United States were usually approved for evacuation. Vietnamese vouched for by American officials—often including their girlfriends, maids, favorite taxi drivers, and in one case musicians in a rock band—were often accepted by sympathetic interviewers. Once approved, the Vietnamese were given a flimsy document bearing the all-important consular seal of the United States. With document in hand, the Vietnamese were lined up to await evacuation flights. One hundred and eighty was the usual number of passengers crammed aboard C-130 transports. Thousands upon thousands of Vietnamese were wandering the streets of Saigon looking for any American who could help them get the stamped document. Most would be unsuccessful. The few thousand who made it inside the airport were the lucky ones.

Rosenblatt and Johnstone set up a parallel evacuation program in the nearby bowling alley. From sympathetic friends in Dodge City they borrowed papers, stamps, and seals. After completing and stamping the documents, Lionel and Craig accompanied their evacuees to the gymnasium and infiltrated them into the long lines of Vietnamese waiting for evacuation flights.

The bowling alley was a hive of activity. "Vietnamese are sprawled everywhere, sleeping on the lanes.... An American construction worker, wearing a cowboy hat, fills out papers for his young Vietnamese companion, who is hanging onto his arm, a worried look on her face. She is obviously a bar girl, her miniskirt hiked high over her glossy patent leather boots. An Embassy official is explaining that it is only necessary that the man sign an affidavit for her support in the United States in order for her to leave the country. He knows full well that this girl is not the only one leaving in this manner. Several enterprising

Americans have signed for entire bars full of girls.... Outside the bowling alley, thousands of Vietnamese and Americans mill about the area. The lucky ones sit in the shade of an occasional roof or tree, their belongings piled around them. Many are well dressed. Some are wealthy, their suitcases curiously heavy from the gold bars they obtained from Chinese merchants in return for their money and valuables."[5]

In three days of intense work, brief naps beneath the racks of tenpins in the bowling alley, and growing tension in Saigon, Rosenblatt and Johnstone evacuated about 200 people. On April 25, they decided it was time to leave. Jim Eckes put them on a planeload of Vietnamese he was evacuating on a Continental flight to Singapore.

* * *

Ron Rogers was another American who came back to Saigon in those last days. Ron worked for the U.S. Agency for International Development (USAID). He first lived in Saigon in 1963 when the Americans were still optimistic about the expanding war. He was now working in Bangkok although he continued to visit Vietnam frequently to manage development projects. On April 24, he was flying to Bangkok from Manila and his Air France flight made a scheduled stop in Saigon. Ron didn't fully credit the reports he had heard about the imminent fall of the country and decided to disembark, take a look for himself, and continue on to Bangkok on a flight the next day.

As he got off the airplane he saw several black Citroën sedans—the official car for senior Vietnamese officials—parked on the tarmac. Vietnamese in business suits got out of each car and scampered up the runway onto the airplane, leaving the cars and drivers behind without a backward look. Ron thought of rats deserting a sinking ship and mused, "Why am I getting off this airplane, while they are getting on?" Traveling around the city the following day confirmed the doom he felt at the airport. Saigon was falling. His option to leave closed. Air France cancelled its flights. He was stuck in Saigon.[6] Rather than call on the Embassy to put him on an evacuation flight, he gathered together Vietnamese friends and colleagues and helped them complete their paperwork to get out.

* * *

The first rockets hit Saigon on the morning of Sunday, April 27, killing six people and announcing loudly that the communist armies were on the outskirts of the city. The rockets were the final confirmation that Saigon would not long stand.

Creativity was the watchword those last few days for Vietnamese who wanted to leave and Americans who wanted to help them. Al Topping, manager of Pan American Airlines in Saigon, adopted 61 Vietnamese employees and 250 of their family members. Then he loaded the Vietnamese into buses, talked — and bribed — his way past the guards at the airport, and loaded his adopted family onto a Pan American 747. They crammed the Vietnamese into seats, bathrooms and aisles, leaving Saigon with 463 passengers. This was Pan Am's last flight from Vietnam.[7] Another creative American was former Green Beret Ellis Edwards of Oklahoma City. He acquired a stack of the evacuation forms from the Embassy and passed them out to hundreds of Vietnamese friends, listing himself and another Oklahoman, General Clyde Watts, as sponsors.[8]

Duong Cong Son, called Sonnie, a 16-year-old girl, told a typical story. Her father was a mechanic and when it became clear that the communists would soon capture Saigon he asked Sonnie and her brother to leave the country. As with many Vietnamese, he believed that their departure would only be temporary. "When the communists had been driven out, I could come back," thought Sonnie. Sonnie had a friend at the American Embassy who put them on a list of eligible evacuees.

On April 28, Sonnie and her brother were picked up by a bus and taken to the airport. At the airport "was a big field with people in it and the sun was very hot and we had to stand in the field. There were loudspeakers paging people and there were vendors trying to sell food and drinks and trying to exchange money. Lots of people were crying and lots of them were shocked because they didn't really know what was happening." Some people said they had been waiting for a week.

Sonnie and her brother were summoned over the loudspeaker and they entered the terminal building. They were searched and they joined a long line. Two Vietnamese military policemen looked over the line to prevent deserters from leaving. "I thought it would be a nice airplane," continued Sonnie. "It was a big C-130. We walked up the back ramp. When we got inside we saw there were no seats. We just had to get in and sit on the floor — like sardines. All of a sudden there were explosions.... Then the airplane started to move with the door still open. I was looking out the door and I saw people running around in all directions shooting crazily into the air.... People all around me on the airplane started screaming and crying.... They didn't even have time to close the door. They just went down the runway with the door open and then we took off.

"We landed at the Philippines at Clark Field. We were taken to a big warehouse. The Americans had everything very well organized for us. We were surprised.

"They put us all in a big waiting area. We had televisions and beds. The next day they told us the communists had taken over Saigon. We were shocked. 'What about our family?' we asked. 'What about Mom and Dad?'"[9]

Vietnamese were trying everything to get out of Vietnam. One Vietnamese pilot loaded his wife and children aboard a small Cessna and headed for the American aircraft carriers offshore. He buzzed the aircraft carrier and dropped a woman's pocketbook on the deck. Inside was a note: "I have my family with our four children aboard. I cannot ditch, please help me!"

The carrier signaled to the Cessna to attempt a landing and the pilot brought it in, set it down perfectly and skidded to a stop a few feet from the end of the deck. The crew of the carrier cheered the virtuoso piloting.[10]

Tran Ngoc Ann — more commonly her name is spelled "Anh"— was less lucky. She was a secretary at the American Embassy and a widow and she readily obtained seats on an evacuation flight for herself and her three young children. She put her children on an evacuation plane, but she went to collect her parents to try to get them out. She was too late.

"When I returned to the Embassy, the crowds trying to enter were tremendous. There was no way to get in; my father tried to climb over the wall, but he couldn't. I went to the docks to inquire about a boat, but they wanted $5,000 and I didn't have any money. I came home and told my father that there was no way out.... Everyone huddled together and cried."[11] Ann remained in Vietnam, was arrested by the North Vietnamese, spent 18 months in a re-education camp and knew nothing of the fate of her sons for 16 years when she finally learned they were living in California.

* * *

Ambassador Graham Martin is blamed for the tardy, arbitrary, and chaotic evacuation that left many Vietnamese behind. Colonel Harry Summers defended him. "Ambassador Martin was in an impossible position. Martin had to maintain the U.S. support for the South Vietnamese government with the idea that they were going to remain in control and the country was not going to collapse. At the same time, he had to plan to evacuate all of his people in case they did collapse. The dilemma was that if he started to evacuate openly, it would undercut the competence of the Vietnamese government, which was his other mission. So, he was damned if he did and damned if he didn't."[12] For Rosenblatt and others, Martin was indifferent to the Vietnamese who had worked for and supported the U.S. over the long years of the war.

Many of the American civilians and military remaining in Saigon settled into a booze-induced lassitude those last few days. A minority worked around the clock to help Vietnamese escape the country. Shep Lowman was among the State Department officers playing a key role in getting Vietnamese out of the country. Shep was a political officer at the Embassy. He was married to a Vietnamese woman and he had an affinity for Buddhist philosophy and Oriental medicine. His first concern was to persuade his wife Hiep to leave the country. Hiep was reluctant, and their friends were reassured by her presence. "Oh, Hiep," they would say, "you're still here. I guess things are not so bad." Lowman knew things were bad, and he finally persuaded Hiep to leave.

Lowman had another problem with a family member. A sister-in-law was pregnant. "I could see myself sitting at my sister-in-law's bedside waiting for her to deliver the baby," said Shep, "as the North Vietnamese army marched in the door." Propitiously, a comfortable seat on a VIP military aircraft bound for the Philippines became available and Lowman got the pregnant woman on board, seated among a coterie of generals and colonels. She had the baby one day after arriving in the Philippines. Unburdened by family concerns, Lowman then devoted his energies to helping friends and Embassy contacts leave the country.

Lowman telephoned Vietnamese to meet him at a large villa about three blocks from the Embassy. The plan was that mini-buses driven by Embassy officers and Vietnamese employees would pass by the villa and other assembly points around the city and bus the Vietnamese to Tan Son Nhut for departure by air.[13]

That plan was overtaken by events at 3:58 A.M. April 29 when rockets and mortar fire began hitting the airfield. Two Marines, Corporal Charles McMahon, Jr., of Woburn, Massachusetts, and Lance Corporal Darwin Judge of Marshalltown, Iowa, became the last American soldiers to be killed on Vietnamese soil. Two rockets hit the gymnasium at Dodge City, wounding several of the 1,500 Vietnamese waiting for evacuation flights. The rockets and mortars continued and the runways at Tan Son Nhut were declared unsafe for American fixed wing aircraft, partially due to the fear that furious Vietnamese soldiers and police ringing the airport would shoot at any planes. "We want to go too," shouted the Vietnamese guards, shooting their guns into the air.[14] Despite the damage to the runway, Vietnamese Air Force pilots continued to take off, many of them flying their aircraft to safety at U-Tapao airbase in Thailand, others making for the aircraft carriers offshore. U.S. helicopters continued to come into Tan Son Nhut during most of the day to carry away several hundred American military personnel and the Vietnamese already inside Fort Dodge, but an alternative had to be sought to evacuate thousands of Vietnamese waiting in the doomed city and clustered around the American Embassy.

Embassy officers quickly arranged the alternative. A tugboat crew and four large barges were hired to load up Vietnamese and ferry them to American warships and merchant vessels waiting offshore. The buses that had been taking Vietnamese to Tan Son Nhut would now be diverted to take people to the barges.

Lowman opened this day — his last in Vietnam — by putting on a suit and tie on the theory that it might make him appear to be a person of importance and help him in dealing with the Vietnamese. Shep went to the villa near the Embassy. He had invited about 100 Vietnamese; 600 were waiting, crowded into every room and standing in the courtyard. Shep shouted to the assembled group that buses would come to the villa to take them to barges on the Saigon River to travel to the American naval vessels waiting offshore. But no buses arrived and, as afternoon came, the streets of Saigon became chaotic. The sounds of artillery hitting the airport and the outskirts were frequent. Finally,

2. Saigon

Lowman told the Vietnamese to make their own way to the barges at the docks. "But perhaps if we wait until tomorrow the buses will come," said a woman.

"No, I don't think so," answered Shep. "You better go now." Many people gave up and went home.[15]

Shep's villa was not the only place the buses missed. One hundred and eighty Vietnamese employees and their family members waited at the office of the United States Information Service (USIS), but the buses never came and the USIS director, Alan Carter, who was not aware of the barges, advised his employees to go home and cover their tracks to avoid being identified by the North Vietnamese as U.S. government employees.

Although they missed Shep Lowman's villa and the USIS office building that last day, Embassy officers such as Ken Moorefield and Joe McBride drove vans around Saigon and picked up Vietnamese at designated spots and took them to the barges. McBride also wore a suit this day, a blue and white striped seersucker that would become sweat-soaked and filthy as his day rolled on. He drove a 15-passenger mini-van and crammed 30 Vietnamese onboard for each trip to the docks. McBride had to stop several times to siphon gasoline out of abandoned cars as the gas stations in Saigon were closed. At his collection point, Joe tried to control a crowd of frantic Vietnamese pushing their way onto his van. A Vietnamese man about 45 years old, by appearance an army officer in mufti, offered to help. All afternoon long, the officer organized the Vietnamese waiting for the buses, lining them up and sorting out bystanders and curiosity seekers from legitimate evacuees—those in the greatest danger and those who had stuck out their necks against the communists.

"It facilitated the job," says McBride. "I couldn't organize people and drive at the same time. This man did the organizing and he did it straight. At the end of the day, I told him this was my last run to the barges and that I had seats on the bus for him and his family. He said his family was too large and all of them wouldn't fit on the bus. I said I would take all those I could. He said no, thanks. He would stay. As I drove away, I waved and shouted thank you. He saluted. I never saw him again. I never knew his name." The man with no name was one of the heroes of the Saigon evacuation.

The barges left the docks late that afternoon to navigate down the Saigon River and into the open sea to rendezvous with the American fleet offshore. The barges had about 6,000 people aboard, but could have taken 20,000 if more had shown up or had been able to force or bribe their way through the police at the gate. As night was falling, McBride drove back to the Embassy and abandoned his van. He worked his way through the Vietnamese crowd surrounding the Embassy, assuring them quietly in Vietnamese, "Don't worry, there'll be enough helicopters for everyone."

The American Marines at the gate refused to let him enter the Embassy. They were afraid that if they opened the gates for Joe the crowd would storm the Embassy. Joe ran into a friend outside the Embassy, a Vietnamese who had

Vietnamese refugees arrive on a U.S. carrier after being evacuated by helicopter from Saigon. April 1975. (National Archives)

previously been a professor at the University of California at Berkeley. "Thank heavens, Joe," said the man. "I know you can get me in." Not so, Joe answered sadly. He couldn't get into the Embassy himself. He advised the friend to go to the docks and try to get on a barge. He never heard of him again.

Joe was wrong that he wouldn't get inside the Embassy — but not by much. Later, Embassy security officers yelled at him over the fence to go to a small side entrance of the Embassy compound. He was asked to "inconspicuously collect" about 30 Americans and their Vietnamese families and shepherd them to the side entrance. Once there, two American Marines, one black and one white, came over the wall into the crowd and pushed and pulled Joe and his 30 lucky Vietnamese toward the armored gate. The Vietnamese were permitted inside one by one as four other Marines pushed the gate shut on the crowd as each passed through. It took half an hour for all to enter; Joe and the two Marines were the last. The two Marines who had gone over the wall to help Joe received commendation medals and were later assigned, as a reward to the U.S. Mission, to the UN in New York.

2. Saigon

Joe was exhausted; he stripped off his sweat-soaked seersucker suit, threw away the tie, wrung out his pants, shirt and coat and put them back on. As he was doing so, about 50 Marines in full combat gear charged out of the Embassy building and deployed at the gate. They were planning to go over the wall and to hold the crowd back while forty CIA Vietnamese "assets" would be escorted into the Embassy for evacuation. The sally into the crowd by the Marines, however, was cancelled at the last minute by the Embassy DCM, who also told McBride, "I don't want you bringing any more Vietnamese into here either." The people outside the Embassy, hoping to be allowed to enter, would be abandoned.

There was nothing left to do. As he walked upstairs, he saw that floor after floor of the Embassy was empty. A few Americans were trashing their offices, determined to leave nothing usable behind. Most of the remaining Americans were grouped outside the Ambassador's office, some of them drowning their sorrows with whiskey. McBride waited his turn, and just before he left Ambassador Martin told him, "I know what you've been doing in the streets and I want to thank you." Joe went to the roof, climbed on a helicopter, and flew away from Vietnam. He saw a city with fires in the outskirts. Lightning flashed from heavy clouds above the helicopter, flares loosed by American fighter planes lit the sky, tracers from ground fire crisscrossed to the north, where 150,000 North Vietnamese soldiers were poised to enter the city.[16]

* * *

Among the worst of the tragic stories of the last days of Saigon is that of Frank Snepp, a CIA analyst in the Embassy and later the author of a book about the evacuation, whose Vietnamese girlfriend came to a sad end. "About forty-eight hours before the end I got a call from a Vietnamese woman I had had an on-and-off relationship with since my first year in Vietnam.... Near the end of 1974 she showed up at my door with a year-old baby boy. I believe it was my own child. So just before the collapse she called and said, 'You've got to evacuate me because the Communists will kill me for running around with an American and having an American child.' I was working on another report for the ambassador so I said, 'Look, Mai Ly, call me back in an hour. I'll do what I can to get you out of the country.'

She said, 'You better because if you don't I'm going to kill myself and this child.' She called back in an hour or so and I was briefing the ambassador and missed the call. On the last day I saw a policeman who knew her and asked him to find out where she was. He sent word back to me that she had killed herself and the kid. I've never been able to verify it, but as I came off the roof of the embassy I was overwhelmed with this numbing guilt. I was focused on trying to persuade a recalcitrant ambassador to pull the plug on the American commitment and I, too, had forgotten that lives were at stake. I should have been out there getting this woman and child out of the country. I had basically become what so many Americans became in Vietnam — all there to do the job but forgetting the human stakes."[17]

* * *

April 30, 1975, dawned hot in Saigon with thin, high, gray clouds. The air was fresh. A thunderstorm during the night heralded the arrival of the monsoon. The calm of the morning air was scarred by tracers from anti-aircraft guns crisscrossing the sky. At the northern edge of the city a column of North Vietnamese tanks rumbled across a bridge and began looking for its objective, the presidential palace. The tank commander was lost. He stopped the column to ask directions from a civilian. Photographer Hoang Van Cuong climbed onto the tank and pointed it in the direction of the palace. "The soldiers were very happy, and they welcomed me as a journalist."[18] The streets in downtown Saigon were quiet, strewn with military uniforms and equipment abandoned by South Vietnamese soldiers but empty of traffic and people — except near the American Embassy.

During the last 24 hours thousands of South Vietnamese had milled and pushed and forced their way through the gates and climbed over the fences around the Embassy. Ken Moorefield recalled: "Hundreds of Vietnamese had swarmed over the walls and were looting the warehouse, the offices, the snack bar. Some were driving embassy cars around and around in almost a maniacal frenzy. On the other side of the walls, crowds were shouting chants against the U.S., celebrating the imminent victory of the communists. In the distance, our jets were still flying cover, chased by tracer rounds."[19]

All the previous afternoon and evening helicopters had come to the Embassy from the American fleet stationed offshore in the South China Sea. Big Chinooks landed in the Embassy parking lot to load up Vietnamese and the smaller Sea Knights landed on the roof of the six-story Embassy building to carry Americans to safety. Now, as day broke, while the looters still raged in the streets and through much of the Embassy compound, only 11 American Marines on the rooftop and 420 non–Americans in an interior courtyard of the Embassy were still waiting to leave. Most of the 420 were Vietnamese employees of the U.S. government, but also waiting in the line were South Korean diplomats and intelligence agents, a German priest, and a Vietnamese fire brigade which had volunteered to stay until the last in case they were needed to fight fires.

During the night Colonel Harry Summers and Captain Stuart Herrington had organized the Vietnamese into "sticks" of 60 persons each, the capacity of each evacuation helicopter. All night long they circulated through the crowd shouting reassuring words, "We're not going to leave you."[20] They believed what they were saying, but before dawn an order came from Washington that all Americans were to leave and the evacuation was to be terminated. The last officials of American Embassy Saigon boarded evacuation helicopters and left the Vietnamese, the South Koreans, the German priest, and 11 Marines behind. The Marines retreated to the roof and barricaded the doors as angry Vietnamese surged into the Embassy building and tried to break down the doors leading to the roof. The Marines waited ... and waited. If another helicopter didn't come they decided they would go down fighting — no surrender, *semper fi* and die.[21]

And then, as the sun rose higher and the heat of the day radiated from the concrete walls of the Embassy, came the chop-chop of a distant helicopter. At 7:51 A.M., a CH-46 Sea Knight from the USS *Okinawa* landed on the roof. The last Marines scrambled on board and the Sea Knight lifted off, struggling to gain altitude over the bends of the Saigon River and then out over the sea to the fleet. A thousand boats of every size and description, from aircraft carriers to sampans and fishing junks dotted the ocean. Many were overloaded with Vietnamese who had journeyed out to meet the American ships rather than wait and hope to be evacuated.

The Marines were the last official Americans to leave Vietnam. Their departure ended the United States' participation in the longest and most divisive foreign war of its history. The American era in the Vietnam War lasted 14 years and cost 58,000 American and between one and three million Vietnamese lives. At 10:20 that morning, the government of South Vietnam announced its surrender on the radio. At noon, the North Vietnamese announced that Saigon had been renamed Ho Chi Minh City and the flag of the Provisional Revolutionary Government of South Vietnam was raised over the presidential palace.

When they talked about the last days before the fall of Saigon to the North Vietnamese Army, the Americans spoke of shame. Major James Kean, the last Marine officer on the Embassy roof said, "Most of all we were ashamed. How did the United States of America get itself in a position where we had to tuck tail and run?"[22] Colonel Summers was more emphatic and personal. "I was so damn mad I couldn't see straight ... I don't think in any other case in my life have I ever lied to anybody ... and that hurt. And, it still hurts. I pledged my word that I would be the last one to leave that Embassy and everyone would get out, and so did the other people who were with me. And then, we were ordered out in spite of it, and that still gripes me. We shouldn't have done that."[23]

The Vietnamese called the last days "the running."

* * *

For most Americans, the helicopter ride from the Embassy ended the story of their evacuation, but for some the ordeal was just beginning. Ron Rogers escaped that last night from Saigon, but he ended up floating around the South China Sea on a merchant vessel. Ron got 17 Vietnamese friends onto evacuation flights and took three more to the Embassy on the morning of April 29 as the end drew near. They joined the hundreds of people awaiting evacuation in a long line snaking around the Embassy swimming pool. Rogers and his three Vietnamese friends finally boarded a helicopter at 9:30 P.M., which took them to the *Midway*. Ron, along with the Vietnamese, was offloaded onto one of the carrier's small boats and transported to a nearby merchant vessel. The sea around the naval flotilla and merchant vessels was crowded with overloaded fishing boats and other small craft. The people on the boats begged to be taken aboard the naval vessels and merchant ships. "The Navy ignored the small boats and refused to board their passengers," Ron recalled. "In response the Vietnamese began to set their boats on fire and throw themselves into the sea. The Navy had the choice of leaving the Vietnamese to die or picking them up. It picked them up. My most vivid memory of the evacuation," said Rogers, "was the sight of a dozen burning boats amidst the flotilla of rescue ships on a hot tropical night in the South China Sea. That captured for me the desperation of the Vietnamese."

Along with 5,000 Vietnamese and 53 Americans and other foreigners, Ron was crammed into the cargo holds of the merchant vessel. "The hold was bare. The first challenge was finding a space to call your own; the second was to find cardboard to put over the ribbed metal plates on the deck. With cardboard padding you could sit or sleep on the deck without the metal ribs cutting into your back and scorching your skin. The third challenge was to find a tin can or another container for water. The temperature in the hold was 107 degrees." Up on the main deck makeshift toilets and salt-water showers were rigged up behind canvas walls with the sewage flowing down wooden troughs to the sea. The lines for the toilets and showers were always long. Drinking water came from a hose hanging into the hold from the main deck. C-rations, the diet of soldiers in the field, were distributed. "We were always hot, thirsty, and hungry. Sleeping on the metal decks of the hold was difficult. We spent as much time as possible up on the main deck of the freighter under canvas awnings set up to provide shade. The holds were a mass of humanity. Tin cans and cardboard were at a premium. Many of the Vietnamese aboard were soldiers. They shouted and threatened to storm the ship to protest the shortage of water. Half a dozen American Marines on board shot their pistols in the air to impose order and additional Marines were brought on board to maintain security."

Instructions were shouted down to the inhabitants of each of the holds that they should elect an English-speaking leader. Ron was elected for his hold. His charges included a motley group of Americans and other foreigners who had lived in Saigon during the war years. His responsibilities were to keep order within his hold, distribute C-rations, and bring problems to the attention of the crew and Marines. Ron's position had one highly valued perquisite: Every morning the leaders met on the bridge with the officers and Marines running the ship. Along the way was a water fountain dispensing chilled water. A few sips of cold water from that fountain were a luxury Ron looked forward to.

Ron's most difficult job was to ensure that C-rations were distributed equitably to everyone in his hold. Frightened and insecure people tried to grab more than their share of food. The weak, the elderly, and the very young were at risk. Nor were Vietnamese the only offenders. A gang of Americans stole boxes of C-rations. Vietnamese soldiers intervened and a fight broke out. Ron had to negotiate the return of the C-rations from the outnumbered Americans and quiet the infuriated Vietnamese.

Rogers and his 5,000 colleagues spent five days on the ship. On May 4, they docked at Subic Bay Naval Base in the Philippines. American authorities came on board. Ron and the other Americans were questioned, their identities and citizenship established, and they were allowed to get off the ship. The Vietnamese stayed on the ship and spent another week in passage to Guam. After disembarking, Ron was taken by helicopter to Manila and to the Enrico Hotel where the Embassy had reserved rooms for American evacuees. "It was heaven," he recalls. "The bellboy took me up to my air-conditioned room and asked if there was anything he could do for me. All I could think of was cold beer and I ordered two San Miguels and drank them in the bathtub as I washed off a week's accumulation of dirt and sweat." A day later he was on an airplane back to Bangkok.

Ron Rogers did not get a hero's welcome. When he reported for work, the director and deputy director of his office berated him for the better part of an hour for his "irresponsibility" and "being absent without leave." His participation in the evacuation, he was told, reflected poorly on his professional reputation and judgment.

Rogers would soon leave Bangkok for a new posting in Afghanistan, his USAID career in Southeast Asia over. He would never forget the cavalier attitude of his superiors in Bangkok toward the Vietnamese and his only regret was that he did not assist more people to escape from Saigon. "I should have passed out evacuation forms like giving candy to kids," he said in retrospect.[24]

* * *

The number of Vietnamese who fled Vietnam in March and April 1975 totaled 130,000. About one-half were evacuated by the United States and one-half left by their own means. Practically none of those who left the country were Montagnards, the highland ethnic groups. The Montagnards had suffered the heaviest casualties and greatest hardships of any people in Vietnam. A Montagnard leader estimated that 200,000 of a total Montagnard population of about one million had been killed, 150,000 were in refugee camps, and 85 percent of their villages had been destroyed.[25] Furthermore, their landscape had been ravaged by the herbicide "Agent Orange" sprayed by the U.S. to destroy forests that might harbor communist soldiers.

A few Montagnards gathered with their families at a villa on April 28 to be evacuated. No buses came. Touneh Han Tho and his family made their way to a U.S. military office where they boarded a helicopter and were transported out to the carrier *Midway*. Navy officers confiscated the ancient Cham swords that Han Tho carried with him as family treasures. Ethnologist Gerald Hickey later wrote letters to the Navy Department to ask that the swords be returned. The Navy said they had been thrown overboard. Hickey did not believe that.[26]

Fraud and theft were common by both Vietnamese and Americans in those last days. Wealthy Vietnamese bribed their way on board the evacuation flights. American con men extorted money from Vietnamese with false promises. Embassy officer Peter Tomsen commented to a military officer that a crisis "brings out the best and worst" in people. The officer said, "I'd put it differently. The pressure shows who the pricks are."[27]

* * *

Most of the Embassy officers involved in the evacuation went on to conventional careers. Lionel Rosenblatt did not. Despite his Harvard education, he was not a stereotypical diplomat. The son of a peripatetic nuclear scientist, he spent two years of his childhood in Israel but most of it moving from place to place in the United States. "My best friend in the sixth grade was black," he said, "but that wasn't remarkable because I was the only white kid in my class." His tastes in music were the heartbreak tunes of Hank Williams and Patsy Cline; in fancy restaurants he was wont to call for a bottle of ketchup to season his food; his hot-weather footwear of choice were plastic shower shoes; and the place he loved most in the world was a primitive Maine cabin without running water or electricity—but it had a telephone, for it is impossible to visualize Rosenblatt without a telephone to his ear, barking away about the subject that was to obsess him: refugees. He cited two influences for his passion: the movie *Casablanca*, which showed him the hopelessness of people trapped in a dangerous situation and the novel *The Ugly American*, which gave him a vision of how America might act to fulfill its best humanitarian instincts.

Rosenblatt had conviction and charisma—and courage. At Harvard he had been one of only five students to enroll in a flight training program in the Army Reserve Officers Training Corps (ROTC) and he briefly contemplated becoming a military pilot. The great majority of his classmates were fiercely anti-military and anti–Vietnam war. And he was genuine—even his many enemies would allow him that. "Enthusiastic, irascible, idealistic, generous, untiring, guilt-ridden and fanatic" was how one detractor characterized him—but four of those seven adjectives are favorable.[28] Rosenblatt took on a cause with ingenuity and bulldog intensity.

A lesson for Americans in the fall of Saigon is that history judges kindly those who put humanity ahead of politics and policy. Contrast Rosenblatt and Johnstone's experience in evacuating 200 Vietnamese with that of Alan Carter, the head of the United States Information Service (USIS) in Saigon. When it came time to think about evacuating USIS's Vietnamese employees, Carter followed the rules. As instructed, he submitted to the Embassy a list of his employees and the members of their families; he assembled all the evacuees at the appointed time and place, and he and his employees waited for a bus that never came to take them to the airport or the barges. Carter finally got out; most of his 180 USIS employees and their families were left behind.

Years later Carter was still white with anger. "Only one episode marks me with embarrassment, rage, and shame and that is the final days of Vietnam. In the last couple days, I never woke up at my villa without a line of Vietnamese out front. I never went to my office without finding a line of people waiting to see me. Those scenes were some of the most wrenching of my life. Here were grown men falling on their knees begging me to get them and/or their families out. I kept saying that I couldn't because we'd been instructed not to while other components of the Embassy were using forged documents to do just that."[29] Carter trusted the system; Rosenblatt, Johnstone, and others did not.

* * *

President Gerald R. Ford summed up the last days of Saigon. "April 1975 was indeed the cruelest month. The passage of time has not dulled the ache of those days, the saddest of my public life. I pray that no future American President is ever faced with the grim options that confronted me as the military situation on the ground deteriorates ... mediating between those who wanted an early exit and others who would go down with all flags flying ... running a desperate race against the clock to rescue as many people as we could before enemy shelling destroyed airport runways ... followed by the heartbreaking realization that, as refugees streamed out onto those runways, we were left with only one alternative — a final evacuation by helicopter from the roof of the U.S. Embassy.

We did the best we could; history will judge whether we could have done better."[30]

3

CAMBODIA: APRIL 1975

Yvette Pierpaoli said of World War II: "I liked the bombings, they were the only time when anyone took care of me ... during the run for the shelter, my mother took me in her arms and I made myself light so she could carry me longer. The rest of the time, I didn't even exist."[1] The daughter of Italian immigrants to France—"macaronis," they were called—Yvette grew up in poverty.

Friendless and unhappy as a child, Yvette retreated into a fantasy world. Her obsession became the faraway country of Cambodia: "I walked, amazed in a dream country ... the river of Tonle Sap, in blossom with golden lotus, and the temples of Angkor.... Here people live in serenity—they know nothing of the words spite, regret, woe."[2] She grew up beautiful with the contradictions of a precocious street gamine, a shrewd manipulator, a quick mind who could talk her way out of any situation, superstitious, and prone to instant—sometimes mistaken—judgments. She hated injustice, hypocrisy, marriage, French intellectuals, and social and bureaucratic niceties. A constellation of ordinary genes lined up to give her unforgettable character and talent.

Yvette made it to her land of dreams in 1967, carrying in her arms her newly-born daughter, Manou, fathered by a Cambodian man she had met in Paris. Her belongings were a few clothes, diapers, a bottle of perfume, and a copy of *Lord Jim*, her favorite novel. Her idealistic notions of Cambodia were almost accurate in those days—especially for the foreigners who lived in the capital city of Phnom Penh. To *farangs*[3] (Europeans and Americans) Cambodia was an idyllic country of indolent, contented peasants, Buddhist temples, emerald-green rice paddies and muddy fish-filled waterways, spiced with an overlay of urban French culture. An American diplomat's wife reflected nostalgically: "In late 1963, when we first arrived in Phnom Penh, the city was peaceful and pleasant. The streets were clean: modern garbage trucks ... made daily rounds; the curbstones lining the main streets and tree-shaded boulevards were frequently whitewashed. The famed ruins of Angkor Wat lay in a park-like setting half a day's drive to the northwest, over an excellent asphalt road."[4] As late as 1970, the journalist Henry Kamm said of Phnom Penh that it "was a tranquil capital of mixed French colonial and Chinese shophouse architecture amid much greenery."[5]

Kindly Cambodians kept Manou fed while Yvette tried to make a living in paradise. A friend offered her a commission if she could sell a small airplane. Yvette launched herself as a businesswoman with her customary audacity. Every day she knocked on doors, baby in arms, and tried to sell the airplane. One day a rich Chinese businessman said yes and her business career was launched. She set up an import and export business, trading in Cambodia's basic commodity: rice. A Swiss man, Kurt Furrer, became her partner and they made a good living through Yvette's street smarts and Kurt's business sense.

To the United States, engaged in a cold war with communism, Cambodia seemed like a comic opera starring Prime Minister Prince Norodom Sihanouk. Sihanouk was noted for playing the saxophone, making films, and chasing women. President Richard Nixon called him "flighty." He seemed prouder of his musical talents than of his political leadership, but a Congressional staffer described him as "one of the few leaders in that area who was in close rapport with what was happening in his own country. He was extremely astute, extremely patriotic ... and far, far ... from the image of a playboy."[6] Journalist Donald Kirk also saw Sihanouk in a different light. "More than any other Cambodian leader ... Sihanouk attempted to meet his countrymen, to communicate with them on all levels, to cut through the barriers separating and alienating the poor from the elite and to imbue in them a sense of participation in the country's future."[7] Of his efforts to develop his country, Sihanouk was to say to Yvette and Lionel Rosenblatt years later, "I sent students off to the Soviet Union, China, and North Korea and they came back good capitalists. It was the students that went to the United States and France who became communists."[8]

Cambodia ruled by Sihanouk was a better place than Cambodia ruled by anybody else. In the 1960s, Sihanouk walked a narrow line of neutrality between the warring United States and North Vietnam, but in 1970 the balancing act of the saxophone-playing prince came to an end. General Lon Nol overthrew him in a coup applauded by the urban elite in Phnom Penh. The rural population, 80 percent of Cambodia's seven million people, continued to revere Sihanouk and many regarded him as Cambodia's only legitimate leader.

The U.S. was happy to see Sihanouk gone. Lon Nol ended Cambodia's neutrality and threw in his lot with the United States. Sihanouk responded from Beijing by forming a government in exile which included among its partners a shadowy rural guerilla group called the Khmer Rouge (KR).

* * *

Cambodia was brought into the Vietnam War in 1969 when the United States secretly began bombing North Vietnamese troops within its borders.[9] The NVA had used eastern Cambodia as a safe haven for the rest and relaxation of its troops fighting in Vietnam. Most of the bombing was carried out by huge

B-52s, which dropped their sticks of bombs over large areas in a technique called carpet-bombing. The majority of NVA war supplies reached South Vietnam through Cambodia, either winding through the mountains of Laos on the Ho Chi Minh trail, by highway from the port of Kompong Som, or by boat and barge up the Mekong River from the South China Sea. Americans rationalized the bombing by saying that the United States was not bombing Cambodia, only North Vietnamese troops in Cambodia. It was a distinction that made no difference to the Cambodian farmers who were hit by the bombs.

The Paris Peace Agreement in 1973 did not bring peace to Cambodia nor an end to the bombing. Instead, prohibited by the agreement from military actions in Vietnam, the U.S. intensified the bombing campaign against the North Vietnamese in Cambodia and also the Khmer Rouge, who were becoming stronger. The bombing extended over nearly every square mile of Cambodia east of the Mekong River and much of the country west of the Mekong. Nobody knows how many civilians were killed. Guesses—and that is all they are—range from 50,000 to 600,000 dead Cambodians with 150,000 possibly the best guess.[10] The bombing campaign lasted until August 1973 when Congress forced Nixon and Kissinger to stop it.

The American bombing and the war between the government and the KR caused many Cambodians to flee their farms to seek safety in the cities. Cambodia, a bystander to the Vietnam War, had a fate that became more tragic than that of the principals. Nobody in the U.S. government knew nor cared much what happened to the people of Cambodia. The durable American diplomat, John Negroponte, expressed American indifference: "I never knew much about Cambodia. I don't think anyone did. I am a Vietnam expert, and I always thought of Cambodia as just an adjunct to the whole damn thing. I knew what I had to know, but I didn't get involved in the gory details."[11]

Yvette's idyllic Cambodia became a memory, although the war was good for her business. She represented Continental Air Services—rumored to be owned by the CIA—and oversaw a crew of hard-drinking Americans and Filipinos and opium-smoking Chinese pilots. Along the way she acquired a reputation. An Australian journalist said, "She's an adventurer with a big heart, works for the CIA."[12] Yvette was pleased with the description, although she said she didn't work for the CIA.[13]

One day, Yvette met a Cambodian woman who told her that the Khmer Rouge had invaded her village and killed all the children. Yvette's mostly leftist friends saw the story as right-wing propaganda, but Yvette was convinced "that no actor, even the best, could have described so much horror with such simplicity."[14]

Once her mind was made up, Yvette was unshakeable: The Khmer Rouge represented horror and evil. She began to help the refugees who were flooding into Phnom Penh. She collected abandoned children to live in her house. Soon there were 20 of them and she fed more at an orphanage abandoned by its adult attendants. She adopted one of the orphans, a three-year-old boy she named Olivier, the most pathetic and traumatized of all the children.[15] She prowled the streets at all hours of the day and night, ignoring the curfew to give comfort, money, and food to homeless people crowding pagodas or living on the streets. She railed against western journalists in Phnom Penh who were pro–Khmer Rouge.

The final offensive of the communist Khmer Rouge against the Lon Nol government began after midnight on January 1, 1975. It coincided — although it was not coordinated with — the North Vietnamese offensive in South Vietnam. The key to the

Cambodian woman and children. This photograph encapsulates the misery of being a refugee. (Berta Romero)

Khmer Rouge victory was cutting the Mekong River supply line that brought to Phnom Penh nearly all its war materials and food — for by this time the bountiful country of Cambodia was importing rice to feed its burgeoning urban population. The barges came up the Mekong from Vietnam. The Khmer Rouge cut the river route by the simple expedient of stationing 5,000 soldiers on the banks of the river and blasting away with rockets and artillery at every barge that appeared. Later, they stretched cables across the river and attached mines, which they detonated from the shore. The last convoy reached the city on January 26.[16] Then, Phnom Penh began to starve. Refugees swelled the city, 600,000 people before the war, to a population of more than 2 million.

Near the end Phnom Penh was a "cesspit of decay" and "a diseased whore." "There was no medicine, few hospital beds and, in a country drowning in blood, none left over for transfusions ... the misery of the many" was "matched by the shameless consumption of the few. While rice prices rose astronomically and, in the shanty towns, thousands of children and old people starved to death, restaurants ... offered *foie gras*, venison, and fine French wines."[17] An iron law applies in famines: the first to die are children under five years old, pregnant mothers, and the elderly. Men with AK-47 rifles rarely starve. That was true in Phnom Penh. The child nutrition center operated by the American charity, World Vision, turned away 1,758 severely malnourished children between December 1974 and February 1975. It only had beds for 235 children.[18]

In the final months of the war, Yvette, her two children, and Kurt retreated to Bangkok, although Yvette flew to Phnom Penh almost every morning to run the business and charter airplanes. Like Lionel Rosenblatt, she made a last minute rescue flight to Saigon, although her mission was business: to evacuate the personnel of the German Embassy. During that visit, in a customary spur of the moment decision, she gave her French passport to a Vietnamese woman she met on the street so the woman and her children could leave the country on an outgoing flight. She then bluffed her way through customs and immigration in Saigon and Bangkok without a passport. She had never met the woman before and never knew her name.

By the end of February 1975, the American ambassador to Cambodia, John Gunther Dean, had lost hope and ordered the evacuation of the dependents and non-essential personnel of the Embassy to Thailand. By early April the airport in Phnom Penh was under constant bombardment and Washington ordered an evacuation of the remaining Embassy staff and other Americans. They would have to leave by helicopter.

On April 11, American journalist Leslie Jacques was told to be at the Embassy the next morning. His Cambodian interpreter drove him. Jacques paid the man his salary, shook his hand, and said good-bye for the last time. About 300 people were assembled at the Embassy, including "agitated and tearful" Cambodians. The evacuation began promptly at nine. "We were led out a back door, past trashcans aflame with Embassy documents and into trucks. The truck I boarded was covered, but the one behind us was a flat-bed: For all their fear of Cambodian rioting, the evacuation's planners had overlooked the point that nothing announced our departure as vividly as all those somber Western faces staring out from the flat-bed truck....

"The trucks stopped at a soccer field. We waited. Helicopters appeared in the sky, and raised huge clouds of dust as they landed. As soon as they touched down, 350 Marines charged out and trotted to the edge of the field ... Cambodians: hundreds of them, mostly children, many shirtless, ran to the field to see what the commotion was about. As I boarded a helicopter, I strained for my last sight of Phnom Penh. Brandishing rifles, the Marines stood hunched over the children, who were nevertheless smiling and waving goodbye. I don't think we deserved the grace with which they reacted to our flight."[19]

The American evacuation of Phnom Penh was a tiny and sedate affair compared to Vietnam. Washington did not open up evacuation to large numbers of Cambodians, suggesting that only high level military and civilian officials and intellectuals should be permitted to leave courtesy of the U.S. Departing on American helicopters that day were 82 Americans, 35 third country nationals, and only 159 Cambodians. The Embassy had anticipated that it would evacuate almost 600 people, but fewer than 300 showed up.[20] About 800 foreigners, including Western journalists, priests, and scholars elected to stay behind in Cambodia. The French kept their embassy open, staffed by one remaining diplomat.

The character of the evacuation was totally different in Phnom Penh than in Saigon. In Vietnam, the demand for evacuation was almost infinite. The fall of Cambodia did not engender the mass panic that the NVA conquest of South Vietnam did. The Vietnamese were accustomed to leaving their homes and taking flight and many of them had done it several times; the Cambodians were less accustomed to war and less sophisticated in the ways of the world. The number of people able to conceive of flight for safety to a strange land was much smaller in Cambodia. The Cambodians hoped that their fellow Cambodians, the Khmer Rouge, would be reasonable. Sihanouk had become the titular head of the Khmer Rouge in opposition to Lon Nol. He was not a violent or vindictive person. Quite the opposite, he personified flexibility and Buddhist amiability. His statements from Beijing indicated that only a few top officials of the Lon Nol government would be executed. Even among those, two turned down Dean's offer of evacuation: Prime Minister Long Boret and Deputy Prime Minister Prince Sisowath Sirik Matak. Long Boret had attended the same French lycée as several of the Khmer Rouge leaders and he anticipated that old school ties would save him. They didn't. He surrendered himself to the Khmer Rouge and, along with several hundred government and military officials, was executed at the Sports Club. On his part, Sirik Matak wrote an extraordinary letter to Ambassador Dean turning down the ambassador's offer to evacuate him.

Dear Excellency and Friend:
I thank you very sincerely for your letter and for your offer to transport me towards freedom. I cannot, alas, leave in such a cowardly fashion. As for you, and in particular for your great country, I never believed for a moment that you would have this sentiment of abandoning a people which has chose liberty. You have refused us your protection, and we can do nothing about it.
You leave, and my wish is that you and your country will find happiness under this sky. But, mark it well, that if I shall die here on the spot and in my country that I love, it is no matter, because we are all born and must die. I have only committed this mistake of believing in you, the Americans.
Please accept, Excellency, my dear friend, my faithful and friendly sentiments.
Sirik Matak.[21]

* * *

Sihanouk later analyzed in a book the factors that determined the outcome of the civil war. A reviewer commented: "Sihanouk elaborates several reasons, among them: the U.S. underestimated support for Sihanouk himself, and underestimated the determination of the Vietnamese to maintain a presence in Cambodia; they underestimated the effects of corruption in the Lon Nol regime; and the U.S. overestimated the effectiveness of the bombing campaign. But Sihanouk does not mention what is arguably one of the most important reasons for Lon Nol's defeat: sheer American indifference. The fate of Cambodia was always a secondary concern to U.S. policymakers. Vietnam was the real arena. Behind most American decisions, one senses that the real question was not 'How will this affect our allies in Cambodia?' but rather 'How will this affect our ability to get out of Vietnam?' It is doubtful that any U.S. action—even a massive U.S. ground force—could have altered the outcome once the full fury of Cambodia's civil war had been unleashed. But American indifference to the fate of the Cambodians made it a foregone conclusion that no dramatic initiatives would ever be undertaken."[22]

If the Cambodians were overly sanguine about the character of the Khmer Rouge, so was the United States and the rest of the world. The American left, which so vociferously opposed the Vietnam War, found democratic and humanitarian virtues in the KR. The venerable *New York Times* and its reporter in Phnom Penh predicted moderation. "Most Cambodians do not talk about a possible massacre and do not expect one," said the newspaper on March 13, 1975. "Since all are Cambodians an accommodation will be found. Khieu Sampan, the best known of the Khmer Rouge leaders, was known for his integrity and would 'move somewhat to the right' on gaining power. A more flexible nationalist socialism or Communism would be the end product."[23]

The U.S. Congress reflected mixed views. Pipe-smoking Millicent Fenwick of New Jersey was prescient, saying on March 6, after a visit there, "There is no doubt that the horror, the terror, of the Khmer Rouge is something that I have never witnessed. Nothing like this has ever been rumored in Vietnam. Nobody knows exactly why this terror has reached the atrocities and the pitch in a place that was supposed to be composed of peaceful people."[24]

Fenwick's premonitions were not the general rule. Congress was too tired of the Vietnam conflict to face up to the possibility that the Khmer Rouge would initiate a bloodbath. A minority report signed by ex–Vice President Hubert Humphrey washed its hands of Cambodia. "By overwhelming majorities, the American public has indicated that it has had enough and that it considers the Cambodian war irrelevant or even detrimental to U.S. interests...." And, refuting the dire threats of a violent Khmer Rouge takeover, he said, "The possibility of a bloodbath has been greatly exaggerated and the entire issue woefully oversimplified."[25]

The Khmer Rouge was to exceed in brutality the direst premonitions. Even in the history of the bloody and bizarre twentieth century, the KR is almost unique and unimaginable.

* * *

The government forces ringing Phnom Penh held out until they ran out of ammunition, but on April 17, five days after the Americans fled, the government surrendered and the Khmer Rouge entered the city. They were welcomed with euphoria. In the words of Francois Ponchaud, a French missionary, "An almost physical sense of relief led to general rejoicing. No more rockets to fear. No more compulsory military service. No more of this rotten, loathed regime."[26] Students, monks, and other people took to the streets, waving white handkerchiefs and banners welcoming peace. Within hours the euphoria was erased.

The Khmer Rouge soldiers were strange and menacing. Photographer Al Rockoff took one of the first pictures of a Khmer Rouge soldier on the streets of Phnom Penh. He seems to be in his early teens, five feet tall, bare-footed, clothed in grimy black pajamas, smoking a cigarette, and has an assault rifle nearly as tall as himself tucked comfortably against his hip. His neck and waist are festooned with belts of grenades and ammunition. Standing nearby, an officer, identifiable by his pistol, wears the customary red-checkered scarf of the Khmer Rouge, sandals, and a broad-brimmed hat. A crowd of onlookers in the background looks on silently and its mood seems apprehensive. The Khmer Rouge soldiers appeared "ill at ease ... [with] a wary, exhausted look." They were from "a different world ... they never smiled.... They didn't even look like Cambodians."[27] It was the recurring nightmare for city people throughout history. The oppressed, despised, uneducated, unfathomable, dark-skinned peasants had taken over the city. These peasants, in the person of the Khmer Rouge soldiers, threatened urban civilization's "eternal inclination to draw lines, invoke boundaries, establish hierarchies, and maintain discriminations."[28]

Within a few hours the KR soldiers shouted the first orders of the new regime in the streets and door to door. Everyone must leave the city. Now. The soldiers said the Americans would bomb the city in retaliation for the fall of the puppet Lon Nol government. The evacuation was for the safety of the people. They would be able to return home in a few days.

"It was a stupefying sight," said Francois Ponchaud, "a human flood pouring out of the city, some people pushing their cars, others with overladen motorcycles or bicycles overflowing with bundles, and others behind little home-made carts. Most were on foot.... The worst part of the whole march was the stopping and starting; there was such a crowd that we could never go forward for more than a few yards at a time before we had to stop again."

The hospitals were not excluded from the evacuation. These were pestilential sinkholes at the best of times: patients shared beds; blood dripped and dried on floors, medicine and food was only available to those whose families had the money to buy it. The Khmer Rouge demanded that everybody leave. "Thousands of the sick and wounded were abandoning the city. They strongest dragged themselves pitifully along, others were carried by friends, some lying on beds pushed by their families with their plasma and IV drips bumping alongside. I shall never forget one cripple who had neither hands nor feet, writhing along the ground like a severed worm. Or a weeping father carrying his 10-year-old daughter wrapped in a sheet tied around his neck like a sling, or the man with his foot dangling at the end of a leg to which it was attached by nothing but the skin."[29]

The five highways leading out of the capital were clogged with people who moved at a snail's pace, leaving their dead and dying behind. It took days for the city to empty. Khmer Rouge along the highways scanned the crowds; confiscated whatever they wanted, questioned suspicious persons, and executed those they believed to have been soldiers and officials of the Lon Nol government. "Sick people were left by their families at the roadside. Others were killed because they could walk no further. Parents who had lost their children cried out in tears, looking for them. The dead were abandoned, covered in flies, sometimes with a piece of cloth thrown over them."[30] The wrath of the Khmer Rouge fell especially hard on the Chinese and Vietnamese minorities living in Cambodia: not only were they city dwellers, they were regarded as capitalist exploiters and foreigners.

The number of people who died in the evacuation of Phnom Penh and other cities is wildly estimated at between 20,000 and 400,000.[31] A Cambodian physician described the casualties of the march with a clinical eye. "We must have passed the body of a child every 200 yards. Most of them died of gastrointestinal afflictions which cause complete dehydration. I had some medication with me, but most children brought to me required massive dosages and lengthy rest afterward. Neither was available. Thinking of all the bodies I saw, plus the sick who came to see me, between 20 and 30 every day, half of whom were not going to live, I figure that between 20,000 and 30,000 people must have died the first month, just in the area described (the route along which he walked to Vietnam)."[32]

If the doctor's estimate of deaths along his route is roughly accurate — and it is as good as can be found — then the total dead among the two million evacuees from Phnom Penh in the first month of the evacuation would be in the range of 100,000 to 150,000, i.e., five main highways multiplied by 20,000 to 30,000 dead along each route.

From later interviews, *Reader's Digest*'s John Barron and Anthony Paul summed up the appearance of Phnom Penh two weeks after the Khmer Rouge took power: "Phnom Penh ... had been transformed into a vast, still wasteland occupied primarily by corpses, stray dogs, pigs, ducks, chickens and ... patrols standing guard to ensure that human life did not return. Around the Soviet hospital lay the remains of nonambulatory patients who had been dumped on the grounds and who had had no friends to take them away before death did so. A few dying souls were propped up against the wall outside, deposited there by relatives who prayed that somebody might help them.... In large sectors of the city not a human voice could be heard. Open doors of empty, looted houses creaked, and banknotes or documents littering the streets rustled in the wind; a starving dog barked forlornly; now and then a pedicab creaked by loaded with bodies to be dumped in the river."[33] One wonders why the dog was starving.

The New York Times summed up the evacuation: "Between two and three million residents of Phnom Penh, Battambang and other big towns—one-third to one-half the population of the country—were forced by the Communists at gunpoint to walk into the countryside in tropical temperatures and monsoon rains without organized provision for food, water, shelter, physical security or medical care. Few, if any, were told that a trek of one to three weeks lay ahead."[34]

The troubles of those who survived the evacuation were just beginning. "After eight days we arrived at a village 60 kilometers northeast of Phnom Penh. Branded as 'new people' or 'April 17 people' we struggled as members of the lowest caste of a supposedly classless society. My father, a French-trained accountant, who had worked at the Industry Ministry, was sent to a re-education camp. All but my youngest brother, a mere 4 years old, were put to hard labor. He would catch small frogs in the evening to fill his empty stomach.... Of the nearly 200 urban families who were settled in the village, only about 50 were left when the Khmer Rouge were driven from power by a Vietnamese invasion on Jan. 7, 1979."[35]

A "new settlement" was the fate of most of the evacuees. "Thousands of these new settlements were hewn out of the bush, scrubland, and jungle. Typically, upon arrival a new villager family would be ordered to construct a hut out of bamboo leaves, whatever could be foraged from the jungle, and then was put in a work group typically comprised of 10 families. The work groups labored from 5 or 6 A.M. in the morning to the midday break and then until 5 or 6 P.M. at night. On moonlit nights, in many areas work continued from 7 to 10 P.M. And this all went on 7 days a week.

"By late summer of 1975, food shortages reached famine level in large portions of the country. Epidemics of cholera, malaria, and dysentery incapacitated a sizable percentage of the new villages. Given the demanding work regimen, the tropical squalor, and the almost total lack of modern medicine, the death rate inevitably was high." Moreover, the Khmer Rouge ordered the execution of all former civil servants and soldiers who had served the previous government.[36]

"The picture," according to *The New York Times*, "begins to emerge of a country that resembles a giant prison camp with the urban supporters of the former regime being worked to death on thin gruel and hard labor and with medical care virtually nonexistent."[37]

* * *

Why did the Khmer Rouge take the extraordinary step of emptying the Cambodian cities? Deputy Prime Minister Ieng Sary offered an explanation in a speech in New York a few months later. He noted that the population of Phnom Penh was swollen with refugees to a population of two to three million. "Before the victory, U.S. imperialism had brought from 30,000 to 40,000 tons of food per month. The problem is to find ways to feed these people by our own means: To find food in Phnom Penh would be to rely on other people.

Therefore we will never ask — we have to solve the problem by ourselves on the basis of peasant's organizations, to work together. To resolve this problem we decided to disperse the people to the countryside."[38]

At first blush, Ieng Sary's assertion seems plausible: Finding and transporting the rice to feed the population of Phnom Penh would have been a challenge. Children were already dying of malnutrition and many adults were weak from long months of short rations. But that the decision to empty the cities was taken on the first day of their victory shows forethought and planning. The Khmer Rouge took no account of the existing rice supply in Phnom Penh — up to a one-month supply, according to some estimates— nor made any effort to moderate the impact of the evacuation by excluding hospital patients, the elderly, and others who could not survive a forced march out of the city into the countryside. It would have been easier to distribute rice to the city-dwellers while they were still in the city rather than to send them to the countryside with promises to bring rice to them.

A more plausible reason for the evacuation of the cities was the Khmer Rouge's fear of counter-revolution. In a speech, Pol Pot himself gave the decision to empty the cities "before the victory was won, that is in February 1975, because we knew that before the smashing of all sorts of enemy spy organizations, our strength was not enough to defend the revolutionary regime."[39] In other words, the revolution was all and the welfare of the inhabitants of the cities was of no concern. What better way to destroy any potential resistance than to scatter the former soldiers, government officials, urban dwellers, and intellectuals before they had an opportunity to organize themselves? Once relocated to rural areas, potential resisters could be more easily controlled.

But the primary reason for the emptying of the cities was the character of the Khmer Rouge themselves. The KR were agrarian revolutionaries. The city represented corruption and oppression to them and to make a new society the old had to be destroyed. Thus, they would empty cities in an action that even their ideological guide, Mao Zedong, had not had the courage to undertake. The Khmer Rouge described their reaction to the city dwellers: "Upon entering Phnom Penh and other cities, the brother and sister combatants of the revolutionary army ... sons and daughters of our workers and peasants ... were taken aback by the overwhelming unspeakable sight of long-haired men and youngsters wearing bizarre clothes making themselves undistinguishable [sic] from the fair sex.... Our people's traditionally clean, sound characteristics and essence were completely absent and abandoned, replaced by imperialistic, pornographic, shameless, perverted, and fanatic traits."[40]

The Khmer Rouge's fanatic puritanism and agrarian communism led to the most radical government in the twentieth century. They abolished money, outlawed religion, burned books, encouraged paranoia; their national anthem spoke of the cleansing power of blood five times in six lines; theft, pre-marital sex, and disobedience were capital offenses; they made Cambodia one vast slave labor camp. Their regime has been compared to *Lord of the Flies*, the novel of a society run by malevolent children unrestrained by law, custom, or religion. No wonder the world disbelieved the wild tales told by the few escapees from the Khmer Rouge.

The evidence of the character of the Khmer Rouge was there for anyone to discern. The Frenchman Francois Ponchaud, who spoke Cambodian and lived in the country for years, said that "ever since 1972 the guerrilla fighters had been sending all the inhabitants of the villages and towns they occupied into the forest to live, often burning their homes so that they would have nothing to come back to."[41] Foreign Service officer Kenneth Quinn, one of Lionel Rosenblatt's lunch group in Washington, wrote a perceptive report in early 1974 about his discussions in Vietnam with Cambodians who had escaped from the "liberated" areas controlled by the Khmer Rouge. Their tales presaged the KR rule over all the country, but his report aroused little attention in Washington and was dismissed as unreliable tales told by refugees. Quinn said that the Khmer Rouge instituted a cooperative agricultural system in the countryside. The Khmer Rouge's policies "as implemented by the new young cadre sent to the villages, was one based on the use of terror, violence and force."[42]

In a rehearsal for the emptying of the cities in 1975, the KR relocated the population to newly formed collectives. "No land is privately owned and no one keeps anything he produces. The hours of work are extremely long and are followed by nighttime indoctrination sessions. No dissent is allowed from existing policies and anyone objecting is arrested or killed. There is no religion allowed in the new sites and all monks are defrocked and ordered to work. Old customs, songs and modes of dress are forbidden along with the possession of any ostentatious property.[43] This process," Quinn continued, "entails stripping away, through terror and other means, the traditional bases, structures and forces which have shaped and guided an individual's life until he is left as an atomized, isolated individual unit; and then rebuilding him according to party doctrine.... Refugees from Kampot and Kandah provinces have said they were so afraid of arrest and execution that even in their own homes they dared not utter a critical word and obediently complied with every ... directive."[44]

Quinn gained his insight by interviewing Cambodians who had fled the Khmer Rouge in 1973. As time went on, however, flight became increasingly difficult and dangerous. "Commune officials were threatened with execution themselves if they let anyone escape and whole families would be killed if one member fled successfully. In one such occurrence the Khmer Communists were said to have shot and executed approximately 700 civilians and surrendered soldiers ... because they tried to flee."[45]

Quinn's reporting was supplemented and verified by one reporter, Donald Kirk of the *Chicago Tribune*, who seemed nearly alone among the dozens of journalists in Cambodia in taking a close hard look at the Khmer Rouge and interviewing refugees who had fled their rule. A refugee told Kirk, "I saw the

Khmer Rouge saw off the neck of a civilian with the sharp edge of a sugar palm leaf. They spent three days cutting his head off. They sawed a little one morning, and then in the evening, and the following day in the morning and the night. They made the victim stand up while they were cutting him in front of hundreds of people. Then they held him up when he could no longer stand."[46]

The reporting of people such as Quinn and Kirk had little impact on the policies of the United States or the Lon Nol government. Cambodia was an orphan kingdom in an indifferent world. Many of the most vociferous critics in Congress of the U.S.–supported government of Cambodia were silent in the face of early evidence that the Khmer Rouge were initiating a monstrous regime. Many academics were vociferous in their support of the Khmer Rouge. A distant revolution often looks attractive.

Cambodia also failed to gain American attention because of the small number of refugees fleeing the Khmer Rouge. The KR sealed the borders by relocating all villages and peasants who lived within five miles of the border, laying land mines, and making the frontier a no-man's land.[47] A trickle escaped. In July 1975, the journalist Henry Kamm visited the border and found about 6,000 Cambodian refugees in three refugee camps. They told him of "fear of hunger, fear of dying by overwork, exposure and the absence of medicine, and fear of being killed" by the Khmer Rouge.[48]

* * *

The westerners remaining in Phnom Penh after the evacuation of the American Embassy, mostly French and journalists, quickly learned that they were not exempt from the wrath of the Khmer Rouge. Al Rockoff, British journalist Jon Swain, Sydney Schanberg, and interpreter Dith Pran were visiting a hospital that first afternoon when they were confronted by Khmer Rouge soldiers who demanded to search their luggage. "As one is taking the camera equipment off my neck and from my shoulder," Rockoff remembered, "another one put a pistol to my right temple, and I saw the two—well, I sensed the two Khmer Rouge behind me move to the side to get away from the splatter."[49] Dith Pran—later the subject of the award-winning film *The Killing Fields*—jumped in quickly and saved the three journalists from execution by claiming they were French newsmen in Phnom Penh to celebrate the great communist victory.

Rockoff, Pran, and other journalists found it advisable to retreat quickly to the French Embassy along with about 600 Cambodians and 800 other foreigners. Among the Cambodians present was Sirik Matak, whose poignant letter to Dean is one of the most enduring documents of the Indochinese war. The living conditions inside the Embassy compound quickly became intolerable. The Embassy lost contact with the outside world when the batteries of portable radios were exhausted. Food ran out and the Khmer Rouge refused to allow any to enter. "Pets, including a U.S. official's gibbon passed on to a friend, were eaten."[50]

The Khmer Rouge demanded that all the Cambodians in the Embassy leave. On April 21, Sirik Matak and others were handed over to the KR. Sirik Matak was executed at the Sports Club. According to Henry Kissinger, he was shot in the stomach, his wound was not treated, and it took three days for him to die.[51] Another account says he was beheaded on the tennis court.[52]

Dith Pran was also turned out of the Embassy, but he blended into the crowd by posing as an unemployed taxi driver—plausible because no taxis were allowed in the new Cambodia. He would survive a labor camp to tell his story.

The foreigners in the French Embassy were sent to Thailand in two overland convoys arriving at the border on May 3 and May 8. With the arrival of the last group of foreigners, the journalists began to write about their experiences. They reported that Phnom Penh was a deserted city. "Abandoned cars and assorted trash marked the trail of the departed population. Every shop had been broken open and looted. Not a single civilian was visible—only the many soldiers camping in the shops and on the sidewalks ... from there to the border we encountered a wasteland of broken bridges, abandoned fields, and forcibly evacuated highway towns."[53] This was the last eyewitness account of Cambodia by western journalists for two years. Cambodia became a forbidden land of silence. Not even the names of most of the leaders of the Khmer Rouge were known to the outside world.

* * *

Yvette, safely ensconced in Bangkok, could not stay away from Cambodia. In mid–May 1975, a month after the Khmer Rouge takeover, she rented a taxi and headed toward the border. When the driver refused to go any further she hired a motorcycle to take her closer, and walking, she entered a forest and then a cleared area in which the houses stood empty. A man in an army uniform riding a bicycle waved her away, "You're crazy, this is Cambodia." Walking back toward Thailand she found a group of 50 Cambodians in a field ringed with barbed war. The Cambodians were terrified because they knew the Khmer Rouge could find them at any moment.[54]

Yvette blamed the plight of the Cambodians at the border on the apathy of the UN High Commissioner for Refugees (UNHCR). The Thai border authorities, terrified of the implications for their country of communist governments as their neighbors, had closed the border and prevented most Cambodians from entering Thailand and finding safety. Yvette began to go to the border regularly to help the Cambodians she found there. She told Kurt they had to make more money in business so they could help more people. In early 1976, Yvette was introduced to Lionel Rosenblatt—probably by Jim Eckes, who knew Yvette well from their mutual association with Continental Air Services. Over time a close working association and mutual admiration would develop between the two. Meanwhile, a trickle of Cambodians continued to escape across the border and tell tales of the savagery of the Khmer Rouge.

Other people also took matters into their own hands. One of the last planes out of Phnom Penh transported 23 orphans to Bangkok. Sue Morton, the wife of a Pepsi Cola executive, housed the orphans for two weeks until they could be transported to the U.S. for adoption. A trickle of Cambodians escaped across the border and told tales of the savagery of the Khmer Rouge. When a missionary found 12 children — unaccompanied minors in the parlance of the humanitarians — wandering near the border and brought them to Bangkok, Sue installed them in her house and found people to adopt them. Sue adopted two of the orphans herself.[55]

One of the early visitors to the Thai border with Cambodia was the peripatetic congressman from New York, Stephen Solarz. In August 1975, the American Embassy's Cambodia watcher, Charles Twining, took Solarz to the border and there he met with Cambodian refugees and heard their stories. What most impressed him was their assertion that the Khmer Rouge killed any Cambodian who wore eyeglasses, the wearing of which they regarded as conclusive evidence that the persons were intellectuals and therefore enemies of the regime. The story that the KR killed Cambodians who wore glasses would become common in the future — but this was the first time it had been heard. Solarz had been an opponent of the Vietnam War, but after his experience at the border he had no illusions about the character of the Khmer Rouge and no patience with the apologists and defenders of the regime in the United States.[56]

4

THE HMONG ESCAPE LAOS

In the dry season the Plain of Jars in Laos would have reminded Jerry Daniels of eastern Montana with its rolling brown hills and big sky. Dusty roads cross the plain and at an intersection is one of the most bombarded places on the planet. The bare countryside is dotted with craters, each about 10 yards in diameter and a yard deep. Locals call them "buffalo swimming pools." In the rainy season water collects in the craters; in the dry season they retain enough moisture to nourish a thriving crop of tulip-shaped purple and white opium poppies. Nearby is a hillside full of large, oblong, hollowed-out rocks, some more than six feet tall. They are called jars and they give the plain its name. The jars are estimated to be 2,000 years old.

An important economic activity on the Plain of Jars is the collection and sale of scrap metal from bombs dropped by the U.S. and Laotian air forces in the 1960s and 1970s. The supply seems endless. The U.S. dropped two million tons of bombs on Laos, hundreds of pounds for every man, woman, and child in the country. In villages piles of twisted bomb parts line the streets. Junk metal dealers load the metal onto trucks and haul it to Vietnam. Five hundred pound bomb casings are used as flowerpots, fences, bathtubs, and to reinforce house foundations. Unexploded bombs and the baseball-sized anti-personnel munitions called "bombies" are still common. UXO (unexploded ordnance) teams— mostly young women wearing body armor — sweep streets, school grounds, and farmland with metal detectors to locate, unearth, and dispose of the still-lethal bombs and bombies.[1] In 2004, 31 years after the U.S. bombing stopped, 66 people were killed and 128 injured in Laos by UXO and landmines.[2] Nobody has any idea how many Laotians died in the bombing during the war years but it was, in the words of Anthony Lewis in *The New York Times*, "the most appalling episode of lawless cruelty in American history."[3]

The Royal Lao government and its ally the United States contested control of the Plain of Jars with the Pathet Lao communists and the North Vietnamese Army from the late 1950s until 1975. The war in Laos was an upside down affair compared to Vietnam. In Vietnam, the U.S. relied on conventional military forces and U.S. soldiers numbered more than 500,000 at their peak.

In Laos, only about 1,000 American military and civilians were present.[4] Most of the Royal Lao Army was ineffective, so an army supported by the CIA and numbering up to 40,000 men — 22,000 Hmong and 18,000 Laotians of other ethnic groups — did most of the fighting. The 40,000 included every part-time warrior, old man, and underage youth able to carry a rifle. In northeastern Laos, General Vang Pao, a Hmong, was the commander. The war in Vietnam was featured on the evening news; the war in Laos was inevitably described as "secret."

Laos was a mythical never-never land of Oz. Its administrative capital, Vientiane, just across the Mekong River from Thailand, was small and sleepy. Its royal capital of Luang Prabang oozed tranquil charm and Buddhist tradition. The Lao were placid and unwarlike. A story, possibly apocryphal, is that the U.S. hired anthropologists early in the 1960s to take a poll and assess how it could win the "hearts and minds" of the Lao. The survey showed that 90 percent of the rural people could not name the country in which they lived and, when asked what kind of economic assistance they needed, overwhelmingly said that they needed help to repair the Buddhist *Wat* (temple) in their village. USAID was, of course, forbidden to assist religion and the wishes of the Lao went unmet. One wonders whether the U.S. might have won the war against communism had it repaired temples rather than dropped bombs.[5]

As in Vietnam and Cambodia, the war in Laos went badly for the Americans. Hmong general Vang Pao said later: "I never imagined that I would be a refugee, because the United States ... supported me in my fight against the communist takeover of my country."[6] If Laos was the land of Oz, General Vang Pao was the Wizard, the charismatic military genius who led his Hmong, Lao Theung, and other soldiers against the Laotian communists, the Pathet Lao, and the formidable North Vietnamese Army. Vang Pao gained a greater reputation in defeat than his enemies did in victory. "He was incredible.... He had no help. He did everything. Ran the goddamn motor pool, the pay of the troops. He was the political leader and the spiritual leader of the Hmong nation.... For Christ sake, on top of that he had six or seven wives and 23 kids."[7]

The people of Laos are divided into the lowland Lao, flatland rice farmers and urban merchants related to the Thai next door, and the highland peoples living in the lofty mountains who practice slash-and-burn agriculture with opium as their cash crop. As in Vietnam, animosity characterizes the relations between highlander and flatlander. The Hmong were the most numerous of the highland peoples in Laos, numbering about 400,000 out of a total population in the country of three million in the 1970s. The Hmong shared the mountainous spine of Indochina with other highland ethnic groups. Unlike the Montagnards in Vietnam, the Hmong were a single people with a single language — albeit with two dialects and 20 clans. Both Montagnard and Hmong were tough and hardy upland rice growers, hunters, and forest gatherers — perfect as guerrilla warriors.

Vang Pao's extraordinary qualities as a soldier and leader were recognized when he was a 14-year-old message runner for French fighting the Japanese in World War II. After the war he was one of very few Hmong trained as policemen and military officers by the French colonialists. He excelled at everything. Vang Pao's military ethic was to lead from the front and, in the words of a CIA agent, "He assumed he was not going to get shot. He just exuded bravery."[8]

By 1961, Colonel Vang Pao was both a leader of the Hmong in their mountain homeland and the highest-ranking Hmong in the Lao Army. He pledged his loyalty to the government and stated his political philosophy to the CIA's Bill Lair: "We own all of these mountains. I've been in touch with the communists. They've been around here for years. But my people cannot live with them. Their life is too different from ours. We have only two choices: we fight them, or we leave. There is nothing else we can do. If you give us the guns," he told the American, "we will fight them."[9] Vang Pao's was not empty talk. In Lair's opinion, Vang Pao "was probably the greatest guerrilla leader in the world." U.S. Air Force general Harry "Heinie" Aderholt was also lavish in his praise: "VP"—as both Americans and Hmong called him—was "better than any American general over there."[10] VP was promoted to general and he became the backbone of the Royal Lao government's resistance to the Pathet Lao and North Vietnamese.

The Wizard had a stellar supporting cast of Americans in Oz. Bill Lair, a quiet, unpretentious, bespectacled Texan, discovered Vang Pao and directed CIA support to him in the early 1960s. Lair—called "Colonel Billy"—was the brains behind 12 Americans, 400 Thai trainers, and thousands of Hmong guerillas in the most successful insurgency ever run by the United States.[11] Lair suffered the usual fate of the innovative pioneer. He was pushed aside for the conventional and buttoned-down. In 1966 a new CIA boss in Laos promised to turn Lair's operation from a "country store to a supermarket." The larger the supermarket became, the less territory Vang Pao and the Hmong controlled. Lair left Laos in 1968, bounced around the Agency for a few years, retired, returned to Texas, and drove a truck for eight years. Ultimately, the U.S. went home and the Wizard and the Hmong were left to suffer the consequences. The conscience of the Americans who served in Southeast Asia was stung by the fate of the Hmong and the Montagnard. They were the admirable, honest, and simple people of the hills, fighting to preserve their land against the grasping, corrupt, and materialistic Vietnamese and Lao.

Edgar M. "Pop" Buell was another legendary American in Laos. He was a short, slight, bald, profane, middle-aged Indiana farmer. In 1960, he had never been out of the United States but after his wife died he looked for a change of scenery and found a job in Laos with the International Voluntary Service (IVS)—a precursor of the Peace Corps—as an agricultural advisor making $75 a month. He stayed on to become "Tan Pop," the "father from the sky." Many

CIA officer Jerry Daniels (seated) and Hmong leader Colonel Moua Sue. (Lionel Rosenblatt collection)

of the Hmong were displaced by the war and others had neither the time nor the security to grow rice so Buell kept the Hmong fed by air-dropping relief supplies, mostly bags of rice, to tens of thousands of them. A generation of Hmong grew up thinking that rice fell from the sky. Pop took money out of his own pocket to pay the bills when the United States treasury ran out of money for its obligations in Laos. On one occasion he withdrew $7,000 from his retirement account and paid the salaries of all the Hmong employees at his field office. He was never reimbursed.[12] Pop's opinion: "For every Hmong that died in the war, one fewer American soldier died."[13]

The American who stuck with the Hmong longest was Jerrold B. Daniels—codename "Hog," which belied his matinee-idol appearance: tall, dark, slender with an air of amused insouciance and a gunfighter's mustache. Jerry claimed to be part American Indian and hailed from Missoula, Montana. While in high school he was a rodeo bull rider, a chess and wrestling champion, and at 17 he became the youngest smokejumper in the U.S. Forest Service. Daniels was recruited by the CIA to work as a loadmaster or "kicker" on cargo planes dropping rice and supplies to allies in Tibet and Laos. In 1965, Daniels, only 24 years old, became Vang Pao's case officer and the American closest to him.

A colleague would say that Daniels "was the most mission-oriented, job-committed, task-driven individual I have ever known. His motto was 'lead me, follow me, or get the hell out of the way.' Jerry was not anti-authority but he was most definitely anti-bureaucratic. Nothing stood between him and completing the mission. Dedicated and hard-charging only begin to describe Jerry.... He was also one of the funniest and most irreverent people one could meet, combining humor and hard work."[14] The Hog—he was called "Mr. Hog" by the Hmong—had both a sense of humor and hidden demons. "Every two or three months, he went to Vientiane or Bangkok and stayed drunk for several days."[15]

Not that Daniel's alcoholic binges were out of the ordinary. Drinking was a major avocation of many of the Americans in Laos. The American CIA agents, diplomats, USAID workers, Air America and Air Force pilots in Laos were a rowdy group who despised the "Rear Echelon Mother Fuckers" (REMFs) who had so much influence over the war in Vietnam. Many of them stayed in Laos year after year. Duty and mission played a part in decisions to stay on as did freedom, excitement, big paychecks, sex, and drugs. In Laos, unconventional warriors escaped from military discipline, uniforms, bureaucracy, and the REMF—imposed rules that made service in Vietnam burdensome for good field operators. They wore cowboy boots or shower shoes, cultivated luxurious mustaches, and spent their nights on leave in hot, seedy bars full of lovely and inexpensive women.

The small Laotian capital city of Vientiane had more than its share of watering holes. Writer Paul Theroux came through here in 1975. "Vientiane is exceptional, but inconvenient. The brothels are cheaper than the hotels, marijuana is cheaper than pipe tobacco, and opium easier to find than a cold glass of beer." Two establishments patronized by Americans have gone down in history. The White Rose was a sleazy place of "darkness, dirty ice, hideous aromas, bad hooch, high prices and very little English."[16] Its floor shows featured naked Lao women, cigars, and billowing smoke from orifices not usually associated with tobacco use. Madame Lulus—officially "Les Rendevous des Amis"—specialized in "warm beer and oral sex." Madame Lulu herself was a "broken down Frenchwoman in her sixties" but her girls were trained to bring in paying customers.[17] The bars acquired fame and even respectability. Many sojourners in Vientiane were given the "The Order of the White Rose," a signed and sealed document thanking them for their dedicated efforts to perform "the mission for which all men were created." The White Rose even sponsored the U.S. Air Force bowling team in Vientiane and bought shoes and shirts for the players, the shirts featuring a white rose printed on the back. Some of the girls showed up at the bowling alley to cheer the team on.[18]

Vang Pao and the CIA are often accused of dealing in opium. The Hmong traditionally grew opium poppies and consumed and traded the drug; the CIA was aware of the drug trade and turned a blind eye. On occasion the U.S. put pressure on the Hmong to stop opium cultivation. Pilot Norm Gardener tells the story of the USAID delegation that came to see Vang Pao and told him he was going to have to stop opium cultivation. "That's a very good idea," Vang Pao responded. He showed the delegation out to his front porch and three or four old people were sitting there. "These people smoke the opium. The reason they smoke the opium is because they're sick. They don't have any hospitals. We don't have any medicines to help these people and we don't have the doctors to help these people, now. Their comfort comes in smoking the opium. If AID was to give us a hospital, give us the doctors, give us the medicine, we could stop growing opium. So, it's up to you." That was the end of the visit.[19]

* * *

Pop Buell was not with the Hmong at the end; he retired in 1974 and stayed for a time in Vientiane working at a school. When the Embassy learned he was on a Pathet Lao hit list, Les Strouse of the CIA–contracted Continental Air Services flew to Vientiane, disguised Pop in a pilot's uniform, drove him to the airport, and took him to Bangkok. Everything he owned fit into three battered suitcases. Pop never returned to the States. He died in Manila on December 29, 1980, while visiting a friend.[20]

The Hmong were tools of the United States in a war perceived to be against a monolithic, international communist conspiracy to take over the world. Admiration for their courage aside, the fate of Laos and the Hmong was of small concern to the geo-politicians in Washington. The attitude of the United States about Cambodia was indifference; about Laos it was ignorance. For example, in May 1975, the Department of State compiled a briefing book about Indochinese refugees for officials to use when testifying before Congress. There is no mention of Laos or Laotian refugees in the thick loose-leaf notebook. The State Department said: "We have acted quickly in establishing a system ... to deal with the large number of refugees who fled Viet-Nam and Cambodia after their collapse."[21] This statement is all the more remarkable because on that very date, May 12, 1975, the flight of the Hmong from Laos had begun. Washington failed to imagine until too late that hundreds of thousands of Vietnamese would wish to come to the United States. It failed to conceive of the possibility of a single Hmong refugee. The war in Laos had always been below the radar screen of all but a few in the U.S. government.

* * *

The Hmong had too few men and too little material to halt the advance of the North Vietnamese Army in Laos, which, by 1970, was estimated to number 67,000.[22] Vang Pao held off the North Vietnamese and the Pathet Lao forces for years by retreating in the dry season when the NVA could use the roads and its machines and attacking in the wet season when the small unit tactics of the Hmong prevailed. His casualties were heavy. By 1973, nearly 20,000 Hmong were estimated to have been killed in combat; 50,000 non-combatants were dead and 120,000 Hmong had been displaced.[23]

The Paris Peace Accord of 1973 and a subsequent agreement imposed by the U.S. on the Royal Lao government doomed the Hmong because American air cover and the military supplies the Hmong needed to continue their fight were prohibited. The highlanders were already hopelessly outmanned. Pop Buell said, "A short time ago we rounded up three hundred fresh recruits. Thirty percent were fourteen years old or less, and ten of them were only ten years old. Another 30 percent were fifteen or sixteen. The remaining 40 percent were forty-five or over. Where were the ones in between? I'll tell you— they're all dead."[24] By May 1975, Cambodia had fallen to the Khmer Rouge, South Vietnam to the North Vietnamese Army, and the remnants of Vang Pao's army were surrounded at Lima Site Twenty Alternate — LS 20A — 30 miles south of the Plain of Jars.

LS 20 A — Long Tieng (alternatively spelled Long Cheng or Tsieng) — was Vang Pao's headquarters, the second largest city in Laos, and "the most secret place on earth."[25] It was in a valley at 3,100 feet elevation, high enough to have chilly nights and cold fog. A runway 4,200 feet long occupied most of the length of the valley. It was a tough airport for pilots. On one side of the runway was Skyline Ridge; on the other were high mountains and just beyond the northwest end of the runway were steep karst outcrops several hundred feet high which looked like the waving mountains in Chinese landscape paintings. On the left hand corner of the runway, in the shadow of the karst, was "Sky," the CIA compound. Here visitors found an office, a bed, breakfast, and a bar. It was an important protocol for American officials abroad never to refer to the CIA by name. In Long Tieng the CIA was "Sky." Daniels named the compound and the organization after his home state of Montana, "Big Sky Country."[26]

"What a place Long Tieng is!" said Jim Schill of USAID. "Tribal soldiers dressed in military garb standing next to traditionally dressed Hmong, with Thai mercenaries still milling about. And the Americans here are mostly CIA operatives with goofy code names like Hog, Mr. Clean, Junkyard.

"The town itself is not much. There's one paved road running through it

Long Tieng, Laos, "the most secret place on earth." Sky (CIA) is on the left at the end of the runway beneath the large Karst outcrop. Vang Pao and Jerry Daniels left Sky by helicopter from the hill on the left of the photograph. (G.R. Jenkin)

and tin shacks on either side with eating shops, food stalls, and living quarters for the multitude of Hmong."[27] In the latter stages of the war only a few Americans continued to visit the besieged Hmong. Most flew in by helicopter or fixed wing aircraft from Vientiane in the mornings and returned in the afternoons. To avoid incidents that would be embarrassing to the United States, the number of visitors was strictly limited.

For Vang Pao the end became certain on May 5, 1975, when he was called before the prime minister of Laos, Souvanna Phouma, and ordered to cooperate with the communists. VP pulled the general's stars off of his collar, threw them on the floor, and stalked out of the room. The Lao government hoped to co-exist with the Pathet Lao in a coalition. The Hmong were expendable. "The Hmong have served me well," Souvanna Phouma would say later, "it is a pity that peace may come only at the price of their liquidation."[28] On May 9, the official Pathet Lao newspaper warned that the Hmong would be exterminated "to the last root."[29]

Jerry Daniels told Vang Pao it was impossible to continue the war.[30] The Americans would not give him the guns and the ammunition he now desperately needed. Both the Lao and American governments had given up. The future of Laos would be communist. With the North Vietnamese Army and the Pathet

4. The Hmong Escape Laos

Lao closing in for the kill, Vang Pao could either go down fighting or flee the country. Daniels, acting under orders from the Embassy, persuaded Vang Pao to leave Laos with the key people in his army. That was easier said than done. Of the 40,000 people in Long Tieng, how many were the American government willing to help escape the advancing communists? On May 8, Jerry proposed to the Embassy that 2,500 Hmong be evacuated from Long Tieng to Udorn, Thailand. Two days later he asked that the number be increased to 3,500. The evacuees would mostly be officers above the rank of captain and their families. The Lao government had promised that Hmong civilians and low-level soldiers would be safe — despite the government becoming more and more a puppet of the communists.

Daniels devised a strategy for the evacuation. However, he had only one 24-seat C-47 at his disposal and one Hmong pilot and the plane could only make two or three trips a day to Udorn. Every day more and more Hmong showed up in Long Tieng. Daniels needed more planes and more pilots. He didn't get help from the Embassy in Vientiane. The situation there was threatening to be a repeat of Danang and Saigon. In the words of General Roswell Round: "The activity and the atmosphere in Vientiane in May 1975 is chaotic.... Our overriding concern ... is for the safety of the remaining Americans ... we are deeply involved in the preparation for a possibly bloody air evacuation of Americans a la Saigon. I have so many things on my mind that there just isn't room for General Vang Pao ... I don't know if anyone at our Embassy is involved in the Hmong air evacuation."[31]

Help came from Brigadier General Heinie Aderholt, commander of the U.S. military assistance group in Bangkok. On Saturday morning, May 10, 1975, Aderholt — who with the departure of General Round from Laos, would be the last American general present in mainland Southeast Asia — received a telephone call at his office. The caller, who refused to give his name, explained that thousands of Hmong were stranded at Long Tieng airstrip in Laos. "The United States has abandoned the Hmong and they're going to be slaughtered if we don't do something!" shouted the caller.

Aderholt wanted to help, but with the American evacuation from Cambodia and Vietnam, the assets of the United States in the region had been drawn down to nearly nothing. Moreover, a direct U.S. military intervention on behalf of the Hmong would be illegal under U.S. law. In extremity, Aderholt turned to Bird Air, the odd, picturesque civilian airline formerly contracted to the United States government in Southeast Asia. He found out that one C-130 transport was still in Thailand, and the pilot, Matt Hoff, was at Don Muang International Airport in Bangkok at that very moment to leave the country on a commercial flight.

Aderholt knew everyone of importance in Southeast Asia and he telephoned the Thai general who ran Don Muang. "Arrest Matt Hoff if you have to," he asked, "and get him to the phone. I need to talk to him." Soon, a very angry Matt Hoff got on the telephone. "You made me miss my flight, Heinie. Now, what the hell is going on?" he shouted.

Aderholt explained the problem. "I want you to fly that C-130 up to Long Tieng and evacuate the Hmong." Hoff was reluctant; his job was over — and nobody wants to be the last to die in a war, least of all a lost war. "Name your price, Matt," said Aderholt.

"Five thousand dollars," said Hoff, a ridiculously high demand.

"Done," said Aderholt. "And five thousand dollars for each of your crew." It was an offer Hoff couldn't refuse. His salary as a Bird Air chief pilot was $3,000 per month. Crew members made $2,000 per month.[32]

Even with Hoff and his C-130, the evacuation would go too slowly as the Pathet Lao and the North Vietnamese armies advanced on Long Tieng. The most powerful nation on earth had a tough time finding airplanes to evacuate the Hmong, and only a single American employee of the CIA — Jerry Daniels — was on the ground in Long Tieng. The REMFs had forgotten that the Hmong had fought on the American side for 14 years and that they were now in the last extremity. Slowly, a few civilian aircraft were assembled. Les Strouse and Allen Rich of Continental Air Services were ordered to take their C-46s — transports of World War II vintage — from Bangkok to Udorn. "Tell us how many people you can carry out of Long Tieng," they were asked. "None," they answered. "It's not safe to bring a load out of Long Tieng with a C-46. You fly cargo in and come out empty." But the two pilots put their heads together and decided that they could take off with 35 people on the airplane and get out of the valley with some maneuvering — but a crash was certain if one of the two engines failed.[33] To lighten the planes they took out all the seats and stretched ropes across the cargo hold to give the passengers, who would sit on the floor, a handhold and to prevent a dangerous shift of weight if they slid toward the back of the plane.[34] Strouse and Rich flew the C-46s into Long Tieng on May 12. Matt Hoff and the C-130 arrived that same day after his plane was "sheep-dipped" — all marks identifying it as U.S.–owned were removed. With these three airplanes in service, the evacuation began at full throttle, but order began to break down as the Hmong in Long Tieng realized an evacuation was taking place and began to fight for places on the departing planes. On his first flight out, Strouse hauled 46 people on his C-46 and Rich took more than 50 — many more than their self-imposed safety limit. On subsequent flights they jammed 65 or more per flight onboard. Rich wrote in his flight log, "Crowd very difficult to control. Approx 14,000 in area. Time very short.... Shooting & fighting on ramp getting bad."[35] Strouse and Rich made three or four flights a day from Long Tieng to Udorn, but they drew the line at flying into Long Tieng at night, "No! Hell no!"[36]

Captain Kue Chaw — code named "Bison" for his solid, stocky build — was on one of the first C-130 flights out. Bison was a radio operator for Sky. He was especially vulnerable and Daniels told him to get his nine-man team out on an early flight. Kue Chaw assembled his team and their families, including his wife and 13 children — three were adopted orphans — and began loading them on the C-130. He stood on the cargo floor of the C-130, about three feet off the ground, and gave a hand to the women and children piling onto the aircraft. A Hmong colonel walked up to the open door of the airplane and objected. "Why are you loading these people?" he asked.

"Orders," Kue Chaw answered.

The colonel pulled a pistol and pointed it at Kue Chaw. "You'll take my orders — and load the people I tell you to."

Bison was a long-time soldier. The French had trained him as a 17-year-old parachutist in the early 1950s. More like an antelope than a bison in those days, Kue Chaw recalled his first parachute jump: "I was so light that it took two hours [a bit of exaggeration there] for me to float down to the ground," he said. "All the other parachutists landed long before me and stood watching me come down. After that whenever I jumped the French loaded me down with equipment so I would fall faster." On this occasion, Kue Chaw pulled his own pistol and pointed it at the colonel and the two faced each other for a few seconds. "I had the advantage," said Kue Chaw. "I was on the airplane and if the colonel shot me I might get to a hospital in Thailand. If I shot him he would be trampled by the crowd and die on the runway." The colonel lowered his firearm and stalked away. Kue Chaw holstered his pistol and continued loading people. But now people were clawing their way on board, trampling the weak. The pilot revved the engine and pressed the button that closed the cargo hatch. Two of Kue Chaw's youngest children, a ten-year-old boy and a girl, were still trying to get on the plane. He caught a last sight of them as the hatch closed and the big airplane began taxiing down the runway. There was no return.

The boy was lucky. Kue Chaw contacted General Aderholt and word went out to Long Tieng to get the boy on an evacuation plane; he caught the last flight from Long Tieng and joined his family in Thailand. The daughter was adopted by another family and remained in Laos. Thirty years later the family and the daughter had never met again. Many Hmong, especially those who worked with Sky, still believe it is too dangerous for them to return to Laos for a visit.[37]

The Hmong were flown from Long Tieng to Udorn Air Force base in Thailand and housed in old barracks at a nearby airbase. There was nothing to eat, and on the first day one of the Hmong went to the market in a nearby village and ordered 600 bags of fried rice for lunch and 600 more bags for dinner.[38] That was the first indication the locals had that they were hosting refugees from Laos.

On May 13, the North Vietnamese and Pathet Lao armies broke through the last outpost leading to Long Tieng. There was no hope now. Daniels planned to get Vang Pao and himself out of the country the next day. Daniels knew that every Hmong eye of the thousands surrounding the airstrip would be watching

Vang Pao and himself. "VP could not be seen getting into an aircraft on the runway with thousands and thousands of Hmong people around. It had to be done secretly," Jack Knotts said. "It was like panic. Like Saigon on the last day."[39]

Daniels enlisted two additional aircraft in his plan. Jack Knotts of Bird Air flew his small Bell 206 helicopter to Long Tieng early that morning and Dave Kouba of Continental Air Services flew in a Porter Pilatus—a single engine, short take-off and landing aircraft. Knotts would fly Vang Pao and Daniels out of Long Tieng in the helicopter; Kouba would be a decoy.

Vang Pao was secreted in a jeep and driven to a small lake on the ridge overlooking the airstrip. Daniels stayed at the airstrip lounging around the Porter with Kouba and drinking Olympia beer, the beer of choice for the CIA in Southeast Asia. He gave every appearance of being a man without a care in the world, but his eyes were sweeping the crowds surrounding the landing strip. "There's a couple of huckleberries around here," Daniels said, referring to potential assassins.[40] Finally, with Hmong attention focused on the transport planes loading people, Daniels jumped into his blue and white Ford Bronco and drove away quickly. Now, it was a race to get out of Long Tieng.

Vang Pao and Daniels met up with the helicopter on top of the ridge. They boarded the helicopter quickly and flew away. Thus were General Vang Pao and CIA agent Jerry Daniels borne into exile. The next day a Pathet Lao battalion walked unopposed into Long Tieng. The secret war in Laos was over.

A few days after Long Tieng fell the Americans left Vientiane and other cities in Laos. The American departure was less violent than that from Saigon. On May 23 Jim Schill and other AID employees were told to take two pieces of luggage, lock their houses and proceed to the Vientiane airport for an evacuation flight to Bangkok. On his way to the airport, Schill saw Pathet Lao everywhere. "Shit," he said. "We are just packing up and leaving.... I was getting out, but what about our employees, supporters, and loyal citizens of this little country that had caught the brunt of our misadventure."[41] The American era in Laos ended as ignominiously as it had in Vietnam and Cambodia. Unlike Vietnam and Cambodia, however, a skeleton staff kept the Embassy open. Laos became communist only gradually. The final step came in December 1975 when the king was deposed and the Peoples Democratic Republic of Laos was declared.

The denouement of life as it was known by Americans in Laos came on Saturday, May 31, when journalists David Andelman and Peter Kann paid a visit to the White Rose, "one of Southeast Asia's renowned watering holes, a must-drop-by rendezvous for spies, adventurers, soldiers of fortune, foreign correspondents, and diplomats of all stripes. It was empty but for us and a handful of the barely cheerful bar girls who were both hostesses and the floor show alike. They had just received the official order that all bars and nightclubs would be closed, orders from the Pathet Lao, who saw them as degenerate symbols of Western imperialism and exploiters of the Laotian people. Balderdash. The girls were heartbroken. But the next morning they would slip across the river to seek refuge in Thailand. This was the last night of the White Rose — a bittersweet moment indeed."[42] Madame Lulu's girls were not so fortunate. They were rounded up by the Pathet Lao and banished to a reeducation camp for 15 years each.[43]

* * *

What nobody anticipated was that the Hmong left behind would follow Vang Pao to Thailand. Some returned to home villages; but a mile-long caravan of Hmong left Long Tieng to walk the dusty road to Vientiane 120 miles away and the easiest route to Thailand. But, when the Hmong got to a bridge over the Lik River (Nam Lik), Lao soldiers had blocked it with a rope barricade. A soldier warned the Hmong to turn around and go back. An old man marched to the front and began to untie the rope. A soldier hit him with the butt of his rifle. The other soldiers began to shoot into the crowd of men, women, and children and advanced with bayonets, killing the wounded. "There was blood everywhere, covering the bridge like fresh paint." The soldiers forced the Hmong back up the road and chased them for 12 kilometers until they arrived at the village of Phon Hong. There, confronted by armed local policemen sympathetic to the Hmong, the soldiers abandoned the pursuit.[44]

The surviving Hmong scattered. Some made their way to a nearby river to hire boats to take them downstream to the Mekong and Thailand. Others made their way by hidden trails through the rugged mountains toward Thailand. Everywhere soldiers robbed and killed them. It was not only oppression by the communists that caused the Hmong to flee. All over the highlands Hmong were starving. The American aid that sustained them had abruptly halted. The experience of the first caravan from Long Tieng made the Hmong cautious. They buried their weapons and traveled at night in small groups on tortuous trails through the rugged mountains that towered up to 9,000 feet.

The stories of this flight are horrendous. Author Sue Murphy Mote tells the story of Chamy Thor, who would later become a college-educated welfare worker in Sacramento, California. Chamy fled with her family and hiked 20 days through the mountains carrying her infant son Johnny. Her group of 150 people ran out of rice and ate snails and rotten fruit. Weaker members, including Chamy's mother, died of malaria, exhaustion, and malnutrition. Soldiers captured Chamy's group before they reached the Mekong; they were roped together and marched to a prison camp in the jungle. By this time only one-half of the original 150 in the group were still alive. Later, the family made another attempt to escape. Traveling in a smaller group, they made it to the Mekong near a village. There, Chamy faced the deepest, darkest nightmare of a parent. Johnny cried. To wake up the village would risk capture and death for all of them. Chamy put her hands over the baby's mouth and nose. "I was very scared, because he kept crying ... and that's why a lot of people they do it until they — there's no sign left." Johnny's life was spared when he quit crying.

These shoeless Hmong refugees have just succeeded in floating or swimming across the Mekong River from Laos into Thailand and are being marched to a detention center. (Berta Romero)

On a raft made out of banana plants tied together with jungle vines, Chamy and her family crossed the river. Like most Hmong, Chamy didn't know how to swim and she held onto the raft with the baby on her back while the men paddled it across the huge, swirling river. When they reached Thailand on the other side, two armed men were waiting for them. One of them stole Chamy's gold necklace. A Thai policeman found them and took them to a refugee camp.[45]

Their experience in crossing the Mekong was typical. Countless Hmong drowned or were shot by Lao soldiers patrolling the river and or by Thai soldiers on the other bank. Of one group of 54 Hmong attempting to cross the Mekong only one person survived, an 11-year-old boy. The rest of the group were gunned down by Pathet Lao soldiers.[46] Despite the dangers, about 40,000 Hmong and other Lao crossed the Mekong by the end of 1975 and more came in succeeding years.[47]

From Thailand, Vang Pao and Daniels sent people to the Thai side of the Mekong to receive those who followed them. The Bison, Kue Chaw, combed the banks of the river helping them find their way to refugee camps. The CIA, it was said, gave $20 million to Thailand for a camp for the Hmong at Ban Vinai.[48] Ban Vinai would be the largest Hmong refugee camp in Thailand for the next 20 years. The government of Thailand, however, was nervous about having Vang Pao in its territory and ordered him to leave. So, the CIA arranged for Vang Pao to go to the U.S. and he left Thailand on June 18, 1975.[49] Jerry Daniels took him to his hometown of Missoula, Montana. Surrounded by rugged mountains, Missoula was a place a Hmong would like. Vang Pao purchased a 402-acre ranch 42 miles south of Missoula. The price was $450,000. The CIA helped him with the purchase and provided him with a pension of $35,000 per year. After getting VP settled in Missoula, Jerry Daniels returned to Thailand. He chose to stay with the Hmong and do what he could to help them.

* * *

Knowledge of the secret war in Laos only slowly came to light. In 1994 ex–CIA director William Colby saluted the Hmong. "For 10 years, Vang Pao's soldiers held the growing North Vietnamese forces to approximately the same battle lines they held in 1962. And significantly for Americans, the 70,000 North Vietnamese engaged in Laos were not available to add to the forces fighting Americans and South Vietnamese in South Vietnam."[50]

And, on May 15, 1997, as described by author Jane Hamilton-Merritt, "3,000 veterans of General Vang Pao's army—Hmong and Lao—dressed in jungle camouflage fatigues, flight suits, nurses uniforms stood at attention on the Mall in Washington, D.C., near the Vietnam Wall.... CIA Station Chiefs paid tribute to the extraordinary contributions of General Vang Pao and his brave forces in the fight for freedom in Southeast Asia and assisted in handing out the Vietnam Veterans National Medal.

"The next day, General Vang Pao and the remnants of his army, again wearing camouflage fatigues, assembled at Arlington National Cemetery. Six deep, they stood at attention for the dedication of the Memorial Monument— a small stone topped with a copper plaque, acknowledging the 'secret war' in Laos—and the Hmong, Lao, and American Advisors who valiantly served freedom's cause in the jungles of Southeast Asia and, in so doing, died in the Lao Theater in the Vietnam War. They will now be forever known and remembered."[51]

5

GUAM:
HALFWAY TO AMERICA

The sentiment in the United States was to put Vietnam behind us. California governor Edmund G. (Jerry) Brown, Jr., said, "We can't be looking 5,000 miles away and at the same time neglecting people who live here." An unsympathetic immigration official named Richard Williams watched planeloads of Vietnamese refugees unload in California and proclaimed, "What a zoo!"[1] Senator George McGovern said, "I think the Vietnamese are better off in Vietnam."[2] Ralph Nader's consumer group charged that the government was not taking precautions to protect Americans from diseases the refugees might spread.[3] *Newsweek* magazine summed up American public opinion: "There seemed to be a wide-spread feeling that the Vietnamese were inassimilable Asian aliens who couldn't have arrived at a worse time—in the middle of a severe economic recession and during a period of soul-searching when Americans did not want to live with human reminders of their country's traumatic experience in Indochina."[4]

* * *

The island of Guam is 2,500 miles east of Saigon and 3,700 miles west of Honolulu. A U.S. territory, Guam is 30 miles long, eight miles wide, and 212 square miles in area. In 1975 the population was 94,000, which did not include the thousands of American soldiers and sailors stationed there. One third of the land area of Guam was taken up by air and naval bases. Andersen Air Force Base on the north end of Guam was the U.S.'s largest base for B-52 bombers, the eight-engine behemoths that attempted to bomb the Vietnamese communists into submission. A B-52 could carry 108 500-pound bombs and fly from Guam to Vietnam and return without refueling. The first B-52 raid on Vietnam left Andersen in June 1965 and B-52s continued to rain bombs down on Vietnam, Laos, and Cambodia until August 1973.

Guam had fine beaches and coral reefs, but the bombing campaign dominated the life of the island. Richard Mackie, a Public Health Service officer, talks about the bombing: "There was no announcement. There was no warning. It just started happening. Every hour, day and night, every house ... would almost shake off its foundation as the deafening roar of three B-52s and a refueling plane would pass a few hundred feet over our heads.... Life became tedious. Sleep was almost impossible. Conversations were continually interrupted. We found ourselves constantly gritting our teeth and staring angrily at the ceiling as each 'sortie' passed overhead."[5] Guam's main highway was jammed day and night with trucks hauling bombs from the port to the airbase.

With the end of the bombing the noise and congestion came to an abrupt halt and the people of Guam believed that the Vietnam War was over for them. But in April 1975, with South Vietnam collapsing, the U.S. was forced to think about what it would do with Vietnamese evacuees. The Department of Defense was in charge of transporting the refugees and needed a place to sort them out before sending them onward to the United States.

The logical place to have warehoused the refugees was Clark Air Force Base and Subic Bay Naval Base in the Philippines, much closer to Vietnam than Guam. A few refugees were taken there, but President Ferdinand Marcos was emphatic: His country would not accept the Vietnamese — nor would any other country in the region. No Asian government wanted a refugee camp on its soil. They feared the refugees would be there forever.[6] Guam solved the problem. Guam governor Ricardo "Ricky" Bordallo offered to house the refugees temporarily in Guam.[7]

On April 23, 1975, the same day that the evacuation from Vietnam kicked into high gear, Rear Admiral George S. (Steve) Morrison, Commander of U.S. Naval Forces on Guam — father of the late rock singer Jim Morrison of The Doors — was ordered "to accept, shelter, process and care for refugees as they were removed from South Vietnam."[8]

Guam was hardly ideal. The military estimated that a maximum of 13,000 refugees could be housed on Guam and that number was exceeded in the first two days of the evacuation. The first refugees to arrive on Guam were "well dressed individuals ... carrying traditional luggage and holding on to the more usual accoutrements of holiday travel including tennis racquets and an occasional bag of golf clubs."[9] They were placed in empty apartments, but the supply was quickly exhausted as aircraft arrived every half hour and each disgorged 100 or more refugees. By April 27, the numbers had reached 20,000, and the refugees no longer looked like they were going to the country club for a round of golf. Often they had only the clothes on their backs. The quality of desperation grew as ships carrying refugees began to arrive at Guam in early May.

* * *

On leaving Vietnam, Lionel Rosenblatt and Craig Johnstone traveled to Guam. The first thing they saw on arrival was a large sign written in Vietnamese at McDonald's which said, "Welcome to Guam, Vietnamese Refugees." For the first time, Lionel had the feeling that things might turn out well. Then, they encountered Admiral Morrison. He had the two suspicious Americans mingling with the refugees brought to his office. They found him seated imperiously behind his desk, eyeing them skeptically while chomping an unlit cigar. Showmanship was not limited to only one generation of the Morrison family. He demanded to know who they were. They told him they were working for the Task Force for Indochinese refugees in Washington and were assisting with the evacuation. While they waited, Morrison called Washington and got the Task Force. Colonel Jerry Rose answered the phone. "I've got two guys from Washington named Johnstone and Rosenblatt here," bellowed the admiral. "They say they're working for you."

Rose might have said, "We've been looking for those two. They went to Saigon against orders. Send them home." Instead, without missing a beat, he said, "Oh, yes. We're glad to hear from you. Johnstone and Rosenblatt are our representatives and your cooperation is appreciated."

The admiral hung up the phone, scowled, and shoved the cigar back in his mouth. "Ok, pretty boys, you seem to be legitimate. Now get out of here."[10] Rosenblatt and Johnstone breathed a sigh of relief. Lionel stayed on in Guam a few more days; Craig departed for Washington in a mission of self-preservation. He told the story of their visit to Saigon to a *Washington Post* reporter and the story appeared on the front page of the newspaper.[11] Suddenly, they were heroes. Publicity about good deeds—scarce enough as the Indochinese countries fell to the communists—helped preserve their jobs. The bureaucracy in Washington did not like heroes who took good publicity away from their seniors, but it was fearful of persecuting them.

The denouement to the Rosenblatt and Johnstone saga came after both returned to Washington. Secretary of State Henry Kissinger called them to his office. Expecting the worst, to their surprise he shook their hands and said, "There has been little of which we can be proud these last few months. But you have brought credit to your country and to the Foreign Service."[12]

Lionel, always quick to take advantage of an opportunity, told the secretary that he wanted to work with the Interagency Task Force for Indochina. Kissinger arched an eyebrow. "That might not be a good career choice." Lionel insisted, and moreover said he wanted to hire 20 Indochinese to help him. Kissinger assented and sent Lionel to meet with Julia Taft, head of the Task Force. Thus, he became the head of the "Office of Special Concerns." The position was perfect, allowing Lionel freedom to determine what were special concerns—meaning he could meddle in everything. His staff soon grew to 42 persons, including 16 Vietnamese and two Cambodians, diplomats, and Vietnam experts.[13]

* * *

The refugees arriving in Guam stepped off airplanes onto buses borrowed from every school on the island and were driven to their quarters. Each person was given a cot, bed sheets and a blanket. Many of the refugees were surprised at how well they were received on Guam. Some were shocked. American principles of equality were strictly enforced. All refugees were treated equally, meaning that all spent a great deal of time waiting in lines for their name or number to come up. Scattered among the refugees were a few American citizens and the Vietnamese wives and families of Americans. They stood in line just like everybody else, complaining vociferously and demanding their rights. Lionel recalled seeing a group of Americans evacuated from Saigon living in a tent and awaiting return to the United States. Everybody was equal for a brief moment of misery in Guam.

Shelter was the first priority and the biggest problem. On day one, April 23, construction battalions—the famous Seabees—rehabilitated "Tin City" at Andersen AFB, a forest of metal quonset huts. Tin City had a capacity of 4,800 people. At Asan Point, the Seabees rehabilitated and installed electricity and water in an abandoned hospital that had not been used for 15 years and wooden barracks left over from World War II.[14] Those two areas were filled up within 24 hours. The Seabees then bulldozed an area christened "Tent City" to accommodate 50,000 refugees. In three days, the Seabees cleared 1,200 acres of brush, "erected nearly 4,000 tents; constructed 22 'Southeast Asia huts' (wood frame and tin roofed buildings); built 150 public showers (each for use by 8 people); erected 750 latrines; constructed eight mess halls ... put up four miles of chain link fence; and provided wiring for electric lights to tents and water lines to showers and laundry facilities."[15] Twenty thousand military personnel were involved as well as untold numbers of civilian volunteers. In addition to the arrival of airplanes full of refugees, other airplanes arrived in a steady stream full of food, shelter materials, and medicine. Guam had no surplus of anything—except good will—to share with the refugees.

On May 7, three merchant ships arrived in Guam. Crammed onto them were 13,000 refugees—the highest number of arrivals on any single day.[16] This group was "farmers, fishermen, local tradesmen and venders, students, and common soldiers ... in one case, an entire fishing village.... Many gave the impression of not knowing where they were or why they were there. Some had simply fled in panic—as the Vietnamese have fled for years...." Once in Guam however, "their destination was the United States. Exactly how many never intended to travel to the Philippines or Guam, much less to continental United States, will never be fully known."[17] Many Vietnamese refugees came to the United States accidentally.

Every day thereafter more refugees arrived on navy and merchant ships and fishing boats. On May 13, the refugee population on the island peaked at 50,450. Many of the refugees had already been transported onward to the United States. The final grand total of Vietnamese refugees transiting Guam in 1975 totaled 111,000.[18] Thousands of additional refugees went to Wake Island and other islands and countries in Asia.

The people of Guam bore up under the refugee influx with good spirits. "Their children could not go to school because their buses were being used by the refugees, they could not swim or fish in their lagoons or beaches, their water supply was severely rationed, travel was limited because of the influx of military vehicles jamming the roads, they were receiving a biweekly fogging with malathion [a pesticide] and they were under threat of several mosquito borne and sewage borne diseases."[19]

Mackie, the Public Health Service officer, worried about an epidemic of dengue fever and — most of all — a typhoon.[20] Guam is typhoon-prone. In an average year three tropical storms and one typhoon pass near or over the island, and about every decade one super-typhoon, with winds in excess of 150 miles an hour, ravages Guam.[21] Even a modest tropical storm and a few inches of rain would have been a disaster for the refugees on Guam. For once the gods smiled. No typhoon hit Guam in 1975.

* * *

Not everybody in Saigon thought that the evacuation from Vietnam was necessary. Employees of the American Friends Service Committee (AFSC) discouraged Vietnamese from evacuating. "We told them what we remembered of the PRG's [the Provision Revolutionary Government of South Vietnam] 10-point program for newly-liberated areas ... two supplicants ... were delighted when we advised them to stay ... they had been panicked into thinking they were likely material for the PRG's bloodbath: the neighbor's daughter, because she'd worked as a secretary for Air Viet Nam, and a Chinese merchant because he'd done business with Americans."[22]

The AFSC representatives remained behind in Saigon until July. They maintained that much of the evacuation was "political" and therefore unnecessary and that Vietnamese refugees who wanted to return home would be welcomed. "The impression we formed in private conversations is that the new government wants the refugees to come back home — if the refugees themselves want to, and if they are ready to work to build the new society. At the same time, there are strong fears that the returnees will include a number of CIA infiltrators. It also seems reasonable to assume that the refugees will have to be prepared to undergo a period of political 'study and practice' on their return."[23]

The AFSC relied on the pronouncements of the People's Revolutionary Government to counsel Vietnamese to stay. In 1969, the PRG had promised pardons and "equal treatment" to South Vietnamese officials and soldiers who were "repentant and sincerely return to the people."[24] Their contention that the new government of Vietnam would welcome returnees was quickly tested. That summer in Guam refugees came forward who said they wanted to return to Vietnam. During the final days the South Vietnamese Navy had gathered its vessels in Saigon harbor, crammed everyone they could fit aboard and headed out to sea, ending up in Guam. One of the crew on board a ship was Commander

Tran Dinh Tru. Tru's wife and three children were still in Vietnam. He had been unable to locate them in the chaos of those last days and had been ordered to steam away without them. Others among the crews of the ships and their passengers were in the same situation.

Tru said, "Everybody now felt secure, relaxed, and ready to focus on their future — all except me."[25] One young woman, who perhaps had made her living as a bar girl in Saigon, left her country without a backward glance. "Thanks to the Viet Cong, I can finally live in the United States."[26] A younger sister wrote Commander Tru that Saigon was hell, "a place nobody wanted to live and from where millions wanted to escape despite the dangers."[27] However, Tru didn't change his mind. Despite warnings that not all was well in Saigon, he wanted to go home and find his wife and family.

Tru was not alone; about 1,500 of the refugees on Guam wanted to go back to Vietnam.[28] Many were, like him, military men who had boarded ships in Saigon and left families behind. On May 3, a group of Vietnamese Air Force pilots were the first to request repatriation and others soon followed suit. For their safety — the anti-communist sentiment among the Vietnamese ran high — those wishing to return to Vietnam were separated from the other refugees. In response to the demand for repatriation by Tru and others, the State Department on May 8 sent a message to refugee camps and embassies stating that refugees who wished to return home could do so. The message said that the United Nations High Commissioner for Refugees (UNHCR) would assume responsibility for returning the refugees.[29]

UNHCR, however, was reluctant to get involved. "The attitude of UNHCR," said Frank Wisner, "was that the Americans merited the refugee crisis as the consequence of its war in Vietnam."[30] Wisner pressed the matter and UNHCR began to work with the Vietnamese, although it avoided calling them "refugees" as that would imply that assisting them was a legal obligation of UNHCR.[31]

International law governs the treatment of refugees. Horrified that so many people fleeing Nazi Germany had been refused entry into other countries and died in concentration camps in World War II, in 1951 the members of the new United Nations negotiated the "Geneva Convention Relating to the Status of Refugees." Article One of the Convention defines a refugee as any person "who, owing to a well-founded fear of being persecuted for reasons of race, religion, nationality, membership of a particular social group or political opinion, is outside the country of his nationality and is unable, or, owing to such fear, unwilling to avail himself of the protection of that country."[32] Thus, to be a refugee and to be protected by the Convention a person had to be outside his home country and to have a well-founded fear of persecution should he return. The U.S. had ratified the Convention — but none of the Southeast Asian countries had.

The negotiators of the Refugee Convention operated with a mental framework that envisioned uncontested borders, functioning governments, and congruent legal systems—none of which applied to the movements of people in the new nations of Asia and Africa. Refugees were seen as mostly being from the educated elite of a country. For example, a journalist who published an article critical of his oppressive government and subsequently fled his country might qualify as a refugee because he would be persecuted if he returned home. A farmer, on the other hand, whose land or crop had been destroyed by the ravages of war, natural disaster, or confiscated by the government might not qualify as a refugee because his problems were economic rather than political. International refugee law was on the side of people who might go to jail for their words rather than the farmer who might starve as a result of his government's action, inaction, or incompetence.

Moreover, the Convention presumed that countries would routinely grant asylum to persons determined to qualify as refugees until such time as they could return home safely, or, if that proved impossible, resettle them permanently in either the country of asylum or a third country. Asylum is a temporary grant of sanctuary given to individuals fleeing persecution. As a matter of fact, none of the Southeast Asian countries would consider accepting Indochinese for resettlement. They had not ratified the Refugee Convention and were under no legal obligation to conform to its provisions.

Refugee law and the role of UNHCR would be stretched beyond the conception of its founders by the Indochinese refugee crisis.[33] Between 1975 and 1980, UNHCR's budget would increase from $80 million to $500 million, money mostly spent for the care and feeding of Indochinese refugees.[34] The transition of UNHCR would be painful and the agency would get few plaudits from activists like Rosenblatt and Yvette Pierpaoli, who saw UNHCR as slow, legalistic, and bureaucratic.

The most important obligation of the nations ratifying the Refugee Convention was to not force a refugee to return to a situation of serious risk in his home country. Article 33 of the Convention says, "States shall not expel or return (*refouler*) a refugee in any manner whatsoever to the frontiers of territories where his life or freedom would be threatened on account of his race, religion, nationality, membership or a particular social group or political opinion."[35] This principle is referred to as "non-refoulement." UNHCR has the responsibility to determine if a person claiming to be a refugee has a *bona fide* right to that status and, if so, UNHCR has the obligation to prevent his refoulement.

Three courses of action are available to UNHCR for dealing with refugees. First, refugees may remain in the country in which they have taken asylum. Secondly, they may be resettled in a third country. Thirdly, they can choose to return to their homeland. Repatriation was the preferred option for UNHCR when dealing with large numbers of refugees. A built-in conflict exists between UNHCR's legal responsibility to prevent refoulement and its operational objective of encouraging refugees to return home. The decision by a refugee to return to his homeland is often a Hobson's choice: live indefinitely in a squalid refugee camp or return home to a dangerous situation. Countries housing unwanted refugees often ensure that life in a refugee camp is as unpleasant as possible to encourage the refugees to repatriate.

UNHCR's preference was to help create the conditions under which refugees would choose to return to their homeland. The agency, reluctantly drawn into the Indochinese refugee crisis, seized on repatriation as its priority. To carry out a repatriation program, UNHCR had to obtain the assurances from the new government of Vietnam that its citizens would be welcomed back. The government duly promised that it would receive "those Vietnamese who had recently been induced to leave their country by false propaganda or who had been taken abroad against their will and wished to be repatriated."[36] But the process was bogged down. Vietnam demanded that UNHCR complete a lengthy questionnaire and compile a dossier on each potential returnee. The UNHCR sent Saigon a first package of 600 completed questionaires.[37] No response was forthcoming. Dissatisfied by the glacial pace of UNHCR, the unresponsiveness of Vietnam, and the demands of the potential returnees on Guam, the U.S. took matters into its own hands. On July 21, Julia Taft, the director of the Interagency Task Force for Indochina, sent a memorandum to Kissinger. Taft reported that demonstrations by the Vietnamese refugees on Guam demanding repatriation would likely occur soon and might become violent.

"We are caught in a difficult position. The Communist authorities in Vietnam have no reason to move quickly and report they are still studying the applications already transmitted. They may have a hand in the present threats of violence but we have no proof of this. The risk of Congressional criticism and bad publicity is constant.

"We should anticipate trouble on July 24 and thereafter." Taft explained that returning the repatriates unilaterally was not a viable option as the U.S. "would be justifiably criticized for failing to ensure the refugees safe return and the UNHCR could withdraw its good offices."[38]

As Taft anticipated, trouble soon broke out, with protests, hunger strikes, and threats of suicide by refugees on Guam. The refugees demanded immediate repatriation and proposed that the U.S. give them a ship and that they return to Vietnam on their own responsibility. The refugees named Commander Tru to command the ship and affirmed that a full crew would be available from those wishing to return.[39]

The idea gained momentum. In September, Taft recommended that the refugees be allowed to return to Vietnam on the *Tuong Tin*, a Vietnamese ship anchored in the harbor in Guam. The *Tuong Tin* was large enough (487 feet and 6,275 tons) to carry all the returnees, but nobody could be sure what kind of reception it might receive in Vietnam. Taft speculated that the ship might even be fired upon. "The international community would be outraged," she said. "Whether this outrage would be directed toward Vietnam for its inhumane treatment or the U.S. for gambling the lives of the repatriates is an unknown."[40] Taft and others were well aware that, in the eyes of many, the U.S. could do no good and Vietnam no harm. Cautious bureaucrats disassociated themselves from the risky operation. Henry Kissinger ducked the decision; Taft got presidential assistant Brent Scowcroft to shepherd the memo to the president.[41]

Julia Vadala Taft, only 33 years old, had been propelled into prominence as head of the Interagency Task Force on Indochina with lunch group member Frank Wisner of the State Department as her deputy. Tall, attractive and congenial, she was the daughter of an Army doctor and a graduate of the University of Colorado. She began her career as the only woman among 17 White House Fellows in the Nixon White House and she later married into the most venerated of all Republican families, the Tafts. She had a decisiveness and courage rare among government officials. She could play the bureaucratic game with the Washington elite, but she also had admiration for mavericks such as Lionel Rosenblatt who had the fortitude to swim against the tide.

President Ford approved giving the *Tuong Tin* to the refugees for their return to Vietnam. In the best tradition of dodging responsibility, UNHCR quickly stated that it was not involved "in any attempt at repatriation which is not conducted according to agreed procedures."[42] In other words, if things went wrong it denied in advance having anything to do with it.

The United States and UNHCR were both well aware that refugee camps full of idle and highly-stressed people become hotbeds of politics and gang politics and that camp bullies, criminals, and demagogues often gain power by strong-arm tactics and intimidation. Thus, it was essential that the real wishes of the individual refugees be ascertained through careful private interviews. The U.S. worried that some of the soldiers, sailors, airmen and civilians stating they desired to return to Vietnam were influenced or ordered to take such a stance by their superiors or camp agitators.

Two Vietnamese experts from Rosenblatt's Office of Special Concerns took on the task of counseling sessions with each potential repatriate and his family. The objective was to ensure that each of the repatriates made his decision to return voluntarily. The only way to do that was to isolate each from his fellows. An processing center was set up with "six isolated interview rooms and three separate exits, so that the choice to return by ship of any individual could be made privately without the knowledge of other repatriates." On entering the interview rooms, the "repatriates were given the latest information on the economic and political situation in South Vietnam.... Repatriates being interviewed were counseled that they could exercise one of three choices. If a repatriate decided to board the ship immediately, he was given a card marked 'A' and escorted through a special corridor to a bus loading area. If he decided he did [not] want to return on the ship but preferred to return to the U.S. refugee system, he was given a card marked 'B' and taken through a separate secret corridor to waiting buses.... If the repatriate wanted more time to consider his decision, he was given a card marked 'C' and escorted through a third corridor to a special room at the top of the outprocessing center to weigh his options.... Altogether forty-five would-be repatriates elected not to return on the ship...." Those declining repatriation were taken back to the camp; those choosing to repatriate were taken directly to the *Tuong Tin*.

Despite the safeguards "it became apparent that the repatriate camp leadership was exerting considerable pressure on all members of the group not to opt out of returning on the ship. While the outprocessing was taking place, a group of specially designated repatriates wearing red arm bands circulated among the rest of the group remaining in the camp and threatened each and every repatriate with severe recriminations against families remaining in Vietnam should anyone decide not to return on the ship. This psychological pressure had considerable impact on some repatriates. Twenty people broke down in tears and suffered severe psychological trauma in making the decision to return. Most of these people did not want to go back but said they had no choice because of fear for their families' safety."[43] The politics of refugee camps are brutal.

The *Tuong Tin* set sail on October 15, despite an advance warning from South Vietnam that the repatriation "was an 'irresponsible maneuver' by the United States."[44] On board were 1,546 Vietnamese, including the crew.[45] Only 128 of the returnees were women.[46] Most were former officers and enlisted men in the Vietnamese Army, Navy, and Air Force who had left their families in Vietnam.[47] The fate of the *Tuong Tin* then became a mystery to the United States for more than a decade. Captain Tru told the unknown story many years later. Tru captained the *Tuong Tin* to near the entrance to the Saigon River and anchored on October 26. He then radioed the Vietnamese Coast Guard.

"We are Vietnamese coming from Guam. Please tell us what we have to do now."

"Where is Guam?" asked the Coast Guard.

That was the beginning of the *Tuong Tin*'s travails. The captain eyed the shore with his binoculars. "Only a few months ago, Cape Vung Tau was so bustling that ships and boats had to scramble to be the next one in line to enter the Saigon River. Now not a soul was on the beach, and all the rundown kiosks along the beach were closed. Streets were empty. A bicycle or two passed by; an occasional boat straggled here and there. It was dreary and dismal...."[48]

Three navy ships escorted the *Tuong Tin* north to Nha Trang. There, interrogators subjected Tru and the other repatriates to endless questions. Why was he picked by the Americans to assume command of the ship? Was he aware that the repatriation was illegal? Was he challenging the authority of the revolutionary government? Or did he have another agenda? He was under constant watch and not allowed to talk to others. Communist governments always seemed to understand very well that people would like to leave, but were perplexed and suspicious when someone returned home.

Police swarmed over the vessel, divided the passengers into groups and loaded them onto two large barges that took them to the docks where a caravan of covered military vehicles were waiting. Tru and two others were taken to a prison and installed in a cell. They were told they would be allowed to rejoin their families when they had learned three lessons: they must "go through the program, internalize the revolutionary policies, and faithfully execute all the work" assigned to them.[49] Tru was given a brief letter from his wife and told that she and the children had attempted to kill themselves when he had disappeared. Then he was subjected to three months of twice-daily interrogations and endless long sessions of writing his "confession."

One day Tru and his colleagues were told that they would be taken to a reeducation camp in the countryside. The camp "featured a few rows of cottages, walls made of leaves, barbed war, and watchtowers on the four corners.... Each of us was given a reed mat to be placed on the makeshift bamboo bed. Each bed had a bamboo shelf for our luggage. A line of barbed wire was strung along each side of the thirty bed rows, and supported by bamboo poles to which we could tie our mosquito nets." Every detail of the life of the inmates of the reeducation camp was regulated "with strict codes of discipline and daily schedules governing everything from wakeup time and morning personal hygiene to mealtime and nightly self-examination sessions.... Like buffaloes, we resiliently and obediently worked the fields on a simple diet provided at a subsistence level: a yam for the morning, two yams or two ears of corn for noon, and two more for the evening." Being deprived of rice was especially difficult. "With this scanty riceless diet, we were forced to labor all day from dawn to dusk, day after day. Living a grim life in the wild, we had to plow the rocky land, slash the trees, drink the filthy water, and scamper like rats in the forest for food."[50]

Many inmates died of eating poison vines and roots or were beaten to death by the soldiers guarding the camp. After three months the inmates were allowed to send one letter a month to their families; months later they were allowed to receive gifts, including food up to a maximum of three kilograms a month of rice. Tru showed pride in the accomplishments of the prisoners. "After one year of harsh labor, hundreds of detainees turned this wild forest into a village of wooden houses with large patches of lush plants and vegetables abundant enough to feed not only the inmates, but also the security guarding the camp."[51]

After 18 months in the camp the inmates were loaded into trucks and sent north to another labor camp in the mountains near the border of Laos. Conditions there were worse. Then late in 1978, Tru and his colleagues were moved south again to a larger camp in which he met some of his old military colleagues. Many of them had confessed to being former soldiers with a promise of amnesty after a brief education course. To the contrary, they found themselves shipped away to camps and condemned to years of imprisonment.

Living conditions improved. On Tet, the New Year, the inmates received a small piece of meat, a bowl of rice, and a marble-sized sweet pastry. Now and then a detainee would be released. Families were allowed to visit. For Tru, the first family visit came six years into his detention. He sat at a table with his wife and three children while an armed guard sat at the end of the table and monitored their conversation. Soon, however, Tru and others were moved again. This time thousands of inmates were loaded onto railroad cars and headed southward. Tru went to Gia Trung camp in the Montagnard highlands. The camp "was run by animal-like hooligans trained in the art of intimidating, beating, and torturing inmates.... Days in this camp were the longest ever, and the pains here, the most excruciating." But, slowly, over the years things got better again with more frequent family visits, more food gifts, and even gift packages from relatives in Australia and the United States. "And more dramatically, since the cadres could savor some imported cigarettes and candies from detainees, they toned down their rhetoric and became less animal like. They, in fact, tried to befriend us so they could partake of the exotic gifts we obtained from our families ... the rules of the game were changed overnight. Americans were no longer imperialists, and we, no longer enemy of the country."[52] Another move to another labor camp ended this soft life for Tru, but the communists had learned pragmatism. At the new camp the prisoners were allowed to continue receiving gifts and food from relatives but they were worked longer and harder then ever. "There was always one more construction project to complete and a shorter deadline to meet ... the wild Viet Nam Cordillera jungle was magically tamed with us as human bulldozers."[53]

On February 13, 1988 — 12 years after being imprisoned — Tran Dinh Tru's name was called out at the morning muster of prisoners. He would be released. "One hour later, I got into an old truck, and bid adieu to my years of harsh labor.... This time the trucks were not covered, and we were not handcuffed. We were free men, at last."[54]

The UNHCR visited Hanoi and Saigon in December 1975 to ascertain what had happened to the Vietnamese who had returned to Vietnam on the *Tuong Tin*. They were told only that the repatriates were detained in a camp outside Saigon. UNHCR also inquired of the Vietnamese when an additional 396 Vietnamese in the United States desiring to return home would be allowed to repatriate. The Vietnamese advised that the time was not ripe to discuss repatriation.[55] That stopped any notion of further repatriation of Vietnamese. Nor did any more Vietnamese come forward requesting repatriation.

Tran Dinh Tru, his wife and three children later immigrated to the United States. The fate of the majority of those returning with him on the *Tuong Tin* is unknown.

* * *

The debate about the Vietnam War in the United States was bitter. Both supporters and opponents painted the motives and the character of the opposing side in the most evil of hues and attributed the most positive of virtues to the side they favored. To the opponents of the American participation in the Vietnam War, Ho Chi Minh was George Washington and the North Vietnamese were gentle nationalists with democratic instincts opposed by the corrupt, kleptocratic South Vietnamese government, a puppet of the imperialistic United States. Socialist Norman Thomas said, in dismay, that some opponents of the war "love the Vietcong more than they love peace."[56] The supporters of the war saw a monolithic communist conspiracy to take over the world and a domino impact: If Vietnam became communist so would all Southeast Asia.

The good-natured entry of the North Vietnamese army into Saigon quelled the fears of the "bloodbath" predicted by many. It was only over a period of years that a less palatable truth emerged. Unlike the Khmer Rouge the North Vietnamese did not take immediate and radical steps to assert their control over the population of the South. Nevertheless, there were large differences between North and South after 21 years of separation. "The December 1975 *Vietnam Courier*, an official government publication, portrayed Vietnam as two distinct, incongruent societies. The South was reported to continue to suffer from what communists consider the neo-colonialist influences and feudal ideology of the United States, while the North was considered ... a progressive environment for growing numbers of a new kind of socialist human being, imbued with patriotism, proletarian internationalism, and socialist virtues. The class of social exploiter had been eliminated in the North, leaving the classes of workers, collectivized peasants, and socialist intellectuals, the last consisting of various groups. In contrast, the South was divided into a working class, peasantry, petit bourgeois, capitalist — or comprador — class, and the remnant of a feudal landlord class."[57]

Among the first steps of the new government in Ho Chi Minh City was the remolding of the character of the South Vietnamese population through the infamous "reeducation" that seemed always to be a part of communist regimes. In 1976, the AFSC representatives saw this as positive. "Re-education is in essence part of the process of unification. Virtually every family had some members on the 'other side' during the war, accounting in large part for the depth and sincerity of the spirit of reconciliation in Viet Nam today."[58] That was a most generous view of the re-education camps.

The reality was that, while Tru's reeducation experience was longer and harsher than most, it was not atypical. Altogether, more than one million people — mostly men and heads of families — were forced into 150 reeducation camps during the first years of communist rule in South Vietnam. About 500,000 of them spent more than 2 years in the camps and 240,000 at least five years.[59] Some of the prisoners were held only a few weeks; others for as long as 15 years. The conditions in the camps resulted in a lot of premature deaths. The communist masters of Vietnam were determined to destroy the old capitalistic society of South Vietnam. The result would be a floodtide of refugees.

6

Resettlement

Julia Taft was worried. She took over the leadership of the Interagency Task Force (IATF) for Indochinese Refugees on May 27, 1975. Thousands of Indochinese, nearly all of them Vietnamese, were arriving daily in the U.S. She had no certainty as to what she would do with them. The State Department hoped that the situation could be internationalized, and that other countries would accept 15,000 Vietnamese for resettlement.[1] That was overly optimistic. The world was indifferent or antagonistic to the plight of the Vietnamese and the United States. Momentarily, Taft had gone from an obscure political position in the Department of Heath, Education, and Welfare (HEW), to one as visible, controversial, and divisive as any in the government.

The IATF consisted of 12 government agencies concerned with Indochinese refugees. The Departments of State and HEW were the most important players, although the Immigration and Naturalization Service (INS) was the final authority in determining if an individual refugee would be granted "parole" into the United States. In reality, INS had little choice but to grant parole. The U.S. couldn't send people involuntarily back to Vietnam. The IATF quickly expanded into a vast undertaking with thousands of employees seconded to it by other agencies and far flung operations that reached from Guam to Washington.

Taft inherited a resettlement program in trouble. First, was the chaotic evacuation, a coda to the disastrous American intervention in Vietnam. Not only were the politicians unenthusiastic, so was the public. A Gallup poll in early May showed that 54 percent of Americans opposed the refugees coming to live in the U.S. versus only 36 percent in favor.[2] "A backlash of unprecedented proportions," said the *Boston Globe*, "is threatening to make the South Vietnamese the first unwanted wave of refugees to reach America's shores since the Statue of Liberty was erected in New York Harbor."[3] Americans who had opposed the war had little compassion for the refugees. Philip Weber of the Indochina Peace Campaign "feared that many refugees would become active in right wing politics and they would serve as 'the next generation' of CIA agents."[4] Representatives of the American Friends Service Committee demonstrated their

Table 1.
Criteria for Admitting Indochinese Refugees on Parole into the United States*

Between 1975 and the adoption of a new Refugee Law by the United States in 1980, nearly all Indochinese refugees entered the U.S. on parole. Parolees had to meet the requirements of one of the categories listed below with Category I taking precedence over Category II, Category II over Category III, etc. For practical purposes, parolees had the same rights and obligations as a person admitted to the U.S. as an immigrant.

Category I	Close relatives of persons in the United States or unaccompanied minors and young adults under 17 years of age.
Category II	Former U.S. government employees.
Category III	Refugees who because of a previous close association with the United States were persecuted or were in fear of being persecuted by the Communist regime; former employees of U.S. foundations, voluntary agencies, and business firms; and spouses and children of persons who would have qualified, but who were dead or unable to escape.
Category IV	Other refugees who because of compelling reasons should be granted parole on humanitarian grounds.

The documentation for applicants was prepared by Department of State Consular officers and caseworkers of the Joint Voluntary Agency (JVA). The International Commission for European Migration (ICEM, later IOM) had responsibility for medical clearances and transportation of refugees. The Immigration and Naturalization Service (INS) had the final decision concerning the eligibility of an individual to be paroled.

*Adapted and simplified from: United States, Cong. House, *Refugees from Indochina: Current Problems and Prospects*, 37–39.

---

undying faith in the good will of the North Vietnamese conquerors. "What we hope is that the refugees here, when they see things calm down over there, will go home to rebuild their lives."[5] Vernon Jordan of the National Urban League interjected a racial element into the debate. "The Vietnamese will not have an easy time adjusting, especially in view of America's traditional racism."[6]

The *Globe* cited three reasons for the unpopularity of the Vietnamese: "They are coming all at once, flooding off military transports ... they are coming at a time of high unemployment (8.9 percent) ... [and] they symbolize a $150 billion war that lasted a decade, rent this nation to its core and ended in America's first military defeat."

Senator Edward M. Kennedy of Massachusetts called a meeting of government task force officials with the charitable organizations responsible for resettlement in early May. It disintegrated into a "shouting match" with the charity leaders accusing the government of being "confused, uncertain and inexperienced in this complicated field." Kennedy's investigation caused him to describe the efforts to receive the refugees in the United States as a "shambles."[7] Thus, Taft inherited a resettlement program that seemed to be running off the tracks. She saw that momentum was crucial in getting the Vietnamese resettled and that delays in the program would work against the public's acceptance of the refugees. She set a goal, at first in her mind and later in public, that the Indochinese refugee program would be finished by Christmas 1975 and that the IATF could be abolished in January 1976. In late May 1975, not many of her colleagues would have agreed that it would be possible to resettle all the Vietnamese in only six months.

Julia Taft's first act was to journey to Fort Indiantown Gap, Pennsylvania, a military base, to meet the first planeload of 341 Vietnamese refugees arriving there from Guam on May 28. A high-level group of Pennsylvania politicians and Washington officials came to greet them. They waited, and waited, for the first plane. Undaunted, Governor Milton Shapp proceeded to give a speech of welcoming to the new arrivals—who hadn't arrived yet—with flourishes of rhetoric that would get him a sound bite on the NBC evening news.[8] When the big transport airplane finally arrived, Taft waited anxiously for the first refugees to step off the plane into the warm Pennsylvania air. The Vietnamese, Taft recalled, had often fled Saigon with no more than they could carry in their hands; many of them had been crowded onto navy ships for the long journey to Guam; others had been jammed aboard merchant vessels lacking every comfort. On Guam they had been housed in tents and quonset huts and now they were concluding a 7,000 mile, 24-hour ride on a crowded and comfortless airplane. "I couldn't imagine what the refugees would look like," said Taft.

The door opened and out stepped the first family: a handsome man, his gorgeous wife dressed in a long, flowing, flowered Vietnamese *ao dai*, and three polite, well-groomed children. They were followed by another equally attractive family, and then another. The crowd responded with admiration. Somebody out there on Guam, perhaps Admiral Morrison, the father of a rock star, had ensured that the Vietnamese made a good first impression. Among those impressed was the head of the Immigration and Naturalization Service (INS) and former commandant of the Marine Corps, Leonard F. Chapman, Jr. Taft recalled him saying, "When I went up to Indiantown Gap I was sure the Vietnamese refugees were going to carry spears and wear no clothes. When I saw these people and I realized what loving couples and families they were, I was so proud of my country and I knew that we should do everything we could to help them." Taft breathed a sign of relief. The INS was often difficult and obstructive. That its chief was enthusiastic would make her job much easier. For Taft, the visit to Indiantown Gap and the reaction of Chapman was the moment she knew that the resettlement program for Vietnamese could succeed.[9]

Taft's optimism was borne out by a change in the mood of the American public. Rosenblatt and Johnson's excursion to Saigon was a front-page story in *The Washington Post* as Americans salvaged what uplifting news they could from the disaster in Saigon.[10] Another heart-warming article in the *Post* told of the ten Vietnamese refugees living in the two-bedroom home of Ken Quinn and his Vietnamese wife. Quinn was doubly distinguished as the Foreign Service officer who had first alerted the Department of State of the character of the Khmer Rouge. Quinn had converted himself temporarily into a social service agency dedicated to enrolling six Vietnamese children in school, finding jobs for the adults—and looking for a bigger house.[11]

* * *

The government designated four military bases as centers for processing refugees and orienting them to the United States after their stay on Guam or other Pacific Ocean islands. The largest was Fort Chaffee in Arkansas, with a capacity of 24,000 refugees, followed by Camp Pendleton in California (capacity 18,000), Fort Indiantown Gap in Pennsylvania (17,000), and Eglin Air Force Base in Florida (6,000).[12]

The military was not altruistic in offering its bases to house the refugees. The Department of Defense charged the $500 million budget of the IATF for every light bulb and gallon of gas expended on its behalf. And the price charged was high. "When I saw the price the Air Force wanted to charge us for transporting refugees," said Frank Wisner, Taft's deputy, "I told them I wanted to borrow the airplanes—not buy them."[13] But the military was essential. It had land and buildings to house refugees and tens of thousands of young, healthy, disciplined soldiers, sailors, Marines, and airmen who could be ordered to turn their full attention to the care and feeding of the refugees.

There was little time to prepare the bases for the arrival of refugees. The first refugees arrived at Camp Pendleton on April 29, followed by arrivals at Chaffee on May 2 and Eglin on May 4. Indiantown Gap was added when it became apparent that the other three bases would be inadequate for the numbers coming to the U.S. Chaffee was the biggest challenge for getting ready for the refugees. Most of the barracks on the huge base were of World War II vintage—rectangular two-story whitewashed buildings of rough-hewn wooden planks, a communal toilet and showers on each floor, coal-fired furnaces for winter heating and no air conditioning. The base was mostly closed; its complement was only 500 soldiers except in the summer when thousands of Army reservists descended on Chaffee for their annual two-week field training.[14] The first task of soldiers on arriving for summer camp was to hack down the weeds and brush that all but enveloped the barracks and carefully root out the snakes, spiders, opossums and other animals that had taken up residence inside.[15]

"They say it's a lot colder here than in Vietnam," said Mrs. Ohnie Calhoun in Arkansas. "With a little luck maybe all those Vietnamese will take pneumonia and die."[16] Southern hospitality quickly prevailed over the likes of Mrs. Calhoun. "When the first contingent of 70 refugees arrived—a group that included six nurses, five lawyers, four plastic surgeons, three physicians and the former head of Air Vietnam—nearly 500 people and a high school band

6. Resettlement

were on hand to greet them."[17] The governor treated them to a speech. A nearby Baptist church put up a welcoming sign.[18]

The mixed reaction to the refugees at Chaffee was repeated at Indiantown Gap. IATF personnel were accosted on the streets of nearby Harrisburg and berated by citizens. Refugees were the targets of angry outbursts at the airport.[19] But, as at Chaffee, this hostility soon ceased and the community coalesced in favor of the refugees.

* * *

The refugees were terrified. Few of them had ever left their homeland. Many were separated from family members, including spouses, children, and parents. They had been forced, with little time for reflection, to make a decision to escape or stay behind. If they fled, they suffered the humiliation and heartbreak of abandoning family members and possessions, bribing officials or clamoring for a piece of paper that allowed them to board an evacuation aircraft, pushing and pulling their way through mobs of people to reach evacuation points and then being herded like cattle onto helicopters or transport planes for rides to unknown destinations. A refugee's decision to abandon his home and his country is one of the most agonizing any person can make — a "dreadful last choice" on the scale of human misery.[20] Refugees are confronted with a new culture, language, and climate in an unfamiliar place in which they may not be welcome.

Nguyen Thi Hue recalled leaving Guam on an airplane loaded with refugees bound for Fort Chaffee. Mid-flight the destination was changed to California. A buzz circulated among the refugees that the flight was being diverted due to anti-refugee riots by Americans at Chaffee. It was a frightened group of refugees that got off the airplane in California, but a few days later they were sent on to Chaffee, the rumors of the riots being greatly exaggerated.[21] Rumors are inevitable and spread like wildfire in the fractured world of refugees. Idleness, especially among men, leads to fantastical illusions, militancy, depression, family violence and a whole range of other disorders.

Despite the long American war in Vietnam, the people of the three Indochinese countries were exotic and unknown to most Americans. In 1964, the Vietnamese population of the United States was only 603 and the number of Cambodians and Laotians fewer still.[22] Few of the 2.4 million American soldiers who served in Vietnam had any meaningful contact with the culture and the people, and many had nothing but derision for the Vietnamese.[23] A few adopted war orphans, Indochinese women married by Americans, and students at American universities comprised the Indochinese in the U.S. before April 1975. The Vietnamese coming to the U.S. in 1975 found few predecessors, but they aided their cause by being attractive, polite, and soft-spoken. Ken Quinn did his part to introduce Americans to Vietnamese. He took his niece to the White House to introduce her to members of the staff. Nobody could resist the small, smiling girl, including President Ford; a photographer took a photo of her with Betty Ford, the First Lady, which appeared on the cover of *Parade* magazine.[24]

* * *

The first English word many Vietnamese learned was "sponsor." That was the essence of the government's strategy to resettle Vietnamese. Citizens, churches, organizations, and employers were urged to sponsor a Vietnamese refugee family. A Vietnamese family that had at least $4,000 in cash per person, were relatives of U.S. citizens or permanent aliens, or had a job offer from a previous employer did not require sponsorship but was released, after processing, from the resettlement centers.[25] The great majority needed sponsors — a person, family, employer, church, or other institution who would be responsible for the newcomer's welfare until he could assume the responsibility himself. The duties of a sponsor were both numerous and expensive. The sponsor "makes a commitment to feed, clothe, and shelter a refugee family until it is self-supporting. The sponsor assists the refugee head of household in finding a job, enrolling the children in school, and in understanding our customs. Ordinarily the health care costs are all the responsibility of the sponsor. However, unemployed refugees are eligible for Medicare coverage which will protect the sponsor from unusual medical liability."[26] The costs of being a sponsor were substantial. The Lutheran resettlement agency, LIRS, estimated them at $5,601 per Vietnamese family.[27]

The IATF contracted nine organizations, called VOLAGs[28] (voluntary agencies), to match refugees with sponsors. The most important were: the U.S. Catholic Conference (USCC), Church World Services (CWS), the International Rescue Committee (IRC), and the Lutheran Immigration and Refugee Service (LIRS). A few state and local governments took on the task of resettlement for themselves. The Chinese Consolidated Benevolent Society was active in helping its ethnic relatives as was the Church of Latter Day Saints, which sought adherents of its faith to resettle.[29]

Frank Wisner, Deputy Director of the IATF, was charged with maintaining good relations between the government and the VOLAGS — and it was a difficult task to deal with these prickly, independent, and often idealistic and impractical organizations. "We were under tremendous pressure to move the refugees from Vietnam to Guam, from Guam to the United States, and out of the resettlement camps in the United States," said Wisner. "The VOLAGs were the essential element in the resettlement program. We had to ensure they got what they needed to do the job."[30]

* * *

"Welcome to the world of refugees. Your life will never be the same." That was the greeting Robert DeVecchi of the International Rescue Committee (IRC) got when he arrived at Fort Chaffee.[31] That proved to be true for hundreds of other Americans working in the resettlement camps. "The employees are caught up in the euphoria of helping others," said a HEW director. "Everyone worked 12-hour shifts, 7 days a week, and it was not uncommon to work 15 or 16 hours at a time."[32]

David Lewis was one of the Americans who worked at Chaffee. Lewis had been a Marine Corps officer who survived 22 months of combat in Vietnam and then worked for AID. When he returned to the U.S. he anticipated that the world would beat a path to his door. He found the opposite to be true. Neither the public nor potential employers were impressed with his Vietnam experience and he was grateful to find a job delivering propane tanks to rural customers in Rhode Island. When he heard of a job working with the Vietnamese refugees with the United States Catholic Conference, he dropped by its offices in Washington. He was interviewed, hired on the spot to be the USCC Representative at Fort Chaffee, and before he quite knew what was happening was on an airplane bound for Fort Smith, the nearest city.

Lewis arrived on May 11, nine days after the first Vietnamese refugees had arrived at the Fort. He rented a car at the airport and along the road he saw a sign in the window of a gasoline station saying, "Watch Out! The Vietnamese will take your jobs." Chaffee was chaos. "Everybody was racing around trying to get organized," said Lewis. "A barracks had been set aside for the USCC and there he met one of the two USCC employees at the base, a retired army staff sergeant named David Hermann. The sergeant, a devout Catholic who later married a Vietnamese woman working at Chaffee, was registering Vietnamese Catholics. Lewis's first decision was to tell him to register every Vietnamese who came to the building whether Catholic or not.[33]

The registration process committed the refugee and his family to a VOLAG and the VOLAG to finding a sponsor and a home in the United States for the family. Lewis benefited from the vast network of the Catholics in the United States: 162 resettlement offices nationwide, tens of thousands of parishes, and a leadership that would sell its program to the nation's Catholics with the slogan, "Every parish take a family."[34] Lewis also reached out to the Buddhists. They were hanging back from registration, uncertain as to what they should do. Lewis met with one of the Buddhist leaders, told him his people were welcome to register with the USCC, put up a Buddhist prayer wheel next to the seal of the USCC on the door of his office, and began to register them. Within a month he had 105 employees and USCC would become the largest resettlement agency at Chaffee and the other resettlement camps. Persuaded by his experience in Vietnam of the importance of ensuring cross-cultural understanding, Lewis hired a Vietnamese interpreter for every American whose job was to interact with refugees.

USCC and Lewis snapped up about 75 percent of the refugees and other agencies complained of "mal-distribution of caseloads."[35] Eventually, USCC began to farm out refugees to the other VOLAGs who also discovered that speed was of the essence in the resettlement program. Instructions from the IATF in Washington always emphasized the need for "expeditious processing" of refugees. The VOLAGs were under pressure to move Vietnamese families from the camps to the American economy as quickly as possible. The U.S. government gave the resettlement agencies 500 dollars per capita for matching refugees with a sponsor and overseeing their well-being during the first few months of their residence in the United States. The more refugees an agency resettled, the more money it received—and USCC was taking most of the refugees and the resettlement money. The Lutherans, regarded by some as the most competent of the agencies, were slower and more meticulous in registering Vietnamese, and they seemed to have an ingrown preference for Vietnamese families who, in the best Protestant tradition, had four members: father, mother, and two children.[36]

Indiantown Gap, the closest reception center to Washington, D.C., was most scrutinized by the media and high officials. The senior civilian officials of the camp included Al Francis, former American Consul in Danang who was still recovering from the beating he had suffered in late March, and Alan Carter, the USIA officer who had seen many of his employees left behind in the chaos of the last days of the Americans in Saigon. Francis and Carter were among 34 State Department and USAID personnel with Vietnam experience who were assigned to Indiantown Gap.[37] The workforce at the camp to service a refugee population that reached 16,500 Vietnamese and 500 Cambodians was 1,800 military personnel, 250 civilian government employees, and 250 volunteers.[38]

Building on the experience gained at Chaffee and the other camps, the authorities at Indiantown Gap imposed a rigid structure on the refugee registration and sponsorship process. Competition among VOLAGS to register and resettle refugees was discouraged. Each refugee and family on arrival at Indiantown Gap was assigned to a VOLAG. To prohibit VOLAGs from shopping for the best clients among the refugees, their personnel were prohibited from visiting the areas in which the refugees lived.[39]

The base was divided into four cantonment areas for housing refugees and two administrative areas. Each cantonment contained up to 120 buildings, mostly wooden barracks and service buildings. Four Catholic chapels, three Buddhist temples, two Protestant chapels, a mess hall for every five barracks, four movie theaters, a hospital, several clinics, an infant feeding area, a telephone exchange, a PX, a locater service, and a bulletin board where Vietnamese could post messages in search of lost relatives and friends were established.[40] The INS, Red Cross, VOLAGs, and other charities had offices in the cantonments or administrative area. A few Cambodian refugees were housed all together in one cantonment.

The American authorities at Indiantown Gap bragged that their camp was more open than any other, but the restrictions on movements of the refugees were draconian. Vietnamese were enjoined not to leave the cantonment area to which they were assigned. "Your being available will speed your processing through the temporary settlement area." And more ominously, "Anyone leaving the prescribed cantonment area controlled by the Military Police are [sic] subject to apprehension which could jeopardize their immigration status. The cantonment area," continued the rules, "will be entered by U.S. personnel only on official business (military in uniform) and with proper pass displayed." The decision to limit the refugees' mobility was seconded by another one to limit the authority or independence of the refugees. The U.S. appointed Vietnamese coordinators for each cantonment and chiefs for each barracks but "it was decided that it would be unwise to give more than minimal authority to the refugees themselves." Another decision was that all refugees were to be treated equally; "there would be no more Colonels or Generals, for example, only 'Mr.'s.'"[41]

Each of the cantonment areas were outlined by white tape. To enter the white taped area, visitors had to show passes to MPs at guard posts. Light blue, red, and yellow passes permitted access to the refugee living areas; pink passes allowed access to certain buildings, but not to refugee living areas.[42] No pass, no entry, no exceptions. Refugees who had visitors were told on public address systems to report to the appropriate building to see the visitor.

The limitation on refugees' movement and access to their living areas caused more than a little heartache to the authorities. Friends, relatives, and potential sponsors of the refugees could not understand why they couldn't simply go the camp to pick up their refugee family and take them home. "We were constantly bombarded by telephone calls and personal visits from people of varying degrees of influence within the Executive Branch and the Congress."[43] And "the frequent visits of VIP's and 'rubberneckers' not only diverted the already limited time and energy of senior officials ... but also contributed to a 'zoo' atmosphere among the refugee population."[44]

The camps performed four services for refugees: First, the refugees were matched with a sponsor; they underwent security and medical examinations to detect security risks and medical problems; and they were introduced to American life and culture through education and language training.

The IATF and the VOLAGs were criticized for the tight control maintained in the camps. While some of those criticisms are valid, one can imagine the circus that would have taken place had the camps been opened to access by every snake-oil salesman, charlatan, politician, oddball organization, ambulance-chasing attorney, and proselytizing evangelist. Moreover, Americans had unfounded but oft-expressed fears on the part of Americans that the refugees were inflicted with exotic tropical diseases. Anti-war organizations opined that many of the refugees worked with the CIA.[45] Apparently past associations with the U.S. made them undesirable and suspicious. Moreover, the refugees needed time to acquire the rudimentary survival skills they needed in the United States and the security and surety of dealing with a limited number of people, organizations, and decisions.

* * *

During the first few days that a refugee was at a camp he was introduced to the VOLAG he had chosen, or been assigned, and interviewed. A case file was built up to match the refugee with a sponsor. Most sponsors were obtained through the head offices of the VOLAGS. For example, Catholic parishes submitted their offers to sponsor a refugee to USCC headquarters and the request was passed along to the resettlement camps. Offers for sponsorship also came through a 24-hour toll free telephone maintained by the State Department, from states, cities, and towns, and by walk-ins at the camps. Many of the offers of sponsorship came from employers who offered to give Vietnamese jobs. Some of these offers were attractive; most, however, were opportunities for minimum wage jobs that were hard to fill—for good reason—even in a high-unemployment period. For the most part, the Vietnamese would follow in the footsteps of other immigrants by taking the least desirable jobs and working their way up.

Indiantown Gap kept records of offers to sponsor refugees. A person, for example, would call into the camp with an offer for sponsorship. The "Sponsorship Coordination Center" would document the offer and pass it along to a VOLAG to be investigated and processed. The Center recorded 1,213 offers of sponsorship of which 759 were eventually accepted and 454 rejected. One hundred ninety-two of the offers were for single men, 104 for single women, and 271 for families. Most of the potential sponsors, however, wanted families of two, three, or four persons and offers were few and far between for families of over eight persons. The opportunities for large or extended Vietnamese families to remain together were very limited. 108 offers of sponsorship were for persons to work as domestic servants; six were offers of marriage. It is unrecorded whether any of the marriage offers were accepted.

Most offers to sponsor Vietnamese in exchange for employment were published in camp newsletters or posted on bulletin boards. Author Gail Kelly recorded a few of the ads for workers published in the camp newspaper at Indiantown Gap.

> Workers for greenhouses in Maryland and North Carolina. Free housing, food assistance, and wages.
>
> Man and wife, owners of a nursing home in Sharon Hill, Pennsylvania, want to sponsor three single ladies age 18 to 30. The couple will provide means for training in nursing and part-time employment at the nursing home.
>
> Two fishermen needed for job in Florida. Position pays $2.10 per hour [the minimum wage at that time] with sponsorship. Housing to be provided in new house trailer plus farm animals and garden. Should be able to sex-sort and count fish.[46]

Among the sponsorships arranged by Fort Chaffee were 11 families numbering 55 persons to work in Jonesboro, Arkansas, in a footwear factory, 11 families with 100 people to go to Kingsport, Tennessee, to work in a garment factory; 76 families and 590 people to work in poultry processing plants in Broken Bow and Grannis, Oklahoma, and 16 families and 42 persons to work in meat packing plants in Wichita, Kansas.[47]

In Oklahoma City, Green Beret Ellis Edwards, who helped hundreds of people escape Vietnam, General Clyde Watts and his son Charlie took on the responsibilities of sponsorship. Edwards in late 1975 had 23 Vietnamese living in his house. Edwards and his group sponsored 750 Vietnamese, got them jobs and help from churches to rent apartments and buy groceries. The only Vietnamese food in Oklahoma City at the time was fish sauce and rice noodles that a man kept in his refrigerator. Suddenly, with the influx of Vietnamese his business flourished. Charlie Watts co-signed loans to enable about 50 Vietnamese to buy automobiles.[48]

The religious VOLAGS—the Catholics, Lutherans and CWS—were less tied to specific job offers in settling refugees. A parish or church often sponsored their clients without a commitment on the part of the refugee to accept a particular job. Geography played a role. The Lutheran church was strongest in the upper Midwest and resettled many refugees in Minnesota and neighboring states—and to this day Minnesota is home to many Indochinese despite its bone-chilling winters. Warm hearts overcame cold winters. Not all sponsorships worked in near-arctic climes. David Lewis recalls one family USCC sent to Bismarck, North Dakota, that fall. The family got off the airplane, felt the chill, got back on the airplane, and disappeared for all time. Failed sponsorships were called break-downs. There were a lot of them.

* * *

One of Julia Taft's biggest problems was California, its governor, Jerry Brown, and its chief Health and Welfare official, Mario Obledo. Taft's predecessor had said that no state would receive more than 10 percent of the Vietnamese refugees. California officials quickly perceived that their state would be the destination of choice for the warmth-loving Vietnamese and tried to hold the Federal Government to that commitment. In fact, as resettlement got rolling, California received about 20 percent of the refugees. Brown and Obledo were unhappy. After listening to Obledo's complaints one day, an exasperated Taft resorted to a threat: "Look, Mario, every Lutheran Church in northern California has offered to accept a refugee family for resettlement. Shall I telephone each of them and tell them that you and Governor Brown don't want them to bring refugees into their state?" With that prospect, Obledo backtracked quickly: "Oh, no. We only want to be sure that the Federal government is paying the bills."[49] The resettlement program continued in California and the state continued to get more than its share of Vietnamese.

* * *

After a slow start the resettlement program raced ahead during the summer of 1975 and tens of thousands of Vietnamese were sent off to new lives in every state in the union and nearly every city. But, as October rolled around, a problem was developing. At Indiantown Gap it was called "Gapitis." About 22,000[50] Vietnamese were still living in the camps and many of these were reluctant to leave. It was not that life in the camps was wonderful, but rather that some Vietnamese, among them the most traditional and least educated, were paralyzed with fear at the thought of leaving the security of the camps and entering American society. The fear was that these refugees would be "unsponsorable" and utterly unsuited for life in America. Additional refugees were turning down sponsorships, "bargaining for the best deal while living in the security of the camps." Still others resisted leaving the camps because they were looking for missing relatives. They feared losing touch with the internal grapevines, the bulletin boards, newspapers, and the social service agencies in the camps charged with helping them find relatives.

Julia Taft laid down the law in stark terms to the VOLAGS on October 20, 1975. Eglin Air Force Base was closed; Camp Pendleton would be closed October 31; Chaffee and Indiantown Gap would be closed December 15. Every day, 393 refugees must be moved out of the remaining camps to meet this schedule. On the subject of sponsorship she said, "In the early days of the program, there was great tolerance and understanding of refugees turning down offers of sponsorship." But not anymore, she warned, "Any refugee now refusing any sponsorship offer from a VOLAG will be required to have his case promptly heard by a 'Sponsorship Review Board.'"[51] The Sponsorship Review Board decided that any refugee refusing a sponsorship would be subjected to "further and continuous counseling until the sponsorship is accepted."[52] Moreover, once refugees had been matched to a sponsor and processed to leave the camp they were forbidden to return. One strike and you're out.

Fort Chaffee in Arkansas—the camp furthest from the glare of national publicity—received the largest number of difficult refugees. The resolution of a problem with "gangs" and "gang leaders" was direct. Their authorities arrested the gang members, found them sponsors in widely separated locales, and sent them away from the camp.[53] Were sponsors informed of the character of their clients? Not likely.

Another problem was a large group of conservative Catholics under the leadership of a charismatic priest named Peter Tran van Khoat. Khoat had a devout following of about 2,000 fishermen and villagers from Vung Tau, a port city near the Mekong delta. Khoat's flock were among those Vietnamese who had piloted their fishing boats offshore in the final days before the fall of Saigon and had been taken aboard U.S. Navy ships. The priest and his followers demanded to be resettled all together in New Orleans. It was a delicate situation. Khoat's followers declined all proposals that they be settled elsewhere. They wanted to remain as a group—and they threatened to resist any alternative.

Their demand violated the policy of spreading Vietnamese refugees around the country to facilitate their integration into American society and to "share the burden." It was also impractical as the number of sponsors in New Orleans was inadequate to accommodate the group. But not only were the priest and his followers insistent, they were also militant.

The authorities feared demonstrations and, when President Ford visited Fort Chaffee on August 10, the priest was apprehended by American authorities and hustled away from the scene of the presidential visit. He was released again after the departure of the president. His detention was perhaps not entirely legal or ethical but it was practical. Public acceptance of the refugees hung on a narrow thread; a protest or riot might inflame public opinion against the refugees and bring to a near halt the resettlement process. The nightmare of everyone working in the program — and politicians in Washington — was that the United States would have tens of thousands of refugees on its hands and nothing to do with them. The generosity of Americans was bountiful for what the public perceived as innocent victims. But, if the refugees were suddenly perceived as pushy, demanding, and ungrateful American public opinion could turn on a dime. So, the militant priest was kept in comfortable custody while the president was visiting.[54]

The solution to the problem of difficult refugees was a slow process of education, compromises and concessions. A priest from New Orleans, Friar Phillip M. Hannan, came up to Chaffee to talk to Khoat and to explain that not all of them could be resettled in the city. The education program was stepped up. In addition to the daily newspapers at the camps, David Lewis set up a radio station at Fort Chaffee. It was a major operation. He had 36 employees at the radio station, including 21 Vietnamese and Cambodians, broadcasting American and Vietnamese music and information all day every day. There were English classes, classes on civics and American government, classes on culture and customs, how to meet, greet, and shake hands with Americans, and currency — what coins were worth and how to use them and to make change.[55] It was all for the purpose of encouraging the Vietnamese to venture into American society — before they were thrown out of the camp. In the case of Khoat's Catholic followers, the government did not protest when the VOLAGS hustled to ensure that the members of the group were mostly settled along the Gulf Coast in close proximity to each other. Beaumont and Lafayette as well as New Orleans accepted additional refugees. "We spent a lot of money helping the fishermen," David Lewis recalls, "including setting up special classes and facilities for them in Beaumont." The saga of the fishermen would continue.

* * *

The most heart-rending problems of refugee camps are the lost children and separated families. In the chaos of evacuation families became separated — husband from wife, and children from parents, or parents put their children on an evacuation flight, hoping to catch a later flight themselves. Camp bulletin boards were plastered with messages addressed to lost relatives or begging for information about missing children. It was a slow and difficult process to track down family members who might be in a different camp in the United States, in Guam, Midway or other Pacific way stations, in a third country such as France or Canada, or often still in Vietnam because the family member had not managed to get out of the country. Once family members were located the policy was to reunite them.

The Red Cross was in charge of the family reunification program. A dozen employees at Chaffee alone were assigned to the program. At Indiantown Gap the Red Cross recorded almost 5,000 cases of missing relatives, friends, and family members. If a family member could not be traced through U.S. and international sources it was assumed that he or she was still in Vietnam. Many of the refugees in the United States were unaware of the fate of relatives left in Vietnam for a decade or more, and some never reconnected with their lost relatives.

Unaccompanied minors, or UAMs, in humanitarian lingo, were the most delicate problem handled at the resettlement camps. The story of the orphans of Cam Ranh is one of many about unaccompanied minors. Cam Ranh Bay had been the location of the largest American naval base in Vietnam. American Baptists supported an orphanage there. Many of the children at the orphanage were not true orphans but had been abandoned by their parents in the maelstrom of war. Thang, for example, had been left at the orphanage in 1972 as a four-year-old boy. He never saw his mother again. The orphanage was not luxurious. The dormitories were crowded and a bowl of soupy rice was the usual meal. As a treat the children were given fresh bread on Sundays.

The staff of the orphanage was Christian and the director, Nguyen Xuan Ha, was a Southern Baptist convert. On April 2, one day before the city was occupied by the North Vietnamese, he fled with 15 staff members and 82 children. Ha bought an old leaky freighter and the children, staff, and an incompetent crew headed out to sea. "We were really packed in," recalled Thang. "I remember it smelled. One of the younger children vomited; everybody was seasick. There was lots of crying. I sat beside a window for three days, watching the sea." The engine on the ship gave out and they were adrift. Finally, a Taiwanese merchant vessel came by and towed them toward the nearest port, which happened to be Singapore. They were afraid their ship would sink, but they arrived safely in Singapore and were quarantined in the harbor for five days until Baptist missionaries secured permission to release them. Then, it was onto airplanes to fly from Singapore to Fort Chaffee where they were quickly processed, spent a few days on a ranch near Houston, and were sent from there to Buckner Children's Home in Dallas.

This story has an improbable ending. An American soldier in Vietnam named John Cope had worked at the orphanage after being discharged from the army and his favorite child was Thang, "a little mischievous child. There was a preschool at the orphanage. He would come down every afternoon and bring his papers to show me. He was cute, but I would have to say that about all the children."

John Cope was working at Fayetteville, about an hour's drive away from Chaffee, in 1975, when he heard that a group of orphans had arrived. He went down to Chaffee and found the orphans. They remembered him. "All the kids rushed him and I couldn't get to him," said Thang. "I went around to his back and pulled on his back pocket. When he saw me, he said, 'I'll never leave you again.'" And Cope was as good as his word. He followed the children to Dallas, became a cook at the Buckner Children's Home and adopted Thang in 1977.[56]

Chaffee had to deal with more than 300 unaccompanied minors, including a few who were servants to wealthy Vietnamese families. Many Americans wanted to adopt refugee children, but many of the children had parents who still might be alive in Vietnam. Thang was typical. His mother might reappear one day to reclaim her child. The same was true of others.

Government authorities were anxious to avoid being accused of kidnapping innocent children. Permitting adoption of these children might be used as anti–American propaganda by both the new Vietnamese government and anti–Vietnam War organizations in the United States. Nevertheless, something had to be done on behalf of the UAMs. The solution found at Chaffee was to place the children in foster homes but foster parents had to sign a document in which they promised not to commence adoption proceedings for at least three years. If the child's parents or other relatives did not appear to reclaim the child during that time, it was considered proof that the child was an orphan eligible for adoption.[57]

* * *

The refugees still at Camp Chaffee that fall were worried by a strange phenomenon. Leaves changed color from green to brown, yellow, and red and they began to fall off the trees. The Vietnamese were worried. They had only seen leaves fall when trees died, and the trees they had seen die in South Vietnam had often been killed by the herbicide Agent Orange sprayed by U.S. planes. They knew that Agent Orange could cause headaches, stomach pains, and other more serious illnesses. The camp management and the radio station rushed to assure the refugees that they were not being poisoned. It was normal for leaves to fall off the trees in autumn — as it was also normal for water buckets left outside overnight to have a film of ice in the morning. The worry of the refugees about the leaves falling was replaced by wonderment and joy when snow covered the camp one morning. "The children played and played and played" in the snow said David Dehart of the USCC radio station.[58]

The snow signaled the end to the resettlement program for the Vietnamese and Cambodians who had fled their countries more than six months ago when the communist armies overthrew their American-supported governments. On December 20—five days late by Julia Taft's timetable—the last 24 refugees from Fort Chaffee departed and the resettlement center closed. Indiantown Gap, Pendleton, and Eglin were already closed. On December 31, 1975, Taft officially abolished the Interagency Task Force for Indochinese refugees. The "evacuation and resettlement" phase of the refugee program was over. 130,000 Indochinese were now living in the United States in every state of the Union.[59] "What began as a tense program ended as a love fest," recalls David Lewis. "The program worked better than anyone could have anticipated. At the end I had churches calling me to request a refugee to sponsor and I had to tell them there were no more refugees. Some of them were furious. It was a rare occasion when everybody worked together and gave of themselves."[60] Julia Taft summed up the 1975 program: "Never before have so many people, from such a different cultural and ethnic background as the Indochina refugees, been brought into American society in so short a period."[61]

The congratulations were warranted—but premature. The closing of the resettlement camps in December 1975 seemed the end of the U.S. involvement with Indochinese refugees. It was just the beginning.

7

INDOCHINESE REFUGEES IN AMERICA

"Half the Vietnamese we intended to get out did not get out — and half who did get out should not have," said a Congressional report.[1] Those, according to the report, who should not have gotten out were "farmers, fishermen, students, street vendors, small shop keepers, local policemen, common soldiers and many others outside the established parole categories." Moreover, not all those who ended up in the United States had really intended to flee Vietnam. "Some had simply fled in panic from conflict and violence — as Vietnamese have fled for years — and had joined a flotilla of small vessels along the coast.... Instructed to 'rescue' Vietnamese on boats deemed not seaworthy, elements of the U.S. 7th Fleet hovered for several days along the coast, scooping up Vietnamese from their boats. Once in the military pipeline, their destination was the United States. Exactly how many never intended to travel to the Philippines or Guam, much less to continental United States, will never be fully known."[2]

The authors were too delicate to mention another group evacuated in sizeable numbers: bar girls — young, enterprising, largely rural and uneducated women who worked in the innumerable bars and massage parlors in Vietnam servicing the sexual thirsts of Vietnamese, American soldiers, and Western civilians living in the country. Many bar girls had developed a taste for things American and had been rescued by their boyfriends during those final days in Saigon. The decision for many bar girls had an economic factor as well. "You think VC like bang-bang?" one girl reportedly asked, seeking insight into the future of her profession.[3]

Bar girls were among the refugees flown to Clark Air Force Base in the Philippines. The Congressional report mentioned obliquely that many of these arriving at Clark were "clearly outside the categories of people targeted for evacuation ... including unattached women and children, maids and others."[4] The U.S. Embassy in Manila "cabled an urgent alarm to Saigon and requested that the flow of such aliens cease." It appears that the Embassy in Manila issued immigrant visas to some of these evacuees and sent others to the U.S. with parole documentation based on made-up stories.[5] One can be shocked at this dishonesty, immorality, and violation of American law — or one can celebrate the humanity and ingenuity of Americans who got their girlfriends and maids out of Vietnam and similarly admire the courage of the women who set out bravely for the New World. With all evacuees — legitimate or not — Washington was in a dilemma: it was morally and politically infeasible to send people back to communist Vietnam who didn't want to go. In official records, bar girls seemed to be hidden away in a category called "service workers." Surveys of the occupational characteristics of the evacuees counted 2,324 service workers as heads of households.[6] Not all of the service workers were bar girls or maids, but many were.

Despite the bar girls, fisherman, and farmers among the refugees, a majority of the Vietnamese who came to the U.S. in 1975 were from the elite. More than 20 percent of the adults had attended a university — about the same percentage as in the United States. By comparison less than one percent of the general population of Vietnam had attended a university.[7] Seventy-five percent of the adult refugees had at least an elementary school education.[8] About one-third of the heads of households had occupations from medical, professional, technical and managerial fields. Only about five percent were farmers and fishermen, as compared to the 70 percent of the Vietnamese population who made a living from the land and the sea. Forty percent of the refugees were Catholic while only 20 percent of South Vietnam's population was Catholic.[9] In the all-crucial area of English language skills, 35 percent of the refugees spoke some English. The integration of the refugees into the U.S. economy proved to be rapid. By 1979, the average Vietnamese worker was making more than the average U.S. worker.[10] That was the favorable side of the statistics. The unfavorable was that about 75 percent of the refugees were employed below their previous occupational level.[11]

Housing for refugees was a problem as large refugee families crowded into sub-standard housing. In San Diego, in one blighted neighborhood, landlords liked to rent to refugees because they didn't make trouble and they didn't know "when they [were] being ripped off." Another said, "The Indochinese are probably the best thing that ever happened" to the neighborhood. "They may not maintain their houses as we do, but they have brought a respect for law and order and a sense of dignity."[12]

The Interagency Task Force summed up the results of the Indochinese refugee resettlement program in 1975:

Refugees resettled in the United States	129,792
Refugees resettled in other countries	6,632
Refugees repatriated to Vietnam (the Tuong Tin)	1,546
Births	822
Deaths	77
Total Refugees processed	138,869[13]

More than 95 percent of the refugees were Vietnamese; the remainder were Cambodian with only a very few Laotians. The U.S. had hoped that third countries would accept many refugees for resettlement, but the State Department reported that "the response of the world community to this tragedy so far has been minimal ... the reaction of most has been either indifferent or negative."[14] Of the 6,632 refugees resettling in other countries, 3,926 went to Canada, 1,877 to France, and the remainder to 28 other countries. Japan, among the most restrictive of countries on immigration, accepted one refugee.[15]

* * *

Refugees had three strategies for coping with their new lives in the U.S.[16] The first was to make little or no attempt to assimilate. Many of the refugees in this group were elderly people who failed to learn English and behaved as much as possible as if they had never left Vietnam. The second was to abandon their Vietnamese heritage and attempt to become 100 percent American in every way. Most of the bar girls fell into this category. The third strategy of coping was the most typical: the refugees preserved as much as possible of their old language and culture while learning the skills they needed to succeed in the United States.

The Vietnamese became economically self-sufficient more quickly than other refugees coming to the U.S. in the 1970s such as Russian Jews and Cubans.[17] Despite the economic success of most refugees, their transition to American life was far from easy. The immigrant to the United States faces a daunting challenge: "to find shelter and work; to learn to speak an unknown language; and to adjust to a drastically changed environment despite the barriers of poverty, prejudice, minority status, pervasive uncertainty, and culture shock."[18] Even the most adaptable of refugees was in a situation of extreme psychological and emotional stress—and one that might continue year after year. In addition, the refugee had lost a past often recalled as pleasant and rewarding. He left behind family and friends, his home, and his identity and status in his culture. Many refugees clung to idealized memories of life in the old country in the good old days.

American society posed threats to firmly held values: children should be respectful and obedient to their elders; older people should be respected and cared for by the family; and all the members of an extended family should live together and collaborate as a unit. U.S. society set these values on their head. Children learned both the language and the culture of the United States more quickly than adults. The wisdom of the elders was mostly irrelevant to the children. Rather than being in a submissive and secondary role in the family, Americanized, English-speaking children became important players. Power relations within the family and community shifted toward the younger and away from the older.

* * *

Among the 822 children of refugees born in the resettlement camps was the son of Lt. Colonel Le Van Me and his wife Sen at Fort Chaffee in the summer of 1975. They named him Quang but everybody called him "Ozark" after the rough wooded hills just beyond the gates of Chaffee.[19] The background of the Le family and their experiences were typical of Vietnamese refugees that year. Sen was from a well-educated Saigon family. Me had been born into a poor farm family but advanced on his merits to become an officer in an elite airborne unit of the South Vietnamese army. He earned a U.S. Silver Star for heroism fighting alongside American Green Berets. The couple and their children escaped Saigon at the last minute on board a South Vietnamese navy ship. They had no time to say goodbye to their parents and other family members. They were picked up in the South China Sea by a U.S. naval vessel, and taken to Guam for a stay of nearly two months and then to Fort Chaffee.

Their life in Chaffee was boring but not difficult. Me volunteered as an English translator. The children "learned English at classes taught by churches and community groups. For fun they watched cartoons and movies such as *Doctor No* and *Jesus Christ Superstar*. They played soccer, saw a professional rodeo, and ate watermelon on the Fourth of July. They stood in line to get immunizations, Social Security cards, and used clothes from the Salvation Army." Me socialized with fellow soldiers and several American Green Berets who visited the family at Chaffee. A warm welcome to the United States didn't overcome the anxiety of the couple. "No future, no money, so sad and scared," said Sen, "but I can work," she assured her husband. "I can work in manufacturing, make toys. I can be a dishwasher or work in the restaurant."

The family was sponsored by the First Baptist Church in Warsaw, Missouri, a farming town of 1,600 people. The church members gave the family a place to live and Me a part-time job as the janitor. Traveling by bus to Warsaw was the most frightening part of their exile. They saw a slice of America they had not known existed: hardscrabble hill country sparsely inhabited by poor people living in run-down frame houses. It was the only time Sen had ever seen her husband cry.

The Le's moved in with the Davidson family in Warsaw while the church members repaired a house for them. Billy Simpkins gave Me a pair of work boots and enrolled him in the community college. Me began his duties as the church janitor, and he was a good one — with a military officer's attention to detail and order. But he knew little of American appliances. Once, when a toilet clogged he called for help and a church member showed him how to use a plunger. Ron Jenkins taught him to drive, but at first he had no car and had to hitchhike to get to his classes in Sedalia, 29 miles away. Sen stayed home most of the time with the four children. She was lonely, no other Vietnamese lived in the small town and only a few in the region. Sen learned to cook. "They sure liked ducks," commented Simpkins.

The Les got along well in Warsaw, their politeness and hard work impressing their friends, but they quickly perceived that job opportunities in Warsaw were slim. Like many Vietnamese families, sunny California appealed to them. Less than a year after arriving in Warsaw they were off to California, driving a 1972 Chevrolet Vega. Three days later they were in San Jose in what would become the heart of Silicone Valley. Many Vietnamese lived there and jobs were abundant. Me's education at the community college in Missouri helped him get a job as an electronics technician at a wage of $4.75 per hour, about double what he could have hoped for in Warsaw. He enrolled in San Jose City College for more education and Sen took accounting courses and within three years the family had purchased a three-bedroom house. It was the archetypal American success story. An immigrant from a troubled land arrives in the United States and from modest beginnings moves quickly to the middle class and prosperity. The children excelled in school. As one friend said, the parents remained foreigners, but the children grew up Americans.

While the Le family was leaving the Ozarks for the brighter opportunities of California other Vietnamese found the region more congenial. Gene Nguyen of Fort Smith, Arkansas, told the story of his father, an unmarried Vietnamese sailor. During four months at Fort Chaffee he learned English and made three good friends who vowed that they would stay together as a group. Like most Vietnamese refugees they were acutely aware of the stigma of living on charity and looked for sponsorships that included jobs. All four were sponsored by a farm family in Noel, Missouri. They worked on the farm for about six weeks, but the family refused to pay them wages. They left in disgust and got jobs at a local grocery store and moved into a house trailer. Nguyen saved enough money for a plane ticket to Maryland, where he intended to enroll in a class to learn to be an automobile mechanic, but when he got to Maryland the class had already begun. So, he got a job at McDonald's and took a bus to work every day. Frugal as he was, McDonald's didn't pay enough and after two months he went back to the Ozarks, rejoined his friends in the trailer park, and resumed work at the grocery store. In a few months he had saved enough to buy a 1968 Oldsmobile and find a better-paying factory job at Emerson Electric in Rogers, Arkansas. There he stayed, later marrying a Vietnamese woman who came to the Ozarks to work in a chicken processing factory. The couple raised a family on their modest incomes. Nguyen said that "the biggest difference between Vietnam and America is that in Vietnam you can work forever and have nothing to show for it, but here he was able to get a house, a car, and raise a family with just a factory job."[20]

The Vietnamese refugees were drawn toward warmer places with good potential for employment or business: California, the Gulf Coast of Texas and Louisiana, and a few large cities. Buffalo, New York, resettled 800 Vietnamese in 1975; by spring 1977 only 200 were left. Some of those leaving went to Louisiana; others to New York City.[21] Governor Jerry Brown's worries that

California would receive more than its share of refugees were well-founded. However, his fear that they would be an economic burden was wrong.

* * *

Failure or success, downward mobility was often the fate of Indochinese refugees in the United States. Author Gail Kelly collected examples. The former director general of the South Vietnamese Ministry of Interior did yardwork for a living. An Air Force colonel worked nights as a watchman and delivered newspapers. A medical doctor became a limousine driver. A bank manager remained within his profession — he became a janitor at a bank.[22]

General Ton Thai Dinh, who began his career as a traffic policeman in Saigon and worked to the top of his profession, told his tale humorously. He was resettled in Washington, D.C. "First I worked at The Wood Shop — a small shop in Georgetown — and did everything, including taking out the garbage." He moved up from that to a job at the Hot Shoppe restaurant cooking french fries. He showed the reporter his pay slip of $85, minus taxes and social security, for a week of work. And he proudly displayed the uniform of his next job with Montgomery County Cars. "Now, I have $200. And I've already paid the rent for next month! I make $2.73 an hour.... You Americans are so democratic. Anyone can make money if they are willing to work. And the rules apply equally to everyone. Punch in! Punch out! Eat quick! Punch in! That's justice! That's liberty!"[23]

Dinh's comments were echoed by a Vietnamese woman in her 40s with two teenage children and several other relatives all housed in a small apartment in the "little Saigon" area of Arlington, Virginia. She worked at three different janitorial and service jobs, putting in a total of about 80 hours a week. The other adults living in the apartment worked similar jobs and hours. The children were awkward in the presence of Americans, but they spoke good English and were doing well in school. The woman asked in puzzlement, "Why aren't all Americans rich? All they have to do is work."[24]

That, of course, is the experience of immigrant groups in the United States. Through choice or chance they come to the United States, work at the most menial jobs and live in squalor and penny-pinching misery. Suddenly, they own homes and businesses in the community in which they live and their children are giving the valedictorian addresses at the graduation ceremonies of their high schools. They are both admired and resented.

The clash between American and Vietnamese values was to be most serious in the story of the Vietnamese fishermen. The Reverend Peter Tran Van Khoat was the self-appointed spiritual leader of the fishermen who caused such a problem for the American authorities at Fort Chaffee. The fishermen were mostly Catholics. In Vietnam, they had lived in a closed theocratic community that Khoat hoped to duplicate in the United States. Khoat was resettled in Port Arthur, Texas. To the average eye, few areas of the United States are less physically attractive than the swampy east Texas coastline where water blends into land with no clear division and oil refineries and chemical plants clog the horizon, but Khoat was enthusiastic. "This land is very good for my people," he told journalist Frances Fitzgerald. "They can grow vegetables and rice; they can fish — they say that fishing is much easier in America because you don't have to go out so deep — and they will grow rich.... They'll buy boats. And I'll build a village called Vung Tau." All this was inspiring, but in 1975 Fitzgerald also picked up a hint of trouble to come. "It has ... not yet occurred to the rural Texans, who hired the Vietnamese as replacements for Mexican 'illegals,' that these people want to end up owning the farms and fishing boats. Nor have the people of Beaumont and Port Arthur ... associated these small, gentle-spoken people with the folks who chewed such great chunks out of the U.S. Army, Air Force, and Marine Corps."[25]

Next to California, Texas was the most popular destination for Vietnamese refugees. Too many Vietnamese resettled in small communities on the Gulf Coast. Barbara Estes, owner of a restaurant in Seadrift, Texas, had it right. "Look, they took and brought 100 of these people into a town of a thousand and that is just too many for a small community like this. If it had been just three or four families, the whole town would have tried to help 'em."[26] Refugees sent to large cities were less than one percent of their population; small Texas coastal towns received up to eight percent of their population in refugees. Seadrift, with 1,200 people, received 100 refugees; Port Isabel, a poor border town of 3,000 with an 85 percent Hispanic population, received 150 Vietnamese. Moreover, in Texas, Vietnamese fishermen competed with local fishermen in a zero-sum game: more fishermen meant a reduced catch.

In Seadrift the Vietnamese achieved a toehold. A local businessman brought in several Vietnamese families and the women proved to be excellent crab pickers. Working on a piece rate basis, they made up to 60 dollars a day, skipping coffee breaks and toiling long hours. The plant manager said they were the "best crab pickers he had ever seen."[27] The Vietnamese pooled their savings and money they had brought from Vietnam — some of the fishermen had left Vietnam with gold bars sewed into their clothing — and bought 15 to 20 crabbing boats.[28]

There was trouble between the Texan and the Vietnamese fishermen from the beginning. A civil rights mediator, Efrain Martinez, explained: "They came from Vietnam where there are no rules or regulations about fishing. You can fish as much as you want and keep whatever you catch. Well, in Texas, to preserve the industry, you can't fish at night and you have to return some stuff. Also, there are open waters and closed waters, and some bays are closed entirely. You also have state regulations and federal regulations, as well as a two hundred-mile limit into the Gulf of Mexico. The Vietnamese didn't pay too much attention to all those laws and customs and what have you. So they began getting in trouble with both the authorities and with the local fishermen."[29]

The Vietnamese were also accused of eating dogs and cats and nailing the feet of ducks and chickens to their boat decks to keep them alive until they wanted to eat them. They didn't understand the American aversion to being crowded or having their boats bumped. In short, the Vietnamese upset the time-honored, laid-back customs of the American fishermen. But there was grudging admiration for them. "A few people here are just jealous," said one Texan.[30] "They're more organized than American fishermen.... They work. That's the problem. They're damn good fishermen."[31]

In 1979 in Seadrift two Vietnamese fishermen shot and killed an American, Billy Joe Aplin. The facts about the incident were in dispute. According to author Robert Lee Mariel, Aplin had been crabbing in the bay along with his family when a Vietnamese crabber set his pots nearby. Outraged by this encroachment, Aplin told the Vietnamese to leave, who did, but came back later with several boatloads full of Vietnamese men who shouted and made threatening gestures at Aplin.

Back on the docks, Aplin recognized one of the men, Nguyen Van Sau, who had threatened him. He hit Sau. Sau went home, got a gun, and came back to the dock with his brother. He confronted Aplin. Aplin threatened him with a knife and Sau shot him five times. The two Vietnamese were charged with murder. The townspeople went on a rampage, burning several Vietnamese-owned boats and a trailer occupied by a Vietnamese family. The Vietnamese community packed up quickly and left Seadrift.

The incident achieved national attention. The Vietnamese received legal help from civil rights organizations and the Ku Klux Klan interjected itself into the dispute on the side of the Anglos. Martinez said of the Klan. "They were very active in the community and might have had some sympathizers. Mainly, they were out-of-towners who would pass by and try to intimidate folks by burning a few crosses shortly after the Vietnamese killed that guy ... they [the townspeople] were afraid to go against the Klan, because they knew these people may be armed and dangerous." A jury was quickly convened in a neighboring country and a five-day trial was conducted in haste. An all-white jury declared the two Vietnamese innocent by reason of self-defense.[32]

In the aftermath of the Aplin killing the people of coastal Texas, despite the deep-seated anger on both sides of the dispute, showed remarkably good sense. Shortly after the trial concluded, the people of Seadrift assembled at the City Council and told the Klan to stay away. "We're not backing the Ku Klux Klan — we don't need to invite any more problems into town."[33]

Another potentially violent situation between the Klan and Vietnamese fishermen was averted in the town of Seabrook, near Houston. Vietnamese fishermen outnumbered the Texan fishermen in Seabrook, owning about 75 boats. The complaints were similar to those in Seadrift. The spokesman for the Texans was a Grand Dragon of the Klan and a six-time-wounded Vietnam veteran, Gene Fisher. Colonel Nguyen Van Nam represented the Vietnamese. After several failed efforts at relieving the tension between the two sides, the mediator Martinez called for a face-to-face meeting in his room at the Holiday Inn. Martinez arranged the meeting by playing on the egos of the two men. Neither would admit to being afraid of the other. Nam showed up with two bodyguards, who waited downstairs, and Fisher had somebody telephoning him every 15 minutes to ensure that he was all right.[34]

Two tough men face-to-face found they didn't have many basic disagreements. The notes that Martinez took of the discussion resulted in a "16-point agreement" between the Vietnamese and Texans. A few months later Klansman James Stanfield was being hired by Vietnamese to repair their boats. Stanfield said to the New York Times that the conflict had never been racial but economic. Both sides now agreed on new regulations to regulate the catch and to put a moratorium on new fishing licenses.[35] The Vietnamese fishermen had become members of the establishment, rather than newcomers. They wanted to preserve their occupation and keep the competition out — just as the Texans did. Should another immigrant group try to break into shrimp fishing in Texas Texans and Vietnamese would probably unite to resist the newcomer. The hard-working Vietnamese fishermen made a place for themselves.

* * *

The Hmong also dreamed of a community in the United States in which they could live together and follow their traditional customs. They had even less chance of achieving their dream. There were fewer of them and they were poorer and less educated.

Mac Thompson in Thailand recalled that the first offer of sponsorship for a Hmong came in November or December 1976. It was from Minneapolis. Mac called in the Hmong selected for the slot, a heavy equipment operator who didn't speak English. The man asked "How many Hmong live in Minneapolis?"

"None," replied Mac.

"How many Lao in Minneapolis?" asked the man, who also spoke Lao.

"None."

"Who am I going to talk to?"

"Somebody has to be first," answered Mac. The man accepted the sponsorship and went off to Minneapolis, a lonely Hmong in a strange town. Rosenblatt and team had a hard-nosed approach. "We weren't running a tourist agency," Lionel said. "If a sponsorship came up and a refugee turned it down he went down to the bottom of the list and stayed in the camp for at least another year before being offered another."[36]

Minnesota would prove to be a fine place for the Hmong to live. Not so Philadelphia.

* * *

Kue Chaw, call sign "Bison," radio operator for Sky and Jerry Daniels in Long Tieng, left Thailand on May 15, 1976, and resettled in Philadelphia along with his wife and 13 children (one daughter had to be left behind and another child passed away while the family was still in Thailand). The family found it difficult. Unemployment, poverty, and crime were high in inner city Philadelphia. The multi-ethnic community was fractured by distrust, hatred, and violence: African Americans, Koreans, Chinese, Ethiopians, Indians—and in 1975 and 1976 Hmong and other Indochinese were added to the mix. The Hmong, the least experienced at urban living, were dumped into a racially charged environment. The African Americans resented them. "We have been here four hundred years and what do we have?" said an African American leader. "Nothing. They came yesterday and they will have all the rights and privileges today that we didn't have in four hundred years."

A refugee responded, "Mostly we have trouble with blacks. We don't have problems with other Americans, because we always try to be nice, but black people they feel we come here and go very fast from nothing to a better job."[37]

Among the mix of refugees, immigrants, and African Americans, the Hmong occupied the bottom of the ladder—but they found work, leaving Philadelphia at three A.M. to cross the river into New Jersey and pick blueberries for 25 cents a pint. They formed work gangs, elected leaders, and became the agricultural workers of choice—similar to their cousins in California who picked strawberries.

What griped Kue Chaw most was that nobody in his neighborhood made any overtures of friendship toward him and his family—"Nobody ever said hello." After four years he had had enough. He undertook a coast-to-coast odyssey to find a place where he could live happily. He found it in the Appalachian foothills of western North Carolina. The green mountains and the lakes and streams reminded him of Laos and the sparse population and mild climate meant he could live an outdoor life. A few other Hmong followed him and soon there was a colony near Hickory, North Carolina.

Kue Chaw found a place to buy—a couple of acres and an old house, land and old houses being very cheap in North Carolina in those days—and set about creating a home that looked like the old days in Laos. He wanted to grow Hmong rice, which is planted on hillsides and on dry land. A sister mailed him a few rice seeds. He didn't know the date to plant the rice in North Carolina so he experimented, planting two seeds on March 1, two more on March 15, two more on April 1, etc. The rice seeds planted on April 1 grew best. He grew the rice to maturity and it produced more seeds for him to plant rice again the following year—on April 1—and to produce more seeds. The following year he grew enough rice to eat and to distribute seed to his Hmong neighbors.

Kue Chaw expanded his tiny rural empire to include chickens, pigeons, and ducks. In a small greenhouse he grew oriental spices: lemon grass, curry leaf, mint, and coriander. He grew Hmong rice, corn, beans, and squash in his garden. He bought a boat and outboard motor and became an expert bass fisherman. Fried bass, spiced with Hmong herbs, was the company meal his wife Mao Moua served. He acquired American friends. "That Kue Chaw," said an old-timer in the neighborhood, "is a real clever fellow." The county named the short dirt track on which he lived "Kue Chaw Street." Several of his children graduated from college. Kue Chaw professed to be happy with his life in the new land and advised fellow Hmong to build their lives in the United States and not dream of going back to Laos to live. "They have learned to like the luxuries in America and they would find it difficult there."[38]

* * *

Reporters occasionally visited General Vang Pao on his ranch in the Bitterroot valley south of Missoula, Montana. One story said he was plowing fields to plant barley; his shoes were caked with dirt and the farmhouse "was so sparsely furnished that a woman who served coffee to a visitor had to bring out a folding chair to hold the cups."

"This country is like my country," the Wizard said happily.[39] He gave no indication of wealth.

VP lived in a modest two-story, frame, white with green trim, all–American farmhouse and about 40 family members lived in other buildings and trailers scattered around the ranch.[40] During his first year on the farm, VP and the young men installed irrigation, took care of livestock, and tended crops. VP hired an American, learned all he could about American farming, and then fired the man. He learned how to fix machinery. The women of the family tended a garden and did the cooking, mainly rice, chicken, and pork. With chickens, ducks, and pigs wandering around the property and a cash crop of barley, Vang Pao's place resembled that of an American homesteader living the simple life in the country.

VP had his complaints. "I have to have permission to have a pig [farm] here. Some people complain it would smell. So, I don't have a pig [farm]. Anything you want to do, you have to go by the law. And even if you go by the law, somebody sues you.... You hear about freedom in America—freedom, freedom, freedom. But you have conditions for everything."

Vang Pao's dream was to buy a parcel of land in North Dakota or Minnesota and settle Hmong on it who would live as they had lived in Laos before the Vietnam War, growing their own food and practicing their traditional culture. It was the old Hmong dream of a homeland or reservation that had been expressed to Lionel Rosenblatt when he first visited them in Thai refugee camps in 1975.

* * *

Vang Pao's dreams almost came true in one country. One of the oddest tales of the diaspora is the story of the Hmong in French Guiana, a French colony in tropical South America, best known for Devils Island, the French penal colony. Its unsavory reputation, a swampy malarial coast, and a rugged interior of hills and tropical rain forest combine to keep it off the main routes of commerce and tourism. The colony had only 200,000 people in an area the size of Maine. Most of the population is Creole: mixed black, white, and American Indian.

A French priest with Lao experience came up with the idea of resettling Hmong in French Guiana and the first group of 45 arrived at the capital city of Cayenne in November 1977. They were loaded into French army trucks and hauled south to a hilly site named Cacao, located about 40 miles inland. More Hmong followed and their population increased to 2,100 by 2005.

The Hmong chose to come to French Guiana rather than the United States or France to live and farm in the rural environment to which they were accustomed. One of the first arrivals said in 2004, "All we ever needed was a forest, somewhere to produce vegetables. We built everything from scratch, all our houses, our farms, everything, until it became our new home."[41]

The Hmong tamed a difficult environment for agriculture in French Guiana. Although they make up only one percent of the population they grow enough vegetables and fruits to supply nearly all the colony's needs. The Hmong grow bananas, citrus fruits, mangos, papaya, watermelon, and other tropical fruits; vegetables such as taro, sweet potato, onions, lettuce, and cabbage; and, of course, rice. The family farm is still the standard and all members of the family work in the fields under the hot sun for several hours a day. Farming has made the Hmong affluent. Many own automobiles, wide-screen televisions, computers, and travel to France and the United States to visit relatives. In 2006, Hmong girl scouts from French Guiana visited Hmong girl scouts in Minnesota.[42]

8

LEFTOVER REFUGEES IN THAILAND

The evacuation from Vietnam and Cambodia, the partial evacuation from Laos, and the resettlement of 130,000 refugees in the United States seemed the end of America's involvement in Indochina. However, as Vietnam receded from American consciousness, a few loose strings remained, especially in Thailand.

MacAlan Thompson, a 34-year-old USAID officer, drove into exile from Vientiane on June 26, 1975, in a Volkswagen bus loaded with his worldly possessions. The American Embassy was drawing down to a skeleton force and surviving uneasily in an unfriendly Laos. Mac took the ferry across the Mekong River at Nong Khai, and drove 400 miles to Bangkok. "Most AID people went back to the States," he said, "but I liked Southeast Asia. So, I checked in at the AID liaison office in an old house on Soi One to see if I could find a job." (Soi is the Thai word for a side street or alleyway. Soi One branched off Sukhumvit Road, one of the main thoroughfares of Bangkok.) "They put me to work shipping the personal effects of AID employees returning to the United States."[1] It was a quiet interlude. Mac's friend Pop Buell had taken up residence in the Chan Fong apartments across the leafy street and Mac liked the cheeseburgers and "sizzling steak," served in the restaurant of the modest two-story Golden Palace Hotel nearby.

The Embassy met Mac's desire to stay in Southeast Asia on August 4 by assigning him to the American Consulate in Udorn to set up a program processing refugees for resettlement in the United States. Thousands of Hmong, Mien, and Yao highlanders, and lowland Lao refugees were crossing the Mekong into northeastern Thailand. The Lao had not been eligible for resettlement until August 1 when the attorney general made up for past neglect by paroling 3,466 for a "Special Lao program."[2]

In addition, Mac was to process for resettlement several hundred Thai Dam and Nung who had crossed from Laos into northeastern Thailand.[3] The Thai Dam and Nung had fled from Vietnam into Laos after the defeat of the

Mac Thompson in Udorn, 1976. Mac was Lionel Rosenblatt's deputy and is shown in a typical pose, buried in refugee case files. (Mac Thompson)

French in 1954 and now they ran again from the communists to Thailand. The Thai Dam were, for the most part, urbanized and educated civil servants and former French soldiers. Many of them had worked for the Americans.[4] They wanted to stay together as a group. A former AID employee in Laos, Arthur Crisfield, took up their cause and had written letters to 30 governors urging them to accept the Thai Dam for resettlement in their state. Iowa's governor Robert Ray responded in the affirmative. Iowa committed to resettle 1,200 Thai Dam over two years. The Embassy in Thailand was tasked to document the Thai Dam for resettlement.[5] However, the policy changed about this time and, unlike the refugees from Saigon and Phnom Penh, any future refugees accepted for resettlement would leave for the United States only after all immigration procedures had been completed and a sponsor was found for them.

The day after his appointment as the first field representative of the Embassy's Office of Refugee Affairs, Mac drove to Udorn near the Lao border and set up office in the American Consulate. The job was overwhelming. Mac had no experience in the arcane world of immigration and refugee law, but he had an encyclopedic memory for facts and figures. He combined an orderly mind with irreverent humor and a love for the simple life of "beer, hamburgers, and bars along a strip in Bangkok called Soi Cowboy."[6] Not surprisingly, he was a risk-taker, jumping out of airplanes long before it became a popular sport.

8. Leftover Refugees in Thailand

Mac first went to Southeast Asia in the mid–1960s as an Army officer after graduating from Oregon State University. Back in the States, he juggled two job possibilities: smoke-jumping in Alaska or the IVS, the same organization that had sent Pop Buell to Laos a few years earlier. An offer from IVS came first. He lived two years in rural Laos building schools. In 1968 he began working with USAID Vientiane in its refugee section. The refugees in Laos at that time — technically internally displaced persons (IDPs) — were Hmong and other Lao who had fled from one part of Laos to another to avoid communist control. Pop Buell was in charge of feeding the refugees in northeast Laos so they could continue to wage the anti-communist battle. This was accomplished by Air America and Continental Air Services airdrops of rice from World War II vintage C-46 aircraft into mountain top hamlets. Mac worked in Vientiane until it fell to the communists in 1975.

In Udorn, Mac united with Jerry "Hog" Daniels who had returned to Thailand after settling General Vang Pao in Montana, or "Hmongtana," as they called it. Mac and Jerry — they shared the same birth date, June 11, 1941— were soon joined by John Tucker, another old Lao hand, low key and unassuming but with a core of idealistic conviction. Tucker had served as a Peace Corps Volunteer in Thailand and worked in Laos for USAID in the provincial cities of Pakse and Savannakhet. In May 1975 the communists held him under house arrest for five days before ordering him to leave the country on an evacuation flight to Udorn, Thailand, with other Americans working for the U.S. He took only a few possessions with him, including a shoebox full of his treasured photographs. But when he arrived in Thailand and opened the shoebox it was full of shoe polish. In his haste he had picked up the wrong box.

Tucker worked on Guam with the Vietnamese refugees there. Distressed to learn that only Vietnamese and Cambodian refugees were allowed to enter the U.S., he wrote a letter to USAID Washington proposing a resettlement program for Lao. By return telegram he received orders to proceed to Thailand to work as a refugee officer processing Lao refugees. "Mac and I were considered oddballs and rebels by AID. The CIA was not pleased with Jerry either. But," he added, "When you see your friends in danger of death, you want to help — and I saw it as an obligation of our country."[7] Assistant Secretary of State Philip Habib expressed that obligation at a congressional hearing: "Many of these people were very closely identified with us. They took part in a chapter of American history which has ended in a disaster not only to them but to their families, and we have felt all along that this imposes a certain obligation on us."[8]

The three refugee officers divided up the work: Mac was informally in charge. Jerry worked with the Hmong and other highland Lao; and John worked with the Thai Dam and lowland Lao. But which Lao should go to the United States? Many Americans believed the highlanders were too backward and uneducated to adjust to American life. The Embassy was not encouraging. A delegation of Hmong met with Ambassador Whitehouse in Bangkok on August 4.

They discussed resettlement in the United States, but the ambassador was noncommittal. An immigration officer told the Hmong they would be denied entry into the United States because they "used to live in the mountains and would never be capable of adapting to American high tech society."[9] The prevailing view was that the Hmong would have to learn to live with their new communist masters in Laos or blend in with the Thai. Ambassador Habib expressed the official Washington position to Congress. The highland peoples "are particularly suited for the area of Thailand, where they will probably remain. They are not ... easily resettleable."[10] Habib's statement notwithstanding, he was considered by Rosenblatt to be one of the most helpful of all the senior State Department officers. The State Department further discouraged Hmong resettlement in a telegram dated September 30, 1975: "Department is concerned by large and growing number of Hmong being included in Lao refugee program. We have previously indicated to Congress that Hmong would not be included in the parole program." The telegram went on to instruct the Embassy that Hmong formerly employed directly by the U.S. or with close relatives in the U.S. might be acceptable but that all others would not.[11] The U.S. government did not want highlanders coming to the United States, even if they had fought and died for the U.S. during the war. The mistaken assumption was that the Thai could be persuaded to resettle the Hmong.

Mac Thompson and Jerry Daniels disagreed. The Hmong deserved the opportunity to resettle in the United States rather than languish in squalid Thai camps. For Jerry Daniels it was personal: "I still remember that I and perhaps other Americans who are representatives of the United States government, have promised you, the Hmong people, that if you fight for us, if we win, things will be fine. But if we lose, we will take care of you."[12] The Hmong trusted his promise. Pop Buell also felt an obligation. In speaking of the Hmong, he was so angry he sputtered: "We have an obligation to these people.... How in the goddamn hell can you use people and then one day tell them 'Goodbye, it's been nice knowing you?' The least goddamn thing somebody could do is to come back in and say, 'I'm sorry.'"[13]

Mac and Jerry had a tough job selling the Hmong for resettlement. Their first opportunity came when Sam Feldman of the Immigration and Naturalization Service (INS) visited Udorn that August. INS had the final word on a refugee's eligibility to enter the United States. Mac and Jerry took him to visit the Nam Pong camp where most of the Hmong were housed. They introduced him to Dr. Yang Dao, the only Hmong PHD in the world at that time. Then they introduced Feldman to English-speaking Hmong military officers wearing American military uniforms and field jackets dripping with patches, awards and medals. The Hmong, it appeared, were not as primitive and unworthy as some believed. A crucial telephone call back to Washington from Feldman helped break the opposition to the Hmong.[14]

While Thompson and Daniels dealt with the highlanders, Tucker traveled around northeastern Thailand and made "river runs" along the Mekong searching for refugees who had just crossed. Tucker told them about the resettlement program and conducted preliminary interviews. The refugees eligible for resettlement under this program were: former U.S. government employees; relatives of U.S. citizens; relatives of permanent resident aliens or of refugees who have already been paroled into the United States; and persons who formerly occupied positions of special sensitivity who would be in danger if they returned to their home countries.[15]

Back in Washington, Lionel Rosenblatt was now head of the Office of Special Concerns for the IATF. In August 1975 a Cambodian employee showed him graphic photographs of dead Cambodian men, women and children. "These are Cambodians who escaped the Khmer Rouge but were killed by a drunken Thai guard while trying to cross the border. Thousands of Cambodians are being held in camps near the border. Nobody is doing anything to help them."[16] Rosenblatt's humanitarian instincts were aroused. Stories were seeping out of Cambodia of horrendous abuses perpetrated by the KR. The Thai had stationed 5,000 police and army along the border to keep out fleeing Cambodians.[17] Nevertheless, reports estimated five to eight thousand Cambodians had crossed into Thailand.[18]

Stirring the political pot by identifying a new refugee problem would not be popular with a nervous Congress and an American public whose goodwill was not boundless. To Washington, the refugee crisis began and ended with the flight of the Vietnamese from Saigon. Turning a blind eye to a few leftover refugees in Southeast Asia was now the preferred track. Nevertheless, Julia Taft agreed that Lionel should go to Thailand to check out the situation. The Embassy was unenthusiastic about his visit. Ambassador Charles Whitehouse had a cautious view of his responsibilities. Arriving in Thailand only in May, Whitehouse had been stunned by anti–American demonstrations and a dressing down by the Thai prime minister.[19] He and Washington were in no mood to rock the boat in Thailand. A National Security Council memorandum to Secretary of State Kissinger advised that the U.S. should not provide "cheap issues" to the Thai.[20] Refugees qualified as a "cheap" issue. Whitehouse's job was to reassure the Thai, shaken by the U.S. loss of Vietnam, of American support and bolster their confidence that they could withstand communist pressure. Crucial was to avoid creating any new problems. Rosenblatt and refugees were problems. Thailand was frightened of hosting anti-communist refugees and thereby arousing the animosity of the new and threatening governments of Vietnam, Cambodia, and Laos. At the same time the country's faith in the United States as a protective ally was undermined.

Thus, the Embassy left Lionel to find his own way, providing him only with a 4-wheel-drive station wagon and a Thai driver. He was not unhappy to be left without interference. He had lived in Thailand and spoke Thai. He headed upcountry to find refugees. It was late October and the monsoon still raged and the red laterite roads near the border were deep in mud and bottomless puddles. Lionel and his driver slipped their way down slimy tracks to several of the 16 refugee camps in Thailand. All were crowded and dirty. The Thai government gave each refugee 500 grams (1.1 pounds) of rice per day and the charitable organizations, the VOLAGs, added a bit more food. There was no soap; dysentery, malnutrition, and malaria were problems.[21] Lionel quickly learned that among the refugees were many former associates of the United States who should be eligible for resettlement. He was also impressed by the terror of the Cambodians that they might be forced back to Cambodia into the arms of the Khmer Rouge. They endured prison conditions in Thailand to avoid that fate.

The Thai government, the UN, and the VOLAGs had not been prepared for the influx of refugees. "Squalid refugee shanty-towns popped up in the border areas and elsewhere." The UN was slowly gearing up but most aid to refugees was coming from Christian organizations in Southeast Asia. A Congressional report concluded that the refugee situation in Thailand would have been "far more desperate, and many thousands of refugees would have died of neglect" had it not been for the work of the charitable organizations.[22] Refugees were still coming out. In one of the more memorable escapes, a helicopter pilot, Lt. Ha, and a sergeant flew from Vietnam to Thailand. They carried a barrel of gasoline with them and somehow refueled in flight. Then, running out of fuel as they got to Thailand, they landed near a gasoline station and filled up again. It was definitely a non-smoking flight.[23]

In Udorn, Lionel met Mac Thompson, Jerry Daniels, and John Tucker. Mac recalled that a "long-haired hippie showed up at their office in the U.S. consulate and said his name was Rosenblatt." Mac was underwhelmed. "So, what is that supposed to mean to me?" But they made a night out of it talking about refugees and Lionel overslept and missed his plane to Bangkok the next morning. Thompson and Daniels suggested he use his extra time to visit a Hmong refugee camp. "I was blown away," said Lionel. "Here were thousands of Hmong, many of whom spoke American military lingo and had names like 'Lucky' and 'Judy' and 'Bison' and who had been soldiers, radio operators, pilots, and CIA operatives in a war unknown to the American public. This was unacceptable. How could the U.S. abandon these people? If the United States owed gratitude to anyone in Southeast Asia it was the Hmong."[24]

The Hmong were not supplicants trying to cadge a way to get to the United States; their preference was to remain in Southeast Asia and they dreamed, encouraged by Vang Pao, of returning to Laos one day and overthrowing the communist government. But, if that proved impossible, they asked that a reservation — similar to an Indian reservation — be created for them in the United States. They wanted to stay together. Rosenblatt left the meeting committed to helping the Hmong. They were the forgotten people.

Until this visit to Thailand, Lionel had perceived himself as temporarily working with refugees and anticipated that he would soon return to regular duties at the State Department. Now, he saw that the Indochinese refugee crisis was far from over. The refugees in Thailand could not be left in limbo. And how many more people were trying to escape their homelands? Lionel was an instinctive champion of the underdog.

Rosenblatt rushed back to Bangkok and drafted a telegram to the State Department in Washington. He described the plight of the refugees and recommended that the U.S. resettlement program take in eligible Cambodian and Laotian refugees—including the Hmong. The Embassy hemmed and hawed and delayed the transmittal of Lionel's telegram. His message would not be popular. One hundred thirty thousand Indochinese were in the United States; surely that was enough. Rosenblatt was having nothing of it. He called Ken Quinn at the National Security Council who, having resettled his Vietnamese relatives, was now back at work. Quinn telephoned Ambassador Whitehouse and inquired politely about Rosenblatt's visit. "The White House," he said, "was anticipating the telegram and would appreciate a report on its status." That broke the logjam at the Embassy. Rosenblatt's telegram was on the wires within hours.[25]

Lionel's report helped persuade Washington that unfinished business remained with refugees in Southeast Asia. Spurred by his report and the quiet efforts of others, the State Department proposed officially in January 1976 that an additional 11,000 Indochinese be admitted into the United States.[26]

* * *

On his return to Washington, Lionel met with Shepard Lowman in the Office of Refugee and Migration Affairs at the State Department. Shep had reunited with his family after the Saigon evacuation. "I was very down," he said. "We had walked away from Vietnam and I left many friends and acquaintances behind. One day I received a telephone call from the State Department. Was I interested in working in the Refugee Office?"[27] He accepted the job temporarily until a better offer came along.

"I didn't know Lionel well," Shep said of their meeting, "but he was persuasive. He said that refugees in Thailand had qualifications for resettlement as good as many we had evacuated from Saigon.

"I argued with him. Congress wouldn't let it happen. Congressman Eilberg said the program was over. The Embassy wasn't interested. The only possibility was for someone—I looked Lionel in the eye—to go to Thailand, set up a refugee program and make the case to Congress that these people merited resettlement in the United States. Lionel agreed immediately—but he threw the ball back at me. He said he would fail in Thailand unless somebody in Washington fought the bureaucratic battles for the refugees. If he went to Thailand, I had to back him up in Washington.

"At the time, I was angling to be head of the Economic section in Jakarta.

The refugee office was a dead end for a career — but Rosenblatt was right. Without Washington support a refugee program would founder in Thailand. So, I agreed to continue to head the refugee office in the States — a job that had no other seekers."

Lowman was a mirror opposite to Rosenblatt — older, laconic, steady, and soft-spoken. Shep became "Mr. Inside," working the refugee issues within the bureaucracy, while Rosenblatt was "Mr. Outside," the field operator, agitator, and advocate. Lowman found a perfect deputy in Henry "Hank" Cushing, a former USAID Vietnam hand. Hank was talkative, crusty, confrontational, and chain-smoking. Hank never pulled punches. Faced with a problem, Shep stayed calm and solved it with patience and persistence. Hank attacked. "Get out and do it! Figure out a way!" was his standard directive. Shep was quiet and tough; Hank was vociferous and tough. He complemented Shep in Washington as Lionel would in Thailand.

"I don't want to take too much credit," said the modest Lowman. "Without Rosenblatt, Cushing, and me the refugee program would have continued. There were enough people of good will in the State Department and the government to guarantee that. But it would have taken months or even years for the program to evolve. The three of us got things going quickly." Money was left over from the budget for the Vietnamese resettlement, but there was a catch. The authorization to spend the money expired on June 30, 1976. Time, therefore, was of the essence.

The additional refugees proposed for resettlement in the United Sates under what the State Department called the Expanded Parole Program would be comprised of three groups: "(1) 3,000 close blood relatives of American citizens or permanent residents; (2) 800 former U.S. government employees and their families; and (3) 7,400 who are clearly vulnerable to persecution if they return home because of their close identification with the United States."[28]

The Indochinese were to enter the United States as "parolees." The attorney general had the authority to designate parolees for humanitarian or public interest reasons. Parole theoretically could be terminated at any time, but for practical purposes parolees had all the rights and privileges of citizens and permanent resident aliens.

In proposing to Congress the admission of 11,000 additional refugees, the State Department gave examples of individuals who would be eligible for the program: the former Queen of Cambodia who did not want to "resettle in France because of pressure on them by left-wing Khmer residing in Paris"; former employees of the Lao Embassy in Thailand and employees of the American Embassy in Vientiane; and the sad case of Colonel Bu Tith of the Cambodian army, whose wife and children had been executed by the Khmer Rouge. Hmong were conspicuously absent from the State Department's list of exemplary refugees. Only Dr. Yang Dao was mentioned as eligible.[29] The Hmong would be stealth parolees.

Lionel's job would be to identify and document individuals and families who qualified for parole under the criteria set out above. He went out to Thailand in early January along with four other State Department employees: Joe Poteet, a secretary, Mike Carr, a junior administrative officer, and two others. UNHCR counted the refugees in Thailand about this time and came up with a total of more than 63,000, including 54,000 Lao, 9,000 Cambodians, and few Vietnamese.[30] About 40,000 of the Lao were highlanders.

Lionel and his staff moved into the AID house on Soi One. Mac Thompson, Daniels and Tucker worked upcountry in Udorn. One of Lionel's first jobs was to get a promise from Jerry Daniels he would be a full time refugee officer and not engage in clandestine activity. Lionel's next task was getting enough employees to handle a formidable workload. Quick hires were the rule: Pajaree Sritham (Tim) a Thai secretary, was interviewed by Mike Carr one day, received a letter offering her a job the next morning, and went to work that afternoon, not going home until late that night. Other Thai would fill critical jobs in administration and as translators and interpreters. Two Thai women with the name of Daeng were distinguished by the refugees they dealt with. They were "Daeng Land" and "Daeng Boat."[31]

Compared to the scruffy Americans, the Thai women working in the refugee office were elegant, beautiful, and sophisticated. The Americans both irritated and amused them with their unruly manners and failure to observe proprieties. One of the stories is about Mac Thompson's car. The Thai employees tried to leave work in the evening before Mac did. His old Volkswagen bus often wouldn't start and he would enlist whoever was around in the office to give him a push. Only reluctantly did the Thai women in the office lend a silk-clad shoulder to push Mac's bus down the street.[32] Mac's VW bus became legendary in refugee camps around Thailand. The Embassy didn't have enough cars and the refugee officers often drove their own.

Lionel also needed additional Americans with Southeast Asian experience to interview refugees. He turned to the Peace Corps. Berta Romero, a volunteer finishing her two-year tour, recalled seeing a notice on the bulletin board at the Peace Corps office in Bangkok advertising jobs working in the refugee program. The salary was $1,000 per month — more than ten times the salary of a Peace Corps volunteer (PCV). Lionel hired 13 volunteers whose tours with the Peace Corps were ending. The next day two of the volunteers, Patty Culpepper and Sally Maxwell, were on the train to Udorn to work for Tucker and Daniels and the others were carving out office space for themselves at Soi One. Berta headed the Cambodian section.[33]

The house on Soi One was a beehive. The nerve center was a blackboard on which a statistical tally of refugees was kept. The numbers were important. INS would keep an exact count of the 11,000 refugees proposed to come to the U.S. Every corner of the building was taken up by desks, file cabinets, typewriters, madly toiling former PCVs, Thai secretaries and typists, and Hmong,

Table 2.
How Refugees Were Processed*

1. Joint Voluntary Agency (JVA) staff pre-screened the refugees with interviews in the camps to determine who might be eligible to enter the U.S. The JVA compiled information about family members, including family members in the U.S., employment with the U.S. government, education, and experience. UNHCR and other organizations often recommended individual refugees to JVA for pre-screening.

2. JVA contacted various organizations to verify refugees' claims concerning family members in the U.S. and former employment with the U.S. Government and to request a security (falcon) clearance.

3. JVA or Embassy Refugee Officers conducted one or more pre–INS interviews to ensure that the evidence in the file was accurate and complete.

4. An INS officer interviewed the refugee again to determine the accuracy and completion of the information in the file. INS then either approved or disapproved the case.

5. The refugee was interviewed again by JVA to obtain information required by resettlement agencies in the U.S. to find a sponsor for the refugee and his family.

6. Once a sponsor was located and JVA was notified, refugees were given a medical examination by ICEM.

7. After the refugee passed the medical examination, ICEM ensured that all documents were assembled and given to the refugee and arranged transportation to the U.S. Refugees traveled on both scheduled and specially chartered aircraft.

The time needed to complete this process varied from as little as three months to as long as several years.

*Adapted from United States, Comptroller General, *Indochinese Refugees: Protection, Care, and Processing Can Be Improved*, 15–16.

Cambodian, Lao, and Vietnamese interpreters. In frivolous serendipity, the American assigned to deal with refugees leaving Vietnam by sea — the forerunners of the famous "boat people" — had his office jammed into a shower stall.

The work space expanded to the driveway in the shade of spreading rain trees or down the street to the restaurant of the Golden Palace Hotel. Here, families were assembled, paperwork spread out on tables, refugees were sworn in, and sizzling steak ordered all around in celebration. A Sino-Thai waitress presided over the restaurant efficiently — except that she took a dislike to Shep Lowman when he visited and always got his order wrong. All were amused that polite, mild-mannered Shep aroused the waitress's ire. Thirty years later the Golden Palace had not changed much; the same waitress was still there, now manager; sizzling steak was no longer on the menu, but the cheeseburgers were as tasty as ever.[34]

A problem with the Hmong and other highlanders, was that couples were not formally married. Lionel arranged to have marriages conducted by an Anglican priest in the Embassy cafeteria. Under international law the Embassy was territory of the United States and marriages conducted there were indisputably legal. Another problem was that many Hmong men had two or three wives, and polygamy was illegal in the U.S. To solve this problem, Jerry Daniels worked out a procedure by which the Hmong husband would designate one woman as his true wife and the second and third wives would live separately in the camp. When second and third wives were no longer on the scene, the Hmong and his designated wife would be eligible for resettlement — now being in compliance with U.S. laws against polygamy. It often took a year or more for Hmong men to divest themselves of second and third wives.[35]

Albert Corcos, the head of the International Committee on European Migration (later renamed the International Organization for Migration) in Bangkok, was a key collaborator. The ICEM gave medical examinations to refugees, arranged transportation, and handled paperwork with the Thai government. Although the Thai fervently wished the refugees out of their country, it still required a steeplechase of rules and procedures. Somebody counted 91 steps — seals, stamps, signatures, and initials — needed from the Thai government to enable a refugee to leave. Corcos performed services beyond the call of duty. Through some financial quirk, so common in the bureaucracy, Lionel had no U.S. government funds readily available to pay the salaries of the ex–Peace Corps volunteers. Corcos loaned him the money from ICEM funds, hoping later to be reimbursed by the U.S. government. A resistance leader in France during World War II, Corcos was 30 years older than most of his American counterparts.[36]

Lionel approached the job with his usual intensity. Even his bosses wilted under his passion. Ambassador Whitehouse recalled, "When I saw Lionel coming down the hall I would duck into an office or go behind a door. I knew he would be coming along with a request I couldn't possibly fill. Lionel pushed me — and the Department long before I had any feeling that Thailand was going to be swamped by a human invasion."[37] Lionel worked Monday to Friday at Soi One and traveled upcountry to the refugee camps on Saturday and Sunday. Mac worked six and one half days a week, taking off Sunday afternoon for a swim and a few beers.

Outside Bangkok, in the remote areas where the refugees were mostly located, the job was hazardous. One refugee worker recalled a taxi ride from Udorn to Loei province twice a week to load buses with Hmong refugees and see them off to Bangkok. There were occasionally clashes in the area between the Thai army and communist guerillas.

The volunteer, Dan Pride, shared his cab on several occasions with a mysterious fellow who "was too god damned important to be sharing a cab with me on the road to Loei." This was Jerry Daniels. Pride, a peacenik who recoiled with horror at the mere mention of the CIA, was awed by Daniels. On his first trip to Loei with Daniels, the Hmong leaders treated Pride to lunch. The Hmong served chicken and Pride was gobbling up a large chunk when he noticed that nobody else was eating much. Daniels told him that the Hmong had killed one of the last three chickens in the camp in his honor. On another occasion when an American had spent all morning trying to organize the refugees for departure.

Daniels breezed into the camp and in five minutes had everything done. "Hustle hustle, hustle.... Fluent Hmong, action and reaction like a spring." Jerry Daniels "was a very brave man. He saw his government engaged in dishonorable behavior [i.e., abandoning the Hmong] toward the friends he had promised so much, and he brilliantly corrected the injustice."[38]

Berta Romero, of Hispanic/Ute/Apache heritage from the tiny town of Espanola, New Mexico, and Rich and Judy Kocher, traveled up and down the border interviewing Cambodian refugees. Berta spoke Thai, not Cambodian, but she learned the Cambodian word for "death" because she heard it so often when she interviewed Cambodians. Over and over again, Cambodians told her that family members were dead — killed by the Khmer Rouge. Some people thought the refugees were lying about the brutality of the Khmer Rouge. The former Peace Corps volunteers didn't.

All the refugee workers suffered from emotional involvement in their cases. Lionel told them, "It's a numbers game. We've got authority to resettle 11,000 refugees from Thailand — Lao, Vietnamese, and Cambodian — and that's how many people we can take — not one less nor one more. You have to decide who is most qualified. We can't take them all." The ex–PCVs compiled family trees of Cambodians and others to have a record in case family members said to be dead or missing showed up later.[39] The essential statistics — those interviewed, approved by INS, etc.— were kept and updated daily by Chris Wharton —"the Wharton Report"— and later Carol Leviton.

Mac Thompson devised a point system to decide which refugees were most worthy of resettlement in the U.S. The refugee who scored the most points went to the head of the resettlement line. As devised, and used for years, the system awarded points for relatives in the U.S., previous service in the military or civil service of the country of origin, and education abroad. For example, an applicant with a spouse in the United States got 10 points; if he had one child in the U.S. he got another 8 points; if he had served in the army of his home country for five years he got another 10 points (2 points for each year of service); if he had spent one year out of Laos for training in the U.S. he got another 3 points. Adding that up, the applicant's total points would determine his position in the refugee queue. A refugee who had never served in the army or civil service, had no relatives abroad, and little education would get no points — and would be very unlikely to be approved for resettlement. Mac could not resist adding a touch of humor to his instructions about applying the point system. If the refugee answered yes to the question of "do you like wine and cheese?" he was referred for resettlement in France; if the refugee said he liked snow he was referred to Canada.[40] Gallows humor relieved the daily tension of agonizing over the fate of refugees.

Rooting out the less qualified, the unqualified, the frauds, and the opportunists caused bitter feelings. All the refugee workers made enemies, especially Jerry Daniels because of his prominence among the Hmong. On at least one occasion, an anonymous letter writer reminded him that for 200 dollars an assassin could be hired in Bangkok.[41]

* * *

Thailand has a reputation for Buddhist Wats (temples), easy-going and smiling charm, canals and floating markets, brightly-colored silk and nimble diplomacy, but Thailand in 1976 was worried about its future. The Thai had to accommodate the new realities of communist control of Indochina. They had two options: reduce their dependence on the United States and lean toward the communists or steer a neutral course, maintaining American support while also being friendly with the new governments in Vietnam, Laos, and Cambodia. It would take all the charm and flexibility of the Thai to navigate these dangerous waters.

Thailand took a hard line on refugees. The government's instructions were, "Should any displaced persons [refugees] attempt to enter the Kingdom, measures should be taken to send them out ... as fast as possible. If it is not possible to repel them, they will be detained in camp."[42] The concerns of the Thai were real. Thailand had sent 12,000 soldiers to Vietnam to fight alongside the Americans. Under the CIA's Bill Lair, Thai police had trained the anti-communist Hmong army in Laos from the early 1960s. Neither the Vietnamese nor the Lao communists would forget this. Domestic insurgencies were simmering in northeast and southern Thailand with an estimated 8,000 home-grown communist guerillas. The Thai, Lao, and Khmer Rouge armies often clashed along the border. The Thai feared that refugee camps would be used as launching pads for attacks into Cambodia and Laos—which they were—and, conversely, that communist agitators would be infiltrated into the refugees to stir up anti–Thai sentiment. Those were good reasons to keep refugees out and to ensure that those who gained entrance to Thailand were confined.

Among Thailand's strengths was the affection for the country by the *farangs* who lived and worked there. Bangkok, known in earlier, quieter days as "the Venice of the East," was a hot, dirty, crowded city noted for good restaurants and bars, massage parlors, attractive women, cheap sex, traffic jams, and kamikaze drivers. The attractions of Bangkok were a contributing factor to the international attention paid the refugees. Thailand was a good place to live and work, and the number of religious groups and humanitarian organizations finding reason to have an office there was, and is, astonishing.

The Thai threatened—and occasionally carried out threats—to push refugees back from their border. A "push back" to Cambodia was a death sentence and might have the same consequences in Laos. Like most things in Thailand, however, the care and protection of refugees was a negotiable matter. The words of the Thai government were often, though not always, harsher than their deeds. The Thai deliberately kept the facilities available to the refugees at the minimum needed to sustain life in a policy called "humane deterrence."

They did not want to encourage more refugees to come and they tried to ensure that the refugees' standard of living was not higher than that of their own people in the border areas. Northeastern Thailand, where most of the refugees were located, was the poorest region of the country.[43]

* * *

The American relationship with UNHCR was strained. UNHCR was not prepared to protect and care for the refugees. It had only four field officers in Thailand and a tiny budget.[44] UNHCR's priority was voluntary repatriation. "Based on our experience, voluntary repatriation can be the happiest of solutions," said High Commissioner Sadruddin Aga Khan. And later he announced, "this present emergency should not last." Aga Khan's faith in repatriation was based on the positive view many people had toward the communist governments in Southeast Asia.[45] Once the new governments of Laos and Vietnam demonstrated their benign nature, they believed, the refugees would return home — and perhaps the reports of Khmer Rouge atrocities in Cambodia were exaggerated. The calculation of UNHCR was wrong. Not a single refugee in Thailand requested repatriation in 1976 or 1977.[46]

UNHCR's alternate solution was local resettlement. UNHCR proposed to help the Thai government resettle the refugees permanently in Thailand. The answer was a flat "no." No promises would persuade Thailand to allow refugees to remain on its soil permanently. The answer from all the other Southeast Asian governments was the same.

Rosenblatt's office and UNHCR in Bangkok often clashed, sometimes seriously. One disagreement resulted when the Thai ordered all refugees to obtain identification cards from UNHCR. Lionel, sensibly enough, posted a notice on the bulletin board outside the Soi One office informing all refugees that they should report to the UNHCR office across town to get ID cards. A flood of undocumented Indochinese descended upon UNHCR. The infuriated head of UNHCR telephoned Lionel and shouted, "How dare you send refugees to UNHCR!"[47]

* * *

Those first few months of 1976 were spent frantically documenting 11,000 Lao, Cambodians, and Vietnamese to go to the U.S. as soon as the attorney general in Washington received the go-ahead from Congress. But passive resistance and bureaucratic foot-dragging delayed the Expanded Parole Program. The opponents of the refugee program claimed that a new round of consultations with Congress was necessary before the Expanded Parole Program could be approved. They won their point.[48]

"Consultations" was a euphemism for delay. Congress and the executive agencies engaged in back-room dealing. "A few voices of dissent were allowed to paralyze the process," said a Congressional report.[49] The paralyzer-in-chief was Congressman Joshua Eilberg of Pennsylvania, the chairman of the House of Representatives' Sub-Committee on Immigration, Citizenship, and International Law. Eilberg tried to block the additional refugees from coming to the U.S. He proposed that 3,000 rather than 11,000 would be sufficient and held up the approval of the Expanded Parole Program for three months.[50] His aim was to delay the process until after June 30, 1976, when funds appropriated by Congress for refugee resettlement would revert to the U.S. Treasury. If so, no additional refugees would be able to come to the U.S. until Congress adopted new legislation, a process that might take months.

Eilberg questioned the motives of the refugees: "It is not reasonable ... to expect the United States to become a haven for the economically oppressed or for those merely seeking to improve their lot in life."[51] He cited newspaper reports to allege slavery and "unsanitary habits" among the refugees.[52] He questioned the effectiveness of UNHCR and the willingness of other countries to accept their share of Indochinese refugees.[53] He referred on several occasions to an alleged "secret agreement" to accept the refugees, apparently referring to Jerry Daniels' promise to take care of the Hmong after a U.S. defeat in Laos.[54] The White House denied the existence of any secret agreements.

Eilberg failed to scuttle the Expanded Parole Program. In Washington fashion, he was eliminated from the bureaucratic loop. On May 5, 1976, Peter Rodino, the chairman of the House Judiciary Committee, the parent body of Eilberg's sub-committee, notified the Department of Justice that "a majority of the members in attendance did not object to the Attorney General granting the parole request."[55] However, the wheels of government move slowly and it was not until the evening of the last day of the fiscal year, June 30, 1976, that the battle was won. "You and your hard working staff," the Department of State cabled the Embassy in Bangkok, "will be interested to know that in a cliffhanger of historic proportions funds were finally obligated." The State Department extended its congratulations to "Rosenblatt, Thompson, Corcos and their staffs ... for a tough job well done."[56]

Congressman Eilberg was not the only opponent of the Expanded Parole Program. In Bangkok, UNHCR's representative, Cesare Berta, shrieked to Ambassador Whitehouse, "This is a catastrophe. This is disastrous."[57] The catastrophe as Berta saw it was that the U.S. resettlement of refugees would be a "pull factor"—encouraging additional Indochinese to make their way to Thailand with the expectation that they would go to the United States. Berta's fears were not realized, at least in the short term. No marked increase in the flow of refugees to Thailand occurred during the following year. Disagreements, however, about "pull factors" and "push factors" and distinctions between "refugees" and "economic migrants" would continue to fester.

* * *

Lionel's job was done. Corcos, ICEM, and Mac Thompson could handle sending the remaining refugees to the U.S. He was exhausted, but a last minute crisis kept him in Thailand for another month. Unknown to Lionel, an American employee of the refugee office had promised resettlement to a refugee boy in exchange for sexual favors. Lionel learned later that State Department Security had been investigating this American for sexual misconduct for more than a year — but nobody had told him. Now, Security arrested the American and sent him back to the U.S. for disciplinary action and prosecution. Lionel was enraged that an American already suspected of sexual indiscretions had been assigned to the refugee office.

The fallout was that the INS declared the refugee boy ineligible to be resettled in the United States. Rosenblatt protested strenuously. The boy had done nothing wrong. The fault was that of a predatory American in a position of authority who had taken advantage of him.

When the INS didn't yield, Rosenblatt staged what was in effect a sit-down strike. He announced that he would not leave Thailand until the boy was permitted to go to the United States. The Embassy was well aware that an aroused Lionel could not be pressured into acquiescence. Finally, the INS was persuaded to yield and the boy was approved to go to the United States. Lionel accompanied him to the airport and saw him onto the airplane to ensure there was no last minute change of mind. Relieved, he left Thailand and returned to Washington. Back in the U.S. however, he discovered that the Justice Department was preparing papers for his indictment. Rosenblatt, the FBI reasoned, must have known what was going on. The State Department rallied to his defense and the Justice Department finally decided it was the better part of valor not to press an indictment against a State Department officer who was both a hero and notoriously unrepentant, stubborn, and outspoken. It would not be the last time that Lionel would have problems with employees. The refugee program attracted all too many people who saw in it an opportunity to benefit sexually or financially.[58]

* * *

Mac Thompson's career almost ended about the same time. He received a letter one morning in Udorn from the USAID director in Bangkok telling him that his employment with AID was terminated, apparently because he was not doing the kind of work that USAID employees are expected to do. He was instructed to depart Thailand within 30 days. Mac digested the letter, went down to the Udorn Hotel, drank a few beers, ate a steak, and reflected that his hard work with refugees during the last year had not earned him the slightest recognition or respect from his organization. Then, later that same day, mysteriously, a telegram arrived from Washington canceling his termination if he accepted an appointment to a much-coveted two-year management course at AID/Washington.

Mac scratched his head, not knowing the details of the management course, asked for his attendance in the course to be delayed so he could complete his job in Thailand, and went back to work. He learned later that an alert friend in Washington, Homer Stutzman, had saved him from being fired by getting him assigned to the management course. Many of the people working with refugees in the 1970s would tell similar stories about the lack of recognition — or downright abuse — they suffered at the hands of their unsympathetic agencies.[59]

9

BEFORE THE DELUGE

Lionel Rosenblatt went back to Washington in August 1976 to cheers and plaudits — but no job awaited him in the Refugee Office of the State Department. Shep Lowman and Hank Cushing capably filled the two senior positions in the office. Lionel was "over-complement," meaning he was still on the payroll of the Department but without a position to call his own. Over-complement employees earn their bi-weekly paychecks in temporary, often make-work duties. An extended period in over-complement carries a stigma. Good officers, says the system, find good jobs. Lionel had no shortage of job offers, but he wanted to continue working with Indochinese refugees.

The refugee program was at low ebb; it seemed its last gasp had been Lionel's 11,000 refugees from Thailand. A few — very few — of the tens of thousands of refugees still in Southeast Asia would be considered for admission to the U.S. Shep, Hank, and Lionel believed that declarations of the demise of the U.S. refugee program in Southeast Asia were premature. Refugees continued to leave the three Indochinese countries and tell horrendous stories of the conditions there. Thousands of former U.S. employees and associates were still in Vietnam and, piecing together reports, many of them had been incarcerated in brutal re-education camps. In Laos, the Hmong, other highlanders, and Lao were being killed as guerillas or herded into reeducation and work camps. Cambodia was a black hole for information but what seeped out suggested that the Khmer Rouge was brutal almost beyond belief.

Lionel needed a place to warehouse himself until a refugee job opened up. Friends helped him get assigned to Chinese language training at the Foreign Service Institute across the Potomac River in Rosslyn, Virginia. For the next ten months, he studied Chinese from nine in the morning until four in the afternoon. Learning Chinese is a full time job: six hours in class daily and two to four hours of study after hours. But nearly every afternoon at four o'clock when Chinese classes ended Lionel caught the shuttle bus to the State Department and worked in the refugee office until nine or ten at night. His night job became even more intense when Richard Holbrooke took over the post of Assistant Secretary of State for Far Eastern Affairs. Holbrooke was a friend, but was perfectly happy to give Lionel the opportunity to work himself to exhaustion.

* * *

Lionel soon got into trouble. The refugee office was now under the Bureau of Human Rights and Humanitarian Affairs, headed by Assistant Secretary of State Patricia M. Derian from Mississippi. Derian shared the goal of all government officials of controlling the information given to the public and the media by her Bureau. However, the refugee officers had become accustomed to seeing themselves as advocates for refugees rather than dispassionate public servants. They enjoyed a close and mutually beneficial relationship with journalists. They steered journalists toward stories that would benefit refugees, but not necessarily the broader aspects of U.S. foreign policy as seen by some senior officials. A news story about the mistreatment of refugees by the Thai government might, for example, result in improvements in the treatment of refugees, but it would also infuriate the Thai government, which would take out its spite by obduracy on other issues of importance to the United States. It was all a question of priorities, and refugees didn't rank high.

Shortly after she took office in August 1977, Derian called together her employees, including her unofficial employee, Lionel Rosenblatt, and made her point: the leaks must stop. All contacts with journalists must be approved and on-message, consistent with the policies of the Bureau of Human Rights and Humanitarian Affairs.

Lionel listened politely, but a few hours later telephoned Henry Kamm of *The New York Times* in Bangkok. He alerted Kamm to reports that Thai police were shooting Lao refugees trying to cross the Mekong River and suggested a story would be appropriate. Kamm agreed and got in touch with the Embassy in Bangkok to get more information, mentioning that Lionel had alerted him to the story. The Embassy had a fit. What was Rosenblatt in Washington doing talking to reporters about events in Thailand? Derian was infuriated and embarrassed. Only hours after she had laid down the law about media contacts, Rosenblatt had defied her. She called Lionel to her office and read him the riot act. He had committed a breach of discipline and professional ethics and he had no future prospects of employment in her Bureau.

Lionel was stricken. He pleaded innocence to Shep. He had had no intention of violating instructions. He had only alerted Kamm to a potential story. Surely, that was not an offense. Shep listened and told him to go back to work, he would handle the problem. A day or two later, after Derian had cooled down, Shep made the case on behalf of Lionel. Whatever his faults, Lionel was indispensable in the refugee program. Soon, Shep hoped to see him assigned to Thailand again as head of the refugee program. Nobody else could do that job as well. Derian relented, and Lionel continued to work in the refugee office, but the incident reinforced his reputation as an undisciplined maverick.[1]

* * *

As 1977 came to an end Shep had growing concerns that the U.S. government was falling behind events, but it was difficult to persuade the bureaucracy in Washington that the Indochinese refugee crisis was still a reality. After the outpouring of 130,000 Vietnamese with the fall of Saigon in April and May 1975, only about 70,000 refugees from all three Indochinese countries arrived in Thailand in 1976 and 1977 — a significant number, but not by any means a crisis.[2] But Shep saw in late 1977 an increase in arrivals and a growing reluctance by the Thai and other Southeast Asians to accept new refugees into their countries.

Shep needed policy firepower to move the U.S. government to pay more attention to refugees. He turned to Leo Cherne, the chairman of the International Rescue Committee (IRC). On November 16, 1977, he flew to New York to meet with Cherne. He had low expectations, but he hoped that Cherne would lend his substantial prestige and that of the IRC to the cause.

Cherne was 65 years old. Born into a poor immigrant Jewish family in Brooklyn, he was a lawyer, businessman, songwriter, sculptor, an advisor to presidents and generals, a vociferous critic of totalitarian governments, and an uncompromising anti-communist. Cherne's organization, the International Rescue Committee, founded by Albert Einstein in the 1930s, was one of the most respected and prestigious of American humanitarian organizations. The IRC had clout with the rich and famous.

Lowman outlined his concerns to Cherne: "It has become difficult to fight for resettlement for more Indochinese refugees. Congress is opposed to paroling more of the refugees and the Attorney General is hesitant to oppose the Congress.[3]

"Four thousand refugees are now coming across the Thai border monthly. One thousand people per month are escaping from Vietnam by sea and those lucky enough to survive are scattered along the shores of Thailand, Malaysia, the Philippines, Indonesia, and even Hong Kong and Australia. Thailand has refugees piling up in camps—and the Thai have said they will turn refugees back unless the United States and other countries guarantee to resettle them. The U.S. resettlement program is near its end. France, Canada, and Australia are now becoming more generous accepting Vietnamese for resettlement than the United States." Refugee resettlement in the United States had fallen to less than 1,000 per month.[4]

The element that worried Shep most was that Vietnamese were leaving the country by boat and turning up on the shores of countries all over Southeast Asia. "Whole families leave Vietnam in small, leaky fishing boats and many drown at sea or are killed by pirates. At sea commercial vessels pretend not to see them and pass them by, because if they have refugees on board none of the countries in the region will let them dock to unload their cargo. If the 'boat people'—as they were called—make land in their own boats, the authorities and police shove them out to sea again."

9. Before the Deluge 123

Cherne's mind was running in the same direction as Shep's. He responded with alacrity. He agreed to push a request to the Carter Administration to parole boat people. He also agreed that the United States needed a long-range refugee policy that would be predictable and would support the Southeastern Asian countries who were groaning under the impact of refugees. The U.S. had to share the burden and stimulate other countries to do their part. Cherne moved fast after the meeting with Shep. He secured the parole of 7,000 boat people within a month and created a star-studded "Citizens Commission on Indochinese Refugees" by the end of the year.

Cherne persuaded banker William Casey — later to become director of the CIA — to be his co-chairman on the Commission. Other luminaries included author James Michener and labor and civil rights leader Bayard Rustin, the ultimate outsider: black, gay, pacifist, and Quaker. In February 1978, Cherne led one-half of the group to Thailand to see boat and land refugees. Casey led the other half to Indonesia, the Philippines, and Hong Kong.

Politics interfered with the Commission's travel. Malaysia, a Muslim country, refused to receive the Casey group if it included Rabbi Marc Tanenbaum. Casey skipped Malaysia. Indonesia, also a Muslim majority country, welcomed the Commission. Cherne and his group visited nine of the 15 refugee camps in Thailand, the highlight being a Buddhist ceremony in the Lao refugee camp in Nong Khai following which Rustin — gospel singing being among his many talents — boomed out "We Shall Overcome."[5] The *farang* present were inspired; the Laotians were puzzled, having as much difficulty finding harmony in Western music as we do in theirs.

At one meeting an American diplomat, John Finney, was introducing the Commission members to Thai officials. He introduced each of the Americans with the honorific *Khun: Khun* Cherne, *Khun* Tanenbaum, etc. While waiting his turn to be introduced, Rustin said to Finney and Bob DeVecchi, "If you call me coon Rustin, I'm going to whop you with my cane."[6]

At Nong Khai the Commission heard of the fate of Laotian, primarily Hmong, refugees attempting to cross the Mekong river into Thailand. Previously, a refugee who made it across the river might be robbed and brutalized and but he was usually taken by the police to a nearby refugee camp. However, on November 15, 1977, the Thai government closed its borders to additional refugees. Police patrols on the river were ordered to apprehend refugees and return them to the Laotian side of the river. Journalists reported that they had seen refugees shot by Laotian border guards as soon as they were returned.

Laotians who eluded the border guards and made it to Thailand were arrested, fined, imprisoned until they could work off the fine, and then assigned to a "detention center." Cherne visited one of the detention centers. Twelve hundred men, women, and children were crammed into an area that sheltered only 200 while the others squatted in the open air. As the Thai government maintained the inmates were "detainees" and illegal immigrants" rather than

Berta Romero (left) and Bayard Rustin (white hat) interview a refugee. Rustin was allergic to official briefings and broke away frequently to talk to refugees. (Berta Romero)

refugees, UNHCR was not allowed access, although charity organizations had been allowed to bring in plastic sheeting and bamboo poles to built shelters.[7]

The Commission members came back to the United States fired up to catalyze action by the American government. Refugees are painfully accustomed to promises from visitors that are never fulfilled. The Citizen's Commission was the exception. Bayard Rustin persuaded the Executive Council of the AFL/CIO labor coalition to support the entry of additional Indochinese refugees. He also wrote a *New York Times* full-page advertisement signed by 80 black leaders titled "Black Americans Urge Admission of the Indo-Chinese Refugees." He said, "If our government lacks compassion for these dispossessed human beings, it is difficult to believe that the same government can have much compassion for America's black minority, or for America's poor."[8] The pastors, priests and rabbis on the commission worked their congregations, as did Bill Casey his congregation of Republican bankers. The Commission's recommendations included:

(1) The United States must adopt a coherent and generous policy for the admission of Indochinese refugees over the long range replacing the practice of reacting belatedly to successive refugee crises.

(2) Such a program will moderate anxieties among Southeast Asian countries which fear that unwanted refugees would be left on their hands; ... and will encourage new countries to join the common endeavor of granting sanctuary.

(3) The special circumstances of boat people, the Vietnamese who have come to Thailand overland, and of Cambodian refugees make it imperative that all existing criteria and categories for their admission to the United States be waived....

(4) The criteria for admitting refugees from Laos to the United States should be eased and applied more generously.... The United States continues to deny the hidden and pervasive character of its role in "the secret war" in Laos.

(5) Let no ships pass by persons of whatever nationality who are in danger of drowning at sea; let no port be closed to their disembarkation and temporary succor; let no merchant ship which has received these refugees be penalized in carrying out its normal function.[9]

Neither Shep nor Lionel could have written a better set of recommendations. And they were timely. Indochinese refugees were again working their way toward the front pages of the newspapers.

* * *

Cherne and the Commission met with Congressman Joshua Eilberg's Subcommittee on Immigration, Citizenship and International Law on March 1. Eilberg and many of his members were initially hostile. As Cherne recalled, the questions came fast and hard. "Hasn't the U.S. done enough already? If we let these refugees in, won't we encourage others to flee? What are other countries doing?"

Cherne credited Monsignor John Ahern and Bayard Rustin for turning the tide. "I find the question of what other countries will do as acutely embarrassing," said Ahern. "It ignores a substantial current history. On Monday I interviewed a gentleman who is a Ugandan refugee in Kenya, one of 60,000. I am not aware that Kenya asked us how many we would take before they took any. The measure of what we do is not what others do, but what we are able to do."

Unsatisfied with the carping of the congressmen, Bayard Rustin stood up and demanded the floor in dramatic fashion. With the thunder of a gospel preacher in his voice, he cited the support from both the labor unions and the African American community for admitting more refugees. "If America can be cruel enough not to admit into this country people who if they are sent elsewhere will be shot, that same cruelty will make it impossible for them—we, us—Americans to deal with the problems in our ghettos and for our poor. This is for me a moral question."[10]

Eilberg and the naysayers were defeated. Cherne, Ahearn, Rustin and group went on to meetings with President Carter. By March 29, a proposal was on the president's desk to admit more Indochinese refugees into the United States.

The payoff for the advocacy of the Cherne Commission and the behind the scenes work of Lowman, Rosenblatt, and others was the decision on June 14, 1978, that the United States would accept 25,000 Indochinese refugees for resettlement during the following year. One half of the refugees would come from the land refugee camps in Thailand and one half would come from boat refugees around Southeast Asia. Lionel had already journeyed out to Thailand in spring 1978 to head the program, now expanding again. The State Department estimated that boat people would continue to leave Vietnam at the rate of 1,600 per month — an estimate vastly lower than the reality to come.[11]

* * *

Shep admired Lionel's feats in Bangkok, but he also knew his template was not replicable in all times and places. Lionel's large and hurried operation had put a huge administrative burden on the Embassy in Thailand. He drained the motor pool of cars, jammed up the communications system, and caused apoplexy among proponents of administrative order and procedures. Back in Washington, the flood of documents, telegrams, requests for security clearances, and refugee case files coming in from Bangkok had forced the State Department to set up a 24-hour-a-day, 7-day-a-week office just to handle the paperwork.

The State Department does not have a large pool of manpower and resources to call upon. A large State Department office might have only 20 or 30 employees. The refugee program in Thailand had a larger budget, more employees, and produced more paper than any other State Department program at any post abroad. By the end of the 1970s refugee programs comprised 20 percent of the total State Department budget and Lionel Rosenblatt, only a mid-level Foreign Service officer, headed the largest and most costly overseas program of the State Department.[12]

Shep, anticipating a revival of the refugee crisis in Southeast Asia, came up with a plan to relieve the State Department of the procedural routine of refugee work. He created the Joint Voluntary Agency or JVA. Shep's concept was that the State Department would contract with a single VOLAG — or nongovernmental organization (NGO) as they were increasingly called — to handle the administrative details of processing refugees within a country. The State Department's role would thus be reduced to funding, policy guidance, and supervision. Shep wanted one VOLAG heading the JVA in each country because to organize a committee or consortium of fractious and competitive charitable organizations would be like herding cats. He picked the non-sectarian International Rescue Committee (IRC) to head the JVA in Thailand. By mid–1978 the JVA was operating in Thailand with about 20 American employees, mostly ex–Peace Corps volunteers, several of whom had worked for Lionel in 1976, whose job was to interview refugees for resettlement at the refugee camps in Thailand. Two dozen local employees supported the Americans.[13] The JVA concept was also quickly applied in other countries of Southeast Asia for Indochinese refugees. Early directors of JVA were Bob DeVecchi Ron Drago, Nan Borton, and Bill Sage.

Coming out of the creation of JVA was also the solution to the problem of finding sponsors to resettle refugees. The first 130,000 from Vietnam were brought to the United States first and sponsors were found later. That was no longer possible under the law. Sponsors now must be found for refugees before they were sent to the U.S. The State Department turned the task of finding sponsors over to the American Council of Voluntary Agencies, a consortium in New York. ACVA found and evaluated sponsors, forwarded information on sponsors to the JVA in the field, handled administrative details, and took over responsibility for the refugee when he landed in the United States. Field officers called ACVA "the meat market."

Bringing the charities into the refugee infrastructure enriched the atmosphere of refugee work. Shep valued the independent judgments of the JVA and the VOLAGs. The JVA, however, didn't like to be reminded that its boss was the Refugee Coordinator of the Embassy in Bangkok and that the government funded it. JVA worked hard to maintain its independence. The outspoken charity officials didn't hold back in blistering criticism of the State Department, its policies, and their Embassy minders. Many of them, in fact, seemed to seek out issues to fight about. Shep was soon spending more than three months every year in Southeast Asia to evaluate the refugee programs and to mediate disputes between the JVA in each country and the Embassies. But the charities, for all their prickly irritations, were the ground-truth the government needed to judge what was right and wrong with the refugee program. They were also a potent force of advocacy for refugees back in the U.S.

JVA's tasks were to make an initial survey of the population of a refugee camp and undertake interviews to determine which refugees might be eligible to go to the U.S. They completed the files on individuals and families and submitted them to the Ethic Affairs officers, such as Tucker and Daniels, and then to the Immigration and Naturalization Service for final interviews and approval or disapproval. It also did the logistics of transporting refugees to the INS for interviews, or helping INS officers visit the refugee camps. JVA matched sponsors to refugees through the "meat market" in New York.

The International Committee on European Migration (ICEM), still headed by Albert Corcos, continued to do cultural training, arrange transportation for refugees to the U.S. and medical examinations. Security clearances were required for each refugee. "Falcon" was the tagline for telegrams requesting security clearances from Washington. Obtaining security clearances was time consuming as clerks for the FBI, CIA and other agencies in Washington ransacked their files for adverse information about people with unfamiliar and exotic Asian names in which the first was sometimes the last. Rarely did the search yield any matching information.

The alliance between the State Department and the JVA was only for the purpose of processing refugees for resettlement in the U.S. Many of the charitable organizations, such as the IRC, who participated in JVA, also had offices in Thailand to provide humanitarian aid and medical care to the refugees. They were often contracted by UNHCR to provide these services in the camps.

* * *

Before going to Bangkok in the spring of 1978, Lionel talked to Assistant Secretary Richard Holbrooke, one of his high-level supporters in the State Department. Holbrooke emphasized that American public opinion was what was keeping the refugee program alive — and all those working with refugees should take every opportunity to bolster public opinion, especially by influencing visitors to refugee camps.

Lionel said he would be too busy to deal with visitors to the camps. Holbrooke rebuked him. "The most important part of your job is building public support for refugees. Welcome visitors and make sure that they go away committed to do something to help refugees."

Lionel took Holbrooke's advice to heart. In Bangkok he made it a point to treat every congressman and visiting VIP, no matter how shallow their interest, with the utmost of personal attention and care. "They all go home and talk about what they've seen," Holbrooke had said. Lionel was to drive his staff up the wall with his endless fretting about petty details arranging for an endless stream of visitors.[14]

The refugee program Rosenblatt took over in Thailand in 1978 was in transition from being the emergency, *ad hoc* program he had created in 1976 to being a long-term effort by the United States, Canada, Australia, France, and other countries. The United Nations and its agencies, notably the United Nations High Commissioner for Refugees (UNHCR) had slowly begun to overcome its earlier indifference to Indochinese refugees. The Indochinese refugees were an international problem that would not go away — although nobody could yet imagine how large a problem they would become. The omens of an expanding refugee and humanitarian crisis were visible before the end of 1978.

* * *

A positive development in 1978 was the defeat of Congressman Joshua Eilberg in the November elections. Eilberg was accused of accepting a "fee" for arranging a government grant. His Pennsylvania constituents voted him out of office. Eilberg subsequently pleaded guilty to the charges, lost his law license, was on probation for five years, and paid a $10,000 fine.[15] There wasn't a wet eye in the halls of the State Department. Many believed that the full scope of

9. Before the Deluge
129

Eilberg's crimes never saw the light of day and that he had gotten off with a slap on the wrist.

Eilerg was replaced as chairman for the Subcommittee on Immigration by Elizabeth Holtzman from New York. Holtzman was strongly favorable toward the refugee program, although her feminism — at the time a new movement — tickled the funny bones of irreverent refugee workers. They called her "Chairperson Holtzperson" to avoid the gender nuance of "Chairman Holtzman." Her two visits to Southeast Asia in 1978 and 1979 with large delegations in tow, while undeniably productive, were wearing on the refugee staff and remembered as the CODELs from Hell — CODEL being a State Department abbreviation for Congressional Delegation.[16]

Bangkok was a popular stopping place for Congressmen and a wise Embassy officer in charge of a CODEL always built in adequate "personal time" so that the members and staff could enjoy the delights of Bangkok, which included bars, bar girls, massage parlors, masseuses, strip clubs, strippers, jewelry, silk shops, and colorful Buddhist temples. If the price of getting them interested in refugee issues was allowing CODELs time to enjoy Bangkok, the refugee workers were amenable. Making sure that visitors had fond memories of their country was also a high priority of the Thai government.

Lionel made sure that all visitors were subjected to an immersion course in refugees. On one occasion he took Congressman Mazzoli from Kentucky, chairman of the Refugee Sub-committee, to a camp to listen to refugees tell their stories. The camp was desolate and the heat was stifling. Sitting in a thatched hut, the congressman swooned in the middle of the interviews, a victim of jet lag and heat, and sprawled out unconscious on the dirt floor. Lionel rushed to his side and shouted in distress, "Mr. Chairman! Mr. Chairman! We have another really interesting case for you. Hello? Hello?" Nothing could deter Lionel from his focus on refugees.[17]

Attention to detail and dedication paid off. The reports of the congressmen and their staffers on their return to the United States were usually positive. Rosenblatt and group, always teetering on the edge of disaster, impressed visitors. As an experienced diplomat once said, "A CODEL will test your faith in democracy."[18] But the refugee office accomplished its objectives. By whatever means employed, congressmen and women and their staffers went home more supportive of the program than when they arrived.

10

CAMBODIA: HOLOCAUST DENIAL

The character of the Khmer Rouge regime was a subject of intense debate in the late 1970s. Many western intellectuals were favorable to the KR or regarded reports of its brutality as tall tales told by refugees. "A genocide myth was being fabricated," they said, by horror stories told by refugees in Bangkok.[1] Revolutionary excesses in Cambodia were inevitable and regrettable, admitted worldly academics, but these could be explained by rage caused by the heavy U.S. bombing of the country from 1969 to 1973.[2]

One sign that not all was well in Cambodia was that 125,000 ethnic Cambodians fled Cambodia for Vietnam between 1975 and 1979. Given the antipathy between the two societies, the flight of Cambodians to Vietnam should have set off scholarly alarm bells. During the same period, 194,000 ethnic Vietnamese and Chinese also left Cambodia for Vietnam.[3] An elementary deduction should be that something is wrong if people flee one country for another, especially if they are going from one poor country to another in which they, the Cambodians and Chinese, are regarded with distaste and suspicion.

With little information seeping out of Cambodia, the intellectuals shrugged off reports of mass murder by the Khmer Rouge. Nor were they alone; most countries and international organizations were similarly unconcerned. Leo Cherne wrote UNHCR in summer 1975 asking for an inquiry about conditions inside Cambodia. The reply was: "It is not within the competence of the UNHCR to make enquiries to which you refer. Possibly the Human Rights commission of the United Nations might be interested in the matter."[4] With insolence and indifference by UNHCR as an example, the scholars dismissed a *Time* magazine article of April 19, 1976, titled "Khmer Rouge: Rampant Terror." The article alleged unbelievably brutal conditions inside Cambodia.

Gareth Porter, a junior scholar out of the Southeast Asian Program at Cornell University, took it upon himself to respond to what he saw as the malicious exaggerations of the *Time* article. Writing in the "U.S./Indochina Report" he charged that horror stories of people being buried alive by bulldozers, suffocated by plastic bags tied over their heads, and other atrocities "all originated from the same four or five Cambodian refugees" in Thailand. He cited three journalists of other publications who were "careful to point out that the refugees are not reliable sources of information on the situation in Cambodia." He rejected the *Time* estimate of 500,000 dead Cambodians as American propaganda. The *Time* article, he lamented, was contributing to the development of a "bloodbath myth" about the Khmer Rouge government in Cambodia.[5]

Porter and other scholars again jumped to the defense of the Khmer Rouge when two books published in early 1977 made even more startling claims than *Time*. The first was *Cambodia Year Zero* by Francois Ponchaud, a French priest who lived in Cambodia from 1965 to 1975, spoke Khmer fluently, and had been an eyewitness to the Khmer Rouge takeover of Phnom Penh. The second book was *Murder of a Gentle Land* by John Barron and Anthony Paul. Barron was a senior editor of *Reader's Digest*, America's best-selling magazine, despised by intellectuals for its muscular patriotism, conservative slant, and appeal to the middle class. Both books charged the Khmer Rouge with mass murder. Ponchaud upped the *Time* estimate of half a million dead Cambodians to 800,000 killed between April 17, 1975, and February 1976 — either directly by the Khmer Rouge or indirectly by starvation and overwork. Barron and Paul estimated an even higher toll of 1.2 million in 1975 and 1976.[6]

Ponchaud's book was persuasive. He was a man of the Left who welcomed the Khmer Rouge revolution, but his experiences during the evacuation of Phnom Penh and his interviews with refugees persuaded him that the KR was committing genocide on their own people. Barron and Paul interviewed refugees in Thailand to compile their estimates. Both books painted a picture of Cambodia so bleak and tragic that people flinched in horror. It was hard to believe that such monstrous stories were true. One million dead? In a country with only seven or eight million people? Surely mankind was not capable of such bizarre and evil behavior.

Many scholars saw the KR as pristine revolutionaries with the admirable objective of freeing the Cambodian poor from the shackles of colonialism, capitalism, and the destructive intervention of the United States of America. In the words of Sophal Ear, a Cambodian-American scholar, this was not a fringe group of Cambodian scholars but "virtually all of them." Ear caustically called their informal meeting of the minds the "Standard Total Academic View on Cambodia (STAV)." The STAV, he said, "hoped for, more than anything, a socialist success story with all the romantic ingredients of peasants, fighting imperialism, and revolution. A cursory examination of the titles to the articles they wrote on Cambodia during that period yields further evidence of their rapture for these elements: 'Consolidating the Revolution,' or 'defining the Revolutionary State,' or 'Social Cohesion in Revolutionary Cambodia,' or 'Rationale for a Rural Policy.'"[7]

A look at two STAV stalwarts, Gareth Porter and Malcolm Caldwell, illuminates the views of the group. Porter discounted refugees as sources for information about Cambodia, but therein was a contradiction. The only two sources of information about events within Cambodia were the government and the refugees. If the refugees were not reliable sources who was? The KR? Porter and the STAV gave free rein to their imagination about what they believed was a true agrarian revolution in Cambodia. They might have asked themselves why the Khmer Rouge did not allow even friendly scholars to visit Cambodia and they might have accorded the same suspicion to information emanating from the Khmer Rouge government as they did to other governments. As author William Shawcross put it, Porter's faith in the words of the Khmer Rouge was surprising for a man who had "spent so long analyzing the lies that governments tell."[8]

Porter and George Hildebrand wrote *Cambodia: Starvation and Revolution*. The book was unabashedly pro–Khmer Rouge and, in the words of Porter's mentor at Cornell, was "undoubtedly the best informed and clearest picture yet to emerge of the desperate economic problems brought about in Cambodia largely as a consequence of American intervention, and of the ways in which that country's new leadership has undertaken to meet them."[9] Porter had the certainty of youth, ideological commitment, and the support of older hands pushing him from behind.

The war of words about the character of the Khmer Rouge would persist until incontrovertible evidence in the form of mountains of skulls and the testimony of tens of thousands of Cambodians removed all doubt of the genocidal character of the KR and quieted the voices of those who denied the Cambodian holocaust.

With the publication of Ponchaud's book and a condensation of Barron and Paul's book in *Reader's Digest* in February 1977, Porter and the other members of the STAV were on the defensive. The U.S. Congress took up the issue in a hearing on May 3, 1977. Stephen Solarz from New York was the principal inquisitor of witnesses who included Porter, Professor Peter Poole of American University, David Chandler, a research associate at Harvard, and John Barron. It seemed three against one: Poole expressed cautious hope that the KR were moderating; Chandler pleaded lack of information and blamed the Khmer Rouge on the United States; Porter defended the Khmer Rouge. Barron was by himself with his claims of Khmer Rouge atrocities.

Barron got right to the point in his prepared statement. "In our judgment a tragedy of terrible proportions has befallen and continues to afflict the people of that land. And I fear that, so long as democratic legislatures throughout the world remain silent about their plight, most are condemned to suffer in inhumane conditions bereft of elementary human rights."[10] Barron said that he and Paul had interviewed more than 300 Cambodian refugees and Paul was still in Thailand collecting up-to-date information. He read a letter, dated March 28, 1977, from Paul:

10. Cambodia

Dear John. I have just returned from a 1,200 kilometer swing through Thailand's camps for Cambodian refugees ... I had expected some evidence of slackening terror in Cambodia. It is true that fewer refugees are escaping from that country into Thailand — the present rate is about 100 a month — but the stories they bring suggest that the killings have not yet stopped.

Paul tells several stories by refugees. Sek, a truck driver, was sent by the KR to Krakor district near Phnom Penh. Because of the accessibility of Krakor, Paul wrote, "If there is any rice in Cambodia, it must be possible to get it to Krakor. If there is any medicine in Cambodia, it must [be] possible to supply it to Krakor. If any community in Cambodia is in touch with the latest directives of the communist administration in Phnom Penh, it is surely Krakor." Krakor had, prior to the KR, had a population of 12,750 people.

Paul continued: "Almost from the beginning, Krakor's scanty food rations began to take their toll. Bodies weakened by malnutrition became increasingly susceptible to tropical diseases. The resultant death toll was swollen by the fairly constant stream of executions — or sudden disappearances — of Cambodians who had for whatever reason offended Angka Loeu, the Khmer Rouge 'Organization on High.'

"Sek remembers that the worst period began late in the dry season of last year [1976] about April or May. The rate of deaths by starvation and disease began picking up. 'By June or July,' says Sek, 'about five people a day were dying ... the famine and plagues were accompanied by an increase in the rate of executions. Sek estimated that, from the end of the dry season to about November of last year, about 600 must have been eliminated. The program embraced soldiers, teachers, students and anyone who knew a foreign language.... 'We often found their bodies later,' says Sek. 'Usually their throats had been cut.'" By December 1976 a KR cadre told Sek and other survivors that they had to work twice as hard because the population of Krakor was now about 6,000, down from 12,750 only 20 months before.

Paul concluded that he and Barron had been too cautious in their book in estimating that 1.2 million people had died in Cambodia. "Krakor's fate," he wrote, "suggests that our earlier estimates of the death toll in Cambodia since April 1975 are underestimated — indeed grossly underestimated."[11]

Barron concluded his remarks by re-stating eloquently the mantra of the human rights advocate. "It is my feeling that, unless we speak out, our silence lends a concurrence. And, by not taking a moral stand, by not denouncing the death of a very large number of people, we, in effect, are communicating to the leadership that they can with impunity continue to do whatever they want."[12]

* * *

Gareth Porter took on the task of refuting the testimony of the *Reader's Digest* editor. He gave the sub-committee a lengthy prepared statement with his interpretation of events in Cambodia. "The situation in postwar Cambodia," he began, "has generated an unprecedented wave of emotional — and at times hysterical — comment. The closing of Cambodia to the foreign press, making the refugees the only source of information used by the media, and the tendency of many refugees to offer the darkest possible picture of the country they fled have combined to provide a fertile ground for wild exaggeration and wholesale falsehood about the government and its policies. The result is the suggestions, now rapidly hardening into conviction, that 1 to 2 million Cambodians have been the victims of a regime led by genocidal maniacs."[13]

Porter admitted there had been violence, disease, and executions in Cambodia under the Khmer Rouge, but he attributed that to "eagerness" on the part of the KR leaders to create a modern economy while maintaining independence from foreign influences. Loss of life and hardship was inevitable, said he, during the revolutionary transformation of the society. "The notion that the leadership of Democratic Kampuchea adopted a policy of physically eliminating whole classes of people, of purging anyone who was connected with the Lon Nol government, or punishing the entire urban population by putting them to work in the countryside after the 'death march' from the cities, is a myth."

Porter then said that refugees were "strongly motivated" to portray Cambodia in the worst light; and the refugees interviewed were often selected by camp leaders, rather than representing a cross section of the population. Many of their "eye witness" accounts on further examination were hearsay and second hand information. Barron and Paul's and Ponchaud's books, he said, "fail to measure up to even the minimum standards of journalism or scholarship, and their overall conclusions and general tone must be regarded as the product of overheated emotions and lack of caution."

In conclusion, Porter discounted the estimates of a million Cambodians who had been killed, starved, or worked to death by the Khmer Rouge. One observer, he said, thought the numbers killed were in the hundreds or thousands rather than the hundreds of thousands. Porter blamed the U.S. for causing "overwhelmingly greater suffering" in Cambodia than the Khmer Rouge and concluded that the "human cost of the revolutionary change is dwarfed by the magnitude of suffering and death which attended the war and its aftermath."[14]

Congressman Solarz led off the questioning of the witnesses. Solarz, a student of the European holocaust of World War II, projected his horror at the slaughter of Jews and others into concerns for the rights of human beings everywhere. He had been one of the first to find his way to the Thai/Cambodian border in August 1975. He had seen and talked to terrified Cambodians who escaped the Khmer Rouge.

Now, he opened up with both barrels at Porter, Chandler, and Poole. He was "appalled" at what had been said about "one of the most monstrous crimes in the history of the human race. To me," he continued, "the holocaust in which

6 million Jews lost their lives at the hands of Hitler is the central existential fact not only of our time, but of human history, because it provides an indication of the depths of depravity to which the human spirit can sink, and I might have hoped that, after Hitler, the world would have finally learned its lesson about genocide, and that holocausts would have been something of the past. Obviously, it hasn't. In its own way, the indifference of the world to the events of Cambodia is almost as appalling as what has happened there.

"Some of the justifications or explanations which we have heard ... have been frankly, in my judgment, cowardly and contemptible. They are, as I see it, very much the same kind of justifications that were offered to justify the murder of the Jews by Hitler in the 1940s."[15]

Solarz demanded what evidence Porter had that the reports of mass deaths in Cambodia were false. Porter cited three sources. The first was a letter to the *Economist* magazine from a man named W.J. Sampson who claimed to have interviewed Cambodian refugees and concluded that only hundreds or thousands of Cambodians had been killed by the KR. Porter did not know Sampson. Solarz commented: "For all you know, this fellow could be a psychotic." The second was an article by Ben Kiernan in an Australian journal, the *Melbourne Journal of Politics*. Kiernan cited contradictions in refugee testimony. Solarz shot back that there were contradictions in every account of human history. The third of Porter's sources were scholarly debates about Ponchaud's book. On this amazingly thin documentation — Porter never mentioned having talked to a single Cambodian — Porter concluded that nothing much was amiss in Cambodia except for revolutionary exuberance.

As the bitter hearing came to an end Porter was unrepentant, Chandler was indignant at the Congressional criticism of him and Poole had reluctantly sided with Barron about the character of the Khmer Rouge. In a rare case of Congressional understatement, Chairman Fraser characterized the hearing as "lively."

Porter's defense of the Khmer Rouge crumbled in the face of facts. Nevertheless, his academic career did not suffer. He became a Congressional aide and a lecturer at the prestigious Johns Hopkins School of Advanced International Studies.[16] He displayed fancy footwork and good timing in shifting his attention away from Cambodia and toward Vietnam.

Porter later became uncomfortable when the subject of Cambodia was discussed. He admitted that he had changed his view "on a number of aspects of the Cambodian situation" and that the Khmer government's policies had levied "unnecessary costs" on Cambodians.[17] Critic Bruce Sharp comments further: "By 1978, even Gareth Porter seemed to want to distance himself.... Interviewed by Ed Bradley for the CBS television documentary 'What Happened to Cambodia,' Porter's eyes dart back and forth when Bradley questions him about the Khmer Rouge regime. He casts his eyes down and stutters slightly. 'My ... my only plea is for some degree of balance in assessing the human suffering that undoubtedly still exists in Cambodia.'"[18]

Porter and others based their denials of the Cambodian holocaust on the grounds that refugee stories could not be believed. But Porter had childlike trust in the words of the Khmer Rouge government. Porter's book, *Cambodia: Starvation and Revolution*, was heavy on KR sources. "The book's last fifty footnotes, from the chapter on 'Cambodia's Agricultural Revolution,' provide an excellent case in point. Out of these 50 citations, there are 43 that pertain to the Khmer Rouge regime. Of these, 33 can be traced directly to the Khmer Rouge sources. Six more come from the official news agency of Communist China, i.e., the Khmer Rouge's wealthiest patron. Two come from an unnamed source, described only as 'a Cambodian economist.' And the remaining two references both come from *Le Monde*: one is a dubious estimate of future rice production, and the other simply notes that, in the future, large rice paddies would be subdivided, 'giving the country the appearance of an enormous checkerboard.'"[19]

* * *

Porter presented his case in the guise of a scholar; but the words objective and balanced were not in the vocabulary of Malcolm Campbell. He was an unabashed cheerleader for the KR. Caldwell, 47 years old, was a lecturer on economic history at the University of London.[20] Caldwell was a communist, unlike many academics whose affection for the Khmer Rouge grew out of their opposition to U.S. intervention in Southeast Asia rather than an ideological commitment to Marxism. Caldwell, in the words of his eulogist, "would have wanted to be remembered as an activist on the British left and an anti-imperialist fighter."[21] Another eulogist said, "Malcolm, one of the staunchest defenders of the Pol Pot regime in the West, viewed that regime through the prism of agrarian revolution. His systematic attempt to deflate Western journalistic reports of mass executions in Kampuchea made him the object of attack from many quarters."[22]

Caldwell was rewarded by the Khmer Rouge for his dedication with an invitation to visit Cambodia in December 1978 along with journalists Elizabeth Becker of *The Washington Post* and Richard Dudman of the *St. Louis Post-Dispatch*. They were the first Western journalists to visit Cambodia in the three years of Khmer Rouge rule. "We traveled in a bubble," recalled Becker. "We had traveled throughout the country, heavily guarded and under near house arrest. I had lived in Cambodia for several years, covering the war, and although the terrain was achingly familiar—the sugar palms, the tough bright green of the rice paddies, and the vast flat skies—the people themselves had seemed alien on this trip. The communist cadre wore black pyjamas. The few peasants I saw wore rags. No one was allowed to talk to me freely."[23] Dudman remembered Phnom Penh as having "the eerie quiet of a dead place—a Hiroshima without the destruction, a Pompeii without the ashes.... My first impression was that the total population of the capital could not be more than a very few thousand. The usual estimate of 20,000 seemed high."[24] The population of Phnom Penh in 1975 has been estimated at about 2 million.

Caldwell had a private meeting with Cambodian prime minister Pol Pot. Becker recalled that he "returned delighted with his time with Cambodia's leader. The two had spent most of the interview discussing revolutionary economic theory, the topic of choice for Caldwell throughout the trip." Pol Pot invited Caldwell to make a return visit next year. Caldwell accepted, although he asked that the visit not be scheduled at Christmas. Christmas! Pol Pot must have despaired of the depth of commitment of his supporters.[25]

Becker and Caldwell last saw each other in the late evening of December 22 at the guest house where they were staying in Phnom Penh. "After dinner, Dudman went to his room to type up notes and Caldwell and I stayed at the table to have our last argument about Cambodia. Caldwell took what he considered the longer view and said the revolution was worth it. I said, on the contrary, I was more convinced of the truth of the refugee stories—which is what I eventually wrote. That night Caldwell tried once more to get me to change my mind."

Becker went to bed but awoke about 11:00 to the sound of gunfire. She stepped out of her bedroom into the dining room and nearly ran into a young Cambodian man with a pistol in hand, an automatic rifle over his shoulder and two bandoliers of ammunition crossed on his chest. He pointed the pistol at her. She ran back into her bedroom, into the bathroom, and threw herself into the bathtub. She heard the sounds of people moving and then more shots. She waited in the bathtub for more than an hour until a Cambodian she knew came to the door. He brought the news that Caldwell was dead. She and Dudman went to Caldwell's room. He had been shot in the chest and in the doorway was another body, this one of a young man who looked like the one who had pointed the pistol at her. Was he killed trying to protect Caldwell—or killed after he murdered Caldwell?[26]

The Khmer Rouge executed the people it said had killed Caldwell, but it has never been determined who killed Malcolm Caldwell and why. That it was not a random act of common criminality is certain in the tightly-controlled land of the KR. Becker theorizes that a high level political enemy of Pol Pot had Caldwell killed to embarrass the Cambodian leader. Perhaps. But why Caldwell? The impact would have been greater if Becker or Dudman—well known journalists—had been killed, and greater still if two had been killed and one spared to take home the story. But, little effort was made to kill the other two. Becker had a pistol pointed at her and a gunman had fired a wild shot in Dudman's direction. We may never know why Caldwell was killed, but a chill swept through the ranks of the STAV who were already in retreat as macabre news seeped out of Cambodia about the Khmer Rouge.

On December 25, 1978, three days after the murder of Malcolm Caldwell, Vietnam invaded Cambodia.

* * *

The question of how many people died at the hands of the Khmer Rouge has been much debated. Of a Cambodia population of seven to eight million, the early estimates of deaths attributed to the KR ranged from several hundreds or thousands by Gareth Porter to 3,314,768 by the Vietnamese invaders.[27] "In the early 1980s, the authorities of the Peoples Republic of Kampuchea [the Vietnamese-supported successor government of the Khmer Rouge] carried out what amounted to a national household survey, aiming to interview every head of household in the entire country about what had happened to their families during the Pol Pot regime."[28] To scholars, the estimate of more than three million dead Cambodians was absurd. Forty percent of the Cambodian population had died at the hands of the Khmer Rouge? Nobody, except Cambodians, believed that.

In the aftermath of the Khmer Rouge, scholars contested the higher estimates and tended to project a minimalist view that the KR had killed less than one million Cambodians. The carefully balanced Time-Life 25-volume series called *The Vietnam Experience* published in 1985 reflects the minimalist view. "It appears that the victims of the Cambodian blood bath may have numbered 1 million or less."[29] Balance, however, is not always synonymous with accuracy.

Over time, the scholars listened to Cambodian survivors rather than their own prejudices. The methodology used by most investigators has been to interview a representative sample of Cambodians, calculate the deaths in their family or deaths that they witnessed, and project the experiences of a few people onto the nation as a whole. As the information base has expanded the number of estimated deaths has gone up. Ben Kiernan, a recanted member of the STAV, interviewed 500 Cambodians in 1980 and estimated the death toll in the country to be 1.5 million, an estimate that he has since increased to 1.7 million.[30]

The most definitive work on counting the victims of the Khmer Rouge was by Craig Etcheson, a former colleague of Kiernan at the Cambodian Genocide Project at Yale University. The two apparently had a falling-out as Etcheson's 1999 essay was deleted from the website of the Genocide Project and Kiernan was scathing in denouncing Etcheson's findings.[31] Whatever academic rivalry caused such animosity between the two cannot be determined, but research by Etcheson stands alone in its sophistication and scope.

Between 1995 and 1999 Etcheson and the Documentation Center of Cambodia mapped and investigated mass graves left behind by the Khmer Rouge. They found 20,492 mass graves and the graves "contain the remains of 1,112,829 victims of execution."[32] This is an astonishing total as most scholars believed that the number of victims of the Khmer Rouge dying of starvation and overwork exceeded those executed. If more than one million people were executed, how many died of other causes that could be attributed to the KR? Etcheson concludes that the Khmer Rouge executed about 1.5 million people and another 1.5 million died of starvation and disease. He said: "We would be driven to the conclusion that not one million, not two million, but rather three million Cambodians died untimely deaths during the Khmer Rouge regime."[33]

11

INDOCHINA: THE PERPETUAL WAR

Vietnam squandered international goodwill. This poor country had defeated the world's most powerful nation. The bloodbath following a communist victory predicted by many seemed to have been a fantasy. Perhaps the new rulers of South Vietnam really were liberators, proponents of a collectivist democracy that would be beneficial to the long-suffering people of Vietnam. From a distance they looked good. The initial pronouncements of the Provisional Revolutionary Government of South Vietnam were moderate. Anti-communist *Time* magazine called the takeover of the country "the most velvety transition of power ever effected by a communist government."[1] North Vietnamese soldiers in Saigon were said to be polite and well-behaved. Nine months after the communist takeover of the South, *Time* spoke of the "slow road to socialism" in Saigon, now Ho Chi Minh City. Wine, women, and black market consumer products were still readily available; flowers, firecrackers, and restrained revelry heralded Tet, the Vietnamese New Year.[2]

A measure of the good feeling toward Vietnam came at the Security Council of the United Nations on August 11, 1975, when 14 Council members voted to admit both Vietnams to the United Nations—thus according a status to Vietnam enjoyed only by the Soviet Union, which had three votes in the UN based on the fiction that Ukraine and Byelorussia were independent countries. The U.S. was the lone dissenter and vetoed the membership application and also vetoed a renewed application later that year.[3] The General Assembly then asked the Security Council to reconsider Vietnam's membership, voting 124-1 in favor of the resolution, the lone dissenter again being the United States.[4]

The issue of whether one or two Vietnams existed was soon resolved: The two were united into the Socialist Republic of Vietnam on July 2, 1976, and the Provisional Revolutionary Government of South Vietnam was abolished. The union was not accomplished without dissent. Truong Nhu Trang, Justice Minister of the PRG, said, "I have no intention of taking part in a regime that was imposing itself on the South after the betrayal of so many promises."[5] Trang was sent to a reeducation camp and later became a refugee.

Vietnam was a favored recipient of economic aid from Western European countries. France and Sweden were the largest donors with grants running into the hundreds of millions of dollars. Holland, Denmark, Belgium, Finland, Norway, and Austria also gave the country millions of dollars in aid and financial assistance.[6]

Even the United States was not entirely negative. One of the most forthright statements came from a report by the staff of the Judiciary Committee of the Senate in July 1976 which proposed healing "the wounds of war" with a "normalization of relations with the people and government of Vietnam." The report recommended that the United States seek reconciliation with Vietnam to help resolve the humanitarian problems resulting from the war and to facilitate peace and stability in the region.[7] Although the Ford Administration was leery of reconciliation, Jimmy Carter was more conciliatory. Shortly after taking office in January 1977 he sent a delegation to Hanoi. He followed that up by sending Richard Holbrooke, Assistant Secretary of State for Far Eastern Affairs, to meet with Vietnamese vice foreign minister Phan Hien in Paris. Holbrooke raised the issue that would drive American relations with Vietnam for nearly two decades: accounting for 2,500 American soldiers who had gone missing in action during the war or, as many believed, were still being held as prisoners of war.[8]

If Vietnam was sincere about reconciling with the U.S., it made a mistake on the POW/MIA issue. Holbrooke promised diplomatic recognition of Vietnam and no opposition to its admission to the United Nations provided that Vietnam cooperated in accounting for missing Americans soldiers. Hien apparently thought Holbrooke's offer came from weakness that could be exploited. He pulled a letter out of his pocket from former President Nixon, dated in 1973 just after the Paris Peace Accord, that promised North Vietnam $3.25 billion dollars in reconstruction assistance. The letter had been kept secret by Nixon and Kissinger, and by this point it had the same value as Nixon's letter of the same time to South Vietnam promising U.S. intervention if North Vietnam broke the peace agreement: none. Holbrooke dismissed the letter, but the Vietnamese persisted, linking cooperation on MIAs with the promised aid.[9]

Did Vietnam really believe that the United States could be bulldozed into providing it with billions in reconstruction assistance — or was it the Vietnamese intention to simply sabotage the talks and the progress toward normalization of relations? There seemed no benefit to Vietnam in sabotaging the talks, but its naiveté was mind-boggling if it expected the U.S. to honor a promise for aid after the North had violated the Paris Peace Accord, destroyed the South Vietnamese government, and sent the U.S. packing in humiliation in helicopters flown off the Embassy roof in Saigon. In the mind of the Americans, the Vietnamese government's demands revealed its true character: it wanted a bribe in exchange for cooperation on a humanitarian matter. Congress quickly voted 266 to 131 to ban any discussions of aid between the U.S. and Vietnam.[10] A Congressional Committee asserted that it opposed "any conditions even faintly resembling blackmail" for information on U.S. missing soldiers.[11] Bitterly split on the Vietnam War, American politicians united to oppose reconciliation until Vietnam was forthcoming in accounting for prisoners of war and Americans missing in action. (Despite the hopes of many, no conclusive evidence of POWs still being held by Hanoi was ever discovered.)

The internal situation of Vietnam likewise was not as benign as first indications. First came an order for reeducation of former members of the South Vietnamese government and military officers. It began as a moderate and reasonable requirement for officials and supporters of the former government to report to a reeducation camp for ten to 30 days, but months and years passed and many never came home. The "velvety" transition to power of the communists evolved into an iron fist. The North's plan for the South was first expressed in July 1976: "We must immediately abolish the comprador bourgeoisie and the remnants of the feudal landlord class, undertake the socialist transformation of private capitalist industry and commerce, agriculture, handicraft and small trade through appropriate measures and steps."[12] With the South polluted by capitalism, the Northern overlords intended to root out the subversive and anti-revolutionary enemies of socialism. Quiet and discreet executions were one method. Scholar Jacqueline Desbarats calculated 65,000 extra-judicial executions in the South by the communists between 1975 and 1985 — and later raised her estimate to 100,000.[13] Reeducation camps were a second technique of ridding the society of its enemies, real and potential. A million or more South Vietnamese were hauled away to the reeducation camps, half of them for years of grueling labor and imprisonment.[14]

Another measure to increase agricultural production and to destroy capitalist remnants in the cities was the relocation of urban dwellers to "New Economic Zones." Vietnam's economy had been severely damaged by the war, especially in the area of agriculture. To make up for the adverse impact of the war on agriculture production, the United States had given South Vietnam 650,000 tons of rice per year — enough food for more than three million people. The loss of this American-supplied rice made it the highest priority of the new government to increase agricultural production. Its leaders were clever enough not to abolish private ownership of farmland immediately. Rather, they established "New Economic Zones" to reclaim land abandoned during the war and to open up land in the mountains used only by the despised Montagnards. The NEZs proved to be less successful in spurring agricultural production than assaulting enemies of the regime — especially the urban dwellers in southern cities. During the war, cities had attracted millions of refugees from the countryside. Now the new government was aiding — or forcing — many of them to go back to the land. The government also took the opportunity to empty the cities of the unemployed, traders, capitalists, failed students, officials of the old regime, relatives of people in reeducation camps, religious minorities, and machinery workers—the last because their mechanical skills would be useful in the countryside.[15]

The conditions in the NEZs were often not much better than those of the reeducation camps. More than one million people from Saigon and other southern cities—their participation was supposedly voluntary—took up residence in farming communities. Passive resistance to the NEZs was high and the program never achieved its goal of relocating four million Southerners during the first five-year plan. Poor planning, lack of rural infrastructure, uncleared jungle and land devastated by Agent Orange or littered with unexploded ordnance contributed to making the program an economic and humanitarian failure.[16]

The hardening fist of the Vietnamese communists fell especially hard on the Chinese. Called Hoa to distinguish them from ethnic Vietnamese, they had migrated from China over the previous 200 years. More than 200,000 Hoa lived in northern Vietnam near the Chinese border. These Chinese were supposedly integrated into Vietnamese society and were mostly farmers, merchants, and often smugglers who maintained contacts on both sides of the border. More than one million Chinese lived in southern Vietnam, especially in Cholon, the sister city of Saigon. In the south, Hoa were primarily engaged in commerce and were more prosperous than the Vietnamese. The Hoa—5 percent of the population—controlled much of the retail trade in the South. As in most of Southeast Asia the Hoa had largely retained their Chinese culture, customs, and nationality and remained a people apart: "Although the Hoa live in Vietnam their hearts are with China."[17] And, as in other countries of the region, they were disliked. They became the prime targets of the campaign to purify the South.

Throughout 1976 and 1977 the Hoa saw their opportunities in Vietnam decline. Discrimination in employment, higher taxes, reduced food rations, and restrictions on their movement reined in and controlled them. Suspicion of them became intense as relations deteriorated between Vietnam and its former patron, China. Hoa near the Chinese border were relocated after having their property confiscated or were expelled to China. In March 1978 the government stepped up the persecution by abolishing private trade. It deployed thousands of police, soldiers, and thugs to ransack shops and businesses in Cholon and other major cities of the south. A few merchants resisted and riots left many people dead. In May, the government introduced a new national currency and hoarders of the old currency—mostly Chinese—were unable to convert most of their old money into the new. About 320,000 Hoa, their businesses confiscated and their livelihoods destroyed, were to be removed from the cities to the NEZs. The Hoa began to leave Vietnam. Between May 9 and 21, 1978, 57,000 left by land for China; by July, 150,000 had left,[18] and by the end of 1979, 250,000 Hoa would seek refuge in China.[19] Many Vietnamese officials and the government encouraged or forced the Hoa to leave and extracted money from them for departure fees and bribes.[20]

Their harsh treatment of the Hoa caused a major decline and dislocation in the Vietnamese economy. What kept Vietnam afloat economically in the late 1970s and into the 1980s were remittances from Vietnamese abroad: $150 million annually from Vietnamese workers in the USSR and Eastern Europe, hundreds of millions annually from Hoa in China and Vietnamese in the United States and other Western countries, and two billion in aid, mostly military, from the Soviet Union.[21]

Author Nayan Chanda made the comment, exaggerated but not unfounded, that China lost more in the Vietnam War than did the United States.[22] Among the mistaken justifications of the United States for its war in Vietnam was that North Vietnam was a puppet doing the bidding of its larger, communist brother to the north. In reality, the Vietnamese had a long history of animosity toward China. Fraternal expressions of socialist brotherhood kept from the public eye the antipathy between China and Vietnam for a long time. But China did not take kindly to the mistreatment of its compatriots—even though the great majority of the Hoa had been born in Vietnam and had never set foot in China. On May 24, 1978, China formally condemned Hanoi for expelling ethnic Chinese, cut off aid, closed its borders with Vietnam, and called Vietnam an "Asian Cuba," i.e., a puppet of the Soviet Union.[23] Once again, when dealing with a major power the Vietnamese had done themselves harm.

One motive for closing its borders was to prevent additional Hoa refugees from entering China. Like other countries in the region China was not anxious to be burdened with a tidal wave of refugees—even if those refugees were ethnic Chinese. Moreover, to avoid the threat of encirclement by unfriendly communist regimes China accelerated its policy of friendship with Cambodia and pursued closer relations with the United States. Vietnam had demonstrated formidable military capabilities in its whirlwind conquest of the South and had acquired a billion dollars or more of U.S. military equipment abandoned by the South Vietnamese Army.

In response, Vietnam edged closer to the Soviet Union, becoming a member of the Soviet economic sphere of influence by joining the Soviet-led Council for Mutual Economic Assistance (COMECON) in June 1978 and signing a treaty of friendship and cooperation with the USSR on November 3, 1978.[24]

* * *

While it took time for the relationship between Vietnam and China to unravel, the Khmer Rouge and Vietnam were at each other's throats immediately. The "domino theory"—the belief that a communist victory in Vietnam would lead to Vietnamese domination of Southeast Asia—proved true in Laos, which become a virtual dependency of Vietnam. And just as the domino theorists predicted, a communist victory in Vietnam coincided with the fall of

Cambodia to the communists like a ripe cherry from a tree. But the KR quickly asserted that they were neither dominos nor cherries.

The ill will between Cambodia and Vietnam went back a long ways. They had contested control of the Mekong Delta for hundreds of years. In the 14th century, the Cambodian empire — the ruins of Angkor reflect its glory — ruled, in addition to Cambodia, the heartland of both southern Vietnam and Thailand. Thereafter, Cambodia lost territory to both Vietnam and Thailand. A large Cambodian minority, called the Krom, was still living in the Mekong delta of Vietnam.

KR forces and the North Vietnamese Army clashed in Cambodia as early as 1973 and firefights between the KR and Vietnamese became frequent all along the disputed borderlands of the two countries. The bellicose Khmer Rouge carried their revolution across the border into Vietnam on raids and extermination campaigns of anti–KR Cambodians and Krom living there. The Vietnamese responded in kind. Indochina in the later 1970s resembled a revolving prayer wheel as refugees ran in circles looking for safety: Vietnamese, Laotians, and Cambodians to the United States; Hoa to China; Cambodians to Vietnam, Laos, and Thailand; Lao, Cambodians, and Vietnamese to Thailand. In fact, at the end of 1978, China and Vietnam had each received and resettled more Indochinese refugees than had the United States.

To avoid being encircled, China undertook a policy of encircling Vietnam. The two countries played politics like snakes entwining each other in a basket. The United States figured in the calculation. China and Vietnam now competed for U.S. favor. In August 1978, a Congressional delegation from the United States visiting Hanoi found the Vietnamese full of goodwill and friendship. Vietnam announced that the remains of 11 missing U.S. soldiers would be returned to the United States.[25] Vietnam, officials said, "was ready to move to "a new stage in the relations between our two peoples."[26] Vietnam dropped its demand for American aid and it appeared that relations between the United States and Vietnam were moving toward normalization.

Diplomatic maneuvering among the U.S., China, Vietnam, the USSR, and Cambodia was frantic that summer and fall of 1978 and Nayan Chanda wryly called the policy of both China and Vietnam "Yankee come home." Unfortunately for Vietnam, China was the bigger prize. Washington did not want to jeopardize its relationship with China by recognizing its bitter enemy, Vietnam. Thus, on December 15, 1978, the United States and the People's Republic of China announced the establishment of full diplomatic relations. Ten days later — and three days after the murder of Malcolm Caldwell in Phnom Penh — Vietnam invaded Cambodia.

Vietnamese tank columns and conventional forces numbering 220,000 men sliced across the border into Cambodia at six different points. Among the Vietnamese were Cambodian refugees who had been organized and trained as soldiers by the Vietnamese. The Khmer Rouge crumbled before the Vietnamese assault and in only two weeks Phnom Penh was captured. On January 10, the Vietnamese created a puppet government in Phnom Penh, headed by Heng Samrin, who had defected from the Khmer Rouge. The Khmer Rouge withdrew to the jungle as resistance fighters. The flight of Chinese Embassy personnel and military advisors from Phnom Penh was as ignominious as that of the Americans from Saigon a few years before. The Vietnamese continued their advance and, by the beginning of the monsoon in May 1979, they occupied nearly the whole country, minus pockets of resistance along the Thai border, where 40,000 Khmer Rouge and other Cambodian resistance forces held out.[27] Cambodian refugees, including armed elements of the Khmer Rouge, crossed the border into Thailand, raising the angst of the Thai to new highs.

Although the Vietnamese invasion liberated Cambodians from the nightmare of the Khmer Rouge, the invasion halted all consideration of establishing normal and friendly relations between the United States and its former foe. Once again, Vietnam had demonstrated impressive military prowess. Thailand seemed next on the agenda of the all-conquering Vietnamese, and the non-communist Southeast Asian countries thought it would be. Through their regional organization, ASEAN, they called for the withdrawal of all foreign troops from Cambodia and all the members of ASEAN, except the Philippines, pledged aid to Thailand if it were attacked.[28] European countries, eager to help Vietnam after its defeat of the Americans, rushed now to cancel aid programs. China was the most aggrieved of all countries, embarrassed by the sudden overthrow of its Cambodian protégé, and maddened by the persecution of ethnic Chinese in Vietnam and the arrogance of the hated Vietnamese.

The Chinese aimed to teach Vietnam a lesson. Chinese leader Deng Xiaoping visited the United States on January 29, 1979, and announced to the astonishment of President Carter that China was going to invade Vietnam. The invasion, as he described it, would be limited in scope and duration and would teach the Vietnamese a lesson and discomfit their Soviet allies. Deng appealed for American moral support and substantially got what he wanted.[29] On February 17, 80,000 Chinese troops invaded Vietnam. Their objectives were the capitals of the five border provinces of Vietnam and by March 5 the Chinese had captured all five capitals. The area of the fighting near the Chinese border, spared in the American bombing campaigns of Vietnam, was destroyed by massive barrages of Chinese artillery and rockets, house-to-house fighting, and deliberate demolition of houses, buildings, and bridges. It was a brief but brutal war. Nayan Chanda was allowed to visit the border areas a few months later. In Vietnam, he "saw a sullen, miserably poor populace trying to rebuild life in the ruins with undamaged bricks from the rubble. The market that had once thrived with an abundant supply of Chinese goods from across the border was now a skimpy collection of listless people selling recycled odds and ends." In China in the border provinces, he saw the other side of the war. "I was struck by the incredible numbers of invalid PLA [Chinese army] soldiers in green uniforms hobbling around with crutches and by the population's total apathy."[30]

With unseemly haste China declared victory and withdrew from Vietnam. The Chinese suffered, by their own admission, 20,000 casualties,[31] and the toll was likely much higher than admitted — possibly 50,000 dead and wounded on each side.[32] The Chinese invasion had not halted the Vietnamese takeover of Cambodia. Vietnam had not even transferred its front-line military units from Cambodia. The Chinese armies had fought mostly militia and garrison soldiers — hardly the best that Vietnam had. The Chinese discovered that the Vietnamese, flush with captured American weapons, were better armed than they were. Vietnam took another hit to its reeling economy, and discovered that its treaty of friendship and cooperation with the Soviet Union was worth hardly the paper it was written on. The Soviets stayed on the sidelines during the war.

* * *

Vietnam lost support among leftists and anti-war activists in the United States. In May 1979, folk singer Joan Baez, one of the most prominent of the former Vietnam War protestors, wrote a letter to 350 of her former colleagues asking them to join her in speaking out against human rights abuses by the government of Vietnam. Only 83 joined her, but they included the luminaries of American anti-war activism: Daniel Berrigan, Cesar Chavez, William Styron and others.[33] Many, however, refused to join her. "I wrote a letter to Jane Fonda about how important I thought her name would be," Joan said to *People* magazine, "and she sent a letter attacking one of our sources as a CIA agent."[34] Baez spoke out in an "Open Letter to the Socialist Republic of Vietnam," published as a full-page advertisement in prominent newspapers:

> Four years ago, the United States ended its 20-years presence in Vietnam. An anniversary that should be cause for celebration is, instead, a time for grieving. With tragic irony, the cruelty, violence and oppression practiced by foreign powers in your country for more than a century continue today under the present regime. Thousands of innocent Vietnamese, many whose only "crimes" are those of conscience, are being arrested, detained and tortured in prisons and re-education camps. Instead of bringing hope and reconciliation to war-torn Vietnam, your government has created a painful nightmare that overshadows significant progress achieved in many areas of Vietnamese society.... We have heard the horror stories from the people of Vietnam — from workers and peasants, Catholic nuns and Buddhist priests, from the boat people, the artists and professionals and those who fought alongside the NLF.
> - The jails are overflowing with thousands upon thousands of "detainees."
> - People disappear and never return.
> - People are shipped to re-education centers, fed a starvation diet of stale rice, forced to squat bound wrist to ankle, suffocated in "connex" boxes.
> - People are used as human mine detectors, clearing live mine fields with their hands and feet.
>
> ... It was an abiding commitment to fundamental principles of human dignity, freedom and self-determination that motivated so many Americans to oppose the

government of South Vietnam and our country's participation in the war. It is that same commitment that compels us to speak out against your brutal disregard of human rights.

As in the 60's, we raise our voices now so that your people may live. We appeal to you to end the imprisonment and torture.... We urge you to reaffirm your stated commitment to the basic principles of freedom and human dignity ... to establish real peace in Vietnam.

Joan Baez
President, Humanitas[35]

The segment of the American population who "loved the Vietcong more than they love peace" responded vociferously to the defection of Baez from their ranks. William Kunstler, a radical activist, said bluntly, "I don't believe in criticizing socialist governments publicly, even if there are human-rights violations. The entire Baez campaign may be a CIA plot."[36] Leonard Weinglass said the Baez ad was a "gross exaggeration." And another diehard, Lowell Finley, criticized Baez's sources: refugees.[37] It was the old excuse: How can you believe a refugee? The question more properly might be: How can you not believe a refugee who has abandoned his home, country, and even members of his family to undertake a near-suicidal journey that leads to a squalid refugee camp in which he may be held prisoner for years?

On June 24, 1979, about 50 persons—missing most of the famous names in the former anti-war movement—responded to Baez with an advertisement in *The New York Times* titled "The Truth About Vietnam." Their argument was "the reeducation program for former Saigon personnel carried out by the Socialist Republic of Vietnam was absolutely necessary and does further recognize and acknowledge the remarkable spirit of moderation, restraint and clemency with which the reeducation program was conducted."

The ad continued: "Vietnam now enjoys human rights as it has never known in history ... the right to a job and safe, healthy working conditions, the right to join trade unions, the right to be free from hunger, from colonialism and racisms. Moreover they [sic] receive — without cost — education, medicine and health care, human rights we in the United States have yet to achieve."[38]

This exchange of public letters, expressing perceptions of Vietnam as far apart as if the speakers were from different planets took place at the peak of the exodus from Vietnam of hundreds of thousands of people fleeing in tiny boats on a dangerous journey to distant shores. Reality does not seem to have intruded upon the consciousness of the signatories of the letter proclaiming the proliferation of human rights in Vietnam.

To those still unpersuaded by the Baez letter, a report in 1981 by Dermot Kinlen, a representative of Amnesty International, made a definitive declaration about conditions in the reeducation camps in Vietnam. "I am satisfied that there is wholesale and widespread violation of human rights in Vietnam. The retention of an uncertain but large number of people without trial in detention and forcing them to do forced labor and subjecting them to indoctrination and depriving them of support and social contact with their families and friends, and providing inadequate medical facilities, and denying them any spiritual administration and allowing them no intellectual exercise other than the absorption of selected texts for the purpose of indoctrination are all negations of human rights."[39]

More colorfully, Kim Ha, a Vietnamese Catholic schoolteacher and mother who had remained behind in Saigon in 1975, said, "If the street light poles could have walked, they would have escaped."[40] Kim would become one of hundreds of thousands who would do just that.

* * *

The Montagnards dropped out of sight in the last days of the Vietnam War and were not to appear again in history for a decade. Their mountain homes were surrounded by communist governments and few of them succeeded in escaping to tell their story to the world. The new communist government in Vietnam wasted little time in demonstrating its intentions toward the Montagnard. The Ministry for Development of Ethnic Minorities was abolished in June 1975; Montagnard leaders who had been allied with the United States and the South Vietnamese government were taken into custody, sent to re-education camps, or executed. The communist's promise of autonomy for the ethnic groups in the highlands was forgotten. From their highland redoubts the Montagnard people continued to struggle.[41]

The theme of the Montagnard struggle is similar to that of the fall of the proverbial tree in the forest. The abuses of the Montagnards were severe but nobody was there to see, hear, and tell the story. The Montagnards were faceless, voiceless, indigenous people who lived and died in obscurity. Nayan Chanda's excellent book *Brother Enemy* covers the history of Indochina in the ten years after the fall of Saigon, but mentions the existence of the Montagnards only once during its pages. That is once more than other books on the subject.

* * *

The Pathet Lao, in true Lao fashion, took their time. After forcing the departure of Vang Pao and Hmong leaders, the Pathet Lao didn't get around to declaring Laos a communist state until December 2, 1975. Then, they abolished a monarchy that dated back 650 years and sent the king, queen, and other members of the royal family off to reside in "seminar camps." The Lao were less brutal but more inefficient than the Vietnamese and the death rate in Lao camps was probably higher than in Vietnam. A larger percentage of the population would flee Laos as refugees than fled from Cambodia and Vietnam.

Unlike Cambodia, Laos accepted its "special relationship" status with Vietnam and also maintained close ties to the Soviet Union. Vietnam maintained a 30,000-man army within the country to counter the continuing resistance of the Hmong and other highland peoples and the Soviet Union replaced the United States as the chief financial benefactor of the impoverished State. Laos became almost a carbon copy of its Vietnamese patron. Laotian seminar camps were comparable to Vietnamese reeducation camps. Although inmates included the king and queen, several other members of the royal family, former government officials and military officers of the Royal Lao government, the majority of the inmates at the seminar camps were Hmong and other highlanders.[42]

War, government repression and mismanagement, and stagnant and declining economies in all three Indochinese countries set the stage for a dramatic flood of refugees in late 1978 and 1979.

* * *

12

THE BOAT PEOPLE COME ASHORE

The first Vietnamese refugee crisis came with the fall of Saigon on April 30, 1975. The second was in 1978 and 1979. The outflow of ethnic Chinese from northern Vietnam to China began in May 1978. A rush of Hoa and ethnic Vietnamese to Southeast Asia began on September 19, 1978. On that date the UNHCR office in Kuala Lumpur, Malaysia, received word that the *Southern Cross*, a small, 950 ton freighter, had rescued 1,220 Vietnamese at sea and wished to put them ashore immediately in Malaysia.[1]

The captain said he was short of water and food. The Malaysian navy delivered aid to the ship by boat and helicopter but, despite the entreaties of UNHCR, refused to let the *Southern Cross* discharge its human cargo. Singapore likewise refused. The captain took matters into his own hands, sailed to an uninhabited Indonesian island, and unloaded his passengers. He then radioed what he had done. The Indonesian government was furious that 1,200 Vietnamese had been dumped on its shores but was subdued by assurances from the United States, Australia, and Canada that they would accept the refugees for resettlement. Indonesia grudgingly transported the refugees to a makeshift camp on Bintan Island, about 50 miles south of Singapore.

Only slowly did the real story of the *Southern Cross* come to light. The ship had left Singapore empty on August 25. The captain anchored the ship 30 miles off the Vietnamese coast where a Vietnamese pilot met it and guided it to shore. Over the next few days, Vietnamese soldiers loaded the passengers. Thus, the *Southern Cross* had not encountered the refugees at sea; it had docked at a Vietnamese port and passengers had been permitted onboard by officials of the government of Vietnam. Moreover, the passengers had paid Vietnamese officials about $2,000 each for exit permits and paid passage on the ship of $600 in gold for adults and $300 for children. The whole affair was arranged by a rich Chinese businessman in Singapore who made a large profit out of the venture, as did the government of Vietnam or its officials. Vietnam vehemently denied reports that it had sold exit permits to its citizens and Western countries initially

12. The Boat People Come Ashore

chose to believe that the outpouring of refugees on the *Southern Cross* was yet another indication of the horrific nature of the Vietnamese regime.[2]

A trickle of refugees had been escaping from Vietnam by boat since the fall of Saigon, but the numbers increased with the success of the *Southern Cross* in making a profit and landing its human cargo. In October the *Hai Hong* departed Vietnam with 2,500 refugees on board. Similar arrangements had been made between the ship owners, government officials in Vietnam, and the passengers. This time, Indonesia declined to allow the *Hai Hong* to land in its territory and the ship ended up sitting off shore in Malaysia. The Malaysians refused to let the passengers disembark and they stayed on board for eight weeks. The impasse was resolved by an agreement that the refugees would be processed for resettlement on board and then taken directly to the airport for travel to resettlement countries.[3]

Canada pledged to process 600 of the refugees for resettlement, but Canada had only two immigration officers in all of Southeast Asia. Ian Hamilton was the chief and his assistant was Scott Mullin, 22 years old and one year out of university. Accustomed to processing 50 or 60 refugees per month, Hamilton and Mullin suddenly were responsible to take on 600. In three days of interviewing from daylight to midnight, Hamilton and Mullin, through a very liberal interpretation of Canada's immigration laws, approved 604 refugees. Four Canadian military transport planes hauled them away.[4]

The working principle of dealing with the boat people, as they were called, was established: "an open door for an open shore."[5] The Southeast Asian countries accepted for temporary asylum the Indochinese refugees who turned up on their shores and the Western countries resettled them. Temporary asylum would be exchanged for permanent resettlement. The Western countries and UNHCR accepted that the boat people were legitimate refugees and had a claim for protection under international law and resettlement to a third country. The Southeast Asian countries perceived their interests as making life as difficult as possible for the refugees to put maximum pressure on the Western countries and the UN to resettle them.

Other ships soon followed. The *Tung An* with 2,300 Vietnamese pulled into Manila Bay and the *Huey Fong* into Hong Kong in December and the response was similar to that of Malaysia and Indonesia. The refugees were held on board until the host countries received assurances that they would be resettled. In the case of the *Tung An*, Philippine authorities did not allow the refugees to disembark for seven months.[6] These were nearly the last of the big ships to transport refugees from Vietnam. Thereafter, refugees turned to flight in smaller craft and at a much greater risk, hoping to sneak ashore in one or another Southeast Asian country. The dangers were enormous. The *Bangkok Post* reported on December 5, 1978, that six boats with Vietnamese refugees had sunk off the Thai and Malaysian coasts in only 11 days with the loss of more than 400 lives.[7] One of these boats attempted to land on the shores of Malaysia but local villagers refused to let it come ashore. Caught in treacherous currents it sank and 200 people drowned.[8] The danger did not deter an increasing number of persons from fleeing Vietnam. In September 1978 the boat refugees topped 8,000 arrivals. In October there were 12,000 and in November 21,000. The refugees included both Hoa and Vietnamese.

What the nations on the receiving end of the seemingly endless stream flowing out of the three Indochina countries feared was being saddled permanently with large numbers of refugees who would be an expense and a political liability. Their concern was not-ill founded. Refugee arrivals in Thailand since 1975 had exceeded departures for resettlement by a large margin.

Thailand Refugee Population

	Arrivals	Departures (Resettlement)	Residual Population
1975	77,241	12,755	64,486
1976	35,558	24,178	75,866
1977	35,750	14,021	97,595
1978	67,429	26,297	138,727

As in Thailand, the refugees arriving in Malaysia were outstripping in numbers those departing for resettlement. At the end of 1978, Malaysia had received 69,252 refugees and only 20,193 had departed.[9] Indonesia was receiving fewer refugees, but the numbers were also increasing there.

* * *

The boat people leaving Vietnam risked hunger, thirst, storms, drowning, pirates, and push-offs, all accounting for an unknown, but large, number of deaths. Those traveling in small boats on which the refugees were both crew and passengers were in the greatest danger. A typical account is that of Lu Phuoc given at a Congressional hearing in 1982.

Phuoc left Vietnam in a seven meter (23 feet) long boat loaded down with 18 people: 11 men, four women, and three children. Two days later one of their two outboard motors broke down and they were boarded and robbed by pirates. Then, their second motor died and they were left drifting and powerless. The next day Thai pirates approached, boarded their vessel, and raped three of the women.

Later, when they had been without food and water for three days, pirates again boarded and gave them food and water but raped two of the women. The saga continued two days later when pirates kidnapped three of the women. One of the women died and the pirates threw the other two overboard. A Thai patrol boat rescued them.

Back on Phuoc's boat, pirates kidnapped one man, a skilled fisherman whom they probably forced into servitude on a fishing boat. Finally, some kindness was shown to the refugees as their boat sank. Thai fishermen rescued and

12. The Boat People Come Ashore

Vietnamese boat people camped on a beach in southern Thailand. Apparently they have been given plastic sheeting to provide shade and protection against monsoon rains while they continue to live on their boats. (Lionel Rosenblatt collection)

fed them and dropped them off at an island. From there they made their way to the nearby mainland. The fishermen said they had once strayed into Vietnamese waters and had been treated kindly and they were returning the kindness. Without the rescue by the fishermen, none of the people on Phuoc's boat may have survived.

The final tally for Phuoc and his colleagues was 17 days at sea, eight pirate attacks, three women raped, one woman dead, one man abducted, fate unknown, and two women abducted and later recovered. When they arrived in Thailand, Phuoc's only possession was the underwear he wore.[10] His story is typical. Phuoc's hardships might have been even greater except that in the latter stages of his journey they had only one woman aboard and she apparently was not attractive to the pirates, and thus was not an inducement for them to board a boat already robbed of everything valuable.

* * *

As if by premonition the old refugee hands regrouped in Southeast Asia in 1978. Lionel Rosenblatt came out to Bangkok from Washington to take over the job of refugee coordinator in the Embassy. Mac Thompson never had his heart in the AID management course in Washington he was attending. Lionel telephoned him in June 1978 from Bangkok and said, "Get your ass out here. I need some help." Mac told AID he was quitting the management course to work with refugees in Thailand. He was told that quitting would ruin his career. He quit anyway. "I thought it would be more fun and useful to be a refugee officer. And it was."[11] Several of the ex–Peace Corps volunteers who had worked with Lionel in 1976 returned to Thailand, including Berta Romero. Morton Abramowitz became U.S. ambassador to Thailand. He was a dedicated pro-refugee ambassador. The team back in Washington was exceptionally strong. Richard Holbrooke was still assistant secretary of state for Far Eastern affairs; his assistant was the very competent Bob Oakley and Shep and Hank ran the Refugee Office.

Jim Schill was a volunteer for refugee work. Thirty-six years old, he was an aw-shucks Iowan with a winning way and an easy manner that barely concealed what he called a "Triple A" personality. He had worked for AID in Vietnam and Laos during the war and at Camp Pendleton during the 1975 refugee crisis. Following that, he had gone off to the Sinai desert to monitor the peace agreement between Egypt and Israel. In March 1978, having returned to Washington, he went by the Refugee Office to express an interest in a job. Shep and Hank took him up on his offer. Schill was bright, skilled in public relations, and adventurous. It took five months, however, to break his assignment in Washington with AID and for him to be on his way to Bangkok to join the refugee section. In 1978, refugees were a low priority in the government.

That lack of priority showed in Thailand. The JVA caseworkers and the Embassy refugee officers such as Daniels, Thompson, and Tucker were working 70 hours a week to process resettlement cases for boat people and submit them to the Immigration and Naturalization Service. INS didn't keep up with the caseload. "Tempers flared," said Jim Schill, "and some INS officers threatened to slow down the process if they felt any more hassled from the State Department officers and the JVA personnel."[12] It was a case of too few American personnel trying to confront a demand for resettlement that was growing out of control.

In December 1978, Jim Schill moved from Thailand to Singapore to get a handle on the influx of boat people there and in Indonesia. Indochinese refugees had become a regional problem. Jim ran into a buzzsaw of Embassy politics. The ambassador in Singapore regarded him as an intruder and tried to put him under the supervision of low-level consular officers. In Indonesia, the Embassy was only processing about 20 refugee resettlement cases per month and the officer in charge was incredulous when Schill proposed that the number be raised to 1,000 per month immediately and 3,000 per month within four months. It was only after a long fight that Schill won his independence from hidebound and hierarchical Embassy procedures.

Jim soon traveled to islands where Vietnamese boat people were said to have turned up. Continental Oil Company had operations on the islands and

12. The Boat People Come Ashore

knew more about the refugees than anyone else. They flew Schill to the Anambas Islands 200 miles northeast of Singapore. What Schill found was worse than he expected. On one small island 4,000 refugees were living in tents improvised from blankets. Most had arrived during the previous three weeks; their only food was what they could buy from local Indonesians, and many of them had little money. They had tried to get to Malaysia, but had been prevented from landing and were towed out to sea by the Malaysian navy. UNHCR was nowhere to be found.

By telephone and telegram Schill informed Washington and UNHCR headquarters in Geneva about the boat people in the Anambas islands. Washington responded quickly, seized by the urgency of the situation. Within two weeks Schill had 12 Americans working for him to begin a resettlement program for the stranded refugees in Indonesia. Singapore forbade any refugee landings within its own territory, but as a base of operations for Indonesia it was closer to the action than any other major city.

Out in the islands again Schill located another 9,000 refugees. His host this time was the Marathon Oil Company. The refugees had attempted to land on their offshore oil platforms. Some of them were in such bad shape that the oil riggers had taken them onto their platforms for a meal before hauling them to nearby islands and leaving them. Many of the refugees would die soon if they didn't receive help. Schill realized with a shock that he was acquainted with some of them from his years working in Vietnam. He collected about 50 pounds of mail from the refugees to forward to relatives abroad and returned to Singapore to report his findings to Washington. He decided it made most sense to assist and process the refugees for resettlement where they were, rather than trying to move them to a more accessible location.

What he needed was transport to the islands rather than having to depend upon the goodwill of the oil companies. He proposed to buy an ancient 48-foot boat and rent a barge to transport goods and teams of people to the Anambas Islands. The cost of the boat and the rental of the barge—$25,000 for the boat and $2,700 per month for the barge—was a tough financial outlay for Washington to accept, but Schill persuaded Shep Lowman to approve the cost. Little did he know that within a few months his operation would grow to 40 people, two office buildings, and a budget of $4 million annually—plus the boat.

The decision of what to name the boat caused a bureaucratic crisis. The head of the JVA in Singapore, Wells Klein of the American Council for Nationality Services (ACNS), wanted to name it *Ivan* in honor of a supporter of his organization. Schill dissented. U.S. government money bought the boat. He wanted a neutral name and proposed *CAT IV*—the abbreviation for Category Four, the immigration category into which most of the refugees would fall. The dispute became bitter and Shep had to mediate. His reverse Solomonic decision was to name the boat *IVAN CAT IV*. Nobody ever called it the *Ivan*, however, save perhaps Wells Klein.[13]

Shep was indefatigable, fighting and usually winning bureaucratic battles in Washington and traveling to Southeast Asia several times a year to keep the proliferating threads of the Indochinese refugee program stitched together in half a dozen countries: Thailand, Malaysia, Singapore, Indonesia, Philippines, and Hong Kong. He ran the program out of a battered briefcase that went everywhere with him. On a rainy night in Singapore, Shep and Lionel were walking down a street. Singapore had wooden manhole covers for storm sewers and in heavy rains the covers floated away. Shep suddenly fell into a storm sewer. Lionel looked down to see him balancing on his elbows and trying to keep from being sucked down the manhole. Instead of reaching out an arm for assistance, Shep held his briefcase up and shouted, "Take the briefcase." Once Lionel had secured the briefcase, Shep accepted Lionel's hand to pull him out of the storm sewer.[14]

In his first month in Singapore Jim Schill's team processed 122 refugees for resettlement in the U.S.; in the second month it was nearly 1,000 and by the fourth month he was up to his goal of 3,000 refugees per month. Schill's comment on his experience was typical of the unorthodox and idealistic government employees drawn to refugee work. "Too often our State Department and USAID officers lack the courage of doing the right thing in spite of the odds and that has hindered many fine officers and critical operations."[15] The same might be true of any profession.

* * *

In December 1978, while Jim Schill was setting up a refugee office in Singapore, the refugee situation in Malaysia was also becoming a disaster. The center of the problem was the small, round island of Bidong located a dozen miles off the northeast coast of Malaysia and 220 miles across the Gulf of Thailand from the nearest landfall in Vietnam.

It was a two-hour traverse to Bidong from the mainland. The UNHCR and the Malaysian Red Crescent Society had leased a fishing boat, but in the monsoon season the water was often rough and the fishermen refused to attempt the passage. Passengers wore life preservers and stayed near the stern of the boat rather than ride in the small cabin to have a better chance for survival if the boat capsized in the heavy seas.

Six months earlier, Bidong, a small, round island barely one-half square mile in area, had been an uninhabited tropical paradise. One hundred and twenty one Vietnamese boat people had been put there by the Malaysians in July 1978; in August another 600 hundred were moved in. The capacity of the island was said to be 4,500 refugees, but by January 1979, the population was 18,000 and growing almost daily as boat people arrived on their own or were towed to the island by the Malaysian navy.[16]

The flat part of Bidong was less than the size of a football field and had a backdrop of steep mountain slopes. Vietnamese refugees crowded onto the

12. The Boat People Come Ashore

island lived in tents and makeshift huts two and three stories high made of salvaged timbers from wrecked boats, plastic sheets, tin cans, and corrugated iron sheets. Their huts extended up and out from the flat area to near the top of the mountain. The island had been nearly stripped of vegetation; tropical cloudbursts sent rivers of filth cascading down the narrow passageways between huts. The refugees collected rainwater for washing clothes and bathed in the sea. Drinking water depended upon the arrival of a barge loaded with tanks holding 106,000 gallons of water. A barge-load was expected to last six days and converted into one gallon per day per person — hardly enough for drinking and cooking, let alone other uses. Four wells had been drilled, but only one produced water fit to drink. The others were polluted by the open trench latrines that overflowed in the monsoon rains.[17] Rice and other food arrived on barges through the choppy seas.

Doctors were abundant, but medicines in short supply. Sanitation was nearly non-existent. One of the unforgettable recollections of refugee camps is the smell of human waste — "There is shit everywhere."[18] In the absence of public sanitation, hepatitis was rampant: 108 cases were reported in one week. Two hundred and twelve sick were treated in one day and almost all had diarrhea. "With 30 doctors for 16,000 people [the population was growing nearly every day], this camp has probably the best doctor-to-patient ratio in the world," said a doctor, "but we are doing no good. We lack everything — medicine to treat the sick, and equipment to solve the fantastic sanitary and hygienic problems."[19] Leo Cherne visited Bidong in January 1978. He called it Hell Isle.[20]

The only good thing about Bidong was the well-organized distribution of water and food. Distribution is often chaotic in refugee camps, but at Bidong elected and appointed refugee leaders took charge. The UN and Malaysian Red Crescent Society provided each newly arriving refugee with a three-day ration of 24 ounces of rice, a can of baked beans, a tin of sardines, and crackers.[21] Then, the food distribution committees took over and doled out food and water to all the refugees regularly.

The refugees were enterprising. An Ngo and his family arrived on Bidong on October 22, 1978, while the island was still only lightly populated. At first they received only cans of chickens and peas to eat and had to dig a well for water. The family, nearly destitute, looked for ways to earn a little money. Ngo traded belongings for wheat flour and became a baker, turning out loaves of bread in a tin cookie box. His wife sold her wedding ring to buy ingredients for pastries and baked and sold them. A few people on Bidong had money and could buy good bread and pastries; most did not.[22]

Many of the refugees on Bidong had tried to land in southern Thailand but had been pushed off or towed away by Thai police and military and forced to continue their dangerous voyage further south to Malaysia. Malaysian authorities greeted them without enthusiasm and towed them to Bidong or other small islands or to one of two or three smaller camps along the coast.

Many of the boats were attacked by pirates en route to Malaysia and an unknown number sank, leaving no trace nor survivors to tell the tale.

Of the asylum countries for Indochinese refugees in Southeast Asia, Malaysia was probably the most difficult. The country was an amalgam of ethnic groups of which the Muslim Malays comprised 53 percent of the population and dominated politics. Chinese, 35 percent of the population in 1975, dominated the economy. Indians were 11 percent of the population.[23] Malaysia was delicately balanced between these three groups and the last thing the country wanted was for that balance to be upset. Many of the new arrivals were Hoa — Chinese, in the eyes of the Malays — and their place of arrival was Malaysia's east coast, the poorest, most conservative, and strongly Muslim region of the country.

JVA and State Department officers lived on the island and interviewed refugees for resettlement in the United States. Refugees were called by loudspeaker every morning for interviews. The procedure for processing a refugee and his family was, first, a preliminary interview by a JVA employee, who was often on Bidong on loan from Church World Service. The JVA collected biographical data and rendered a recommendation on the refugee's eligibility for resettlement in the United States. The refugee might be referred to another country — France, Canada, or Australia — if resettlement there seemed more feasible because of family connections. Refugees with serious health problems were often referred to Switzerland, which accepted mostly refugees with health and disability problems. The JVA also referred cases to the Red Cross or Red Crescent to attempt to find missing family members.

The JVA file would be passed on to a State Department refugee officer who would verify the information, resolve any unanswered questions and problems and approve the case for transmittal to the Immigration and Naturalization Service (INS). Offices were long, open-sided tin-roofed huts and furnishings were a rough plank table and chair along with several battered file cabinets. The JVA and other refugee workers slept on the same table they used for interviewing during the day.

The refugee case was passed to INS when the interviewers were satisfied that it was sufficient to make a case for resettlement for the refugee family. This was not always easy. INS interviewers were hard. Journalist Mike Connolly described one INS employee, Harold Boyce of Burlington, Vermont, assigned to Bidong for two months. Boyce showed up for work every morning in Bermuda shorts, a colorful shirt, and sandals. He stared balefully over his spectacles and searched for lies and inconsistencies in a refugee's story that had been missed by the more sympathetic JVA and State Department interviewers. "I scare hell out of them," he said. INS officers often had little knowledge of the culture of the people they were interviewing. But they had the ultimate decision as to whether the refugee was permitted to go to the U.S. It was an endless cycle: the refugee and his family were interviewed first by JVA, then by the State Department, and finally by INS, and if he was approved and also passed security and medical clearances he would, at long last, after a wait of months or even years, be put on an airplane for the United States. Journalist Mike Connolly described those who interviewed refugees as "men who play God."[24]

The first boat people on the *Southern Cross* and *Hai Hong* had generated rapid action by the international community, but now, the initial shock over, it took from six to 12 months for a refugee to be processed and sent off to new home — usually the U.S., Australia, Canada, or France. It was a numbers game. The quotas for resettlement in the U.S. — 7,000 per month for all Indochinese refugees at this time — and other countries had to be divided up among Vietnamese, Laotians, and Cambodians all over Southeast Asia. Thus, the number of people who could be processed and leave Bidong every month was small. Top priority went to the oldest people and to unaccompanied children who had left Vietnam without their parents or had lost them at sea. More new refugees were arriving than leaving.

One of the refugees was Dr. Tuan Ti Tran, a U.S.–educated micro-biologist. Tran told the story of his flight from Vietnam in November 1978 with his children, Ahn, a girl, age 12, and Fong, a boy, age eight. Dr. Tuan spent a year arranging a passage outside Vietnam. His wife, the couple decided, would stay behind. For all the family to disappear suddenly would set off a search by the Vietnamese authorities. If his wife was present they might believe the story that he and the children were visiting relatives and would soon return.

Tran and his two children were taken by truck, bus, and taxi to a safe house on the Saigon waterfront. They boarded an 18-meter-long fishing boat along with 200 other refugees. They were put in the hold and told to stay there and the boat chugged out of the harbor. The boat was so heavily loaded there was hardly any freeboard.

Three days at sea and the boat began to sink as the bilge pumps failed. The refugees hailed a passing fishing boat and several of the refugees leaped off the sinking boat to board the fishing boat. They were beaten with iron pipes and their bodies were thrown into the sea. The "fishermen" were Thai pirates. The pirates boarded and searched their boat for valuables. Tran does not mention any of the women being raped but gang rape was the usual fate of attractive women. When the pirates had finished taking all the valuables they could find, they threw the refugees into the sea. Those who could swim — Tran and his children could — made it back to their boat. Tran said that 32 people drowned.

Back on board their damaged and leaking boat, now lightened by the absence of refugees who had been killed or drowned, they drifted for a day before sighting the mountains on the coast of Malaysia. They were fortunate to be found by a UNHCR boat and towed to Bidong.

Tran and his children's troubles were not over yet. He had no money or food and for three weeks he begged food from other people already on the island. Then, duly registered, Tran began to receive a food ration. He built a small shelter out of a plastic sheet for himself and his children. Dr. Tuan was on Bidong only four months. An English speaking Ph.D., he was given a high priority and was soon offered resettlement in Canada. The worst part of his stay on Bidong was when the children realized that their mother was not going to be joining them. When Tran was interviewed in Montreal after his arrival in Canada he still had had no contact with his wife.[25]

To the refugee workers it appeared that the whole population of southern Vietnam was leaving the country. By June 1979 Bidong Island had a population of 40,000 who had arrived in 453 boats.[26] The island was said to be the most heavily populated place on earth. The Malaysians became more and more hostile to the refugees, and on June 11 they closed Bidong to additional arrivals and backed up their words with a naval blockade.

By the end of June 1979, the boat people were scattered all over Southeast Asia and north as far as Hong Kong. Malaysia was hosting 75,000, Hong Kong 59,000, Indonesia 43,000, Thailand 10,000, and the Philippines 5,000.[27] The refugees kept coming. No end was in sight. Something had to be done.

* * *

13

SOLVING THE BOAT PEOPLE CRISIS

The large and growing numbers of Vietnamese boat people turning up on the shores of Southeast Asian countries month after month stimulated a frantic round of diplomacy. The effort to stem the tide began in December 1978 when UNHCR convened an emergency meeting in Geneva. Vietnam attended the meeting but claimed to be powerless to stop the exodus of its citizens. This, despite growing evidence that the Vietnamese were profiting handsomely, while ridding themselves of their one million ethnic Chinese and other malcontents. A CIA report described the system: "Vietnam has created an elaborate but efficient machinery to process refugees. The Politburo oversees the program, and the Public Security Bureau — the political police — carries it out. Internal policies that discriminated against Sino-Vietnamese began in the spring of 1978, and many were given the choice of moving to primitive New Economic Zones or leaving the country. Those who choose to leave often deal with a middleman who in turn deals with the Public Security Bureau. Vietnamese officials certify the passenger list for each boat, collect an exit fee, and set the date of departure. The middleman, who is often a Chinese businessman, arranges for the boat, enlists the passengers, and collects the passage money."[1]

A *Far Eastern Economic Review* article detailed the price for leaving Vietnam. Adults paid ten taels (about $3,000) with children five to 15 going for half price. Children under five years old were free. A large part of this fee found its way into the pocket of Vietnamese officials, usually the provincial police chief who provided documents permitting a boat to depart.[2] Thus, the income from 10,000 adult refugees leaving Vietnam in a given month could amount to thirty million dollars — a sum in which the recipients of the money had only the expense of procuring old boats and the refugees took all the risk. The money for leaving often came from Vietnamese relatives in the U.S. and other countries. One estimate is that Vietnam made about $3 billion in 1979, including refugees and remittances sent back by family members living in the West and China.[3]

Some evidence also indicates that Vietnam encouraged the boat people to leave because the southerners resisted the collectivist policies of their northern conquerors. Thus, the foreign minister said in 1979 that "most refugees are from the south.... In 1975 we forbade them to go out. We were criticized by the West. We thought it over. We decided to give them the freedom to go. Now [they] say we are exporting refugees."[4]

Despite the lucrative practice of selling permissions to leave, Vietnam had reasons to cooperate with UNHCR. It had its own internal refugee problem, hosting 150,000 Cambodians and 170,000 Vietnamese and Chinese who fled the Khmer Rouge to take up residence in Vietnam. Vietnam was receiving financial help from UNHCR to help care for them.[5] In the aftermath of its invasion of Cambodia on Christmas 1978, many countries cancelled aid to Vietnam. Thus, Vietnam needed financial help to care for its refugee influx and to keep its lifelines to the international community.

The five members of the Association of Southeast Asian Nations, ASEAN (Thailand, Malaysia, Singapore, Indonesia, and the Philippines), agreed that Indochinese refugees would not be allowed to remain in their countries permanently and only reluctantly did they permit them to enter temporarily. They called themselves "countries of transit" and insisted that they "not be burdened with any residual problem" of refugees.[6] They rebuffed every international suggestion that they should resettle some of the refugees. A CIA analysis said it bluntly: "No ASEAN state will accept for resettlement any of the Vietnamese refugees."[7]

Singapore was the most adamant. Prime Minister Lee Kuan Yew said on February 17, 1979, "You've got to grow calluses on your heart or you just bleed to death." This from Singapore, a Chinese majority state that might have been expected to have some sympathy with the ethnic Chinese leaving Vietnam. His foreign minister amplified the point: "The flow of the boat people poses the non-communist world, including the ASEAN countries, with a moral dilemma. We could respond on humanitarian or moral grounds by accepting and resettling these desperate people. But by doing so we would not only be encouraging those responsible to force even more refugees to flee ... those countries which give way to their humanitarian instincts would saddle themselves with unmanageable political, social and economic problems that the sudden absorption of hundreds of thousands of alien people must inevitably bring in its wake."[8]

Lee called for more pressure on Vietnam to stop the flow of refugees: "The latest exodus of 'boat people' and 'ship people' is the result of acts of cold calculation, measured in gold."[9] Vietnam, which might have otherwise been lauded for eliminating the noxious KR regime, found itself ever more isolated internationally because of its production of refugees. The ASEAN countries also ramped up their pressure on the Western countries, especially the U.S.

The blunt talk of Singaporean leaders was matched by that of Malaysian leaders. The United States, said the deputy prime minister, wanted the ASEAN countries to accept all refugees arriving on their shores with no questions asked. Then, he added sarcastically, the United States "has the luxury of spending several months asking the refugees if they have tuberculosis, if they speak English, and so on, before it decides whether to accept them or not."[10] The Southeast Asian countries demanded actions and not just humanitarian hand-wringing. They wanted the Americans and other resettlement countries to take all the refugees—not just the most desirable ones—and they wanted it to happen quickly. The United States on its part tried to get an international consensus on burden-sharing by persuading other countries to accept more refugees.

The boat people arriving in Southeast Asia peaked, reaching a new high of 56,941 in June 1979. The ASEAN countries hardened their line. On June 30 they announced that they had "reached the limit of their endurance and decided that they would not accept any new arrivals." Malaysia had turned back or expelled 53,000 refugees during the year and now the Malaysian foreign minister said that Malaysia would also expel the 75,000 refugees in the country "unless they are resettled within a reasonable time period." The UNHCR High Commissioner concluded ominously that "the problem has clearly run ahead of the solutions."[11] The CIA estimated that the number of boat people fleeing Vietnam would total at least 250,000 more during the last half of 1979 if solutions were not found.[12]

Urgency was essential. The Malaysian push-offs of 15,000 boat people in June signaled that the Southeast Asian countries had had enough. It was up to the world to decide whether the boat people should be saved or left to drown or starve. Four years after the last American left Vietnam from the roof of the Embassy in Saigon the refugee problem had become a humanitarian catastrophe of worldwide import.

The United States and the UN were forced to respond. President Jimmy Carter led the way. At the Tokyo Economic Summit conference on June 28, 1979, Carter announced that the U.S. would double its intake of Indochinese refugees from 7,000 to 14,000 per month.[13] He also ordered four U.S. Naval vessels in the South China Sea to watch for boat people and rescue them.[14] Not the least of the pressures on Carter to increase the U.S. involvement with the refugees was from a group of men and women from the international community living in Japan who, under the leadership of Sue Morton, formed an organization they named Refugees International. They took out a full-page ad in the *Japan Times* and lobbied the attendees at the conference 24 hours a day from their office in the Okura Hotel. Sue had lived in Bangkok earlier and had adopted two Cambodian refugee children.[15]

The Tokyo Summit was followed by a special United Nations conference on refugees. Sixty-five countries met in Geneva on July 20 and 21, 1979. UNHCR set the stage by summing up the issue. Since 1975, more than 575,000 Indochinese refugees had left their home countries. Of these, 202,000 had been resettled in third countries. Remaining in camps were 373,000 of whom 204,000 were Vietnamese boat people.[16] The number of boat people was increasing by 50,000 per month.

Vice President Walter Mondale headed the U.S. delegation as a symbol of the importance the U.S. placed on the subject. The briefness of the meeting and the immediacy of the crisis left little time for posturing. China criticized Vietnam most stridently. It accused Vietnam of "militarism, genocide, creating and exporting refugees, causing human disasters and spreading anti–Chinese sentiment in Southeast Asia."[17] Most of the other delegations avoided the rhetoric and focused on the humanitarian issues.

In response to the demands of the Southeast Asian countries receiving the boat people, the Western countries pledged to increase their resettlement of Indochinese refugees from 125,000 to 260,000 in the following 12 months. In addition, they pledged $160 million in contributions to UNHCR for the care, feeding, and protection of the refugees. The United States restated its pledge to double its intake of refugees from 7,000 to 14,000 per month for one year. To placate the receiving countries, the U.S. also promised to assist in the establishment of refugee processing centers which would facilitate the movement of refugees from camps to the U.S. and other locations.[18]

The government of Vietnam, to the surprise of everybody, responded positively by announcing a moratorium on refugees, pledging its efforts to stop the mass exodus of boat people for a reasonable period, and promoting orderly departures. Even more surprising was that the crisis of the boat people ended at almost precisely the time of the Geneva Conference. After an outflow of 56,000 in June, the numbers of boat people turning up on Southeast Asian shores in July was only 17,000, partially attributed to the monsoon season which made travel on the sea more difficult, but mostly because of the new cooperative attitude by Vietnam. Or had it run out of people able to pay the steep price to leave and brave the dangers at sea? The numbers declined to 9,000 in September and October, and further to less than 3,000 in the following months.[19] The worst of the humanitarian crisis, to the relief of the world, was suddenly over.

Living up to the promises made in Geneva would be difficult, but Thailand, Malaysia, and other Southeastern Asian countries would ensure those promises were kept by the West. To accomplish this a large number of people in Southeast Asia to process refugees for resettlement would be required. In Thailand, Lionel Rosenblatt now oversaw the largest and most expensive State Department program in the world—185 employees—and Lionel was only a middle grade State Department employee.[20]

The U.S. rate of resettlement jumped from 5,882 in June to more than 15,000 in September 1979 and continued at an average monthly rate of 14,000 for the following year. As the intake of refugees to third countries increased, the camp population of the boat people dropped from 371,000 to 252,000 by

13. Solving the Boat People Crisis

February 1980. The crisis was over. What remained was a humanitarian problem of serious magnitude, but one that was manageable, albeit still only with continued strenuous efforts for another decade.[21]

* * *

In March 1979, UNHCR had reached an agreement with Vietnam for the orderly departure of its citizens who wished to leave. In May, Vietnam said that 10,000 per month would be allowed to leave. The initial results of the program were far less impressive, but the Orderly Departure Program (ODP) would be a major factor in decreasing the near-suicidal flight by Vietnamese boat people.

The demand for the program was high in the United States, especially from families who had relatives in Vietnam. By October, the State Department had petitions for 9,000 Vietnamese to be admitted to the program. The problems in getting the program moving were twofold: first, the U.S. had all its refugee allocation numbers—14,000 per month—tied up in moving refugees out of camps in Southeast Asia. To reduce the number of refugees taken from camps would cause consternation in Thailand, Malaysia, and other host countries. Second, the government of Vietnam was very slow in granting exit permits to its citizens approved for the program. By the end of September 1979, only 220 had been approved. Corruption and the necessity of paying a steep bribe for an exit permit probably had a lot to do with the small number of persons getting approval. Nevertheless, a reason for the decline in the numbers of boat people was that Vietnamese now had some hope they would be able to leave their home country for the U.S. in due course.[22]

The Orderly Departure Program was not implemented without controversy. Critics saw it as the UNHCR assisting Vietnam to get rid of an unwanted minority, the residents in Vietnam of Chinese descent.[23] Moreover, it was alleged that UNHCR paid a price to work in Vietnam—nearly fourteen million dollars to assist Vietnam with its refugees from Cambodia.[24]

Despite a slow start, the ODP became the keystone of a program that encouraged relatively safe and organized immigration from Vietnam to Western countries. The boat people would continue to leave Vietnam in significant numbers, however, until 1994.[25]

* * *

One of the innovations coming out of the negotiations to solve the refugee crisis was the creation of refugee processing centers (RPCs) in the Philippines and Indonesia. The priority of the Southeast Asian countries was to ensure that they would not be burdened with leftover refugees. Thus came the idea to establish a center that would process refugees guaranteed resettlement. The Malaysian home minister, in the usual tone of Malaysian officials, proposed on June 26, 1979, that such a center be set up in U.S.–controlled territory because the refugee crisis was "the hangover" of the U.S. war in Indochina and, sarcastically, "because the United States is the loudest proponent of human rights and humanitarian principles."[26]

The Bataan peninsula is famous in World War II history for the brave and futile defense of American and Filipino soldiers against the all-victorious Japanese army in the dark days after Pearl Harbor. In 1980, it became the site of the Refugee Processing Center, the creation of which had been encouraged by Shep Lowman, who was still managing the U.S. response to Indochinese refugees from his new position as the first deputy assistant secretary of state of the new Bureau of Refugee Programs in the Department of State. The Indochinese refugee program by 1980 was no longer just a temporary activity of the State Department but had acquired a permanent place in the bureaucracy.

The RPC came about with an agreement on November 13, 1979, between the government of the Philippines and UNHCR. The Philippines donated the land to locate the RPC in a remote area to minimize local impact. The UNHCR agreed to build housing and administrative facilities and to administer the RPC.[27] Japan contributed medical equipment.[28] UNHCR, along with several contracted VOLAGs, ran the centers. The State Department perceived the RPC as a way of demonstrating to the restive countries of Southeast Asia that the international community was taking its commitment to resettle the refugees seriously. The Philippines made it crystal clear that the RPC was to be only a way station, not a permanent roosting place for refugees. A smaller RPC was established on Galang Island in Indonesia.

The Refugee Processing Center in the Philippines was located on a mountain ridge that overlooked beautiful beaches and the sea. The refugees enjoyed a great deal of freedom of movement — a relief to most after having spent months or years in prison-like camps.[29] The RPC had a capacity of 17,200 refugees and the goal was to move 3,000 refugees per month to resettlement countries, replacing them with the same number from camps in other Southeast Asian countries. In addition to pacifying the Southeast Asian countries, the RPC prepared the refugees for life in a resettlement country. The preparation had three elements. First, the refugees studied English and were oriented to life in the United States which would be the destination for most of them. Secondly, the refugees themselves took over much of the responsibility for maintenance and improvement of the camp and its facilities, and third, refugees were encouraged to volunteer to work in the camp on functions such as orientation for new arrivals, counseling, administration, health, and sanitation Theoretically, a refugee gained points to qualify for resettlement through his participation in camp programs. In actual fact, no refugee was held back from resettlement because he didn't acquire enough points.[30] The political expediency of moving refugees was more important than enforcing rules.

The camp population was divided along ethnic lines with separate areas for Vietnamese, highland and lowland Lao, and Cambodians. The first effort was to mix the population, but this arrangement didn't work, so ethnic-based communities were established, each with its own set of leaders reporting up a chain of command to a Philippine administrator and a UNHCR representative. Frictions with the local community were minimized by the sparse population in the region of the RPC. A Congressional study, however, identified a problem. The Hmong and other Lao highlanders went out of the camp into the nearby forests to forage for food. This was a source of irritation for the local Filipinos. Moreover, the Hmong were picking and eating mushrooms that proved to be poisonous. When the camp authorities advised the Hmong not to eat the mushrooms, some of them disregarded the warning, suspecting it was only a ruse to keep them from foraging.[31]

* * *

Piracy was the most serious of the many hazards to the boat people, whose leaky and decrepit boats were usually indefensible, slow, and easy to board for the worst elements among tens of thousands of fishermen in the Gulf of Thailand. Most of the pirates were Thai and Malay fishermen who took advantage of an easy catch on the high seas.

Father Joe Devlin, a Catholic priest working with the boat people in Songkhla, Thailand, described the piracy problem in late 1979. "Every morning we would go down to the beach and there would be bodies — men, women, and children — washed ashore during the night. Sometimes there were hundreds of them, like pieces of wood. Some of them were girls who had been raped and then thrown into the sea by pirates to drown ... the bodies were always there."[32]

A typical story of encounters by boat people with pirates was that of Lien, a 21-year-old Vietnamese woman. Lien and her family were members of a group of 79 people — 35 men, 21 women, and 23 children — crowded aboard a 40-foot boat leaving Vietnam. Their voyage would take 27 days. Their first problem was a shortage of water, which they collected from monsoon rains, and a lack of shelter on the small boat from those same rains.

Ten days out of Vietnam the motor on their boat quit. The men used planks for oars. That same day pirates boarded their boat. Ten men, armed with knives and hammers, robbed them of everything they had of value. They attempted to row their boat for another nine days, running out of food, and were then attacked by pirates a second time. This time, Lien and another girl were raped. "They told us we were lucky," said Lien. "Many of the men here never saw their wives and daughters again. They put us back on the boat and left."

In the days to come, more than fifty ships passed their boat by as they desperately hailed for assistance. Finally, an Argentine freighter stopped, took them on board, and transported them to Bangkok, from where they were sent to a refugee camp in southern Thailand.[33]

The international community was slow to recognize the piracy problem.

Table 3.
Piracy Statistics for Boat People Arriving in Thailand*

	1981	1982	1983
No. of boats arrived	455	218	138
No. of people arrived	15,095	5,913	3,171
Deaths from pirate attacks	571	155	43
No. of abductees	243	157	89
No. of rape victims	599	179	85
No. of missing persons	n.a.	443	153
No. of boats attacked	352	141	77
No. of attacks	1149	381	173
Ave. no. of attacks per attacked boat	3.2	2.7	2.3

Note: These statistics compiled solely on reports by boat people. Statistics are not available for 1978 to 1980 when the number of boat people was larger and piracy was probably more rampant. Most of the abductees were young women who were probably also rape victims although the statistics in this table are mutually exclusive.

Deaths in the table are only from piracy. Many other deaths among boat people were reported from starvation, illness, accidents, and boats sinking.

*Source: UNHCR, http://www.vietka.com/Vietnamese_Boat_People/HorribleStatistics.htm, May 20, 2009.

It was not until the number of boat people from Vietnam slowed in late 1979 that the relief workers caught their breath and had time to listen to refugees tell of their experiences with pirates in the Gulf of Thailand.

Ted Schweitzer, born in Mark Twain's hometown of Hannibal, Missouri, was a former schoolteacher married to a Thai woman. UNHCR contracted him to work as a field officer in a boat people camp in southern Thailand. Soon after his arrival, on November 16, 1979, a helicopter pilot for an offshore oil company told him of seeing refugees on Ko Kra, one of a group of small islands 35 miles off shore. Schweitzer asked the pilot to fly him over the island. They saw refugees but also boats—probably pirates—near the island and bodies floating in the water. The pilot declined to land. "I'm not hired to fly combat missions," he said.[34]

Schweitzer persuaded the Thai Marine police to take him to the island and he brought back 157 men, women, and children to Songkhla. He spoke Thai and he listened to the refugee stories. Pirates had attacked their boat and threw them overboard near the island. Seventeen people drowned trying to swim to the island. Then, as the survivors perched on the uninhabited island, pirate boats returned day after day—as many as 50 in one day—to rape the women.

Schweitzer returned to the island several times in the next two months to rescue additional Vietnamese who had washed up on Ko Kra or had been left there by pirates. In January 1980, he rented an old fishing boat and its crew to go out to the island. It was night when they arrived; the seas were rough and the boat was unable to land. Schweitzer swam ashore, arriving exhausted with his legs cut by the sharp coral. At daybreak, two Vietnamese men found him on the rocks near the beach. They told him, "The robber men are here and they are raping the girls." They helped him climb a cliff overlooking a beach where he saw about 50 drunken men — pirates. They were raping Vietnamese girls.

The Vietnamese told Schweitzer that many more women and girls were hiding in the thick grass and caves on the island, but the pirates had tortured the men to reveal their locations. Schweitzer decided to take action. He gathered together about 35 men and marched to the beach. Speaking Thai, he shouted at the pirates that he worked for the United Nations and that the Vietnamese were under his protection. He told the pirates to leave the island immediately. The pirates were unimpressed; they attacked him with lead pipes, beating him until he was bleeding and unconscious—but they left.

When Schweitzer woke up, the pirate boats were still lingering offshore and dozens of panic-stricken Vietnamese, fearing the pirates would return, were begging him for help. He collected all the refugees on the island, including one young woman who had taken refuge in a cave for 18 days and others who were too weak to walk. Then, he organized a human chain to swim to his boat offshore, loaded up 88 refugees, and transported them to Songkla on the overloaded fishing boat.

Schweitzer returned to Ko Kra many more times during the next several months, rescuing 1,250 refugees and earning a place in the pantheon of refugee heroes. At least 160 refugees died on the island. Schweitzer, his kidneys nearly destroyed by beatings and his health failing, finally left Southeast Asia for a desk job in Geneva. His personal story inspired the UN and donors to take seriously the danger to refugees from pirates. The UN provided a patrol boat and the U.S. funded increased sea and air surveillance.[35] But there were thousands of fishing boats in the Gulf of Thailand and the problem of pirates persisted.

It will never be known how many of the Vietnamese boat people perished at sea of hunger, thirst, shipwreck, and pirates. Estimates run from ten to 50 percent of the 500,000 boat people fleeing Vietnam from 1975 to 1981 with something nearer the lower figure being more probable.[36] Under even this most optimistic scenario, however, 50,000 boat people lost their lives during those years. The number of rapes added up to several thousand but are difficult to quantify as many traumatized women did not report rape. Probably too, several thousand women were kidnapped and were sold to brothels or killed when their captors tired of them. The experience of one girl, Thuy, aged 15, illustrates their fate. When pirates rammed their boat killing 65 persons, Thuy and another woman were held captive as sex slaves for nearly four months, raped multiple times every day, and were passed among the sailors of at least 14 fishing boats before being dumped on a Thai beach.[37]

The UNHCR only began to compile statistics on pirate attacks in 1981, at which time the flow of refugees from Vietnam had already dropped to a fraction of those leaving in late 1978 and 1979. Even so, the statistics, compiled from refugee accounts of their experiences, are frightful. Between 1981 and 1985, the UN documented 2,347 cases of rape, murder, and kidnapping and only 32 pirates were convicted of these crimes.[38] The international community never really solved the piracy problem, although by 1991 about 100 pirates had been prosecuted and the problem had ceased, along with the flow of boat people.

14

THE PUSH BACK AT PREAH VIHEAR

The plight of the boat people received most of the attention of governments, the UN, and charitable organizations—VOLAGS or Voluntary Agencies—during the first eight months of 1979, but building during the year was another humanitarian crisis of equal or greater magnitude: the rush of Cambodians to the borders of Thailand and the threat of mass starvation inside Cambodia.

The Khmer Rouge had kept such a tight rein on the population, including depopulating the border and sprinkling it with minefields, that few people were able to flee.[1] Cambodian refugees escaping to Thailand from 1975 to the end of 1978 totaled only about 34,000 by UNHCR count.[2] But the invasion of Cambodia by Vietnam on Christmas day 1978, the takeover of most of the country by the Vietnamese army, and the installation of a Vietnamese-sponsored government in Phnom Penh led to massive dislocations of Cambodians. The Khmer Rouge retreated into the rugged and forested Cardamom Mountains near the border with Thailand. Northward, but still along the border, the Khmer Serei, a collection of anti-communist and right wing opposition groups, resisted the Vietnamese, although they fought among themselves as much as they did against the Vietnamese. The border east of the city of Aranyaprathet was the dividing line between the two: The Khmer Rouge were south of Aran; the Khmer Serei were north of Aran.

The Thai and other Southeast Asian countries were frightened by the Vietnamese invasion of Cambodia. A Thai academic, Khien Theeravit, cited four unfavorable consequences for Thailand of the Vietnamese occupation of Cambodia. It eliminated Cambodia as a buffer state between Vietnam and Thailand, threatened to embroil Thailand in a war with Vietnam, caused a large refugee flow to Thailand, and catalyzed the growth of military influence in the government of Thailand.[3] To see Vietnamese soldiers on their borders was a Thai nightmare. Thus, it suited them that parts of western Cambodia were still controlled by anti–Vietnamese forces. Monstrous as were the Khmer Rouge, the Thai did not consider them a potent threat. In mid–1979, Thai policy was to allow anti-Vietnamese armed groups, including the KR, to enter Thailand and rest and regroup temporarily before reentering Cambodia. However, the Thai prevented, as much as possible, the entrance into Thailand of Cambodian non-combatants—people who sought food and safety. Thailand sought to stem any potential flood of indigent Cambodians trying to cross its border.[4]

Politics and refugees clash. Thailand did not recognize the people arriving from Cambodia, Vietnam, and Laos as refugees, but called them "displaced persons" or "illegal migrants." The Thai feared that among the refugees would be spies and agitators sent by the communists to stir up trouble in Thailand and that cross-border clashes would lead to war with Vietnam. The Thai government also had to accommodate public opinion, especially in the sensitive border zones, which was heavily against the refugees. Thai farmers and villages in poor northeastern Thailand might become jealous and restive if they saw refugees receiving food and other assistance that they did not.

Thai policy toward refugees was "humane deterrence" in which Thailand attempted to make the life of refugees as difficult as possible in order to discourage additional people that might be attracted if Thailand was envisioned as a land of milk and honey. Thailand had never ratified the Refugee Convention and did not feel bound by its provisions. Moreover, Thailand was similarly unenthusiastic about resettlement programs by the United States and others as they might also be a pull factor for refugees. Thailand, other Southeast Asian countries, the United States, China, and most Europeans opposed the Vietnamese-imposed government in Phnom Penh and that made them uncomfortable bedfellows with the horrendous, genocidal Khmer Rouge. It made for uncomfortable politics that those who wanted to help the refugees found themselves also helping the Khmer Rouge.

The Thai have a national genius toward vagueness, compromise, and amiability that conceals a harder core of conviction that is no stranger to violence and repression. Those more severe traits were often displayed at the border. Thailand would not be saddled permanently with hundreds of thousands of refugees nor would it cede control over the Indochinese refugees to foreigners and foreign humanitarian organizations who wanted to assist the Cambodians as the outflow from Cambodia increased in 1979. There was method to their harshness. Thailand feared becoming the next domino to fall to communism. And the Thai feared that the Cambodians fleeing the Vietnamese would seep into Thai society.

The foreigners working with the Thai learned to interpret the Thai position based on their actions as opposed to their rhetoric, which was often contradictory depending upon the audience for which it was intended. The foreigners also learned quickly that public criticism of Thailand and Thai policy toward refugees was counterproductive. Much better was to cultivate Thai officials carefully, pick away at their more objectionable policies and use their dislike of saying "no" to one's own advantage. Personal relations were important;

14. The Push Back at Preah Vihear

a foreigner who irritated the Thai was the recipient of polite smiles, exquisite courtesies, well-concealed backstabs, and semi-promises that were never fulfilled. In Thailand, the rule is for even bitter enemies to preserve surface courtesies and keep conflict in the background.

Thailand, the United States, and China were in accord in opposing the Vietnamese-installed government in Phnom Penh. Vietnam was a threat to Thailand; a government in Cambodia owing allegiance to Vietnam raised the level of the threat. China made little secret of its military and economic support for anti–Vietnamese Cambodian armed groups and factions.

* * *

In Malaysia and other Southeast Asian countries, also non-signatories to the Refugee Convention, the governments and local populations often "pushed off" boatloads of arriving refugees, leaving them to suffer pirate attacks, weather, and shortages of food and water until they found a place to land. In Thailand, where most refugees arrived by land, refugees were often "pushed back" to Cambodia. The largest and most infamous of the "push backs" occurred in June 1979 near a famous temple named Preah Vihear on the border of Cambodia and Thailand.

Yvette Pierpaoli, the French "adventurer" and lover of Cambodia, had set up business in Bangkok with her partner Kurt Furrer after the Khmer Rouge takeover. Soon, they were making money hand over fist, but Yvette spent many weekends on the border. She carried rice and medicine to Cambodian refugees she found, and hid starving children beneath rags in the back seat of her car. She took the children to hospitals in Bangkok and, when they were well, found them a place to live or returned them to their parents or other relatives, if possible. Her house in Bangkok became a haven for lost children and Cambodian refugees. Had it not been for her own children, Manou and Olivier, she would have joined the armed resistance to the Khmer Rouge.[5] She and Lionel Rosenblatt became good friends and informal colleagues in refugee work. Yvette made an instant judgment that Lionel was a rare government official who truly cared about refugees and she put trust and confidence in him.

* * *

Lionel and Yvette were different. Yvette wanted to save individuals. She heard that a man who had worked for her in Cambodia and four starving children were hiding in a pagoda. She asked Lionel for help. He was angry. They had to save as many people as possible, not just focus on a few individuals. But he took down the names of the children and the man and promised to try to help. Yvette prayed to a Buddhist saint and promised to donate two tons of dried fish to refugees if the children were saved. Lionel answered her prayer. He reconsidered, called her back, and said he would help. A monk collected the children and with Lionel's help brought them to Bangkok.

More often than not Lionel did not obey his own rule of saving many people rather than a few. His boss, American ambassador Mort Abramowitz, recalls wryly the many telephone calls he received from Lionel pleading the case for a single refugee or refugee family.[6] In the midst of mass misery, relief workers, for their own mental state, seized on giving their special attention to one person or one family. It personalized their work, rather than submerging their emotions in favor of an undifferentiated mass of people.

On June 4, 1979, Yvette heard rumors that the Thai were going to force a large number of Cambodians back across the border. The next day she drove to the border armed with fake documents she had manufactured that bore an impressive seal made by an ink-soaked slice of potato. She saw several hundred Cambodians imprisoned behind barbed wire by soldiers. She rushed back to Bangkok to try to generate action to prevent the forced repatriation of the Cambodians, and a few days later Lionel went out to the border with her.

The night of June 12, Lionel called Yvette and asked her to go to the border with him immediately. He brought her up to date on the way to Wat Ko, a Buddhist temple, near the border city of Aranyaprathet. The Thai were going to force a large number of Cambodians back across the border, but France, the United States, and Australia had obtained agreement to choose 1,200 refugees for resettlement from among those who were being repatriated. Their job was to pick out 1,200 refugees among 6,000 being held at the temple. They had three hours to choose those they would save, make a list of them, and load them onto 22 orange buses. One hundred other buses would haul the remainder of the refugees away to an unknown location. Four of them would make the selection: an Australian, a Frenchman, Lionel, and Yvette. John Crowley and Rich Kocher from Lionel's office had been on the border for several weeks making lists of potentially eligible refugees and those lists gave the four some guidance.

The refugees realized that their chances for survival were better with the four foreigners than with the Thai soldiers surrounding the Wat. For the next three hours, separated by a barbed wire fence from thousands of screaming and panic-stricken refugees held in the temple—Thai soldiers beating back the Cambodians with their rifle butts—the four *farangs* picked out refugees, noted their names, and directed them to buses. Yvette made her choices almost at random: an old man, because he deserved to die in bed, and a young woman with a child, because the child reminded her of Manou. The soldiers kept count of the people she selected. They told her when she had picked 300. Most of the soldiers then entered the Wat and pushed all the Cambodians who remained toward the 100 buses that would carry them away in a different direction.

With only a single Thai soldier beside her, Yvette relied on the dramatics that served her so well. She simulated a dead faint, falling into the arms of the embarrassed soldier, and while he was distracted by Yvette in his arms, an additional five refugees sneaked out of the wire enclosure. A woman and a child boarded the buses; three men disappeared into the mists of the early dawn.

14. The Push Back at Preah Vihear 175

John Crowley organized the bus caravan while Yvette and the other refugee workers rushed to their cars to lead the buses toward Bangkok before the Thai soldiers changed their minds. They had 1,296 refugees with them. All four of them had cheated and exceeded their quota of 300 each. All of them had plastic bags full of messages written by the refugees behind the barbed wire and tossed out to them. Some were names, others were letters to relatives in the U.S. or France, or to President Jimmy Carter begging his intervention on their behalf. For many of the writers those scrawled notes would be their last will and testament.[7]

Lionel watched the convoy depart and then scoured the hospital in Aranyaprathet to locate any refugees who might be there to take them with him to Bangkok. He found a Cambodian woman and her newly born baby and loaded them into his car. But, he broke the key off in the ignition, so he commandeered a nearby UNHCR car and drove it to Bangkok with the woman and her baby. UNHCR complained not only that he had stolen one of their cars but that he had returned it in poor condition.[8] The refugees who Lionel, Yvette and the others had saved were taken to the Lumpini Transit Center in a park only a few blocks from the Embassy in Bangkok. From there, they would be processed for travel to the United States and other countries. The Thai initially objected to the refugees being taken to Lumpini, but Mac Thompson, as only he could do, smoothed the way with a bottle of Jack Daniels and an amiable drink with Thai officials.[9]

Several days later Yvette found out what had happened to the Cambodians who had been loaded onto buses by the soldiers. The soldiers had told the refugees they were being taken to a transit camp and from there they would go to the United States. At first, it seemed plausible as the buses headed west toward Bangkok, but then they turned north and east. The buses and trucks headed toward an unknown destination. Soldiers guarded them to make sure that no one escaped. Mac Thompson may have been the first person to discover where the refugees were going. He tried to follow the bus caravan, but he was stopped by a Thai army roadblock. He reported back to Lionel that the refugees were going in the direction of Wat Preah Vihear on the Thai Cambodian border. Mac stationed himself under a shade tree along the road leading to Preah Vihear and counted buses to estimate the number of refugees being taken there.[10]

Phreah Vihear is one of the premier monuments remaining of Cambodia's most glorious period, the Khmer empire of Angkor in the 9th through the 15th century. It tops an escarpment in a spectacular setting almost 2,000 feet above the Cambodian plain. Resting on the border, its ownership is disputed between Thailand and Cambodia. It took three days for all the 40,000 plus refugees gathered all along the border to arrive.[11] Thai soldiers had sealed off Preah Vihear so there would be no prying eyes. The refugees were unloaded at night, forced to follow a trail going down the nearly vertical mountainside toward the Cambodian plains beyond and were told not to stray to either side because minefields lined the trail. Vietnamese soldiers, they were told, would meet them at the further end of the trail. The Cambodians were relieved by the Thai soldiers of any goods or money they had and anyone who protested or refused to go down the trail was beaten or shot. A survivor described the ordeal:

> There was no path to follow; we had to go through the bush. The way that we were to go down was only a cliff. Some people hid on top of the mountain and survived. Others were shot or pushed over the cliff. Most of the people began to climb down using vines as ropes. They tied their children to their back or strapped them across their chests. As the people climbed down, the soldiers threw big rocks over the cliff.
>
> Closer to the bottom, there was a strong terrible smell. We began to see the bodies of those who had died there before us. The first people to reach the bottom walked out into the field and it was then that the first mines began to go off. Many people were killed here too.[12]

Former soldiers of Lon Nol had been the first to be pushed down the cliffs. Their bodies marked a safe path about three feet wide through mine fields. Those who followed them stepped over the bodies. Many young men who left the trail to get water from pools near the trail were killed by mines, but one young man, a former employee of the American Embassy in Phnom Penh, cleared a trail to the water by crawling on his belly and feeling in the soil for the tiny shiny metal disks on top of mines, then marking the location of the mines with scraps of paper.[13]

A Vietnamese soldier on the Cambodian side of the border also described the scene: "The Thai soldiers began firing their guns into the crowd of civilians to make them move faster. We watched as people were cut down by gunfire and we heard sobbing and screams for help. A terrible scene unfolded in front of our eyes ... the column of civilians walked right into the minefield.... We heard terrible screams and moans from inside the minefield." The Vietnamese soldiers met the refugees in the minefield and led the survivors to safety near a lake about two kilometers inside Cambodia.[14]

Back in Bangkok, Yvette heard of the events at Preah Vihear and took the story to the director of the International Red Cross, the ICRC, in Thailand. Her dislike of officials comes out in the story of their meeting, "His tie matched the color of his curtains." She tried to generate a response from him to no avail. The stoic Swiss pointed out that rules prevented him from acting. Yvette had no respect for rules or those who enforced them. To be fair to the ICRC, while the character of the organization was the opposite of the white-hot passion of Yvette, it protested the push-back and its Thai director, Francis Amar, was recalled to Geneva at the insistence of the Thai government. By contrast, the UNHCR—charged with protecting refugees—did nothing, although individual UNHCR employees protested the inaction. The Swedish ambassador in Thailand summed up the reaction: "The international community has shown a notorious lack of interest in this question."[15]

On June 22, two Cambodian survivors of Preah Vihear found their way

14. The Push Back at Preah Vihear

to Yvette's house in Bangkok and told what had happened to the refugees. Yvette called reporter Henry Kamm, who wrote an article about the push back in *The New York Times*. From the accounts of survivors who made their way back to Thailand a story can be pieced together. It took three days for one of the survivors to cross the minefields at the foot of the cliffs and find the Vietnamese soldiers inside Cambodia. Most of the refugees had no food and water was hard to find. "The crowd was very dense. It was impossible to number the victims of the land mines. The wounded people were moaning. The most difficult part of the walk was near the dead bodies."[16]

About 10,000 of the refugees clustered at the foot of the cliffs below Preah Vihear and there they stayed for a week or more, too frightened to continue their journey through the mine fields, foraging for food in the forest and drinking rainwater. Many of them were killed by mines; others died of exposure and disease in the cold monsoon rains. Some tried to return to Thailand and were shot; others bought food from the Thai border guards or ate what was sent in to them on trails cleared of mines by the Vietnamese.

Yvette tried to get permission from the Thai government to transport 21 tons of rice under the auspices of Catholic Relief Services to try to get it to the refugees who had been pushed down the mountainside. Finally, on June 30, she had the permissions and she and Lionel took a night train and a taxi to as near as they could get to Preah Vihear. Then, the two of them tried to work out a way to get the rice to the surviving refugees below Preah Vihear. They failed, but, near the border, through the kindness of poor Thai farmers sheltering Cambodians and Thai soldiers who did not relish their grisly work, they received hundreds of notes from surviving Cambodians.

Lionel and Yvette returned to Bangkok defeated, but their work and that of other humanitarians, Thai and foreign, caused the Thai government to relent. The government allowed the rice Yvette had sent to the border to be distributed and granted the right of temporary asylum in Bangkok to the survivors. Lionel and Yvette gave the Thai government a list of the names they had collected and a Thai official journeyed to Preah Vihear. In a single day's work he compiled a list of 922 survivors. The Thai army collected the survivors and brought them to Bangkok to the transit center with the agreement that they would be resettled abroad within 60 days.[17]

It will never be known how many Cambodians pushed down the cliffs at Preah Vihear died. A UNHCR report on July 3 estimated that 42,000 Cambodians had been pushed back. Thirty-two thousand, UNHCR estimated, found their way across the minefield to the Vietnamese soldiers on the other side; 3,000 died; and 7,000 were still trapped at the foot of the cliffs. How many of that 7,000 made it to safety is unknown.[18] Some of them found their way into Cambodia and the relative safety of Vietnamese-controlled areas; a few were able to sneak back into Thailand. Lionel and Yvette found several of them being protected by Thai farmers.

Why was the pushback at Preah Vihear so elaborate when it could have been simple? The Thai were pushing back Cambodian refugees daily. It was a simple process. "When we want to push back the refugees," said a Thai official, "border authorities simply inform Vietnamese officials on the other side of the border by loudspeaker that we're going to send back the refugees. When they okay them, we allow the refugees to walk across."[19] So, why the elaborate and dramatic busing of refugees from camps to a famous temple on the border of Cambodia? Why, if secrecy was essential, did the Thai government allow Pierpaoli, Rosenblatt and others to save a few people at Wat Ko? Court Robinson, a refugee scholar, and others agreed that it was a demonstration to the international community that Thailand was not going to accept the refugee burden from Cambodia alone.[20] Help, or watch Cambodians pushed back to die was the message. The gesture worked. The world became aware of the plight of the Cambodians, and public opinion galvanized in favor of helping them.[21] Like the Malaysians with their push-offs of boat people, the Thai achieved their objective. They would not be left in the lurch with hundreds of thousands of Cambodians to protect and feed who would be a potential security risk and financial drain on their country. The international community would pay the bills for their upkeep, resettle large numbers of Cambodians, and spend the next dozen years devising means by which Cambodians could return safely to their country.

* * *

The best-known survivor of the Cambodian holocaust was photographer Dith Pran. As recounted in Chapter Three, he saved the lives of journalists Al Rockoff, Jon Swain, and Sydney Schanberg on April 17, 1975, when KR soldiers threatened to execute them. His experiences over the next four years were the subject of an award-winning movie, *The Killing Fields*, which brought home to a large international audience the realities of the Khmer Rouge regime.

Pran was a resourceful, fast-talking, bright young man, the kind of assistant often called a "fixer." He divined that his best chance of survival under the Khmer Rouge lay in erasing every trace of his past. "He threw away his regular Western-style street clothes and put on a working-class disguise, that of a lowly taxi-driver — dirty shirt, short pants, sandals, a traditional Cambodian neckerchief." He got his hair cut short and threw away the 2,600 dollars the Western journalists had given him —"Money was useless in the new Cambodia and could only incriminate him."[22]

"'If you tell the truth, or argue even a little, they kill you' was Pran's simple rule of survival. 'They told us all people are one class now, only working-class, peasants.' So he censored his thoughts and watched his vocabulary, keeping it crude and limited, to conceal his education and journalistic past. He talked as little as possible, and then softly and obsequiously." Pran made his way through Khmer Rouge checkpoints to a small village 20 miles east of his hometown of Siem Reap, famous as the location of the famous ruin of Angkor. There he would stay for two and one half years working in the fields and attempting to survive on a starvation diet. "They did not kill people in front of us.... They took them away at night and murdered them with big sticks and hoes, to save bullets."

To avoid starvation was his greatest challenge. Once he crept into the rice paddies at night to gather a few grains of rice to eat. He was caught and beaten and the leaders of the community debated executing him. He was spared because he had ingratiated himself with one of them. Pran estimated that ten percent of the Cambodian population starved to death in 1975 and early 1976, but as the food situation improved, the killings increased. Pran fled one commune for another after hearing that the second was not so rigidly communist. He wheedled his way into a good position at the second commune as a personal slave of the chief, who seemed to have lost his dedication to the Khmer Rouge.

The Vietnamese invasion gave Pran his opportunity for escape as well as providing the same opportunity to hundreds of thousands of other Cambodians. On January 10, 1979, the Vietnamese conquered Siem Reap. They encouraged Cambodians in the nearby communes to return home and Pran walked the 20 miles to Siem Reap to look for his family. He described meeting his sister:

> From a distance, we could not immediately recognize each other; we were both very thin, wore old torn clothes and walked barefoot. I had lost almost all my teeth because of poor diet, and my feet and legs were badly infected because I had so often waded in animal manure when I worked in the rice fields. My sister had also worked in a labor camp. At these camps, malaria was common and she and I both caught it. I suffered attacks every week. I would get sudden chills, or the sweats, or high fevers, sometimes several times a day.... My sister has suffered far more than I. She saw a daughter and our father starve to death and our young brother taken away. She still has nightmares.[23]

The toll of Pran's family: His father had died of starvation; his mother had survived. One sister had been killed; another had survived but one of her four children had died of starvation. His three brothers had all been executed. Their bones were probably in the "killing fields" near Siem Reap where he saw the bones of thousands. "In the water wells, the bodies were like soup bones in broth.... And you could always tell the killing grounds because the grass grew taller and greener where the bodies were buried."[24]

For a few months Pran prospered under Vietnamese rule. With little competition because so few educated Cambodians had survived, he became a puppet mayor of Siem Reap, dressing in a uniform, sporting a rifle, and giving speeches to the populace. But the Vietnamese became aware that he had been a journalist who had worked for the Americans and he was dismissed from his position and felt endangered once again because of his past. On July 29, 1979, he left Siem Reap with 11 other men to attempt an escape to Thailand. The Thai border was about 70 miles away. The dangers of their journey were "roving bands of Khmer Rouge guerillas, Vietnamese patrols, deadly punji traps (sharpened bamboo stakes smeared with toxic matter and covered with leaves and brush) and unmarked mine fields."[25] Two of the men with him were killed by a land mine and he was hit in his side by flying shrapnel. Reaching the border at last, Pran waited an agonizing 17 days for an opportunity to sneak across. Had he been apprehended by Thai authorities he would likely have been "pushed back" into Cambodia and died at the hands of the Khmer Rouge or the Vietnamese or of starvation. Pran succeeded in getting into one of the border camps.

Pran found upon arrival at the border camp that he was already a well-known person. The JVA workers kept a watch list of Cambodians who, if they survived, might show up at the camps, and due to *The New York Times*, the JVA had kept an eye open for Pran for more than two years. Thus it was that Judy Kocher knew who Pran was when she received a letter from him and she helped him send out a message to the *Times*. Pran requested help to get out of the camp and "a donation."[26] He was something of a celebrity. His former boss, Syd Schanberg, flew out to meet him and the Embassy people pushed to help Pran get out of the camps and on his way to America as quickly as possible. Schanberg, no shrinking violet, made himself thoroughly unpopular with the Embassy and refugee officers by loudly demanding special treatment for Pran. The Embassy believed it had done everything it could without going beyond the bounds of what the Thai government would tolerate and got Pran on his way to the U.S. as quickly as possible.

Pran survived — where many had not — with pluck, luck, discipline, and an ability to size up a situation and take advantage of it. He pushed the horrors he had witnessed into dark corners of his mind but he acknowledged years later the terror in the night that left him crying in the arms of his wife.[27]

Pran's story was repeated a thousand-fold by other Cambodians who survived the Khmer Rouge. Judy Kocher (whose husband Rich was also in JVA), like most of the refugee workers, could not avoid sometimes becoming directly involved in assisting individuals. Judy sneaked two battered Cambodian boys out of the camp and took them to her house in Bangkok to live for a few days. Before they departed for the United States, Judy took them shopping. The boys owned nothing more than the tattered clothes they were wearing. She recalls their sad smiles as they tried on new clothes. They had never been in a department store before, but they wanted to arrive in the U.S. looking "normal."

This story has a sequel. Two years later, the mother of one of the boys escaped to Thailand. She told Judy that her son was in the United States but she didn't know where. Judy recognized the name and connected her with her son. Later, the woman pressed a small pendant into Judy's hand. It was the only thing of value she owned. She wanted Judy to have it for reconnecting her with her son. Judy accepted the pendant as memento of a sad beginning with a happy ending. The other boy — who had witnessed his whole family being beaten to death in Cambodia — wrote Judy eight years later to thank her while he was a student at Oregon State University.[28]

* * *

Preah Vihear and the flight of refugees such as Dith Pran was only the beginning. Had the KR remained in power in 1979 hundreds of thousands of Cambodians would probably have starved to death or been killed and like a tree falling in an empty forest their deaths would have gone unnoticed outside the country, surviving only as tales told by refugees. Vietnamese rule released the Cambodians from their bondage and, free to roam, they sought to cheat death by running toward Thailand in search of rice and international assistance. Most Cambodians had been on starvation rations for four years when the Vietnamese invaded. The disruptions caused by the invasion and the subsequent war between the Vietnamese-imposed government in Phnom Penh and the Khmer Rouge pushed the country toward famine.

Cambodia has two rice harvest seasons. The most important is the monsoon season crop planted at the beginning of the monsoon season in May or June harvested six months later in December and January. The second is the dry season crop, planted in November on lands still wet from the just-concluded monsoon and harvested in February. The monsoon crop accounts for about 85 percent of rice production.[29] The Vietnamese invasion interrupted the harvest of the monsoon crop in December and January and the dry season crop in February. As more and more of the country was liberated from the Khmer Rouge, millions of Cambodians in communes returned home to the farm or to the cities, searched for relatives or wandered in pursuit of wisps of hope that somewhere they would find friends, relatives, work, and food. Cambodia in the spring and summer of 1979 was one vast migration of people, mostly on foot, from one place to another. As a result, little rice was planted. By fall, fragmentary reports from inside Cambodia suggested that famine stalked the land and that soon Cambodia would be in danger of a famine that would kill hundreds of thousands of people.

15

SA KAEO AND KHAO I DANG HOLDING CENTERS

The international effort to save Cambodians from mass starvation in late 1979 and 1980 was probably the most complex and expensive humanitarian operation the international community had ever undertaken. Relief expenditures amounted to $500 million dollars in little more than one year.[1] The United States was the largest donor of money and food. The relief operation was fraught with controversy and back-biting among the governments, UN agencies, and charitable organizations who cooperated and competed in bringing help to Cambodians in Thailand and inside Cambodia.

The Vietnamese launched an offensive in September 1979 against the remaining Khmer Rouge strongholds and the KR retreated to near the Thai border, taking many non-combatants with them. After Preah Vihear, the Thai had ceased pushing large numbers of Cambodians back across the border, but now instead prevented them from entering Thailand. Informal encampments up and down the borders of the two countries sprang up quickly, the inhabitants drawn by the lure of Thailand just across the barbed wire barriers patrolled by Thai soldiers. The refugees—although they were not legally refugees because they had not crossed an international boundary—came to escape the Vietnamese and find food. A few, especially the survivors of the Cambodian middle class, hoped to escape the killing fields of their country and join relatives abroad or find a new life in the West.

It suited the Thai that the Khmer Rouge and other resistance forces such as the Free Khmer (Khmer Serei) stood between their country and the Vietnamese army. The joke among relief workers was that the greatest obstacle the formidable Vietnamese army would face if it invaded Thailand was the traffic in Bangkok. The policy of Thailand toward the Cambodians was influenced by American diplomacy in Bangkok led by Ambassador Morton I. Abramowitz and Refugee Coordinator Lionel Rosenblatt and by the promises of resettlement for Indochinese made by Vice President Walter Mondale at the Geneva Conference in July.

15. Sa Kaeo and Khao I Dang Holding Centers

On the other side of the equation was the new Vietnamese-installed Heng Samrin government in Phnom Penh. Controlling about 70 percent of Cambodia's land and people, the 200,000-man Vietnamese army in Cambodia sought to exterminate the remnants of the Khmer Rouge and other resistance movements. They believed, with reason, that any assistance or safe harbor given by Thailand to combatants in the border camps would strengthen the resistance to them. At the same time, Heng Samrin and his government, mostly ex–Khmer Rouge, had taken power in a devastated country whose people were in danger of starvation. Vietnam itself was in sad economic shape. The Soviet Union and its bloc would help, but the cornucopia of the food, medicine, and equipment Cambodia needed was the West and its relief organizations. Cambodia would try to obtain Western food and goods, but avoid the importation of Western influence and ideas. On July 3, 1979, Hun Sen, the foreign minister, made the first request for aid to the World Food Program. His description made the situation inside Cambodia seem even more ominous than observers had feared. Two million two hundred fifty thousand people were menaced by famine, he said, and Cambodia required 162,000 tons of rice, 8,100 tons of vegetable oil, and 15,000 tons of sugar. Hun Sen proposed that the modalities of the aid be discussed and agreed upon with the Cambodian Ambassador in Hanoi, and conspicuously did not invite UN officials to visit Phnom Penh.[2]

The shocking statement from Hun Sen that over two million Cambodians faced starvation combined with the growing number of obviously malnourished and diseased Cambodians arriving at the Thai border galvanized the relief community into action. What developed was a three-pronged relief effort. The first effort was to provide food, medical care, and protection to the tens of thousands of Cambodians who had succeeded in entering Thailand, plus any more which might succeed in crossing the border. The second was to provide assistance to the growing number of Cambodians clustered near the Thai border who were unable, because of the Thai border guards, or unwilling to cross into Thailand. Third, was to address the plight of the millions of Cambodians in the interior of the country.

* * *

In late September 1979, the Thai government worked out procedures with UN agencies to help the Cambodians rushing to the border and obviously in severe straits. The World Food Program (WFP), they agreed, would import and deliver food to Thai warehouses. The UN Children's Fund (UNICEF) would transport food and other humanitarian goods to the border and distribute the food. The International Red Cross (ICRC) would be in charge of medical care and the Joint Mission of ICRC and UNICEF would coordinate and monitor the aid program.[3] The UN agencies would sub-contract many of these functions to the VOLAGs (non-governmental charity organizations) flooding into Thailand. Not part of this command structure, but nevertheless the dominant player, was the American Embassy in Bangkok. The United States was the largest donor, had the most influence with the Thai government, and, with its staff of experienced personnel and expertise, was the most knowledgeable about what was happening up and down the border.

Absent from any major role in this arrangement was UNHCR. The Americans criticized UNHCR for being slow to build up its presence in Thailand and timid in its defense of refugees. One American official threatened to publicly take the refugee agency to task for its poor performance.[4] Despite the poor relations between the U.S. and UNHCR, Lionel recognized that the agency's presence and prestige were essential. When a new field officer of UNHCR, Mark Malloch Brown, arrived in Thailand in September 1979, Lionel woke up the young Englishman while he was still sleeping off jet lag in his hotel room and gave him an unrequested but impressive briefing on the border situation, including more than a few suggestions as to what UNHCR's proper role should be.[5]

The first contact of relief agencies—and one of the few face-to-face contacts Westerners had ever had with the Khmer Rouge—came on September 17 when two officials of ICRC and one from UNICEF journeyed a few miles into Cambodia on elephant back hauling with them 500 kilograms of dry milk and 300 kilos of medicine. They found appalling conditions. Thousands were starving. An "epidemic of cerebral malaria had decimated the population. Many of the refugees no longer had the strength to move from their sanctuaries, and many others were malnourished to the point where they could not digest the food given them."[6]

Lionel's wife, Ann Grosvenor-Rosenblatt, was on the first medical team to journey to the border. Ann, a recent graduate from nursing school, was working for the International Rescue Committee with the Hmong in northern Thailand when she heard stories of the plight of the Cambodians. Along with a Filipino physician, Levi Roque, she journeyed to Aranyaprathet, the nearest Thai city to the Cambodian border. There she joined a group of 15 international medical personnel: six from Doctors without Borders, just off an airplane from France, five from IRC, and four from World Vision. They were briefed quickly by Robert Ashe of Christian Outreach, who had worked on the border since 1975, and were broken into two teams each to go to KR encampments on the border.

Ann's group consisted of Roque, another doctor, and four nurses—American, Filipino, Canadian, and French. With a Thai military escort to guide them, Levi drove to the border in a pickup truck, the others riding in the back, all quickly covered with the red laterite dust of Thailand's scrubby and poor northeastern region. They found the encampment of Cambodians in open fields surrounded by tall grass. The *farangs* were anxious; the camp was Khmer Rouge who had fled the Vietnamese, bringing with them — or forcing to come — their families and supporters. Most of them, men and women, were dressed in the

15. Sa Kaeo and Khao I Dang Holding Centers

Ann Grosvenor-Rosenblatt. Ann, a newly graduated nurse, was a member of the first medical team working on the Cambodian border and she worked for the International Rescue Committee. Ann caught tuberculosis while working in the refugee camps. (Lionel Rosenblatt collection)

KR uniform: loose black pajamas and shirts, rubber-tired sandals, and red and white checked scarves that served as hats, slings for babies, and shopping bags. Thirty thousand refugees were estimated to be at this encampment.

The medical team set up a clinic on the tailgate of the pickup. Pencil-thin Cambodian men and women came out of the tall grass at the edge of the field to watch them. Others clustered around bags of donated rice stacked in the field or escaped the sun under shelters of blue plastic sheets. A Khmer-speaking Thai soldier announced that the medical clinic was open and patients arrived and were formed into two lines in the hot sun, the Cambodians squatting on their haunches.

Ann and Frederica gave each person in line a cursory examination. Angie, a Filipina, and Martha dispensed high-protein biscuits and medicine. The two doctors searched the fields for people too weak to come to the clinic. Most of the patients complained of chills and fever and were obviously near starvation. The nurses passed out fansidar, which both treats and prevents malaria, and iron and folic acid tablets.

Ann was called away to tend to a woman too weak to walk. She was near death. Cambodians carried her back to the shade of the pickup truck. Ann gave her an iron injection and protein biscuits—having little hope that the young woman would survive. She was surprised the next day when the woman was standing in line for the clinic. Ann saw another woman crawling on her hands and knees, digging up roots and eating them. Twice during the day, Ann set up IVs for dying men, hanging the tubes from tree branches. She never knew whether those men survived or not.

The doctors and nurses were not allowed to remain in the camp overnight and made the long trip back to Aran in the afternoon. They were famished because they hadn't felt comfortable eating in front of the starving refugees. The next morning they were off again to the encampment. Concerned that refugees might return every day for medicine and overdose themselves, they worked out a system of marking each person who had received medicine with a dab of orange paint on his forearm.

On the third day, the Thai soldiers helped them set up a tent—eight bamboo poles covered by a tarpaulin, and a Thai medical team arrived to staff a field hospital. The international medical team set up three tables in front of the medical tent to pass out medicine. The Thai soldiers by now were interested in the operation and helped give the patients oral rehydration salts. Roque's prescriptions were simple. He wrote the prescription for each patient on his forearm with a red marking pen: "V" meant vitamins, "C" was combantrin (for worms), "F" was fansidar, and "FE" was iron. The Thai medical teams also gave Cambodian women an injection of Depo-provera, a contraceptive banned in the United States.[7]

Patients were brought to the hospital in litters carried by Cambodians on their shoulders. Many had wounds infested with maggots. Soon, there were 60 malaria patients in the hospital and Ann realized that the patients they had been seeing in their open air clinic every day had been the strongest refugees, able to get to the clinic and wait in line. Several Cambodian women came forward and declared themselves to be nurses' aides and were put to work. One old man died in a pool of excrement at the side of the field hospital.

To the excitement of the medical team, a truck arrived one day with boxes of donated goods from abroad. They tore into the boxes to see what they contained that would assist them in doing their job. The first box contained a device that warmed up shaving cream. The other boxes had similarly useless items. They shut the boxes up and pushed them to the side to fester and decay in the hot Thai sun and the torrential monsoon rains. That day, their fifth at the border, they left early. The Thai, they heard, had agreed to set up a camp inside Thailand for Cambodians and would bring these and other Cambodians camped along the border to the camp.[8]

The situation Ann witnessed on the border was repeated elsewhere. About 200,000 Cambodians were estimated to be on the border attempting to enter

15. Sa Kaeo and Khao I Dang Holding Centers

Thailand.[9] On October 18, 1979, Thai prime minister Kriangsak was shocked when he saw the appalling condition of the Cambodians on a visit to the border. Two days later, taking a political risk, he changed the government's policy. He announced an "open door" policy granting temporary asylum to Cambodians inside Thailand; Thailand would still not recognize them as refugees but it would rescue them from the border and place them in "holding centers." On October 22, a Thai colonel called UNHCR and said that the government had decided to admit 90,000 Cambodians who were camped on the border. The Thai military planned to begin moving them to a location near the town of Sa Kaeo within 48 hours. Sa Kaeo Holding Center was about 40 miles west of the border near the town of the same name and 130 miles by road east of Bangkok.

The brand-new, 26-year-old UNHCR officer, Mark Malloch Brown, rushed to Sa Kaeo to prepare to meet the first arrivals.[10] The site for the holding center was a poorly-drained rice field 33 acres in size. Operating out of a suitcase full of money and documents in the trunk of his car, Mark contracted for the site to be bulldozed; tents for shelter, hospitals, and latrines erected; and food and water to be stockpiled — but there was far too little time to prepare adequately for the arrival of the refugees. That first day, October 24, 8,000 refugees arrived in an endless stream of buses and trucks from the border; by the end of the first week Sa Kaeo had 32,000 residents.[11]

Ann and her medical team were at Sa Kaeo when the first refugees arrived from the border.[12] A busload of volunteers came up from the American Embassy in Bangkok, among them Sheppie Abramowitz, the wife of the ambassador, who had taken charge of the volunteer effort. Sheppie and Mark got into an altercation on some matter of procedure. Mark didn't realize until later that he was shouting at the wife of the American ambassador. Sheppie, on her part, regarded the incident as proof that Mark was no shrinking violet, but a young man to be respected.[13] Sheppie's volunteers would be absolutely essential for the survival of the Cambodians during the first few critical days at Sa Kaeo.

Susan Lenderking, an Australian married to an American diplomat, was among the group. Susan had a nine-month-old baby at home. She and the other volunteers arrived at an empty rice field at Sa Kaeo. A bulldozer was pushing soil around to improve drainage and a backhoe dug trench latrines around the periphery of the camp. Water would have to be trucked in until three wells were completed.[14] Tents were being erected and food was arriving to be distributed to the arriving refugees, but most of the new arrivals would have to sleep on the ground without any shelter. While Thailand is tropical, the monsoon rains are chilling and, after a hiatus, the monsoon resumed and made dusty Sa Kaeo a mudbath.

The arriving refugees were lined up by the Thai soldiers and marched into the camp, which was still little more than an empty rice paddy. Susan had expected health problems among the Cambodians, but the reality was worse

This Cambodian woman is probably one of the Khmer Rouge coming to Sa Kaeo Holding Center in October 1979. She is attempting to draw water from a UN water tank, but is apparently too weak to stand. The paper in her hand is probably a registration form. (Photographer unknown. Susan and Bill Lenderking collection)

than she had expected. The nurses inspected each of the refugees as they passed from the trucks to the camp and they sent any refugee who appeared to be seriously ill or malnourished to the improvised hospital tent. Very few aid personnel were as yet on the site. Susan recalls only a single doctor, probably Levi Roque, in Sa Kaeo that first day. The doctor improvised a hospital by stringing a wire from a bulldozer to a tent pole and draping canvas over the wire. It was a roof and afforded some protection from the rains, but that was all. Roque also strung a plastic tube between the bulldozer and a tent pole. This was to carry a glucose/saline solution to treat malnourished refugees. There were no beds in the makeshift hospital. Straw mats were laid out on the ground under the roof.

A *Time* reporter saw a group of Khmer Rouge soldiers mixed in with the refugees. They were nearly as bad off as the non-combatants. "They did not look like human beings ... but rather like wild animals, completely brutalized.

They slept huddled side by side like beasts in a cage. They seldom spoke and kept their eyes cast downward. They seemed so pathetic that it was almost possible to forget the abominable cruelties they had committed."[15]

Two thousand sick and dying refugees were brought to the hospital in the first few days of Sa Kaeo. Several hundred other refugees probably died without ever reaching the hospital, usually of exposure and hypothermia, aggravated by malnutrition, during nights spent on the sodden, monsoon-soaked ground. Some women resisted taking their babies to the hospital. Ann speculated that they had already given up hope that the children would survive and their priority was to search for husbands and family members. In many cases the mothers were correct. Many women begged for infant formula to bottle-feed their babies. They were convinced that the Western-made formula would save their babies. The volunteers and interpreters tried to persuade them to breast-feed. Lack of clean water meant that bottle-feeding of babies was a last resort. Quickly, programs began for supplemental feeding to lactating mothers.

In Susan Lenderking's opinion, Levi Roque, the Filipino doctor, was the hero of those first few days at Sa Kaeo. He went from patient to patient and wrote his instructions with a marking pen on their chests—men, women, and children alike. There were no paper or medical files. Patients were hooked up to IVs if they were unable to eat or drink. At that time in the U.S., nurses were not allowed to begin intravenous therapy, but Ann soon found herself doing it for dozens of patients. Susan, who had no medical training whatsoever, was taught to give injections. Her instructions were to "plump up" the flesh before giving the injection, but often she could find no part of the body that had a bit of flesh to plump up. Journalists and photographers were persuaded to carry buckets of electrolyte fluid from patient to patient and hold a tin cupful to their lips. Many of the patients were beyond drinking on their own. A few of the journalists were also prevailed upon to donate blood.

For the first time in her life, Susan was present as people breathed their last. She recalled the terrible stillness of the dead when the almost imperceptible rise and fall of their chests ceased altogether and a death rattle sounded in their throats. In the morning, men with wheelbarrows came and piled bodies on the wheelbarrow and took them away for disposal at a nearby temple. At the same time as patients were dying in the hospital tent, came the sound of babies being born in a nearby tent. Ann Rosenblatt tied off the umbilical cord of one baby with a string she plucked from where it was holding up an IV line.

In the midst of the chaos of the first few days of Sa Kaeo the tail end of the monsoon struck with renewed fury and the camp became an ocean of mud. Susan Lenderking estimated that the deaths amounted to 100 a day in those first few days when nobody was counting. A tally of the dead was begun on October 28 and during the next ten days, after more medical personnel had arrived, an average of 28 per day died. That translates into a death rate of about

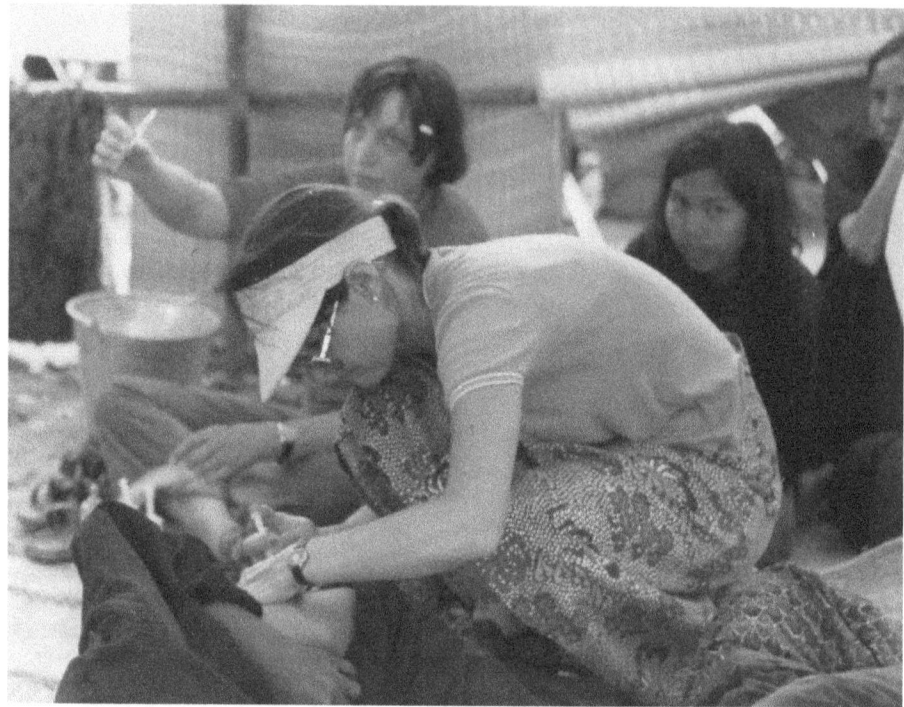

Susan Lenderking gives an injection to a Cambodian refugee at Sa Kaeo. Susan, who had no previous medical training or experience, had trouble finding enough flesh on the emaciated refugees to insert a needle. (Susan Lenderking)

one person per 1,000 persons per day, which, if continued, would mean that about 37 percent of the people would die within one year.[16] And, the official count of deaths probably missed many who never got to the hospital. A *Time* reporter saw four dead bodies in Sa Kaeo during a one hour visit. One of them was lying in the main track through the camp, a blanket over it, nobody paying any attention. Another body was of a woman in rigor mortis whose husband had covered her with a yellow cloth.[17]

A Thai employee of UNHCR, Supawan, later Supawan Green, was sent to Sa Kaeo in those early days to work with unaccompanied minor children. Arriving at the camp amidst the chaos, she couldn't find the Children's Center where she was supposed to work. So, she began working at a feeding tent where an organization called Food for the Hungry was distributing milk to the refugees. She worked in an open tent where two big stoves boiled milk in giant pots. Then, they put the pots of boiled milk on a truck and drove around the camp giving it out to any refugees who could find a container — tin cans, plastic bags, and dirty pots served. As many Asians are lactose intolerant, milk was a poor choice of food for the refugees, probably contributing to the rampant diarrhea in the camp. Much of the food contributed by well-meaning people in refugee crises is inappropriate or unusable.

Supawan eventually found the Children's Center where 300 unaccompanied minors ranging from one day to 15 years old were housed and cared for. "There were no smiles: Every little face showed fear, sadness, sorrow, depression, confusion, insecurity and looked totally lost."[18] Many of the children were beyond saving. Supawan's job was to find surviving parents or other relatives to look after the children. Some of the children had been left at the Children's Center by their parents who thought the child had a better chance to survive as an orphan than with the family.

Supawan carried the body of one deceased child to the makeshift morgue in a big blue UNHCR tent. Inside the tent was a neat stack of bodies ten bodies wide and five feet high. "The bodies were all wrapped up and in different sizes. I could see hair and feet stick out from some loose ends. Some feet were tied with strings attached to labels."[19]

Within a few days the medical situation and living conditions for the refugees became better. Doctors and nurses arrived from VOLAGs in Bangkok and abroad and the number of medical personnel increased to as many as 60 doctors and 170 nurses and aides.[20] As the late-arriving organizations and professionals took over they dismissed the American Embassy and other volunteers and their work.[21] But for a few days at Sa Kaeo, a crew of unpaid amateurs held the place together and saved countless lives. Susan went home to tend to her baby; Ann stayed on as an employee. Sa Kaeo improved rapidly, by the standards of those who had been there at the beginning.

With the plight of the refugees in Sa Kaeo spread all over the newspapers and TV came a flood of visitors: congressmen, VIPs, and even a president's wife, Rosalynn Carter. Lionel and his associates, especially John Crowley, sold the program to the visitors. It was a challenge: "Lionel is very disorganized, but somehow it doesn't matter. In the end he is extraordinarily effective," said a colleague.[22] But, conditions were still so bad that when Rosalynn Carter visited Sa Kaeo in mid–November it hardly seemed that the situation had improved. She found a sea of starving refugees lying on the ground on mats or dirty blankets or rags or seeking shelter under the improvised tents of the ubiquitous blue plastic sheets passed out by the UN. They were "all bones and no flesh; and others with cracked feet and swollen as though to burst. All with serious diseases, such as malaria, dysentery, and tuberculosis. All wretching, feverish, and silent." Some were too weak to even respond to her when she spoke to them. The children were the worst. One boy, four months old, weighed four pounds. A starving little girl held her dying sister in her arms.

Carter's visit had immediate benefits for the refugee program. A doctor told her that only a few children in the camp between one and five years old survived—they died during that crucial period after being weaned from the breast until they could fend in some fashion for themselves. The statistics bear

Rosalynn Carter visits Sa Kaeo. Lionel Rosenblatt is (center, white shirt) beside Mrs. Carter (white skirt). Richard Holbrooke (in suit, wearing glasses) is at left center. Visitors to refugee camps usually draw a crowd. (Lionel Rosenblatt collection)

out his statement. Only 2,700 of almost 32,000 refugees in Sa Keo were children under the age of five. In normal circumstances in Cambodia, that would be about one half the expected number of children of those ages. And more people were dying outside the hospital than inside it. The emergency measures taken in the hospital saved them for the moment, but, weakened, they often soon died of exposure or disease.[23]

The U.S. immediately sent 45 metric tons of corn/soya milk—which in the rushed acronym-rich world of disaster relief was known as CSM—to Sa Kaeo for supplementary feeding of children. Large boiling pots of the nutritious gruel—better than the milk that had been used in the beginning—became a fixture in the camps. After cooking, the CSM was ladled out into cups for children over six months old. A large cup of about ten ounces was the normal ration for children and it provided more than 300 calories plus abundant protein and fat.[24] Forty-five tons was enough to provide supplementary feeding for 6,000 children for a month—and this first shipment was quickly followed by others. The U.S. also sent a plane from Washington, D.C., with a water purification unit, medical personnel, tents, and rolls of the ubiquitous plastic sheeting for emergency shelter. The U.S. also came up with a budget for the Cambodian relief program of $105 million for the first year.[25] It would end up costing much more than that.

The tardiness of UN relief agencies arriving in Sa Kaeo was noted by many, including Ambassador Abramowitz and Lionel Rosenblatt. They agreed that, while Mark Malloch Brown's performance had been outstanding, UNHCR had been poorly prepared to take care of the refugees. A relief worker wrote to UNHCR, "I have not seen, in many years ... of experience, a situation as humanly degrading as exists in Sa Kaeo. There isn't the remotest vestige of privacy as men, women, and children defecate in full view of and within feet of the camp living areas."[26] UNICEF and ICRC also came in for criticism, the suspicion being that they feared jeopardizing their relationships with the new Cambodian government if they played an active and visible role.[27] Never reticent, Lionel's office drew up a list of 11 shortcomings of the ICRC's medical program at Sa Kaeo. These included the failure to bring medical teams from Geneva and to establish a field hospital until nearly two weeks after the refugees arrived at the camp.[28]

The American Embassy volunteers, mostly wives without medical training, were crucial in saving hundreds of lives in Sa Kaeo in those first few chaotic days. For Sheppie Abramowitz the experience at Sa Kaeo was no one-time experience. On her return to Bangkok, she appropriated a corner of Lionel's office, set up a desk, and worked as hard as any paid employee. Visitors were shocked to see the American ambassador's wife toiling away in the cluttered corner of a shabby office.[29]

As the staff of medical personnel increased and the care given refugees improved, the camp began experiencing the problems always confronted in humanitarian emergencies. Doctors and nurses came from a dozen countries and miscommunication was frequent. Western-trained doctors and nurses usually lacked experience in situations like Sa Kaeo. Many had never treated—or even seen—malaria and starvation. Hans Nothdurft described the situation, "Almost all the teams had difficulty in establishing appropriate priorities and in relating to the needs for, and levels of, medical care appropriate for a refugee situation. They had to deal with an inherent reluctance 'to help many people a little rather than a few people a lot.' The repeated calls for x-ray facilities, for more laboratory support, and the preference for expensive drug regimens reflect medical and cultural values of developed countries."[30]

Few of the newly-arrived relief workers were attuned to local sensitivities. The poor Thai farmers who looked across the barbed wire at the refugees had little access to medical care and none at all to sophisticated Western-style care. The Thai government was insistent that the appearance the refugees were being treated better than their own people be avoided. The "welfare cadillac" syndrome operates in all countries; an appearance that a person fares better with the support of charity than he does through the sweat of his labor can have devastating consequences on the public acceptance of social programs, refugees, and immigrants.

In the frantic haste to save Cambodian lives it was only slowly that the relief workers realized that the people they were aiding in Sa Kaeo were Khmer Rouge, their supporters, and people under their control. That made many of them uneasy.

* * *

The disadvantages of Sa Kaeo—its small size, tendency to flood, and the rising tide of starving Cambodians—led within a month to finding an alternative for newer arrivals. A new and larger camp was needed and in early November, Ambassador Morton Abramowitz and the Thai foreign minister personally went to the border and picked out a site for the new camp.[31] Khao I Dang, a few miles north of Aranyaprathet and about six miles from the Cambodian border, was opened on November 21, having been built in only four days in another fast job by UNHCR's Mark Malloch Brown. Mark would become known as the mayor of Khao I Dang. The principal problem was a shortage of water, which had to be brought in by tank truck from miles away at a high cost.[32] But even with water shortages, in the first ten weeks of its operation, the refugee population at Khao I Dang zoomed to 112,000 and at its peak it reached 140,000 people.[33] The refugees there had a different character than those at Sa Kaeo who were either Khmer Rouge or under the control of the Khmer Rouge. The inmates at Khao I Dang were mostly people fleeing from the Khmer Rouge or fighting against them, belonging to the Khmer Serei—a loosely-organized anticommunist coalition. Many charitable organizations were more enthusiastic about helping the Khmer Serei or any other group other than the Khmer Rouge.

The war along the border between the KR and other resistance groups and the Vietnamese invaders of Cambodia was brutal. A Red Cross representative once told the Khmer Rouge that his job was to visit prisoners of war and investigate their complaints that they were not being treated in accordance with the Geneva Convention. A KR representative responded that "no Vietnamese soldier has yet complained after we cut off his head."[34]

15. Sa Kaeo and Khao I Dang Holding Centers

Ambassador Morton Abramowitz (left) and Lionel Rosenblatt (second from left) visit a refugee camp on the Cambodian border. On the right are two unidentified refugee workers. (Lionel Rosenblatt collection)

Khao I Dang would later come to be regarded as a luxury refugee camp, the "last haven of the Phnom Penh bourgeoisie"[35] and a "Refugee Hilton."[36] It housed mostly middle-class, educated Cambodians who had survived the Khmer Rouge; its political leanings were anti-communist. After years of pretending to be uneducated, of trying to blend into the peasant population of Cambodia, the educated Cambodians slowly came out of their shells and emerged as leaders, teachers, and doctors. These were people aid workers could empathize with. Cambodian refugees had finally penetrated the world's consciousness and a stream of charity workers, journalists, job-seekers, missionaries, and disaster junkies descended upon the camp. Medical personnel always seem to be the most essential people early in the crisis and the most numerous as the crisis wears on. Soon, the prevailing view among the refugee workers became "We're up to here in fucking medical teams."[37] The refugees were poked, prodded, measured, interviewed, photographed, and suffered all manner of indignities to satisfy the well-meaning doctors, scientists, and professors who had a research project to complete. That is the way of humanitarian crises: too little too late, followed by too much. Khao I Dang and Sa Kaeo holding centers would eventually have, in addition to 150,000 refugees, hundreds of workers from charitable and international organizations and the Thai Red Cross.[38]

In another of its sudden policy shifts, the Thai government in early 1980 announced the end of its "open door" policy.[39] It would no longer facilitate the entry of Cambodians into Thailand. Most Cambodians would remain on the border. One reason cited for the change in policy was the poor international response to Thailand's request for assistance for the refugees. That was an excuse; the outpouring of aid had been substantial. A second was that life in Sa Kaeo and Khao I Daeng was dangerous. "Murders, rapes, armed robberies and other crimes frequently occurred at Khao I Dang while ... Sa Kaeo was completely controlled by the Khmer Rouge, who ran their own 'courts,' prevented the refugees from holding religious services and tried to compel them to re-enter Cambodia and join the Khmer Rouge." The Thai government set up a special military unit to police the camps.[40]

Not long after the Thai government closed the border to more entrants, Mark Malloch Brown was traveling near the border in a jeep when he saw a squad of Thai soldiers, bayonets fixed, forcing a group of recently-arrived Cambodians to return from whence they came. Mark jumped out of his jeep, looked over the refugees and spotted an emaciated young girl holding a tiny baby wrapped up in a red cloth. "I'm taking this woman and baby with me," he said. "They'll die if you make them go back." The Thai soldiers reluctantly assented. He took them to the hospital at Khao I Dang and after weeks of medical care both survived.

This story has a happy ending. Ever since she had adopted two Cambodian children in 1975, Sue Morton, the founder of Refugees International, had made innumerable trips to the border searching for surviving relatives of the two children she had adopted. The girl rescued by Mark turned out to be the sister of her adopted son. Both had survived the Khmer Rouge. Most of their other family members were dead. Family connections were often made as a result of chance.[41] JVA workers such as Charlene Day, Berta Romero, and Judy Kocher made these unlikely family reunions possible.

Other than a skeleton force of emergency medical personnel, the relief workers were not allowed by the Thai government to remain in either Sa Kaeo or Khao I Dang overnight. They all lived in Aranyaprathet and were driven to the camp at eight o'clock every morning and at five in the afternoon they were driven back to Aran.[42] They customarily worked ten days on and then a day off. The ban on their presence in the camps after dark was ostensibly for their safety, but it also prevented them from seeing what happened after dark. All the Thai camps were closed. Refugees were unable to leave without permission from the armed soldiers surrounding the camps. Work parties of refugees were organized outside the camps, but armed guards accompanied them.

* * *

15. Sa Kaeo and Khao I Dang Holding Centers

The humanitarian situation at Sa Kaeo, Khao I Dang, and the much smaller holding center at Kamput, was quickly stabilized at a low level of misery—the death rate at Sa Kaeo had dropped by more than 90 percent six weeks after the camp had opened. The pressing humanitarian problems were solved in a few weeks; access to the camps was easy from Bangkok; resources were adequate; and workers flooded in from all over the world. Within a short time more than 100 relief organizations were working in the camps and on the border.[43]

The town of Aranyaprathet became the center of the relief effort. A writer described Aran as a mixture of Amarillo, Texas, and Saigon before the fall. The refugee workers hung out at a restaurant called Prols. They wore sunglasses and black hats, listened to Simon and Garfunkel, ate hamburgers and drank Singha beer. Many of them had research grants to study some facet of the Cambodian refugee crisis; others were the job-seekers and disaster junkies who show up at every humanitarian crisis. It is the norm in humanitarian emergencies for resources to fluctuate between critically scarce to overly abundant.

A different type of human being also frequented the Cambodian border those days and the bars of Aranyaprathet: the pot hunters. A few Cambodians scoured the ruins of Angkor and other sites of Cambodian civilization and brought the pots, statues, and murals to the border to sell. Rumors were rife that some of the richest men and the most famous museums in the world had agents on the border to buy antiquities—of which those from the ninth and tenth centuries were most desired.[44]

* * *

The refugees at Sa Kaeo reunited the old controversy between UNHCR and the United States about repatriation versus resettlement of refugees. UNHCR argued that voluntary repatriation of the Cambodians was now feasible with the majority of the country under the control of the Vietnamese army and the Vietnamese-installed government. The Khmer Rouge leaders at Sa Kaeo agreed. They wanted their fighters back in Cambodia to combat the Vietnamese. The Thai also agreed; they wanted to be rid of the refugees, and they were interested in strengthening the resistance to the Vietnamese. Martin Barber made the persuasive argument that what remained of the Cambodian middle and educated classes was in the refugee camps, especially Khao I Dang. Taking those skilled people for resettlement abroad would make Cambodia's survival more difficult and would dim its future prospects for success as a country.[45]

The other side of the argument was enunciated by Rosenblatt. "Give the refugees the choice," he said, "between being resettled or returning to their home country—or remaining for the time being in refugee camps." The refugees were not pawns whose future should be determined by international civil servants or governments. Moreover, Rosenblatt feared that repatriation would be seized upon as a viable alternative to refugee resettlement and the resettlement program would lose the support of the U.S. and other governments.[46] ICRC and UNICEF opposed the repatriation effort, questioning whether the refugees could go home safely.

The test between the two points of views came at Sa Kaeo in June 1980. UNHCR, the Embassy, and the Thai government set up a voluntary repatriation program, interviewing refugees with the aim of determining who wished to return to Cambodia and who did not. However, it was difficult to ascertain an individual's true desires because Khmer Rouge operatives hung around the tents where the interviews took place and chanted a ditty, "If you decide to stay at Sa Kaeo, you'll end up two feet under the ground." Another KR tactic was to infiltrate interpreters into the refugee interviews to mistranslate what the refugee was saying and ensure that Thai officials always believed that the refugee had said he wished to repatriate. Lionel and John Crowley observed the process to try to guarantee that the decisions of the refugees were not coerced or misinterpreted by the Khmer Rouge.[47]

But the Khmer Rouge did not have an uncontested rein in the internal politics at Sa Kaeo. A Buddhist group — made up of former KR operatives — sprang up, built a makeshift temple, a *Wat*, in the camp, and defied the Khmer Rouge. The Buddhists resisted repatriation and on June 13 published a newsletter. "No one has to go," they said. "UNHCR, the Buddhist Wat, and others are prepared to help anyone who is put under pressure to go [back to Cambodia]." The Buddhists declared the Wat a sanctuary for people needing protection from the KR.[48]

Thai authorities were infuriated at this challenge to their carefully orchestrated plan to rid themselves of many thousands of Cambodian refugees. The night before the repatriation was to take place they kidnapped four of the leaders at the Wat and spirited them away, across the Cambodian border. This was to break the back of the resistance to the repatriation. Mark Malloch Brown rode to the rescue, his trusty steed a battered Toyota Corolla. He rushed to the border, flourished his UNHCR credentials, and demanded to know where the kidnapped Buddhists had been taken. He found out they were in a temple just across the border in Cambodia and drove there, but he got stuck in the mud and was delayed. He finally collected the Buddhists and rushed back to Sa Kaeo with them, arriving just when the repatriates were to climb on the buses to be taken back to Cambodia. Lionel was waiting for him and together they paraded the rescued Buddhists before the inhabitants of the camp. The reappearance of the Buddhists was a moral boost and an alternative to KR rule for the Cambodians in the camp who did not wish to return to Cambodia.

The midnight ride of Mark Malloch Brown, the oversight by Rosenblatt and Crowley, and the opposition of the Buddhists to the Khmer Rouge prevented thousands of Cambodians from being repatriated against their will to Cambodia. The total number of repatriates from Sa Kaeo between June 17 and 26, 1980, was 7,464, less than one third the population of the camp. From Khao

15. Sa Kaeo and Khao I Dang Holding Centers

I Dang during the same period only 1,626 chose to repatriate out of a population of about 140,000. At least 1,500 of the repatriates were Khmer rouge soldiers or die-hard cadres.[49]

Thus, UNHCR and the Thai government's hope for large "voluntary" repatriations of Cambodian refugees proved false — especially since most of those going back were Khmer Rouge and their families and supporters. For many years into the future the choices available to Cambodian refugees in the holding centers in Thailand was resettlement abroad or continued stagnation in the centers. A few Cambodians chose to return home from Thailand, but not until 1993 would Khao I Dang, the largest camp for Cambodian refugees in Thailand, be closed and the Cambodian refugee crisis officially come to an end.

16

THE LAND BRIDGE AND CAMBODIAN FAMINE

Sa Kaeo and Khao I Dang holding centers in Thailand housed 150,000 Cambodian refugees. Far more Cambodians rushed to a narrow strip of borderland between Thailand and Cambodia. Thai police and military prevented their entry into Thailand and the refugees at the border congregated into informal camps. The number lurking near the border or attempting to cross reached, according to a UN estimate, 750,000 by the end of 1979. About 400,000 of these were in the border camps.[1] It was a fluctuating population as people came and went from the interior of Cambodia. Estimates of numbers were no more than guesses. The humanitarian situation in the holding centers stabilized, but reaching the Cambodians in the border camps was more difficult and became controversial.

As described by British relief worker Robert Ashe, the border camps appeared almost overnight for three reasons. First, in order to trade in the black market; second, to escape harassment by the Vietnamese and/or to seek resettlement in a third country; and, third, to search for food.[2]

Cambodians controlled by the Khmer Rouge were grouped mainly in two camps just inside Cambodia about 20 miles south of Aranyaprathet. The camps, named after nearby Thai villages, were Nong Pru and Tap Prik, with 10,000 residents each in early 1980. Twenty to 40 miles north of Aran were four large camps and four or more smaller camps ruled by anti-communist Khmer Serei and pro–Sihanouk resistance movements. The most northerly of the large border camps was near the Thai village of Ban Sangae. The camp had about 30,000 more or less permanent residents, along with tens of thousands of temporary visitors coming to get rice distributed by relief agencies. Moving south was Camp 007 or Nong Samet, near the Thai village of the same name, which had between 60,000 and 200,000 residents. Next, was camp 204 near Mak Mun of similar size, "a settlement in which squalor was widespread, sanitation non-existent, and a sense of human degradation pervasive."[3] A warlord and black marketer named Van Saren ran the camp for his own benefit, confiscating and

16. The Land Bridge and Cambodian Famine

Cambodian border camp. Squalid encampments of refugees sprung up on the Thai/Cambodian border in late 1979. Many of these people returned to their homes in 1980 with a sack or two of rice to enable them to survive until the next rice crop. (Lionel Rosenblatt collection)

selling rice intended for free distribution. Next to the south was Nong Chang, the most accessible of the camps. Nong Chang had about 13,000 more or less permanent residents, but an estimated 6,000 visitors per day came to haul away rice to their families and villages inside Cambodia.[4]

The fears by some that the Cambodians had lost their entrepreneurial spirit during the Khmer Rouge years were quickly dispelled. Many of the Cambodians had buried gold with the coming of the Khmer Rouge. Now, recovering their gold, or finding something else to sell, they came to the border in search of consumer goods. Open-air markets sprang up in the camps and the Thai villages near the border to exchange merchandise and food for Cambodian gold. The markets brought in an estimated one half million dollars per day, sufficient to attract a motley crowd of speculators and crooks.[5]

In Nong Chan, Ashe ran the cross-border feeding program called the Land Bridge. He gained the cooperation of the camp's leader, Kong Sileah, a supporter of Prince Sihanouk. On December 12, 1979, Kong Sileah and Ashe initiated the food distribution program for a few hundred Cambodians who had come to the border in search of food. The Land Bridge had the dual objective

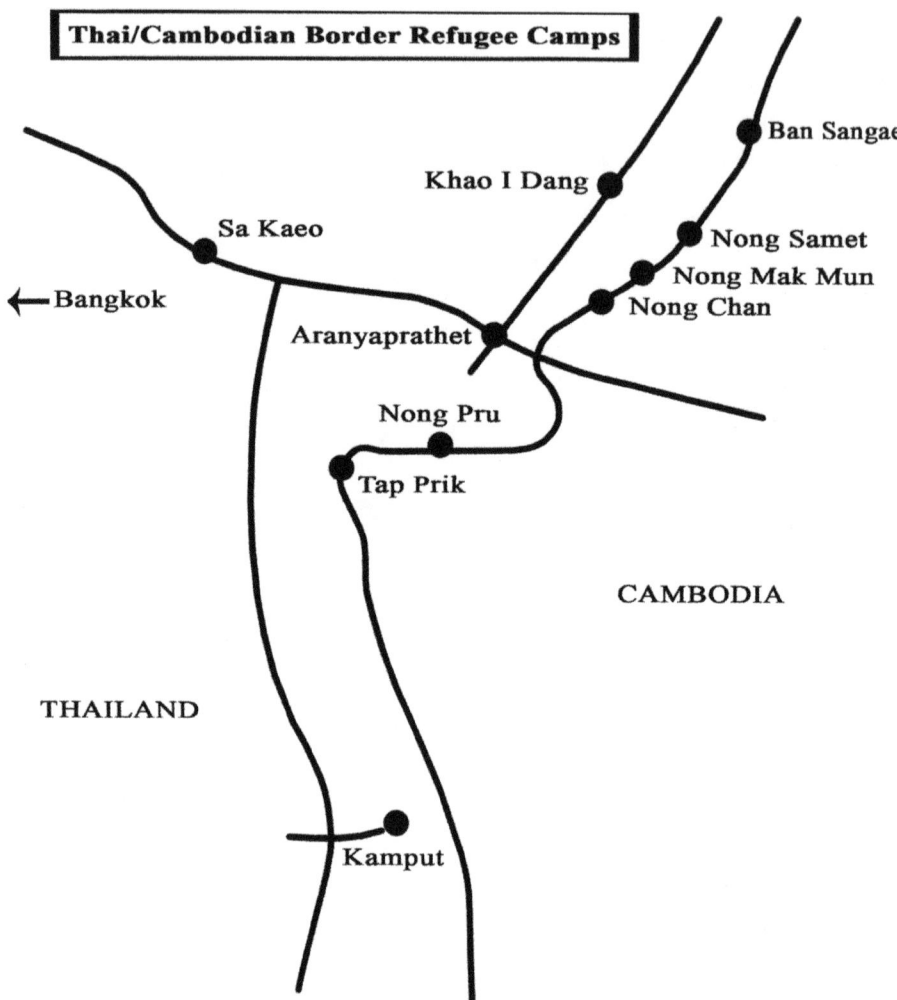

Map adapted from "Emergency Refugee Health Care," US HHS 4, by Kathryn Kelly-Hensley.

of giving food directly to Cambodians while undercutting the black market in food, especially that of Van Saren in Mak Mun. Van Saren did not let the threat to his livelihood go unchallenged. On December 30, the price of black market rice falling, his soldiers attacked Nong Chang and closed down the Land Bridge for a few days.

The cross-border aid program mushroomed and in May 1980, it was precisely calculated that 106,210 people had come to the border for food in one week and that the Land Bridge food operations were feeding 902,370 people.[6]

16. The Land Bridge and Cambodian Famine

The Land Bridge at the Cambodian Border, spring 1980. Bags of rice are stacked up to distribute to Cambodians who came to the border to pick up rice and take it home with them. The Land Bridge helped prevent both a famine in Cambodia and an influx of refugees into Thailand. (Lionel Rosenblatt collection)

The Land Bridge channeled 44,000 tons of food and 23,000 tons of rice seed into Cambodia between December 1979 and September 1980.[7] That was enough to put 100 pounds of rice and 50 pounds of seed into the hands of each of one million people during those months— about one-third of the total food needed by those million people to survive and enough seed for each of them to sow more than one acre and produce twenty-fold of rice — to put it in biblical terms.[8] Kurt Furrer, Yvette Pierpaoli's business partner, was a key supplier of rice for the Land Bridge, but Kurt showed a reluctance to cooperate that puzzled other participants at the time.[9] The reasons for his reluctance and hesitation would later become clear.

U.S. Ambassador Abramowitz visited three border camps in early 1980. "At Nong Chan ... there are now some 7,000 to 10,000 refugees, only 900 of whom permanently live there. The remainder are all transients, drawn by word of mouth to the border for food over the last six days. The feeding operation is run by a remarkable Englishman, Robert Ashe, who makes sure each refugee gets 30 kilos of rice to take back.... The Cambodians have established a huge parking lot of bullock carts and bicycles.

"A less ordered and less equitable but similar scene goes on at the two major border concentrations opposite Nong Samet and Mak Mun. Here refugees come both for food from international relief agencies and to partake of the more varied delights of the large private markets.... I talked to a number of bullock drivers and bicyclists. Some are taking back large amounts of food to families and others to sell."[10] People came, got their rice, went home, and returned again in a couple of months for another 30 kilos. After receiving rice, most people also got in line to receive rice seed to be planted with the onset of the monsoon in May or June.[11]

In response to the Cambodian crisis, Ambassador Abramowitz created the Kampuchean Emergency Group (KEG) headed by Lionel Rosenblatt. Lionel acquired, in addition to Mac Thompson, a second deputy: Lt. Col. Mike Eiland, a former Special Forces officer and Vietnam veteran. Eiland was broad gauged. He had a Master's degree in economics and had written his thesis on the unlikely subject of traditional agriculture in Southeast Asia.[12] Mike arrived in Bangkok just after Christmas 1979. He had an ear infection, fever, and chills and was exhausted after a long flight across the Pacific. Lionel met him at the airport at midnight, took him to a hotel, expressed profound sympathy for his delicate medical condition, and told him that a car would come by for him at 6:30 A.M. to take him to Aranyaprathet for his first visit to the border.[13] Eiland survived and eventually recovered — and came to appreciate Lionel's dedication to refugee work.

KEG established its headquarters in a large white house in Aranyaprathet. In keeping with the symbolism of KEG, Eiland named the headquarters the "Taphouse." A popular brothel two doors away attracted numbers of the many relief workers in Aran. KEG's personnel — American (especially Rich Ruebensall), Thai, and Cambodian — ceaselessly patrolled up and down the border, finding new and needy refugees, evaluating the security situation, solving problems, often dodging gunfire between Cambodian factions, and evaluating the effectiveness of aid now flowing in large quantities to the border.

KEG personnel avoided contact with the Khmer Rouge border camps. However, on one occasion, Mike, a journalist, and a high-level Defense Department official decided to visit the Khmer Rouge. The three concocted the story that they were East German diplomats and crossed the border and entered a KR camp. Greeted with formality and a guest book, they signed themselves in as Hans, Hansel, and Gretel and all went well until one of the KR soldiers exclaimed, "Wonderful! I studied medicine in East Germany. We can speak German." They each muttered a few words of broken German and kept silent the rest of the visit. As they were leaving they heard the KR medical student say, "They said they were Germans, but I think they were Americans."[14]

Even the critics of KEG agreed it had the most extensive and reliable intelligence about what was happening on both sides of the Cambodian border. That knowledge was parlayed into influence with aid donors and diplomacy in

16. The Land Bridge and Cambodian Famine

The Land Bridge. These Cambodians have shouldered 30-kilogram bags of rice to carry home with them. Many of them had walked for days to get to the border. (Lionel Rosenblatt collection)

Bangkok as Abramowitz and Rosenblatt nudged the Thai out of their more recalcitrant positions. The prominence of the Americans further ruffled the feathers of the UN agencies which saw their role of primacy in humanitarian aid usurped. The U.S. was also far and away the largest financial contributor to the humanitarian relief effort, supporting both the UN agencies and private charitable organizations.

To suspicious VOLAGs and international organizations, the American objective was to force the Vietnamese to withdraw from Cambodia and its humanitarian actions were to further that objective.[15] The presence of Vietnam War veterans in the KEG program aroused the suspicion of the UN and VOLAG aid community that the United States had ulterior motives in its assistance to Cambodians. U.S. objectives as outlined in a memo were (1) aiding and protecting Cambodian refugees; (2) supporting anti–Vietnamese resistance forces; and (3) promoting resettlement of Cambodians in the U.S.[16] KEG's role was only to achieve the first of those objectives—to aid and protect Cambodian refugees—but the second objective of the U.S. government—supporting anti–Vietnamese resistance forces—rubbed humanitarians the wrong way. Most of the Europeans involved, and many of the Americans, had fiercely opposed the U.S. war in Vietnam and had affection for Vietnam, which had now further endeared itself to them by overthrowing the Khmer Rouge. That some of them had defended the Khmer Rouge only a year or two earlier they readily forgot. Lionel's objective of promoting resettlement was also controversial for many organizations, especially UNHCR, which thought that a resettlement program would pull more Cambodians to Thailand and deplete the country's already critically short supply of trained and educated people.[17] Some relief workers even believed that the Land Bridge was a U.S. plot to draw Cambodian farmers off their land and bring them to the border to get them away from Vietnamese control.[18]

While KEG, on top of the food chain, was the common target for criticism, the fractious situation of the Cambodians near the border was duplicated by the behavior of the relief organizations. "By early 1980," said Charles Twining of the State Department, "it was all turf battles." The alphabet soup of international agencies—UNHCR, UNICEF, WFP, and ICRC—fought for their interests and the private charitable organizations competed for a share of the projects, programs, and money.[19]

The poor relationships among the organizations working on the Cambodian border prompted Abramowitz to express despair. Rosenblatt sent him a memorandum on February 8, 1980, promising to try to heal some of the open wounds. "We admittedly have rubbed raw spots on some of the people we try to energize ... we may want to draw back somewhat from our day-to-day nagging."

Lionel, however, was unyielding on using U.S. leverage on the aid organizations to ensure that Cambodians got the food they needed to survive. "We will lower our expectations and our decibel output. But ... in a profound way our involvement has been responsible for the breathing spell now being given the Cambodians, and we cannot afford to turn our backs because the relief effort is buffeted about from various quarters.... We can step back a bit, but we cannot disengage."[20] In other words, Lionel's priority would remain the care, feeding, and survival of the refugees—not good relations with prickly, turf-conscious international aid agencies. Lionel now spent much of his time in Bangkok, he and Abramowitz continually prodding and persuading the Thai to support, or at least not obstruct, the aid effort along the border. His wife, Ann, continued working in the refugee camps.

By a strange turn of events, the United States now seemed to be on the side of the Khmer Rouge in its struggle against the Vietnamese invaders and the Vietnamese-installed government in Phnom Penh. In what has been called a "Faustian pact," the U.S., China, and most Western countries refused to recognize the new government of Cambodia and voted to maintain the Khmer Rouge as the legitimate representative of Cambodia in the UN.[21] China was infuriated that its Khmer Rouge acolytes had been overthrown; America protected its relationship with China and joined the non-communist Southeast

16. The Land Bridge and Cambodian Famine

Asian countries in the objective of ensuring that the power and influence of Vietnam did not spread outside the borders of the old Indochina. As one State Department official said, "The U.S was both revolted from a humanitarian standpoint by the Khmer Rouge and revolted from a political standpoint by the Vietnamese."[22] Humanitarian revulsion was outweighed by political revulsion.

Cambodian opinion was best expressed, as usual, by Prince Norodom Sihanouk, who did so in a stinging letter to the prime minister of Vietnam. "Your government tried to justify the invasion of Cambodia by altruistic and humanitarian claims, which would be noble if they were serious." But Vietnam had instead installed in Phnom Penh "a little team of communist Khmers at its service of which, in an authoritative manner, it made the 'government' of Popular Kampuchea. It is with this 'government' which came in the baggage of its army, controlled at every level by Vietnamese civil and military authorities and with[out] a popular base of any kind."[23]

Lionel Rosenblatt got similar views in a conversation with a Cambodian refugee. "Who do you want?" Lionel asked. "Do you want Pol Pot back?"

"Heavens no," was the response.

"Do you want to continue with Heng Samrin?"

"Oh, no, he brings the Vietnamese." Fear and hatred of the Vietnamese is a given in Cambodia.

"What do you want?" Lionel asked.

"Norodom Sihanouk," was the reply. The former king, prince, and prime minister was still the only man who could command the loyalty and affection of most Cambodians.[24] Lionel's personal opinion, expressed half in jest, was that the Vietnamese should get the Nobel Peace Prize for ousting the Khmer Rouge.[25] His energy, enthusiasm, and commitment won over many of those who suspected he was a CIA agent in disguise.[26] When was it exactly that he had time to be a spy?

* * *

Among many problems with weather, bad roads, thieving warlords, interagency disputes, and often-uncooperative Thai authorities, the worst problem for relief workers on the border was security. "At times workers had to enter the trenches when there was small-arms fire overhead."[27] Moreover, when the aid workers evacuated the area, they left food behind which fell into the hands of the strongest faction on the scene. Most of the time the conflict was between competing rebel factions, united only in opposition to the Vietnamese. However, sometimes the Vietnamese army also attacked the border camps. On June 23, 1980, the Vietnamese attacked and overran the border camps at Mak Mun and Nong Chan and engaged the Thai army inside Thailand. The Vietnamese arrested Robert Ashe and held him briefly for questioning.[28] The ensuing battles left several hundred people dead, including Thai and Vietnamese soldiers and Cambodian refugees and closed down the food distribution program to

The Land Bridge. Bullock carts filled with rice head home to the interior of Cambodia while others arrive to collect rice and rice seed. (Lionel Rosenblatt collection)

the border camps. The Vietnamese withdrew after several days to their former positions five miles inside Cambodia.

The primary reason for the Vietnamese attack was the repatriation by UNHCR of Khmer Rouge fighters, described in the previous chapter.[29] The Vietnamese tolerated the border camps and the food flowing across the border into Cambodia. They tolerated Cambodians going to the border to get food and other goods to return to their homes inside Cambodia. But they would not tolerate military operations launched against them from inside Thailand nor the repatriation of any sizeable numbers of their chief enemy, the Khmer Rouge.

The border incursion by Vietnam had enormous consequences. ICRC and UNICEF withdrew from the border feeding operation. The reasons they gave were (1) the border operation's high profile was provocative to the Vietnamese and the Cambodian government; (2) it promoted black market trade in food and other items; and (3) it strengthened the opposition to the Vietnamese occupation, especially from the Khmer Rouge. Scholar Court Robinson observed that, except for the second point, the United States wanted the border operation to continue for precisely the same reasons.[30] UNICEF later resumed food aid to the border camps; ICRC never did. The Vietnamese incursion, however, was the beginning of the end of the Land Bridge feeding program. It had accomplished its objectives in 1980 — to provide food and seed to one million

16. The Land Bridge and Cambodian Famine

Cambodians in western Cambodia. The Land Bridge continued to distribute rice and rice seed into 1981 but Cambodian rice production doubled in 1980 compared to 1979 and the need for large scale assistance across the border declined.[31]

* * *

The first two prongs of the aid effort to stave off mass starvation of Cambodians were the holding centers in Thailand and the Land Bridge. The third prong was aid inside Cambodia in cooperation with the Vietnamese-installed government of Heng Samrin. This was the preferred option of international agencies such as the International Red Cross (ICRC), UNICEF, and independent minded — often reflexively anti–American — VOLAGS such as the British OXFAM.

ICRC and UNICEF officials predicted famine in Cambodia after a tightly-controlled July 1979 visit to Phnom Penh. "2.25 Million Cambodians Are Said to Face Starvation," screamed a front-page *New York Times* article on August 8. The UN and Red Cross officials painted a dire picture of starving children and abandoned rice fields, although they had not actually seen much of either. An OXFAM representative visiting Cambodia in October talked publicly of "emaciated walking–Belsen–type skeletons."[32] OXFAM on October 10, 1979, at a Congressional hearing, had said, "It is indisputable that 3 to 4 million Cambodians face starvation."[33] Less well publicized was a visit about the same time of another OXFAM representative who found difficult conditions but concluded that it was possible that "the rural population of Cambodia could scrape through without food aid."[34] But nobody wanted to contradict publicly the conventional wisdom that starvation had descended — or would soon — descend on the Cambodian people.

The starving refugees at the border and at Sa Kaeo that September and October solidified in the minds of relief agencies and the public that the Cambodian people were in danger of extinction. On October 15, President Jimmy Carter said, "A human tragedy of horrifying proportions is unfolding in Cambodia, with millions of people facing illness or death from starvation."[35]

The holy grail of the relief worker is to be credited as the leading individual or organization in blunting a famine or humanitarian disaster. Thus, a natural tendency among competitive aid organizations was to carve out a piece of the disaster pie and cling to it fiercely, repelling all challengers. Just as on the border, there was much rivalry in the relief efforts inside Cambodia. With American dominance on the border, operations inside Cambodia seemed to independent-minded aid organizations a much more heroic alternative for preventing a holocaust of starvation. The competition to get to Phnom Penh and pioneer the relief effort there was enormous, but the negotiations with the Cambodian government were tiresome.

OXFAM readily accepted the Cambodian government's demand to channel all its assistance through the government in Phnom Penh.³⁶ ICRC looked quickly for excuses to terminate its role in the Land Bridge, and UNICEF kept a low and reluctant profile in its border operations. The aid agencies believed that participation in the Land Bridge jeopardized their desire to work inside Cambodia.

The holy grail of Cambodia was huge — one of the largest relief operations of all time. The agencies calculated that 30,000 tons of food imports per month were necessary — an enormous quantity that would be enough to meet the needs of the 2.25 million people in Cambodia judged to be in danger of starvation. Thus, the agencies proposed to bring into Cambodia as much rice per month as the Land Bridge would do in half a year — and the Land Bridge had access to good ports and highways in Thailand.

It was a daunting task and the aid partners — ICRC, UNICEF, OXFAM, and several other VOLAGs — had problems getting aid flowing to Cambodia. Initially, the government would not allow them to set up offices in Phnom Penh. That problem finally solved; they found that the Cambodian transportation infrastructure after four years of Khmer Rouge rule was degraded to the point of non-existence. The Cambodians in power in Phnom Penh were ex–Khmer Rouge, hardly progressive and enlightened individuals. The Vietnamese, now numbering 200,000 soldiers in the country, were looking over their shoulders. Both of them had profound suspicions of the West. "We should consider the intentions of the international organizations that are providing us assistance," said a Cambodian official. "Most of them are imperialists who seize everything.... The goal is to impose their influence on cadres and staff of the ministries and offices and on the people.... They make domestic contacts and deeply infiltrate various localities, factories, and ministerial offices. Some enter the houses of cadres and staff and give them equipment in order to recruit them.... Seeing this kind of opportunism, we shouldn't be afraid, but should be extremely vigilant and use the opportunity to request valuable assistance from them."³⁷

Delays in getting aid distributed in Cambodia caused consternation among relief agencies and consequent finger-pointing. Phnom Penh resisted the entreaties of the ICRC and UNICEF. OXFAM was untainted by any association with aid to the refugees on the border and pledged to channel all assistance through Phnom Penh.³⁸

OXFAM aid, however, was small compared to what the ICRC and UNICEF had to offer. A compromise was eventually reached on September 28, 1979, in which the Cambodian government agreed to ignore the border operations in Thailand and the international agencies reduced their usual standards for monitoring the distribution of aid, thus giving the government the authority to use imported food and other humanitarian aid in any way it wished.³⁹ The aid program was budgeted at $104 million for one year, including $52 million for food, of which the total imported would be 10,000 tons in October, 20,000 tons in

November, and 30,000 tons per month beginning in December.[40] To even come close to achieving this total would require enormous improvements in the degraded Cambodian infrastructure. The actual amount of food arriving in Cambodia never reached the goal of 30,000 tons per month — and, in fact, not that much was needed.

Daily aid flights from Bangkok began on October 13 and Western aid increased to 1,000 tons per day by December 1, mostly through the port of Kampong Som, now Sihanoukville. However, the government strictly limited the numbers of aid workers in Phnom Penh. A program the size contemplated needed hundreds, but only 60 aid workers— six from American NGOs—were allowed in the country. They were all required to live in two hotels and none were allowed to operate motor vehicles. There were no telephone or telegraph connections with the outside world. An official guide monitored all conversations. All trips outside Phnom Penh required permission and it was difficult to get. Doctors and nurses sent in by OXFAM and other organizations were not allowed to practice medicine.[41] What the relief workers found was that the Vietnamese were firmly in control of Cambodia and would allow no competition for power from either Cambodians or foreigners whatever their expertise or their resources. Their motto might have been "better red than expert."[42]

With the increased flow of food to Cambodia came also logistical problems. Only a single locomotive operated on the railroad from Kampong Som to Phnom Penh. The government had only a limited number of vehicles. On December 7, 1979, UNICEF said that while the people of Phnom Penh were receiving food, less than 10 percent of that intended for the countryside was being delivered. The bulk of the aid was being stored in now-bulging warehouses. The World Food Program decreased goals for food deliveries from 30,000 tons per month to 13,000 tons until deliveries could catch up with arrivals.[43]

The Vietnamese proved again to be their own worst enemy. They deserved plaudits for overthrowing the Khmer Rouge and a forthcoming attitude toward the relief effort, now headline news around the world, regained for them some of the positive image they had lost with the outflow of the boat people. Instead, they were vilified for their inefficiency or outright indifference to distributing aid. Aid workers in Phnom Penh, however, had to be wary of criticizing the Cambodian government for fear of being expelled, so they blamed the failings of the United States and the Western countries.[44] Public criticism, they believed, especially by the United States, caused the Phnom Penh government to be more suspicious of foreigners and therefore made their job of distributing aid more difficult.

* * *

At the same time the Cambodian government was urgently appealing for aid it was also issuing contrary statements. Contradicting their own prediction of a famine, a Vietnamese official said, "This so-called famine is a trap, a Chinese plot ... the West is playing it up to supply food and ammunition to the Pol Pot forces."[45] The specter of immediate famine in Cambodia began to fade in December 1979, while aid efforts on the border and inside the country were just beginning. An OXFAM representative visiting Cambodia said, "I saw no evidence of famine, starvation, or serious hunger. In fact I found it hard to believe that there had ever been famine or starvation on a massive scale in the parts of Cambodia that I visited." The aid agencies began to modify their fundraising literature subtly to put more emphasis on the long-term development needs of Cambodia. But "the fundraising machinery was unstoppable" as the reality of famine in Cambodia was now imprinted on the public's mind.[46]

In evaluating why the aid program inside Cambodia was so difficult to implement, *The Economist* cited three theories. First, was that the Vietnamese and their Cambodian clients were trying, but simply not capable of distributing food in a timely and efficient manner. Second, was that the Vietnamese deliberately blocked the distribution of food to reduce any possible resistance to their rule by the Cambodian populace. This theory was bolstered by the fact that it seemed that there were abundant military vehicles in Cambodia to undertake food distribution, but they were not being used for that purpose. The third theory was that the Vietnamese were stockpiling food, anticipating a shortage later in 1980. With 20 percent of the Cambodian population either in Thailand or being fed from Thailand and a quantity of Russian grain on hand, the Vietnamese may have exaggerated the gravity of the situation to prepare for a worsening food situation in the future. *The Economist* pointed out that the three theories were not mutually exclusive and that some truth might be found in each of them.[47]

* * *

The Cambodian relief effort re-ignited the passions of the Vietnam War with a war of words between the American government, UN agencies, and charitable organizations about each other's policies, intentions, and character. The animosities between the relief workers working inside Cambodia — especially OXFAM — and those working on the border came to a head in a December 19, 1979, Congressional hearing in Washington.

The congressmen responded bitterly to a charge by columnist Mary McGrory that "if the Carter Administration put as much effort into feeding the Cambodian people as it does into trying to discredit the Cambodian government, the famine would be over in a month."[48] That was salt in the wounds of Congress, several members of which had recently visited Cambodia and had undergone the searing experience of visiting refugee camps on the border. They had voted tens of millions of dollars in aid for Cambodia and most of the food reaching Cambodians was American.

Leo Cherne, head of the Citizens Commission, said that Mary McGrory's

16. The Land Bridge and Cambodian Famine   213

accusations were shocking and false. He put his finger on the roots of the controversy: "There remains a continuing division among the American people about America's previous role in Vietnam and Cambodia. That ... feeds certain perhaps unconscious desires to see a picture one way rather than another."[49] Congresswoman Millicent Fenwick gave a wry example of the impact of the controversy. Few people, she said, are prepared to accept that Pol Pot was a hideous dictator and also that the Vietnamese army is not an unmitigated blessing to the Cambodian people. In other words, in the opinions of many, if you were anti–Pol Pot you had to be pro–Vietnamese or the reverse. It was the old Vietnam War syndrome. Black and white.

Richard Holbrooke summed up U.S. policy toward aiding the Cambodians: Get food into Cambodia regardless of the political implications; send more food to the border and hope that it gets into Cambodia by "informal networks" rather than the Khmer Rouge, and help UNHCR and the Thai government deal with the pressure of refugees. Strip away the red tape, the politics, and get people fed.[50] Holbrooke vehemently denied that U.S. policies had delayed the arrival in Cambodia of a single grain of rice. "The problem," he said, "inside Cambodia is distribution. There is a lot of food in that country that has come in that hasn't gotten to the people."[51] He also noted the incongruity of the international community having to beg the government in Phnom Penh to be allowed to distribute food to prevent mass starvation.[52]

Holbrooke then took an indirect shot at those criticizing the Land Bridge at the border by reading from a message sent by Ambassador Abramowitz to Washington. "This [the border]," said Abramowitz, "is the obvious place the international relief effort is working best at the moment. We should do our utmost to expedite this effort...."[53] The corollary to that view, shared by many, was that the concurrent effort to bring food into Cambodia through cooperation with the Vietnamese-installed government was not working well.

A statement by an ICRC official working inside Cambodia confirmed the American view. On December 5, *The New York Times* reported that an international relief official said that 80 to 90 percent of the food and other aid delivered to Cambodia was still in warehouses, undistributed. ICRC threatened to pull out of the country if the performance of the government didn't improve. On December 6 the White House charged the Vietnamese and Cambodians with "delay and diversion of humanitarian efforts."[54] The relief organizations in Cambodia found their programs under fire.

Representatives of OXFAM, Church World Services, and the American Friends Service Committee defended their Cambodian programs to Congress. OXFAM reported on a three-day visit to the Cambodian countryside its representative had taken in November, accompanied by government officials. However, remarkable on this occasion was that in the lengthy report the OXFAM representative mentions seeing only a handful of severely malnourished Cambodians during his travels. This in a country in which a famine threatening millions of people — the extinction of the Cambodian people — had been predicted![55] Instead of starvation of a "hideously wide-spread nature," OXFAM observed only that "the nutritional status of people is bad but not disastrous" and that "the general climate of nutrition and health had improved slightly ... there were very considerable areas of rice under cultivation and almost ready to be harvested ... we were told that food is assured until late March 1980."[56] OXFAM does not speculate why the situation might have improved. The Land Bridge to western Cambodia had not yet been started and the amount of food that had arrived in Cambodia from Western countries had not yet reached significant totals. It seemed that the predictions of immediate famine in Cambodia had been exaggerated. Aid organizations, which had appealed to the public and governments for resources to meet a famine, subtly changed their appeal to emphasize the diverse needs of a ravaged country.

OXFAM's informative report at the Congressional hearing was marred by its counter-attack on those who criticized the performance of the aid agencies in Cambodia and the Cambodian government. It cited critical reports by the French government, the State Department, and the BBC as damaging relations with the government and the aid program and fell back on the tried and true tactic of blaming refugees on the border of Thailand for the "orchestrated account of the situation" by "the refugees going there" who "have a strong axe to grind."[57] It was an old story. An organization choosing to cooperate with a totalitarian government has to pull its punches and avoid criticism of its host if it wishes to continue working in the country. And it must defend its client government from criticism.

The members of Congress struck back hard, calling into question the assertions by the VOLAGs. Especially damning was the threat of the ICRC to pull out of Cambodia because food aid was being stockpiled and not distributed. The ICRC, cranky and contentious, is the closest thing the world has to an objective humanitarian agency untouched by politics and prejudice. Pipe smoking Millicent Fenwick made the telling observation to the three charities that "not one of you in these three very fine reports has mentioned the strain that it must be on the country to have 200,000 occupying troops"— the Vietnamese army. Yet, the women members of Congress who had visited Cambodia had reported "Vietnamese troops were in control of the airports, Vietnamese soldiers in control of the buildings; they are all over. So you don't see them?" she asked. OXFAM ducked the question.[58]

* * *

Was the threat of famine in Cambodia as severe as earlier reports had claimed? Did the skeletons reaching Sa Kaeo Holding Center in Thailand represent the norm of the condition of all Cambodians, or were they an aberration, a group of a few tens of thousand of people on the run from Vietnamese army? Were the Cambodian people at risk of extinction or mass starvation?

16. The Land Bridge and Cambodian Famine

It is clear now that the famine expected by many in late 1979 never occurred. Hardship yes, doubtless isolated cases of starvation, especially in conflicted areas, but famine, no. Quite possibly, however, the food aid for Cambodia which began on a sizeable scale in December 1979 and continued until 1981 prevented a famine in 1980 and 1981. The rice harvest in January and February 1980 was small and would not have lasted through the year until the next major harvest had not it been supplemented by imported rice. The needs, however, were less than the 30,000 tons per month and the number of threatened people was less than the 2.25 million initially estimated by the international aid agencies.

William Shawcross in his book *Quality of Mercy* calculated that the total amount of food aid, rice and corn, distributed in rural areas in Cambodia in 1980 was 4,000 to 5,000 tons per month — roughly 50,000 tons for the entire year. Perhaps another 50,000 tons was distributed to government workers in Phnom Penh and other cities.[59] A benefit of the urban distribution program was that the government did not have to take rice from the farmers to feed the cities. Add to that the same amount distributed over the Land Bridge and the total rice distributed in Cambodia in 1980 was about 150,000 tons. The Soviet Union also contributed corn to Cambodia, although the amount cannot be determined. It is likely, however, that — contrary to the wishes of the international aid agencies — a significant portion of the food aid to Cambodia fed the occupying Vietnamese army or possibly was transported to Vietnam to feed a population there that was by no means prosperous.[60]

Rice production in Cambodia in 1980 totaled between 600,000 and 700,000 tons and thus the food aid added more than 20 percent to the rice supply of Cambodia. That was an important addition, although there is no way to determine how much of the imported rice was essential to prevent serious malnutrition and starvation and how much was, in essence, surplus to the basic needs of the people. One can be certain, however, that the imported rice was eaten by someone. The Cambodian people had been on short rations for a long time. Another factor limiting the total amount of rice needed was that there may not have been as many Cambodians as the international community believed. The full extent of Khmer Rouge genocide was not yet fully known and aid agencies estimated the total population of Cambodia at about seven million. It seems, however, that it was only about six million and, thus, the total needs of the country were less than projected.[61]

The distribution of rice seed over the Land Bridge and to a lesser extent through the aid agencies in Phnom Penh was as important as the food distribution. Nearly 50,000 tons of seed were sent into Cambodia during the first five months of 1980 for the planting season in May and June. The result was good. The next harvest in January and February 1981 saw rice production double over the preceding year. The threat of a major famine in Cambodia had been averted.[62] Both the land bridge and the food aid program inside Cambodia had worked.

* * *

For all the back-biting and ideological wrangling among the aid agencies and the overly dire predictions of famine, the Cambodian relief operation from 1979 to 1981 was a huge and remarkably successful operation. In size and scope, perhaps only the humanitarian aid program for Bangladesh from 1971 to 1975 rivaled it. Undoubtedly much of the food distributed across the Land Bridge ended up with Khmer Rouge or Khmer Serei soldiers and food distributed through the government in Phnom Penh ended up feeding the Vietnamese army. But thousands upon thousands of ordinary farmers showed up at the border to haul away bags of rice, rice seed, and farm implements. There can be no doubt that the food distributed at the border strengthened the Khmer Rouge — who were starving when aid first reached them — and the Khmer Serei and other resistance groups. At the same time, the food brought into Cambodia and distributed by the Vietnamese-installed government and the aid agencies working there undoubtedly helped the Vietnamese solidify their control over much of the country. In other words, all sides of the wars in Cambodia benefited from humanitarian relief.

In 1980, the people clustered on the Thai border began to return home. By the end of 1980, UNHCR announced that more than 200,000 Cambodians who had been living in the border camps had returned home. But Thailand still had more than 150,000 Cambodian refugees within its borders.[63]

Unfortunately, Cambodia would continue to be wracked by civil war and not until 1991 would a peace agreement be signed among all the contending forces in Cambodia. Afterwards, at long last, nearly all Cambodians were able to return home to a land ravaged by the wars of so many decades. Cambodia has never really returned to being the pleasant green land that Yvette Pierpaoli found when she arrived there in 1967.

17

BEING A REFUGEE

A refugee camp is a prison. In the most liberal of camp environments, refugees have freedom of movement and can shop or work in the local community outside the camps. However, in Southeast Asia, movements in and out of the camps were usually controlled and some camps were encircled by barbed wire and had armed soldiers patrolling the perimeters. To visit the outside world, the refugee had to bribe the guards or sneak under or over the wire. Within their constricted world, refugees were dependent upon aid organizations for their daily bread. The soldiers, government and UN officials, and foreign aid workers usually did not speak their language or understand much about their culture and customs. Many of the foreigners had an agenda. Proselytizing Christians pushed their beliefs upon the refugees. Equally present, but more subtle, were missionaries of secular culture who indoctrinated the refugees with theories of education, women's rights, nutrition, medical practices, pre- and post-natal care, capitalism, anti- or pro-communism, and anti- or pro-Christianity. Southeast Asians had a cultural tradition of agreeable vagueness that often persuaded *farangs* they were succeeding in enlightening their charges. The refugees were masters of survival and they adapted quickly to maximize their benefits in the environment in which they found themselves.

Refugees stood in line endlessly to receive food rations, building material, used clothing, and medical treatment. Doctors stuck needles into them to extract blood and collected bottles of their feces and urine. The food given them was often unfamiliar. Long-nosed foreigners constantly tried to make their children drink milk or swallow disgusting gruel. There was little privacy and often not enough water for bathing. Group latrines and showers were disgusting, dangerous because of male predators, and embarrassing to modest Indochinese women. When JVA, embassies, or INS showed up at the camp for interviews, the refugees would attempt to say a word or give a letter to the mysterious foreigners who held in their hands the power to decide their destiny. What to say during the interview was debated at great length among the refugees who looked for the magic word that would gain them an offer to resettle in the United States, France, Canada, or Australia, or occasionally some other country.

Table 4.
Refugee Camp Population in Thailand*

End of Year

1975	64,846
1976	75,866
1977	97,595
1978	138,727
1979	259,167
1980	258,680
1981 (July 31)	232,107

Refugee Population in Thailand by Ethnic Group†
July 31, 1981

Cambodian	123,131
Lowland Lao	39,259
Highland Lao	55,785
Vietnamese	13,932
Total	232,107

*U.S. Congress, Senate, *Refugee Problems in Southeast Asia* (1981 staff report), 23.
†Ibid.

If one refugee was approved for resettlement after telling an interviewer that the communists killed his water buffalo, one could be certain that others would tell the same story. Not all, nor even most of the refugees really longed for a new home in the U.S., but the old one had become intolerable.

In the case of the Hmong and other highlanders, the foreigners had an inexplicable interest in the relationships of their family members, trying to fit the highlanders into the Western concept of a nuclear family. The highlanders learned to describe their children to the satisfaction of the foreigners. "Same belly" they would say to distinguish children born of the same mother from those of a second or third wife or adopted, as many Hmong children were, due to the large number of adults killed in the war.[1] The foreigners were extremely careful not to admit any refugee into the United States who had two wives.

The worse trauma of the refugee was being separated from family members and friends. In the Cambodian camps some people spent day after day looking for and asking for news of the fate of fathers, mothers, sons, and daughters. For every happy reunion, a dozen people never learned the fate of the missing.

* * *

One of the best stories of an escape from Vietnam, life in a refugee camp on the Cambodian border, and travel to the United States is told by a Vietnamese-American with the anglicized name of Kim Ha in her book, *Stormy Escape*. While most Vietnamese refugees fled by boat, a few attempted the overland passage to Thailand through Cambodia or Laos. Kim, her husband Vinh, and their four children — ages four to ten — were among them.[2]

Kim and Vinh, Catholics and moderately well-to-do, stayed in Vietnam in 1975 but soon became disillusioned with the communists. Life in a declining economy with a repressive government and fear of being sent to re-education camps or exiled to live in New Economic Zones, persuaded the Ha family to escape. In June 1978 they attempted to leave by boat. They were caught. Kim and the children were jailed for three days, her husband for several months. Kim was dismissed from her teaching job and her ration card was confiscated. Without a ration card she could not buy food cheaply in the government stores, only on the black market at higher prices.

It took them more than a year to find another opportunity to escape. Frightened of what they had heard of the hardships of the boat people they decided to try to get to Thailand overland. They became smugglers and vagabonds as cover for their plans. Vinh traveled all over the country looking for opportunities to get out; ten times, Kim relates, he was cheated, abandoned, or betrayed. At last, he found an opportunity in Go Dau, a town on the Cambodian border. With the Khmer Rouge overthrown in early 1979 and a pro–Vietnamese government now in Cambodia, cross-border trade and traffic in people was flourishing. Vinh became a noodle merchant, taking noodles on a bus to Go Dau to trade for cigarettes and other items from Cambodia and made the contacts the family needed to cross the border. While Vinh was setting up the escape, Kim taught the children a few English phrases — "I am hungry, I am sick, I need help" — and made them memorize the addresses of relatives in the United States. If the parents died during the escape she hoped that the children would be able to seek help and to identify themselves.

Kim was five months pregnant on March 27, 1980, when the couple and their children boarded a bus in Saigon for Go Dau. It was the dry season and travel was easier than during the monsoon. The cost of their escape was ten ounces of gold. Five they paid in advance to the guides; five more would be given the guides by Kim's sister in Saigon if they were successful. The couple had $840 in U.S. currency and a few gold coins sewed into their clothing.

The crossing into Cambodia was difficult. The guides separated the family with the husband crossing first, while Kim and the children waited through an agonizing night, not knowing if Vinh had succeeded and fearful that they would be murdered by their guides. Finally, they were loaded onto motorcycles and sped down dark, rural paths running between rice paddies. Leaving the motorcycles behind, they were guided across the border on foot, stumbling through fields and forests in a nightmare rush to evade discovery. The dawn brought good news: Vinh was waiting for them in the first town in Cambodia. They boarded trucks full of Vietnamese escapees to continue their journey to Thailand.

Kim's greatest fear was that she would become separated from her children in the confusion, darkness, and chaos of their flight. It nearly happened on several occasions, once when their truck left her behind with two of her children still on board. Luckily the children had the presence of mind to jump off the back of the truck and the family was reunited—but on foot. Moreover, Kim feared discovery whenever the children spoke in Vietnamese. She remained silent as much as possible.

The Ha family crossed Cambodia over the next two weeks. It was an exhausting and dangerous traverse by foot, train, truck, and bullock cart. Along the way they encountered other Vietnamese refugees attempting the same journey. Kind Cambodians saved them on several occasions. The family was thrice abandoned by guides and fleeced of every last gold coin and dollar—including a strip search by a Cambodian soldier who took their last $240 and then mercifully returned a $20 bill. Kim said of the crossing, "Everybody was robbed at one time or another." The robbers were both Vietnamese and "Para," a generic term loosely applied to any Cambodian soldiers.[3] Kim was fortunate not to be raped as well as robbed—or at least she does not report being raped. Perhaps her pregnancy discouraged rapists.

The danger increased as the family got closer to Thailand. The Vietnamese controlled the cities; near the border with Thailand were the Khmer Rouge, Khmer Serei, and other groups. The only thing that Cambodian soldiers of these groups had in common was opposition to the Vietnamese invaders.

Almost within sight of Thailand, after a slow cart ride down rutted and dusty highways lined with abandoned rice fields overgrown with jungle, the Ha family, weakened by thirst and hunger, met their last and most serious challenge. They passed through the last Vietnamese army checkpoint, bribing the guards with two chickens, and entered no-mans land along the border—a strip about five miles wide. Traffic on the road increased. Vietnamese and Cambodian refugees headed toward Thailand while merchants came back on foot, bicycle or carts loaded down with textiles, cigarettes, and sacks of rice. The merchants brought rice from Thailand and took refugees back, thus making money both ways.

Suddenly, two young armed men jumped in front of them and forced the family off the cart and into the jungle. They searched them. "They bent me over so they could do a full body search for gold or diamonds," said Kim. "Their fingers inside me felt as big as bananas ... then they forced my mouth open to see if I had any gold rings hidden there." They found only the $20 bill. After being hit by rifle butts and shoved and pushed, the Ha family was released, only to run into another group of armed men a short distance down the road. They went through the same ordeal all over again. These last outrages were a surprise—they had been told that they would be welcomed by Thailand.

Resuming their journey penniless, violated, and terrified, the family soon came upon a military outpost. Inside a hut alongside the road four men wearing blue jeans and T-shirts questioned them in English. Kim had documents showing that her mother was in the U.S. and that she was a Christian. When the four men saw their connection with the United States, Ha said they were treated better than the other refugees.

But "better treatment" consisted of another strip search and probe for hidden gold and the theft of the last possessions of the family: Vinh's blue jeans, two pens, and medicines. Then they were led to a bamboo hut where they joined 30 other Vietnamese refugees. Cambodians trying to cross the border were housed in another hut a short distance away. A woman told Kim that two nights before Para had come to the hut at night and dragged a Vietnamese girl away, raped, then shot and killed her. The Ha family was dreading the onset of night, but late that afternoon the soldiers came to their hut and led them and the other members of their group in single file through mine fields for about one mile to a large bamboo gate. Through the gate they saw the flag — red cross on a white field — of the ICRC, International Red Cross. The Ha family had arrived at Nong Chan camp, the home of the Land Bridge where Robert Ashe and others distributed rice to Cambodians who came to the border. "We are saved," said Kim. She was overly optimistic. The border camps were controlled internally by armed Cambodian groups resisting the government in Phnom Penh and externally by the Thai military, which prevented the inhabitants from entering Thailand.

In reaching Nong Chan, the Ha family was probably more fortunate than the average refugees. All the members of the family had arrived at the Thai border alive and together. The worst was over. But what followed would also be an ordeal.

* * *

The residents of Nong Chan were assisted by the ICRC, the UN Children's Fund (UNICEF), and several VOLAGS. In keeping with the Thai assertion that the inhabitants of the border camps were not refugees, UNHCR was not allowed to work there. The relief workers did not stay in the camps at night.

On entering Nong Chan, Kim and her family were issued blankets, food, and blue UN tents, large enough to house several families. They were settled into an area of the camp reserved for Vietnamese. They were in good spirits, chatting with the other refugees, exchanging experiences, and asking about lost relatives and friends. Vinh cooked rice and dried fish and they ate heartily for the first time in many days.

However, a visit to the communal latrine dispelled any notion of comfort. One trench toilet served 340 people. And the illusion of safety was dispelled that evening. Camp leaders told them: "Don't move. Don't talk loudly. This place is dangerous." The Has spent an uneasy night. Every night the Para came to the tents, shined flashlights over the sleeping Vietnamese, picked out attractive young women, and dragged the women away to be raped. Kim was touched, her sarong pulled up to have her body examined. Fortunately, the Para "did not pay any attention to a dirty pregnant woman."[4] At night the Para — presumably the anti–Vietnamese Khmer Serei — controlled Nong Chang.

The flies, filth, mosquitoes and malaria, the rapes, the nightly gun battles among different groups of Cambodian and Thai soldiers, and shortages of food soon made the Ha family wonder why they had fled Vietnam. When a Thai soldier was killed in a gunfight, the government suspended deliveries of food and water to the camp for a day. It was the dry season, and the daily ration of water was only two liters per person — barely enough for drinking, but not enough to wash. Extra water was available to those with money to pay for it; the Has had no money, not even enough to buy a container that didn't leak. Other refugees with money bought and traded cigarettes, rice, cooking oil and blankets. Stolen medicine was available from black marketers who sold it at high prices. In the squalid and desperate conditions of a refugee camp the worst characteristics of humans come out — and the weak, the poor, the old, and the young are the most vulnerable.

The ICRC distributed food and water and Western doctors and nurses worked in the hospital and health centers. But to complain about the Para, the black marketers, the refugee leaders, or the Thai was to risk retaliation. The refugees remained silent. One night, after Kim and her family had been in Nong Chang about a week, the refugees rose up against the Para and drove them away. Retaliation was certain and, to protect the Vietnamese, the next day the Red Cross arranged for them to be trucked to a newly established camp, Northwest 9, reserved for Vietnamese land arrivals. The Thai government located NW 9 well inside Cambodia to keep the dreaded Vietnamese off Thai soil.[5] The camp was said to be safer and better organized than Nong Chan — itself being considered the safest and best organized of the border camps.

The refugees arrived at NW 9 in good spirits, which were quickly dashed. There was nothing there except grass and trees and a few other refugees. The Ha family was assigned a spot in a tent two meters wide by two meters long, large enough only for the family to lie down and stretch out to sleep. Food was scarce; at night artillery and rockets thundered. One night, when the shelling got close, the refugees panicked, forced their way through the barbed wire, and scattered into the Thai countryside. They were rounded up by Thai soldiers and brought back. In their absence, their food, water and other possessions had been stolen from their tents. NW 9 was a closed camp; any refugee going outside the barbed wire fence was liable to be shot by Thai soldiers. Nobody came in or went out except relief workers, Thai soldiers, and now and then a delegation of foreign visitors or journalists. Merchants, black-marketers, Para, and others were kept out; the refugee's needs were met by the international relief agencies.

Food, medical care, and sanitation slowly improved. Kim wrote letters to friends and relatives in the United States and received responses. Vinh worked hard in the labor corps of the camp to earn six liters of extra water every work day and the Has soon had enough to bathe their children occasionally, reuse the water to wash clothes, then use it a third time to water beans they had planted. "Wealth or poverty was judged by how much water you had." Later, when the monsoon began, too much water became a problem, flooding tents and causing clouds of mosquitoes and an upsurge in malaria. The population of NW 9 reached about 3,000 as new Vietnamese came in almost daily.

Refugees wrote letters, or had them written for them, to family members abroad or in other camps and to anyone else who might be able to help them. Refugee workers always came home from visiting the camps with sacks full of letters and they were usually conscientious in ensuring that they were posted. Two months after arriving in NW 9 Kim received a letter from a former supervisor in a Christian organization in Saigon she had worked for. Inside was 2,000 Thai *baht*, equivalent to $100. The Has first purchase with their new wealth was sugar. They invited their friends to a celebration and ate sugared green beans, coffee made of roasted and ground green beans, rice, and cigarettes. It was a feast. But the money, and additional money the Has received from relatives, didn't go far in the refugee camp. Corruption among camp leaders was rampant; one refugee, who worked in an ICRC warehouse, was said to have made $10,000 selling stolen relief goods at high prices. A way around the restriction on leaving the camp was quickly found by comely young Vietnamese women who exchanged favors with Thai soldiers, got permission to leave the camp, bought goods in nearby markets, and sold them to the refugees. Whoever said that adversity brings out the best in people never visited a refugee camp in which survival is paramount.

The most frequented place in every refugee camp is the bulletin board. The official bulletin board had notices, camp news, and announcements posted. A second was for messages by refugees. Here, families asked for information about family members, left notes telling how they could be found, and posted messages to relatives and friends and photos of lost children and other relatives. Many joyful reunions of families came about from messages on the board. Often the families had been separated for years only to find themselves, however different their experiences, in the same camp. But most often letters, notes, and photos remained for months on the bulletin board without any response. The agony of not knowing was the most excruciating of the traumas of the refugees.

Noted in a congressional report was that the "most insidious problem, which is to be found in even the most physically comfortable camp, is that of boredom and enforced idleness." Violence and family problems were one consequence.[6] The most vulnerable refugees were the elderly, of whom there were few, children without parents (unaccompanied minors), and single, unaccompanied women. Single women needed men to fight for their food and water and ward off other men. Sexual liaisons for convenience and protection were common.

The Vietnamese refugees in NW 9 created a society out of the hardship. A refugee priest held Catholic services. Special feeding centers were set up for orphans, children, and pregnant women. English classes began. Refugees gathered at night and sang Vietnamese and Western songs and Christian hymns. A sense of humor came out of the hardship. The refugees named their smelly latrine "Uncle Ho's tomb"—after the late Ho Chi Minh. The main road through NW 9 was named "Sunset Boulevard."

In July, after three months in the camp, the Has were among 141 Vietnamese who were informed they would be permitted to leave NW 9 to live in a holding center and to be processed for resettlement, mostly in the United States. These first departees had succeeded in contacting relatives, friends, and former employers and securing them as sponsors. On August 1, 1980, Vinh, Kim, and their five children — Kim had just given birth — and others crossed a bamboo bridge across a ditch and entered Thailand. The 3,000 they left behind waved goodbye with bitter smiles. The Ha family was lucky; the Thai government normally prohibited resettlement from NW 9 to discourage Vietnamese from coming to Thailand and seeking resettlement.[7]

The Ha family and the other Vietnamese were met by the ICRC, loaded onto buses, and taken to Panat Nikhom Holding Center near the city of Chonburi, southeast of Bangkok. The Vietnamese were orderly, in contrast to the chaotic departures from camps hosting Cambodians, the most desperate and traumatized of the Indochinese refugees. In Cambodian camps, the air of desperation was palpable. "Thousands of people mobbed the busses, and there were sometimes dozens of claimants for every name.... Fights broke out, people got hurt."[8] It took all day for refugee officers and leaders to sort out the mess, decide who belonged on the buses, and who was an imposter and would be removed, by force if necessary.

The Panat Nikhom Holding Center to which the Ha family was taken was new, neat, and clean with raised barracks-like houses and plots for the refugees to plant vegetables. Just outside the gate was a market where Thai merchants had set up stalls to sell food and other items. The Ha family visited the market to enjoy the unheard-of luxury of eating bowls of noodles and drinking Coca-Cola.

The Has and three other refugee families occupied one of the barracks, making a total of 19 people. The water well was only 100 feet away, and water was not rationed. That was another luxury. So too was the food. A chicken and fresh vegetables were given to be shared by the residents of each hut every day to complement rations of salt, *nuc maam* (fish sauce) and, of course, rice. Latrines were cleaner, more abundant and more private than those in NW 9. A loudspeaker played Cambodian music all day, irritating the Vietnamese; most of the people in the holding center were Cambodian. Refugees were free to leave the holding center and explore the market and the nearby rice paddies and town. However, if the refugees were tempted to escape the holding center, they quickly learned that it would go hard on any Vietnamese refugee attempting to live in Thailand. Cambodians, many of whom spoke Thai, had less trouble living in Thailand; but they too would forfeit a chance to be resettled if they left the camp. Every day the holding center received visitors, mostly Westerners from international organizations, churches, and aid agencies. Money divided the refugees. Those who had it lived in a manner that seemed grand to those who did not. The Has were among those who had little money, but they received small amounts of money from charities. Kim received $200 from her mother in the United States, delivered to her personally by an American Embassy employee, Georgia Guldam.

In what would be called today post-traumatic stress disorder, many refugees began to see ghosts, symbolic of the horrors they had gone through. One woman claimed to have been nearly strangled by a ghost; after dark the refugees only went to the latrine in groups; ghosts beckoned like sirens for people to follow them outside their houses into the night. "The ghosts were very real to us," said Kim.[9]

A concern of the resettlement countries was that the refugees would bring communicable diseases with them. Each refugee was given a medical examination, a chest x-ray, and was screened for diseases. Tuberculosis, venereal disease, leprosy, and mental disorders excluded the refugee from further consideration until such time as the condition was treated successfully. Other than the impact of malnutrition, the refugees were mostly free of infectious diseases. Only the hardiest had survived. Nevertheless, in the U.S., refugees were blamed unfairly for a cholera outbreak in Louisiana, and seven cases of diphtheria among arriving refugees were discovered in California. The rate of hepatitis B was also higher among refugees than in the general population of the U.S.[10]

After two months in the holding center, the Has were transferred to Rangsit Transit Center, the next stop for them on the way to the United States. They had been interviewed, their bona fides as refugees checked out through interviews with the JVA, a security check run on them, they had passed their medical examinations, and all was well for them to continue on to the U.S. Still needed, however, was final processing and approval by the Immigration and Naturalization Service. Rangsit was a camp of four-story apartment buildings, dirty, reeking with urine from the overcrowded bathrooms, and expensive if a refugee wanted to supplement meager rations by purchasing food outside the camp. Cambodians in one building and Vietnamese in another fought and argued. The endless paperwork and interviews before departure for the United States continued every day. ICEM alone had a list of 30 procedures that must be accomplished before the refugee family could be on its way.[11]

The Ha family made it through Rangsit quickly. On October 15, 1980, they were bused to Bangkok International Airport, and loaded onto a passenger airliner with other refugees—Laotian, Cambodian, and Vietnamese. Each family carried two folders. The first included their chest x-rays and medical records; the second the entry documents from the INS and the voluntary agency that was in charge of getting them resettled in the U.S.[12]

On the flight, the flight attendants were courteous; the refugees were in high spirits—only slightly dampened when they overnighted in Hong Kong in "the worst motel" that Kim had ever seen.[13] Also dampening was the announcement over the public address system on their subsequent flight across the Pacific that "There are a lot of Vietnamese refugees on this plane. Please be careful. Lock your luggage and watch your bags. Otherwise, it could be lost." Kim, an English speaker and university graduate, was shocked. She had just learned that, to many people, Indochinese refugees were regarded with suspicion and disdain. They would have to prove to Americans that they were worthy of respect. Most of them have done so splendidly.

* * *

The border camps for Cambodian refugees had a different atmosphere than those for Lao in northern and northeastern Thailand. Nong Khai camp across the river from Vientiane housed mostly ethnic Lao, usually about 30,000 of them. Of similar size was Ban Vinai, in isolated northern Thailand, which was the largest Hmong settlement that had ever existed. If one had to choose a refugee camp in which to live, Ban Vinai in the early 1980s would have been a good choice. Visitors were often shocked by the crowded, dirty conditions, but the camp had its attractions. Although the camps were closed, the barbed wire and armed guards characteristic of camps along the Cambodian border were less oppressive and the atmosphere more relaxed. The JVA workers, such as Charlene Day Howell, were permitted to live in the camp and resided very simply in wooden barracks. They ate Hmong food and lived not very differently than the refugees themselves, usually spending about three weeks at a time and then taking their case files with them to Bangkok for a week of administrative duties and rest.[14]

Ban Vinai was set among lush, wooded hills. The Hmong lived in individual huts built of scrap wood and bamboo or long houses built on stilts; several wells and a lake provided adequate water; and sanitation was not any worse than it would have been in their home villages. They had enough land to grow small fields of upland rice and squash and beans. They kept turkeys and chickens; the women planted flower gardens in pots and a few of the refugees kept pet birds in cages. The Hmong received rice, fish, and canned biscuits from relief agencies. The children and young men played soccer. Buddhist *wats* and Christian churches appeared — usually thatched roof huts open on the side with an altar and room for a few dozen people to sit on the dirt or plank floor.

Ban Vinai was a beehive of commercial activity. Young men pedaled rickshaws; women wove handicrafts to sell for a pittance to tourist shops; soft drink venders, noodle carts and food stalls abounded. Traditional healers and shamans set up shop and letter writers did a booming business as refugees wrote letters to UNHCR, refugee workers, and the president of the United States, searching for the words that would gain them attention from the long-nosed *farangs* who seemed all important. A minority of the refugees had money, but most depended upon an occasional day of work and the rations passed out by the VOLAGs and the Thai government. At Nong Khai camp two refugees gave tennis lessons — a popular game among the Lao elite — at the camp's tennis courts.[15]

Coordination is a much repeated word by aid workers, but it generally means that others should coordinate while your organization does what it wants to do. The aid organizations working in the camps held endless coordination meetings. A summary of one at Nong Khai comes from Dr. Karen Olness from Minnesota. "Meeting set for ten A.M., began at eleven, and lasted until two.... There was inconclusive discussion of fact that half the toilets in camp were currently overflowing, that the original contract for toilet pumping was inadequate.... There followed discussion of need for garbage removal and general clean-up.... Representative of Norwegian Church Relief bemoaned lack of competition among VOLAGs for the garbage business.... Under health matters, IRC medical director reported that most medical problems in camp were related to inadequate sanitation. There was a brief discussion of the unsatisfactory food situation in camp, and difficulty of monitoring its distribution and quantity.... Adjournment."[16]

What the meeting illustrated is that a person who could fix a toilet was often the most valuable employee that a VOLAG could find. Idealistic young men and women with liberal arts degrees from prestigious universities often found themselves engaged in latrine sanitation and garbage disposal in refugee camps.

The capability of refugees to administer themselves and keep their camp clean and well running varied from place to place. Torn loose from their familiar environment and communities, focused intensely on their personal survival and that of their families, refugees often had little sense of cooperation toward meeting common goals. Competent and selfless leadership among the refugees was indispensable, but often lacking, as petty criminals and bully-boy gangs ruled in many camps. The *farangs* knew little about what happened in the camps at night — and for most their knowledge about happenings during the day was filtered through an interpreter who often had his own agenda to promote.

Ban Vinai was better organized than most refugee camps as the Hmong clung to their traditional leadership. The camp was divided into seven centers, each with its own leader, all reporting to a head man who, in 1980, was Vang Neng, a cousin of General Vang Pao. When Vang Neng was approved for resettlement in the United States in the camp some of his followers and the JVA protested. He was, in their opinion, an indispensable leader. Mac Thompson ignored the protests, but JVA and the VOLAGs took the issue all the way to the

Farewell to friends and relatives. Buses were sent to the refugee camps to transport refugees to Bangkok for final processing en route to the United States. (Paul Paquette)

Embassy Deputy Chief of Mission. Vang Neng was prevailed upon to remain longer in the camp as the leader, but later departed. The camp and its refugees survived without him.[17]

"In general," Lionel said to a reporter, "the camp conditions are not that bad. Where you get the bad cases is before they get to the camp." The new arrivals from Laos, especially the Hmong, were often malnourished and suffering from malaria.[18] The Lao had a tough initiation to refugee life. Before enjoying the relative comforts of Ban Vinai, new arrivals who swam or floated across the wide Mekong were taken by Thai police to a detention center called the So Ko Tou. It looked "like a run-down cavalry fort in a Grade B cowboy movie. High walls of wood and corrugated roofing enclose an area of about one acre, where up to four thousand people live in makeshift shacks.... There is filth everywhere."[19] The refugees endured the detention center for weeks or months before they were sent onward, the Lao to nearby Nong Khai refugee camp and the Hmong to Ban Vinai.

In contrast to Cambodians and Vietnamese, the Hmong were not enthusiastic about resettlement. "No shows" when the buses came to the camp every three or four days to take refugees to Bangkok and onward passage to the United States were often high. The arrival of the buses at the Hmong camps was a sad day of impending separation rather than jubilation. The Hmong were terrified at the prospect of going to the United States. Their primary sources of information were the photographs and cassette tapes sent them by relatives and friends in the U.S. What they heard sounded like a lonely existence in a culture incomprehensible to them.[20] The Hmong wanted to go back home to Laos and they were often encouraged by their leaders, including Vang Pao, to remain in the camps in expectation of going home, overthrowing the communist government, and resuming their former life in the Lao highlands. Language was one of the most difficult problems for all refugees. An active literacy program taught Hmong literacy in their own language along with English, but acquiring fluency in a new language is one of the most difficult of all intellectual tasks, especially for elders.

Despite their fears, most Hmong approved for resettlement would eventually climb on the buses when their names were called and undergo a 12-hour ride to Bangkok where they would be housed in an overcrowded transit camp for a day or two until being taken to the airport and sent to the United States. The refugees made a brief stopover at an Air Force base for a final medical checkup, immigration and customs, and then they separated with each family going to a different city where they were met at the airport by their sponsor. Life in the United States had begun.

For many refugees the most difficult problem was their facelessness in their new land. "He's been a big man in Laos, a big man in the camp," said Rosenblatt of one. "But when he gets to the U.S., he's going to be just another refugee without a skill." The Hmong also had another concern — they wanted to remember that they were Hmong.[21]

In 1980 "yellow rain" was added to the problems of the Hmong. On May 20, according to a victim, a bomb was dropped by a helicopter on a Hmong village in Laos. The bomb released a cloud of yellow powder that settled on the village and its inhabitants. The villagers immediately suffered nausea, vomiting, bleeding, red and swollen eyes, and blisters on their bodies. Fifteen died within three hours and nine later for a total of 24; all the animals in the village died.

Nineteen people escaped the village and six weeks later were interviewed at Ban Vinai by Gary West, a researcher from the U.S. Centers for Disease Control. One man was in the hospital; others had "unusual rashes." Three refugees were "severely debilitated." West had no expertise with the effects of poison gas but he concluded that the physical condition of several of the Hmong supported "the possibility of a toxic exposure."[22] Additional evidence would be obtained and many more Hmong would describe similar medical problems and symptoms over the next several months

Thus began the "yellow rain" controversy which divided the American people along the same ideological lines as had the Vietnam War. In 1981, Secretary of State Alexander Haig accused the Soviet Union and its allies of using chemical weapons in Southeast Asia. A team of scientists concluded, however, that yellow rain was honeybee feces.[23] It never became clear whether yellow rain was chemical weapons, bee feces, both or neither. Most of the knowledgeable people, including Jerry Daniels, were skeptical of the evidence that the Lao government was using chemical weapons against the Hmong.[24]

The highland Lao refugees distrusted Western medicine. The Hmong initially rejected the vaccinations and other medical treatment offered by World Vision, an American VOLAG, preferring to rely on their own shamans and traditional medicine.[25] Western doctors, they complained, spent only a short time with each patient and did not explain what they were doing. Traditional Hmong medicine was holistic; the shaman combined elements of psychology, myth, folklore, religion, and medicinal plants to heal his patient. Medical care in the camps, especially the highlander camps, operated on four levels. "There were thatch-hut pharmacies where any drug, expired or not, was available without a prescription. There were private 'clinics' mostly selling injections at about a dollar a shot. There were traditional healers of many sorts—herbalists, exorcists, and religious guides." The camp hospital run by the *farangs* was often the last stop on the refugee's quest to be cured of what ailed him.[26]

Many of the ailments of the refugees were psychological and psychosomatic—and quite possibly the traditional healers did a better job than did the technically competent but culturally unaware foreigners. The average refugee had seen one hundred times more death, brutality, danger, and misery than the average American. His escape from that was to be thrust into a bewildering new culture, first at the refugee camp and secondly in his country of resettlement. That Hmong and other refugees suffered from culture shock and mysterious and serious illnesses was inevitable.[27]

* * *

Distributing food to people in refugee camps is the most basic of services provided by relief organizations and, oddly enough, is probably the most difficult. If the camp is "open," and the refugees can enter and leave more or less freely, often there are problems with local people, non-refugees, getting into food lines for bags of whatever is being distributed. Refugee workers combat this by not announcing food distributions in advance and distributing at odd hours. Three A.M. was the usual time for food distributions in camps for Afghan refugees in the 1990s. If word leaked out in advance about a planned distribution of food people would come from miles around, claim to be refugees, and present an authentic-looking ration card to get a bag of wheat.[28]

Food distribution could be dangerous. A truck full of food pulling into a refugee camp can cause a scramble in which the strong get the food and the weak get trampled. In the chaotic world of Indochinese refugee camps with tens of thousands of refugees the challenge was to ensure that all refugees, especially the most vulnerable—the weak and sick, elderly, pregnant women, and unaccompanied children—got their share. In a refugee camp, food is power, and he who has it exercises control over his fellows. The problem of achieving a reasonably adequate and equitable food distribution was worst in the Cambodian camps. Warlords, crooks, and self-styled leaders dominated the camps. Control of the food supply was one of their most potent and lucrative weapons. A household survey in Mak Mun, the most notorious of the border camps, indicated that 89 percent of the rice distributed never reached the intended recipients, the individual households.[29] The impact of this failure was mitigated by the fact that the warlord running the camp vastly inflated the population estimates and more rice was being distributed than was needed. The extra rice was sold or hoarded against a rainy day in which distributions might cease or the armed men in the camp might embark on a campaign against the Vietnamese army or rival armed groups.

Relief workers were faced with choosing which refugees in the camp would be their allies in distributing food. The *farangs* were neither numerous enough nor inclined to undertake all the labor involved in loading, transporting, storing, and distributing food. They tended to bypass the traditional leaders in the camps because they were corrupt, and instead aimed to set up a parallel system using refugees on their own payroll. But relief workers came and went so often that an old hand was one who counted his experience in weeks rather than days. Few of the foreigners had the time, inclination, or language skills to learn the political dynamics of a camp.

The ration for each adult refugee per day, as determined by the UN agencies, was 500 grams of rice (about 1.1. pounds), 50 grams of legumes (almost 2 ounces), 30 grams each (about one ounce) of dried fish and vegetable oil, and salt.[30] A refugee with money could supplement this monotonous ration with food purchased in the markets of the camp. About the only measurement the relief agencies had for determining whether sufficient food was reaching each person in the camp was the incidence of malnutrition and other nutrition-related problems. A growing number of malnourished women and young children was a sure indicator that the food distribution system wasn't working.

At the border camps in Cambodia it took relief agencies more than six months of trial and error to discover that direct distribution to women only was the best means of ensuring food got to those who most needed it. The first large scale direct distribution to women was planned like a military campaign by UNICEF and CARE and involved camp leaders and a large number of Cambodians playing key roles. On July 19, 1980, each of 16,000 women were given rations for three persons for four days. Direct distribution to women then became standard practice.[31]

* * *

One of the features of every refugee camp is the supplemental feeding center. Unaccompanied women with small children, children under five years old, and the elderly are nearly always the first to die in a humanitarian crisis. They are the people among the refugee population least able to compete for food and other services. Men with AK-47s can almost always find food.

A team running a feeding center at Sa Kaeo described its program.[32] The center served about 150 patients and was staffed by five nurses, a pediatrician, a nutritionist, and numerous volunteers, both refugees and people from the Thai and foreign communities. The workers included speakers of Khmer, Thai, French, Finnish, Danish, and English. Four tents with 24 sleeping mats each accommodated up to 48 persons per tent — with two children in a bed if necessary. To ensure good drainage of monsoon rains, the floors of the tents were gravel overlaid with wooden planks. Each patient received two blankets. Keeping them off the wet ground and warm was important for recovery.

Patients unable to eat were fed by injection and feeding tubes; those able to eat but severely malnourished were given a high-protein, high-calorie, low-bulk liquid food mix called K-Mix-II. Each patient was given six feedings per day. Even starving people, however, can be resistant to food they are unfamiliar with — especially if administered to them by large, frightening people with strange demeanors and uncertain motives — and patients were moved as quickly as possible to a diet of fried rice with egg or chopped meat. Motherless infants were spoon-fed formula. Families were not allowed to eat with their children

These Mien women pose in their finery for a photographer at a refugee camp in Nan province, Thailand. (Paul Paquette)

in the feeding centers or bring in food to them. Ravaged stomachs might not tolerate the sort of food the mothers thought they needed. There were cultural clashes about how the malnourished were fed as traditional wisdom clashed with modern technology.

Once the patient was deemed able to leave the hospital, he was encouraged to return for checkups and continued to receive daily bowlfuls of porridge from boiling cauldrons of CSM or CSB (corn soya blend) porridge.

* * *

The most isolated of the refugee camps in Thailand were in Nan province in the far north of the country. These camps housed refugees from several different highland groups in Laos. Paul Paquette, who worked for JVA in Nan from 1978 to 1980, recalled one cultural misunderstanding that occurred between a refugee family and an Immigration and Naturalization Service officer. As opposed to Embassy and JVA officers, many of whom had years of experience in Southeast Asia and fluency in at least one local language, INS officers were sent on temporary duty to Thailand from their regular postings, which might be in Iowa, or Miami, or Salt Lake City. They worked for a few weeks at the camps giving approval or rejecting refugees for resettlement in the U.S. At a Nan camp on one occasion an INS officer angrily rejected the resettlement application of a highland family because he said it was fraudulent. The woman was in her late 30s and her supposed husband was in his early 20s—and the woman didn't even know her last name. Paquette had to explain diplomatically to the INS officer that men in that group often married older women and that, traditionally, that group of highlanders didn't have last names. To conform to Western naming customs, JVA officers asked couples to choose a last name—and this woman had apparently forgotten the name chosen for her. Paul finally persuaded the INS officer to reverse his decision and permit the family to come to the U.S. This was the kind of misunderstanding that often occurred.[33]

Perhaps the most crucial bit of cultural information taught the refugees just before they departed for the United States was how to find the bathroom on the airplane that would fly them to the United States, how to lock the door, and how to use a Western toilet.[34]

18

THE END OF THE BEGINNING

The resettlement programs for Indochinese refugees run by the United States and other countries, the regime of international cooperation that came about with agonizing slowness, and the improvement — improvement being a relative term — in the human rights and economic situation within the three Indochinese countries all contributed to a mitigation of the refugee crisis in the early 1980s. The Vietnamese boat people were still coming, but in manageable numbers; the threat of famine lessened in Cambodia and Cambodians began returning home from the border; Lao arrivals in Thailand in 1982 were down to 2,000 a month compared with 5,000 a month in 1980.[1] Indochinese refugee issues would loom large for another dozen years, but a humanitarian disaster that threatened massive numbers of lives subsided. By April 1982, Poul Hartling, the UNHCR High Commissioner, declared the beginning of the end of the Indochinese refugee crisis.[2]

During 1980 the number of refugees in Southeast Asian camps declined for the first time in five years. More than 20,000 Indochinese were being resettled every month around the world. The boat people in camps in Southeastern Asian countries plus Hong Kong fell from a high of 250,000 in July 1979 to one-half that in 1980. Thailand counted 259,000 refugees in 1980: 143,000 Cambodians in Sa Kaeo and Khao I Dang holding centers, 12,000 Vietnamese, and 104,000 highland and lowland Lao. Still clustered along the border were 400,000 Cambodians, although this number mainly consisted of transients coming to the border to get food and seed and take it home with them. This number declined as conditions improved inside Cambodia.[3]

"A deceptive feeling of security, calm, and permanence pervaded the border area in December 1982," said an American refugee officer. "The border camps were then neat, clean, well run and orderly — a remarkable change from the dirty, insecure, near anarchic camps of 1979 and 1980. The houses were well built and substantial. Lush fruit and vegetable gardens were everywhere. The raising of pigs, ducks, chickens, and other livestock was increasing. There were

Table 5.
Indochinese Refugees — April 1975–August 1982*

Asylum Countries	Arrivals	
Boat Refugees:		
Malaysia	177,000	
Hong Kong	114,000	
Indonesia	75,000	
Thailand	70,000	
Philippines	30,000	
Singapore	28,000	
Macau	7,000	
Other	38,000	
Total Boat		539,000
Land Refugees:		
Thailand: Cambodian	212,000	
Thailand: Highland Lao	126,000	
Thailand: Lowland Lao	152,000	
Thailand: Vietnamese	23,000	
Total Land		513,000
Orderly Departure Program		23,000
Vietnam to U.S. in 1975		125,000
Vietnam to China in 1978/1979		263,000
Grand Total of Refugees		1,463,000

Note: Totals do not include more than 300,000 Cambodians, Vietnamese, and ethnic Chinese departing Cambodia for Vietnam and Laos from 1975 to 1979. Nor does total include several hundred thousand Cambodians sheltering in border camps in 1979 and 1980.

*"Refugee Reports," Oct. 22, 1982. Derived from State Department Records.

well-functioning schools and clinics.... Most of the warlords who formerly controlled the border camps had been killed, had disappeared, or had gone to Bangkok or France to live on the wealth they had acquired."[4] This idyllic snapshot of the border was clouded by periodic outbreaks of violence that would keep the border in flux until the 1990s.

* * *

The appointees of the Reagan administration taking office in 1981 were less emotionally committed to Indochinese refugees than those of the Carter administration and also had burgeoning Cuban and Haitian refugee crises to deal with. From Congress came renewed opposition. Senator Walter Huddleston of Kentucky claimed that many of the Indochinese were "economic opportunists" rather than people fleeing political and communist oppression.[5] He was backed up by INS officers, one of whom wrote in February 1980, "It is time that we recognized that the outflow of refugees from Vietnam ... has been given impetus by the major role being played by the U.S. in their resettlement.... It has become an endless stream with the hoped-for destination for most being the

U.S.—Shangri-La."⁶ The INS bolstered its case with a survey carried out by the American Consulate in Songkhla, Thailand, that showed 70 percent of the boat people arriving there cited economic problems as their principal reason for leaving Vietnam.⁷ Senator Huddleston also cited UNHCR opposition to the large U.S. resettlement program. Martin Barber, the UNHCR representative in Bangkok, stated the case, "I could never see how we were contributing to the solution of Cambodia's refugee problems by flying its few remaining qualified people to new homes thousands of miles away."⁸

Ambassador Abramowitz in Bangkok was so concerned about this growing opposition to refugees that he visited a refugee camp and interviewed 16 Indochinese to satisfy himself that they had valid claims to be fleeing persecution.⁹ And Abramowitz fired off a stinging telegram to Washington that said, "I have been simmering for the last two weeks while watching the outrageous way in which INS has been handling Cambodian refugees."¹⁰ Abramowitz, in turn, was accused by Huddleston of having "bullied" INS into accepting large numbers of Cambodians for resettlement who were not true refugees.¹¹ It was the old problem of determining who was and who was not a refugee. Did economic motives disqualify a person? UNHCR, in theory, did not believe so: "the fact that a person has an economic motive should not of itself prejudice his claim to refugee status, for 'such [economic] motives are often revealed in practice to mean that the individual has been denied the right in his own land to earn his living in peace or in the occupation, skill, or profession in which he is qualified.'"¹² That was the liberal interpretation of refugee law; the conservative interpretation, increasingly cited by opponents of refugee resettlement, was that a person must suffer "confinement, torture or death inflicted on account of race, religion, or political viewpoint" in order to be a refugee.¹³ Leo Cherne observed that the contention that the Indochinese were economic migrants rather than refugees was "orchestrated" in part by UNHCR, OXFAM, the American Friends Service Committee and others "who, for philosophical reasons, wish to diminish the status of the refugees ... with a view to refurbishing the reputation of Vietnam."¹⁴

The less generous attitude of the State Department was reflected in a speech drafted for new Under Secretary Walter J. Stoessel to give to the Senate Judiciary Committee on September 22, 1981. Stoessel supported Thailand's policy of "humane deterrence," which aimed to discourage future refugees by prison-like conditions in refugee camps. He applauded the fact that "Ethnic Lao have been placed in separate more austere camps where voluntary agencies are not permitted to provide them with additional services and where delegations from resettlement nations are not permitted to interview them for the purpose of resettlement processing." Stoessel advocated "longer stays in camp before resettlement."¹⁵ The department also concurred in a reduction of Indochinese refugee quotas—or ceilings as they came to be called. Congress cut the ceiling from a high of 168,000 in 1980 and 1981 to 96,000 in 1982, 64,000 in 1983, and

Table 6.
Indochinese Refugees Resettled by Country
April 1975–July 31, 1981*

1.	United States	515,029
2.	China	265,588
3.	France	77,787
4.	Canada	77,317
5.	Australia	54,623
6.	Germany	19,102
7.	United Kingdom	15,239
8.	Switzerland	8,930
9.	Belgium	4,429
10.	Netherlands	4,278
11.	New Zealand	3,994
12.	Italy	2,982
13.	Sweden	2,669
14.	Norway	2,641
15.	Denmark	2,081
16.	Argentina	1,281
17.	Others	17,367
	Grand Total	1,075,337

*United States, Cong. House, *Refugee Problems in Southeast Asia*, 1981: a staff report, 12. Small errors in arithmetic corrected by the author.

50,000 in 1983.[16] (The actual numbers on Indochinese admitted into the U.S. in each of these years were substantially under the ceilings.)

UNHCR had long argued against resettlement. UNHCR's Barber stated the case: "a refugee camp would never be emptied, because there were always new arrivals keen to follow their relatives and friends to a new home in the West."[17] That statement does not seem to be true for the great majority of refugees fleeing Vietnam in 1978 and 1979 and Cambodia in 1979 and 1980, the years of greatest exodus. Nor was it true of the Hmong and other Lao crossing into Thailand. The refugees had adequate — in fact compelling — reasons to undertake their dangerous trek or voyage to a new land and an uncertain future. Leo Cherne and the Citizen's Commission on Indochinese Refugees struck back at the naysayers. "The boat people, we are told by some, brave the risk of seeing their children drown and their wives and daughters raped by pirates for no other reasons than their hope of economic betterment. And not so long ago it was considered necessary to continue the fighting in Indochina to prevent a bloodbath. The bloodbath happened in Cambodia and three million people perished. Are we now to deny refugee status to those Cambodians who escaped when escape became possible."[18] The advocacy of Cherne and others kept the refugee program afloat when detractors, such as Senator Huddleston, would have cut it further and faster. Nevertheless, Lionel Rosenblatt recalled that the watchword of the State Department in 1981 was to "manage down" the refugee numbers.[19]

Congress passed legislation creating a Bureau of Refugee Affairs at State in 1980, giving refugee affairs increased stature and recognition. However, for cautious Washington bureaucrats the refugee workers in Southeast Asia were too pro-refugee, too undisciplined and individualistic, and, one suspects, too knowledgeable of the region and too expert at their jobs. Cynics have said that once a new government office becomes stable enough to put drapes on the windows its usefulness and efficiency have ceased. Bureaucratic somnolence is induced, innovation is discouraged, process becomes paramount, and nonconforming rebels and malcontents are exiled. Lionel's operation in Thailand never gave much thought to drapes.

* * *

On the heels of growing resistance in Congress and the State Department came an incident that motivated some in the State Department to ensure that the refugee workers in Southeast Asia were not major players in the Washington bureaucracy. Different versions of the story were told, but Jim Schill gave the most complete account. Jim was back in Washington in 1981 working in the new Refugee Bureau. The maximum number of Indochinese refugees eligible for admission into the United States in fiscal year 1981, ending September 30, 1981, was a maximum of 14,000 per month. However, by August only an average of 10,000 per month had entered the U.S. that year. Schill, apparently unfamiliar with the implicit U.S. policy of "managing down" refugee resettlement, made the reasonable assumption that flexibility in catching up for shortfalls in the earlier part of the year was justifiable.[20] Moreover, the embassies in Southeast Asian countries reported they had many refugees processed and waiting to travel to the U.S. Schill sent a telegram to the embassies telling them to send the additional refugees, without asking how many might be sent. He got many more than he had bargained for. Twenty-one thousand Indochinese arrived in the U.S. in September.[21] INS and Congress threw a fit, the resettlement program in the U.S. was overwhelmed, and the leaders of the Bureau of Refugee Affairs were embarrassed. Moreover, the suspicion was that the old guard of refugee workers had pulled a fast one on the bureaucracy by sneaking in thousands of additional refugees. Schill's boss Hank Cushing, who had been shot and nearly killed by an intruder in his house earlier that year, took most of the blame and Congressional inquiries made his life miserable for weeks.[22]

For once Lionel Rosenblatt could not be fingered as the culprit behind the great refugee invasion of September 1981. He had left his job in Bangkok earlier that year and returned to the States. However, there may have been suspicions that he had engineered the event behind the scenes. One of the new officials in the Refugee Bureau told him that for a short-term gain, the refugee workers — through their zeal — had given the enemies of the refugee program, both inside and outside the Department, a club to beat them with. Rosenblatt and others defended themselves by saying that fine-tuning refugee admissions

18. The End of the Beginning 239

was like trying to turn an ocean liner—a long lead time was needed. Flights were arranged, tickets purchased, and sponsors in the U.S. complained or lost interest if their refugee families did not arrive promptly. Moreover, it was unconscionable to keep refugees waiting month after month in camps after they had been approved for resettlement and slots were available within the ceilings approved by Congress.

On his return to Washington, Lionel had assumed he would be offered an important job in the Refugee Bureau, perhaps taking over as Deputy Assistant Secretary for Resettlement from Shep Lowman. What he got was frozen out. No job at all was offered him and he found himself walking the halls of the State Department looking for a position. Lionel, however, had many friends and supporters and he soon landed a prestigious one-year fellowship to promote good relationships between communities and refugees in the United States—a job that suited him admirably. However, the handwriting was on the wall. His career as the State Department's best-known refugee officer was over.[23]

Rosenblatt left the State Department in the late 1980s to become the head of Refugees International, the free-wheeling, passionate organization that Sue Morton had created. In that job, he became known for his fearless and forthright critiques of UN and U.S. policies toward refugees. He expanded his reach to encompass Bosnians, Rwandans, and others in the 1990s, but always kept a careful eye on the Indochinese refugees now growing old in camps in Southeast Asia.

Lionel's closest collaborator, Shep Lowman, also soon departed refugee work. In 1982 he was off to Honduras as Deputy Chief of Mission. He then retired and preceded Rosenblatt as President of Refugees International. His long time comrade in arms, Hank Cushing, left the refugee bureau in May 1982.

* * *

Refugee crises bring out the best and the worst of humans. Refugee workers in Southeast Asia recalled their experience as the most satisfying time in their careers. But refugee and emergency work also bring out the worst. The temptations are strong to pocket money or to trade favors with powerless refugees for sex. Yvette Pierpaoli ran into one of the bad eggs in the refugee basket.

One day in Bangkok in 1979, a USAID official named George Warner, 47 years old, called at the office of SUSINDO, Yvette and Kurt Furrer's company.[24] Warner demanded a ten percent commission on all rice purchased by SUSINDO for refugees. Cooperate, he said, or he would ruin SUSINDO's reputation. Kurt and Yvette were appalled, Yvette because she could not imagine anything more evil than cheating on food meant for refugees and Kurt because he, a rigorous Swiss, deplored corruption. Yvette consulted with Lionel and they told Ambassador Abramowitz. A team of USAID inspectors from Washington descended secretly on Bangkok. They told Yvette and Kurt to pay Warner the kickbacks he demanded and they would swoop in and arrest him. The USAID inspectors proved to be the Keystone Kops and, for reasons beyond the comprehension of Yvette, they didn't attempt to arrest Warner.

Six months later, the FBI appeared with renewed interest to get Warner and muscled a now disillusioned and reluctant Kurt and Yvette into cooperation. Cooperate, the FBI said, or they would sabotage SUSINDO. Warner steered a $4.8 million contract for seed rice to SUSINDO and Kurt agreed, with the FBI's concurrence, to pay $138,000 in a kickback to Warner. Soon, Kurt found himself in a Washington hotel room, wired for sound, with $45,000 to pay Warner as the last installment of his fee for arranging the transaction. The plan was for Kurt to invite Warner to his room, pay him the kickback while being recorded for sound and video and then the FBI would swoop in and arrest Warner with the recordings as evidence.[25]

It worked more or less as planned but the next day the *Washington Post* reported "U.S. Official Is Accused of Accepting Kickback in Cambodia Aid Program," which also implicated Kurt and Yvette in the crime.[26] Instead of heroes, they found themselves the target of suspicions in Bangkok. The Swedish government, the UN, ICRC, and most humanitarian organizations cancelled business with them. SUSINDO, the most honest, principled, idealistic supplier of rice to Cambodian refugees was suddenly on everyone's black list. Old friends passed Yvette on the street without speaking.

Finally, the U.S. Department of Justice released a letter that cleared Kurt and Yvette of wrongdoing and commended them for their role in the Warner case. They settled back into the good graces of the international community of Thailand — except that the ultra cautious ICRC never did business with them again.

They had a new worry, however. Now identified as the people who had informed on Warner they worried that they might be assassinated by his Thai cronies. The American Embassy offered them bodyguards. Kurt refused. Yvette also refused because she had lost all faith in the Americans. She hired a Thai bodyguard; she was almost as afraid of him as she was of assassins. The denouement of this story is unsatisfying and tragic. The FBI's recording of Warner accepting the bribe was defective. Warner escaped prosecution for serious crimes and ended up pleading guilty to a lesser charge and being fined $40,000.[27]

About a year later, Kurt Furrer dropped dead of a heart attack on an airplane en route to Bangkok. Yvette blamed his heart attack on the extraordinary strain he had undergone in the Warner affair.[28] Disgusted with the business world, Yvette took her exit. She moved back to France, the homeland she had once spurned in favor of Cambodia. Without Kurt to protect her, she was soon cheated out of her business. She went home as she had left: broke.[29]

When Lionel became president of Refugees International in 1989 Yvette was the first person he hired and she fit admirably into her job as a traveling advocate for refugees around the world. However, on a wet and stormy day in

18. The End of the Beginning

Lionel Rosenblatt and Yvette Pierpaoli at Angkor Wat in Cambodia in 1997. Yvette was killed in an automobile accident in Albania in 1999. (Larry Thompson)

Albania in 1999, the driver of the taxi she had rented to travel to a refugee camp for Kosovars skidded over a cliff. She died in the accident.[30] She was buried in France. Lionel Rosenblatt and her friend, the novelist John Le Carré, spoke at her funeral. Le Carré would later dedicate his book *The Constant Gardener* to Yvette.

* * *

On April 30, 1982, Jim Schill in Washington received a telephone call from John Tucker. Jerry Daniels had been found dead in his Bangkok apartment. Daniels had been dead for several days when his body was discovered. His death was blamed on a gas water heater that had leaked gas into the room.

John Tucker and Schill accompanied Jerry's remains to Missoula. On arrival, they were greeted by General Vang Pao and 15 Hmong and CIA mourners, including several of the Hog's colleagues: Glassman, Lucky, Zack, Judy, and Mr. Clean. Jerry's brother Big Dan was there to pick up the casket in his pickup truck and take it to the mortuary. The Hmong asked for the casket to be opened to view the remains. The mortician said no, the casket was sealed by order of the Embassy in Bangkok. The closed casket aroused speculation among the Hmong that Daniels had been murdered or that his death had been faked by the CIA and a still living Daniels was off to some other country on a new and secret mission.[31]

The Hmong held a traditional funeral for Jerry and wrote the following eulogy to him:

In Memory

From 1961 until the Communist takeover of Laos, our friend Jerry Daniels, dedicated his every ounce of energy towards helping the Hmong, the free people of Laos, improve the quality of our lives. Jerry gladly accepted life in our rural villages in order to better understand our problems, aspirations and dreams. Jerry shared with us the dream that one day life would return to normal and the Hmong people would be able to once again enjoy the beauty and serenity of the high mountains of Laos.

Sadly, the dream was not to be. In 1975, the anti-Communist government of Laos fell to the invaders and the Hmong people along with our American friend had to flee for our lives to seek refuge in Thailand.

Jerry continued to serve the people he loved as a State Department official at the American Embassy in Bangkok. Jerry saw to it that the Hmong were given the opportunity to come to the U.S. to begin a new life. We have the courage to meet the challenges which we must face because our friend Jerry taught us well. Jerry was not only our mentor, but our friend as well. He dedicated more than twenty years of his life to us and we grew to know him well. Not only in name, but in spirit too. I guess we love Jerry so much because we always knew that he honestly cared.

Jerry's life came to a premature end in Bangkok, still serving the people he had

Jerry Daniels' tombstone in Missoula, Montana. The stone is engraved with a Hmong scene from highland Laos. (Mac Thompson collection)

18. The End of the Beginning 243

grown to love. We all owe Jerry a lot and will miss him very much. Each of us in our own way will wish our friend a sad farewell.

So until we meet again — Goodbye old friend.[32]

* * *

Mac Thompson was the last of the old refugee workers still on station in Southeast Asia. The great refugee invasion of September 1981 was followed by the INS "Reign of Terror" in 1982. The dispute centered on INS interviews of 20,000 Cambodians in Kamput camp. Many had been interviewed by JVA and the State Department and declared eligible for resettlement, but Cambodians had long been subjected to more stringent questioning of their eligibility for resettlement in the United States than other Indochinese.[33] Hmong had fought on the side of the U.S. in the long war against the North Vietnamese; many Vietnamese had worked closely with the United States and Americans had closer ties with Vietnamese than with Cambodians. Moreover, UNHCR continued to maintain that the repatriation of Cambodians was feasible — or would be feasible soon.

JVA had always been proud of its record in preparing cases for INS. More than 90 percent of its cases had customarily been approved. However, teams of INS interviewers arriving in Thailand in March 1982 to approve refugees at Kamput began turning down Cambodians for resettlement at rates of 30 and 50 percent.[34] JVA interviewers were enraged at the harsh treatment of Cambodians by INS officers who spent a few weeks in the camps — perhaps their first visit ever to Southeast Asia — and left behind devastation when they departed to be replaced by another team that was equally harsh and arbitrary.

INS interviewers maintained that the Cambodians did not meet the definition of "refugee" — one who had a reasonable fear of "confinement, torture or death inflicted on account of race, religion, or political viewpoint" if they were returned to Cambodia. That very restrictive definition had never been applied so rigorously to Indochinese — nor to other people around the world who had fled communist regimes. The general rule had been that Indochinese who reached a UNHCR-recognized camp were considered refugees (but not those who were in Cambodian border camps). Now, INS wanted to make a determination for Cambodians on a case-by-case basis in which each and every refugee would have to prove that he had a well-founded fear of persecution if he returned to Cambodia.[35] Fears of being killed in the crossfire of opposing armies or starving to death were no longer enough to establish a Cambodian's bona fides as a refugee. Although some of the INS officers were good guys — and a couple of them were women — they were often bullying, demanding, and behaved like petty tyrants.

Complaints from Mac and Mike Eiland led to an INS internal investigation which confirmed that its officials had been abusive to refugees. Instructions were sent to the field that INS officers were to be polite and courteous—

Table 7.
Indochinese Resettled in the United States*

Fiscal Year	Cambodian	Lao Highland	Lao Lowland	Vietnamese	Total
1975	4,600	300	500	125,000	130,400
1976	1,100	3,000	7,100	3,200	14,400
1977	300	1,700	400	1,900	4,300
1978	1,300	3,900	4,100	11,100	20,400
1979	6,000	11,300	18,900	44,500	80,700
1980	16,000	27,200	28,300	95,200	166,700
1981	27,100	3,700	15,600	86,100	132,500
1982	20,100	2,600	6,800	42,600	72,100
Total	76,500	53,700	81,700	409,600	621,500

*"Refugee Reports," December 18, 1987, derived from U.S. Gov. totals; Heim, 47. Numbers differ slightly depending upon the source.

but the opposite occurred. Approval rates at Kamput plummeted to new lows in October 1982 with 63 percent of refugee applications rejected one week.[36] Even telegrams from Washington and a visit to the camp by the attorney general, William French Smith, failed to solve the problem.

Mac spent November and December 1982 working at Kamput as the temporary head of the JVA there and living nearby. It was a near war, and the biggest challenge of Mac's career as he slowly and painfully persuaded, jollied, cajoled, and threatened the INS to get the resettlement program back on track. The war with INS was also fought in Washington. Mac telephoned Mike Eiland in Bangkok every evening with his tales of INS transgressions. Mike passed on the information to refugee advocates back in Washington, including Lionel, to demonstrate that INS representatives in Kamput were defying the guidance of their own agency. Mac lost 20 pounds during this ordeal, but by Christmas he was winning the battle and left Thailand to spend his first Christmas in the United States in 14 years.[37]

Mac came back after Christmas to continue the struggle with a somewhat chastened INS. The refugee advocates finally won the war with an assist from the White House and allies in Congress. On May 13, 1983, the White House issued a NSSD — National Security Study Directive — that demanded "proper and effective processing" of Indochinese refugees. In the careful and tortured prose of government, the NSSD ordered a review of refugee cases rejected by INS, including "those who fled Cambodia because of occurrences during the Pol Pot regime, former members of the military, those with close relatives in the United States, and persons who refuse to work with the new regime in Cambodia." Furthermore, unaccompanied minors, deserters, and evaders of military service in communist Vietnam were to have their cases reviewed. Additional

18. The End of the Beginning

training and "rotation" were prescribed for INS officers in Southeast Asia. "Rotation" meant that several INS agents were quickly transferred out of Southeast Asia. It was a resounding victory, ensuring the continuation of a significant Indochinese refugee resettlement program for the next decade.

Lionel attributed the victory to the work of Congressional staffer Jim Towey and Dick Childress of the National Security Council.[38] Senator Mark Hatfield's staffer, Jim Towey, was the most important ally of the refugee program in Congress.

* * *

It is fitting to close with a story of the Montagnards, the shy people of the Indochinese highlands. Few of the Montagnards had the opportunity to become refugees. They were trapped after the fall of Saigon. They continued their old war with the Vietnamese, but by 1977 they were decimated. About 10,000 of them — men, women, and children — took refuge in remote Mondulkiri province in Cambodia. There they led a precarious existence sandwiched between Vietnam and the Khmer Rouge. Most perished, but in 1986, 212 Montagnards escaped to Thailand and were subsequently resettled in Raleigh, North Carolina.[39]

Although shut out of the State Department's refugee bureau, Lionel never lost his commitment to the people who had helped the U.S. during the Vietnam War. In 1992, in a last major moment of satisfaction, he had the opportunity to help another group of Montagnards. The UN discovered a group of 400 in Mondulkiri. Lionel telephoned Sergio Vieira de Miello, a Brazilian heading the UN in Cambodia.[40] The Montagnards were in a dangerous position, he told Sergio. They might be attacked by the Vietnamese army very soon and forced back to Vietnam. What could the UN do? Sergio said he could bring the Montagnards to Phnom Penh, but only if he could tell the Cambodian government that they were in transit to the United States. Lionel promised he would arrange for the Montagnards to go to the U.S.— a promise he had no authority to make. Sergio took him at his word and they two concluded the deal with a verbal handshake.

Sergio went to Mondulkiri and negotiated an agreement with the Montagnards to surrender their weapons. They were airlifted by helicopter to Phnom Penh. Then, he sent a hand-written fax to Lionel in the United States:

Dear Lionel,
Operation concluded!
They were disarmed between last night and this morning (144 weapons) dissolved as a political/military organization and were relocated.... The ball is in your court. Please help with expedited processing.[41]

Lionel sprang into action and found a rare unanimity in the U.S. government about helping the Montagnards. Dennis Grace, the head of JVA, immediately sent JVA representatives to Phnom Penh to interview the Montagnards and prepare their cases for INS. In record time, INS responded positively and the Montagnards were flown to safety in Greensboro, North Carolina. Lionel was, as always, the agitator devoted to overcoming government lassitude and indifference about refugees. For both Sergio (whose distinguished career with the UN would end in 2003 when he died in the bombing of UN headquarters in Baghdad) and Lionel the rescue of the Montagnards was among their proudest moments.

* * *

The Indochinese refugee program in the 1970s attracted Americans from both ends of the political spectrum. Some, especially ex–Peace Corps volunteers working for JVA, were peaceniks who deplored the Vietnam War. On the opposite side were those who had played large roles in fighting that war, such as Colonel Mike Eiland and CIA agent Jerry Daniels. Lionel Rosenblatt collaborated with both the left and right of the political spectrum with equal facility. The refugee workers proved that a good heart depends on the individual, not on political orientation or occupation. Ambassador Morton Abramowitz spoke for all the refugee workers when he said that in the U.S. refugee program, "we have stepped on toes, displeased some with greater attachment to bureaucratic or narrow national interests, and incurred the wrath of those who see only sinister motives behind American purposes.... So be it. The misery and death along the Cambodian border ... demanded no less as did the memory of our ineffectiveness in the face of the Nazi holocaust."[42]

Just about everybody who worked with Indochinese refugees during those critical years of the late 1970s and early 1980s agreed that they had never worked harder at a job they loved. It was not easy; the pay was poor, especially if calculated on an hourly basis, and the bureaucratic rules and regulations that governed them were complex, onerous, and infuriating. They faced daily challenges, often in isolated places and within the sound of gunfire. They witnessed death, starvation, disease, and terror at close hand. Some were motivated by guilt, others by religious conviction, still others by adventure. Some were unabashed do-gooders while others recoiled at that description of themselves. Rosenblatt himself said his motivation was to clean up the mess left after a war. "During the Vietnam War, we spent billions of dollars. We ought to have been willing to spend some money and effort on the human aftermath."[43]

The refugee resettlement program had a profound impact on American foreign policy. In 1975, when Indochina fell to the communists, many anticipated that the other countries of the region would fall like dominos to communist pressure. By 1981 it had become clear that they would not. In the words of a State Department memorandum, the greatest contribution that the U.S. made to the stability of Southeast Asia had been to take the refugee burden off the backs of Thailand, Malaysia, and Indonesia. What could not have been done with arms and money was accomplished through the refugee program. Doing

18. The End of the Beginning

the right thing, as is often true, had favorable political consequences.[44] The refugee program was a glorious moment of commitment for the men and women in Southeast Asia in the chaotic and tragic years that followed the Vietnam War. This has been their story.

* * *

Chapter Notes

The World Wide Web is now a major source. Through its wonders, material is often available in more than one format. For example, books and articles are often republished in whole or in part on the WWW, and sometimes on more than one website. In endnotes in which I cite web pages as the source, it should be understood that the material may also be available elsewhere and in other formats.

Introduction

1. Robinson, *Terms of Refuge*, 295.
2. Department of the Army, "After Action Report: Indiantown Gap," author's files.

Chapter 1

1. Military units of the Provisional Revolutionary Government (PRG), the Viet Cong, were with the NVA, but they were a force of secondary importance. I use the word "refugee" in the popular sense, meaning people fleeing a war or insurrection. Technically and legally, a person must cross an international border to become a "refugee" and those remaining in their homeland are properly called "internally displaced persons" or "internal refugees." My loose use of the word "refugees," however, conforms to general usage. A discussion of the legal term "refugee" and its implications follows in a later chapter. <http://www.riciok.com/Cease_Fire/last_christmas.htm> Accessed April 16, 2009.
2. *Washington Post*, January 22, 1975, A-12.
3. Wisner, interview.
4. United States, Cong. House, *Refugees from Indochina*, 157.
5. Snepp, page 296. Much of this chapter also derives from interviews with Rosenblatt.
6. Wisner, interview.
7. <http://www.mtholyoke.edu/acad/intrel/pentagon3/doc253.htm> Accessed April 17, 2009; Text also found in *The Pentagon Papers*, Gravel Edition, Vol. 3, 694–702.
8. <http://news.bbc.co.uk/1/hi/world/asia-pacific/716609.stm> Accessed April 16. 2009.
9. <http://www.afa.org/magazine/April 2000/0400saigon.asp> Accessed December 18, 2005.
10. Robinson, *Terms of Refuge*, 15–17.
11. Scott, 72.
12. Phil McCombs, "Stranglehold: A Reporter's Personal Story of Saigon's Final Weeks," *Washington Post Magazine*, April 25, 1985, 10.
13. Willenson, 302.
14. Ibid., 303.
15. Freeman, 258.
16. CIA station chief Thomas Polgar in Willenson, 291–292.
17. Walter J. Boyne, "The Fall of Saigon." <http://www.afa.org/magazine/april2000/0400saigon.asp>
18. Douglas Brinkley, "Of Ladders and Letters," *Time*, April 24, 2000. <http://www.time.com/time/asia/magazine/2000/0424/history.vietnam.html>
19. Quinn, interview.
20. United States, Cong. House, *The Vietnam-Cambodia Emergency, 1975, Part III — Vietnam Evacuation: Testimony of Ambassador Graham A. Martin*, 542, 543.
21. United States, Cong. House, *Refugees from Indochina*, 107.
22. Ibid., 157.
23. McManaway, interview.
24. Ibid.; Interagency Task Force, "Report to the Congress," June 15, 1976, 14, author's files.
25. Butler, 196.
26. Halberstadt, 15.
27. Memorandum of Conversation, April 5, 1975, author's files.

28. *Washington Post*, April 11, 1975, A-12.
29. *Washington Post*, May 5, 1975, A-1.
30. Butler, 263.
31. White House Telegram from Kissinger to Martin, April 17, 1975, author's files. I have not attempted to delve into the bureaucratic complexities of the decision to parole the Vietnamese.
32. Isaacs, 434–435.
33. <http://www.historyplace.com/speeches/ford-tulane.htm> Accessed July 24, 2009.

Chapter 2

1. Rosenblatt, interview, plus his written notes about the flight, author's files.
2. Nguyen Thi Hue, interview.
3. McBride, interview.
4. Rosenblatt, interview.
5. Dirck Halstead, "White Christmas," *The Digital Journalist*. <http://digitaljournalist.org/issue0005/ch3.htm> Accessed June 18, 2006.
6. Rogers, interview.
7. <http://paavn.org/about.html1.html> Accessed April 1, 2007.
8. <http://www.raoulwallenberg.net/?en/press/3873.htm> Accessed April 1, 2007.
9. *Washington Post Magazine*, April 21, 1985, 19–21.
10. Dirck Halstead, "White Christmas," *The Digital Journalist*. <http://www.digitaljournalist.org/issue0005/ch8.htm> Accessed June 18, 2006.
11. Public Broadcasting System, "Vietnam Passage: Journeys from War to Peace." <http://www.pbs.org/vietnampasssge/index.html> Accessed April 1, 2007.
12. Summers, "Last Days in Vietnam."
13. Lowman, interview.
14. Lavalle, 93.
15. Lowman, interview.
16. McBride, interview.
17. Appy, 503–504.
18. Public Broadcasting System, "Vietnam Passage: The Stories: Cuong." <http://www.pbs.org/vietnampassage/Stories/stories.coung.02.html> Accessed July 3, 2006.
19. George J. Church, "Saigon: The Final 10 days," *Time*, April 24, 1995. <http://www.wellesley.edu/Polisci/wj/Vietnam/Readings/saigonfall.htm> Accessed July 3, 2006.
20. Ibid.
21. Henderson, 356.
22. <http://news.bbc.co.uk/1/low/world/asia-pacific/716609.stm> Accessed December 5, 2005.
23. Summers, "Last Days in Vietnam," 70–71. <http://www.clemson.edu/caah/history/FacultyPages/EdMoise/end.html> Accessed December 21, 2005.
24. Rogers, interview.
25. Hickey, 335.
26. Ibid., 357–358.
27. Tomsen, author's files.
28. Alexander Casella, "Refugees Awaken Ghosts of Vietnam." <http://www.usaforunhcr.org/archives.cfm?ID=3365&catid=2&cat=Hot%20News>
29. Carter, 14, 39. <http://www.clemson.edu/caah/history/FacultyPages/EdMoise/end.html> Accessed December 21, 2005.
30. "President Ford's Letter to the Fall of Saigon Marines." <http://www.fallofsaigon.org/ford.htm> Accessed December 28, 2005.

Chapter 3

1. Most details about Pierpaoli in this chapter are from her autobiography, *Mother to a Thousand Children*, in an unpublished English translation (it was published in French as *La Femme Aux Milles Enfants*). Page numbers are from the English translation. The author also draws on his memory of many discussions with Yvette.
2. Pierpaoli, 13.
3. Variations of the word *farang* are used in the languages of many countries of Asia to refer, sometimes derisively, to Europeans and Americans. The word derives from "Frank," the medieval word for the French.
4. <http://www.unc.edu/depts/diplomat/archives_roll/2001_10-12/bergesen_riot/bergesen_riot.html> Accessed May 22, 2006.
5. Kamm, 35.
6. <http://www.senate.gov/artandhistory/history/resources/pdf/valeo_interview__03.pdf> Accessed June 1, 2005.
7. Kirk, 73.
8. Rosenblatt, interview. In 1996 Rosenblatt and Pierpaoli lead a delegation of Refugees International board members who met with Sihanouk.
9. Recent disclosures indicate the bombing might have begun in 1965. <http://www.walrusmagazine.com/articles/2006.10-history-bombing-cambodia/>
10. <http://www.fpif.org/pdf/gac/0211coldam.pdf> Accessed July 20, 2009.
11. Shawcross, *Sideshow*, 269.
12. Pierpaoli, 43.
13. Author's conversations with Pierpaoli.
14. Pierpaoli, 72.
15. The boy, Olivier, grew up to be a chef in France and now owns his own restaurant.
16. Short, 262.
17. Ibid., 264.
18. Shawcross, *Sideshow*, 348.
19. Jacques, 284–287.
20. Deac, 7.
21. Reprinted in many sources, including Loescher and Scanlan, 104.

22. <http://www.mekong.net/cambodia/sihanouk.htm> Accessed August 14, 2006.
23. Sydney Schanberg, "Enigmatic Cambodians," *The New York Times*, March 13, 1975, A-1.
24. Supplemental assistance for Cambodia report, March 12, 1975, Folder 14, Box 06, Douglas Pike Collection: Unit 15 — Cambodia, The Vietnam Archive, Texas Tech University, 4.
25. Ibid., 23, 24.
26. Ponchaud, 4, 5.
27. Short, 268.
28. Crossan, xii.
29. Ponchaud, 6–7.
30. Ponchaud, as quoted in Short, 272.
31. Kiernan, *The Pol Pot Regime,* 49; Barron and Paul, 203.
32. United States, Cong. House, *Human Rights in Cambodia,* 10.
33. Barron and Paul, 38–39.
34. "Cambodia's Crime," *The New York Times*, July 9, 1975, 30.
35. Ker Munthit <http://www.asianweek.com/2000_04_20/news_phnompenh.html> Accessed August 14, 2006.
36. United States, Cong. House, *Human Rights in Cambodia,* 10–11.
37. "Cambodia's Crime," *The New York Times*, July 9, 1975, 30.
38. Mean Sangkhim, "Democratic Kampuchea: An Updated View," *Southeast Asian Affairs*, 4, 1977. Extracted from PCI Full Text, published by ProQuest Information and Learning Company.
39. William Shawcross, "The Third Indochina War," *New York Review of Books*, April 6, 1978.
40. Sophal Ear, "The Khmer Rouge Cannon 1975–1979: The Standard Total Academic View on Cambodia." Quoted from Foreign Broadcasting Information Service, May 15, 1977. <http://jim.com/canon.htm> Accessed July 25, 2006.
41. Ponchaud, 21.
42. Quinn, 86, attributed to a speech by Pol Pot.
43. Ibid., 87.
44. Barron and Paul, 59–60.
45. Quinn, 94–95.
46. Ibid., 90.
47. Twining, in United States. Cong. House, *Human Rights in Cambodia,* 5, said that the KR had established a no-man's land 25 miles wide at the border.
48. Henry Kamm, "Cambodian Refugees Tell of Revolutionary Upheaval," *The New York Times*, July 15, 1975, 1, 10.
49. CNN.com transcripts. May 26, 2000. <http://transcripts.cnn.com/TRANSCRIPTS/0005/26/nr.oo.html> Accessed July 31, 2005.
50. Deac, 227.
51. Kissinger, 529–530.
52. Maguire, 41.
53. Sydney H. Schanberg, "Evacuation Convoy to Thailand: Arduous Trip Through the Secret Cambodia," *The New York Times*, May 8, 1975, 14.
54. Pierpaoli, 114.
55. Morton, interview.
56. Solarz, interview.

Chapter 4

1. Author's observations, 1997.
2. "Lao People's Democratic Republic," *LM Monitor*, 2005. <http://www.icbl.org/lm/2005/laos.html> Accessed May 15, 2006.
3. *The New York Times*, July 9, 1973, 33.
4. Estimate derived from consultation with Mac Thompson.
5. A story heard by the author about 1969.
6. Hamilton-Merritt, 351.
7. Interview with Norman Gardner, March 14, 2001, Norman Gardner Collection, The Vietnam Archive, Texas Tech University, 33. Actually, Vang Pao had 28 children.
8. Tony Kennedy and Paul McEnroe, "The Covert Wars of Vang Pao," *Minneapolis–St. Paul Star Tribune*, July 2, 2005. <http://www.startribune.com/1742/v-print/story/34839.html>
9. Warner, 45.
10. Kennedy and McEnroe.
11. "Once Upon a Time in the CIA," documentary film by Roger Warner. <http://www.montgomerylaw.net/ciadoc.html> Accessed May 24, 2006. A shorter version of his film is on Youtube.com.
12. "Edgar Buell," Hmong National Development, Inc. <http://www.hndlink.org/mrpop.htm> Accessed June 4, 2006.
13. As remembered by John Tucker.
14. <http://www.smokejumpers.com/smokejumper_magazine/item.php?articles_id=299&magazine_editions_id=19> Accessed July 25, 2009.
15. Parker, 38–39.
16. "Vientiane by Night," *CP Media: The Asia Experts*. <http://www.cpamedia.com/travel/vientiane_by_night/> Accessed July 14, 2006.
17. Ibid.
18. Eugene Rossel, "Laos: A Personal View." <http://home.earthlink.net/~aircommando1/LaosEDR.htm> Accessed March 12, 2006.
19. Interview with Norman Gardner, March 14, 2001, Norman Gardner Collection, The Vietnam Archive, Texas Tech University, 33; July 30, 2009.
20. Les Strouse, "The Last Nerve Wracking Flight out of Laos," *Mekong Express Mail*, March

2003, 3; December 4, 2005; Warner, 345; Mac Thompson, personal correspondence.
21. IATF Briefing book, May 12, 1975, author's files.
22. <http:///www.air-america.org/About/History.shtml> Accessed April 24, 2006. This number has been questioned.
23. Robinson, *Terms of Refuge*, 13.
24. <http://www.thaitourism.com/articles/05_04_2.asp> Accessed April 24, 2006.
25. Robbins, 56.
26. Morrison, 15.
27. Ibid., 17. Also Schill, interview.
28. Quincy, 361.
29. Yang Dao in Santoli, 261–262.
30. Most of the following story of the evacuation of the Hmong is from Morrison's *Sky Is Falling*.
31. Morrison, 72.
32. Trest, 252; Morrison, 109–111; Aderholt, interview, Bird Air Documents, author's files.
33. Morrison, 89.
34. Les Strouse, "The Last Nerve Wracking Flight Out of Laos," *Mekong Express Mail*, March 2003, 3, December 4, 2005.
35. Morrison, 201.
36. Ibid., 135.
37. Kue Chaw, interview.
38. Morrison, 80.
39. Tony Kennedy and Paul McEnroe, "The Covert Wars of Vang Pao," *Minneapolis–St. Paul Star Tribune*, July 2, 2005. <http://www.startribune.com/1742/v-printstory/34839.html> Accessed March 24, 2007.
40. Morrison, 171.
41. Schill, 98–99.
42. David A. Andelman, "Laos Falls to the Communists. I Was There," *American Heritage.com*. <http://www.americanheritage.com/articles/web/20051202-communism-catfish-vietnam-thailand-cambodia-pathet-lao-cia-bangkok-vientiane.shtml> Accessed June 18, 2006.
43. "Vientiane by Night," *CPA Media*. <http://www.cpamedia.com/travel/vientiane_by_night/> Accessed June18, 2006.
44. Quincy, 373–375. Or Pong Song per Quincy.
45. Mote, 37–40.
46. <http://openweb.tvnews.vanderbilt.edu/1978-8/1978-08-23-NBC-13.html> Accessed June 18, 2006.
47. Quincy, 376.
48. Unconfirmed. Widely believed by refugee workers.
49. "Vang Pao Leaves Asia," *The New York Times* (1857–Current file); June 18, 1975; ProQuest Historical Newspapers *The New York Times* (1851–2003), 5.
50. "Dedicated to the U.S. Secret Army in Laos, 1961–1973," Arlington National Cemetery website. <http://wwm w.arlingtoncemetery.net/laosmem.htm.> Accessed June 14, 2006. The figure of 70,000 has been questioned.
51. Ibid.

Chapter 5

1. *Newsweek*, May 5, 1975, 30.
2. *Newsweek*, May 12, 1975, 37.
3. Mackie, 26.
4. *Newsweek*, May 5, 1975, 30.
5. Mackie, 7–8.
6. To put it bureaucratically, as did Henry Kissinger, "negotiations with foreign governments for alternate staging areas were becoming so protracted and sharply conditioned as to make this alternative impractical." *Pacific Daily News* quoted from Mackie, 13.
7. Moos and Morrison, 34.
8. Ibid.
9. Ibid.
10. Rosenblatt, interview.
11. *Washington Post*, May 5, 1975, A-1.
12. Kissinger, 544.
13. Rosenblatt, interview.
14. Kelly Nicholas, "Navy, residents remember Operation New Life," *Pacific Navigator*, April 22, 2005. <http://www.guampdn.com/guampublishing/navigator/data/EEEuEuplAyaUFCNQAB.htm> Accessed July 20, 2006.
15. Moos and Morrison, 43.
16. Nicholas.
17. United States, Cong. House, *Indochina Evacuation and Refugee Problems, Part IV*, 5.
18. David V. Cristomo, "Guam Hosts Refugees in 1975," *Pacific Daily News*. <http://www.guampdn.com/apps/pbcs.dll/article?AID=/20050718/NEWSO1/507180301/1002&temp> Accessed July 18, 2005.
19. Mackie, 57.
20. Ibid., 53.
21. <http://www.guampdn.com/guampublishing/special-secetions/agum-2005/welcome2.htm> Some of the highest winds ever recorded took place on Guam in 1997: 236 miles per hour.
22. "Camp Experiences of Indochinese Refugees in the United States," American Friends Service Committee, Summer 1975, author's files.
23. Ibid.
24. Doyle and Maitland, 13.
25. Tran Dinh Tru and To Hong Duc, *My Mistep and Mishap under the Cyclops*, February 2002, 33. Unpublished manuscript.
26. Ibid., 34.
27. Ibid., 37.
28. Tru says 3,000, but the actual number indicating an interest in repatriation was less than 2,000.
29. "Indochina Refugee Resettlement," *The

Department of State: Special Report, No. 20, August 1975, 6, author's files.
30. Wisner, interview.
31. Loescher and Scanlan, 109. Plus, documents in United States, Cong. House, *Refugees from Indochina*.
32. "Basic Facts." <http://www.unhcr.org/cgi-bin/texis/vtx/basics/opendoc.htm?tbl=BASICS&id=3b0280294> Accessed July 22, 2005. My description of international refugee law is as brief and simple as I can make it.
33. Previous refugee crises, especially refugees from Bangladesh in the early 1970s, presaged Indochina, but in size, complexity and duration the Indochinese refugee crisis was unique.
34. UNHCR, *State of the World's Refugees*, 79.
35. UNHCR, "Protecting Refugees." <http://www.unhcr.org/cgi-bin/texis/vtx/protect?id=3c0794574> Accessed July 22, 2005.
36. Loescher, 191.
37. United States. Cong. House, *Indochina Evacuation and Refugee Problems: Part IV*, 56–62.
38. "Repatriates for Vietnam and Cambodia," Memorandum from Julia Vadala Taft to the Secretary of State, July 21, 1975, author's files.
39. Tru, 58.
40. "Vietnamese and Cambodian Refugees Repatriates," Memorandum from Julia Vadala Taft to the Secretary of State, September 11, 1975, author's files.
41. Taft, interview.
42. "UNHCR Position on the Presidential Decision to Make Available a Ship for the Voluntary Repatriation on Guam," statement issued by UNHCR, Geneva, September 30, 1975, author's files.
43. "After Action Report: Office of Special Concerns," December 23, 1975. Tab "C" "Repatriation," author's files.
44. "Guam Refugee Ship in Vietnam Waters," *The New York Times*, October 28, 1975, 11.
45. Number as cited in "Report to the Congress: HEW Refugee Task Force," March 15, 1976, 31.
46. "Profile of Guam Repatriate Population," author's files.
47. Ibid., "After Action Report."
48. Tru, 129–130.
49. Ibid., 146.
50. Ibid., 167.
51. Ibid., 169.
52. Ibid., 175–176.
53. Ibid., 176.
54. Ibid., 178.
55. United States, Cong. House, *Refugees from Indochina*, 472.
56. Podhoretz, 88.
57. *Country Studies: Vietnam. After 1975.* <http://www.country-studies.com/vietnam/vietnam-after-1975.html> Accessed August 12, 2006.
58. Sophie and Paul Quinn-Judge, "Viet Nam: Reunification and Reconciliation," *US/Indochina Report*, Indochina Resource Center, April 30, 1976.
59. Doyle and Maitland, 19.

Chapter 6

1. IATF Briefing book, May 12, 1975, author's files.
2. "A Cool and Wary Reception," *Time*, May 12, 1976.
3. David Nyhan, "A Questionable Welcome for the Wave of Refugees," *Boston Globe*, May 4, 1975. Quoted from United States Cong. House, *Indochinese Evacuation and Refugee Problems*, 113–114.
4. Nyhan.
5. Ibid.
6. "Forum," *Time*, May 26, 1975.
7. Nyhan.
8. Television News Archive, "NBC Evening News," May 28, 1975.
9. Taft, interview and oral history.
10. *Washington Post*, May 5, A-1.
11. Ron Shaffer and Doug Brown, "Refugees Start Settling Here," *The Washington Post*, May 9, 1975, A-1.
12. "Indochina Refugee Resettlement," *Department of State: Special Report, No. 20*, August 1975, 2.
13. Wisner, interview.
14. "Environmental Impact Assessment: Vietnamese Evacuation and Refugee Program," 11–12, author's files.
15. Personal experiences of the author.
16. *Newsweek*, May 12, 1975, 32.
17. Ibid., 38.
18. Rosenblatt, interview.
19. *Indiantown Gap*, 80.
20. <http://dougdawg.blogspot.com/2006/10/asian-district-today-story_23.html> Accessed April 1, 2007.
21. Nguyen Thi Hue, interview.
22. Peter Nguyen, "A History Left Behind." <http://www.hotaspho.com/html/history.htm> Accessed August 27, 2006.
23. *History Magazine* says 2.59 million. <http://www.vhfcn.org/stat.html> Accessed August 20, 2009.
24. Quinn, interview.
25. *Indiantown Gap*, Annex, Friedman report, 20.
26. Kelly, 132.
27. Ibid.
28. The term VOLAG has since fallen into

disuse and NGO (Non Governmental Organization) is now more commonly used.
29. Kelly, 135.
30. Wisner, interview.
31. Jonathan Saruk, "The Star Talks to Robert P. DeVecchi, Believer in Second Chances," June 16, 2005. <http://archive.easthamptonsar.com/ehquery/20050616.news.htm> Accessed September 3, 2006.
32. *After Action Report*, Fort Chaffee, I-62.
33. Lewis, interview.
34. July 17, 1975, letter from John E. McCarthy, Director USCC, to Julia Taft, author's files.
35. United States, Cong. House, *Refugees from Indochina*, 411–412.
36. *Indiantown Gap*, 85.
37. *Indiantown Gap*, Annex, page 5, Friedman report.
38. Ibid., 3.
39. *Indiantown Gap*, 50.
40. Compiled from various reports in *Indiantown Gap*.
41. *Indiantown Gap*, 71.
42. *Indiantown Gap*, Annex, Policy Guidance No. 3.
43. *Indiantown Gap*, 51.
44. *Indiantown Gap*, Annex A.
45. American Friends Service Committee, 35.
46. Kelly, *From Vietnam to America*, 143–144.
47. *After Action Report*, Fort Chaffee, I-12.
48. Jennifer L. Brown, "Vietnamese Refugees find Second Home in Oklahoma City," *Shawnee [OK] News-Star*, September 29, 2002. <http://www.news-star.com/stories/092902/New_48.shtml> September 12, 2006.
49. Taft, interview and oral history.
50. Taft Memo, October 20, 1975.
51. Ibid.
52. "Plan for Counseling," *Indiantown Gap*, Memo of October 31, 1975.
53. *After Action report*, Fort Chaffee, K-83.
54. Lewis, interview.
55. <http://www.uafortsmith.edu/CLH/InterviewWithDavidDehart?skin=text>
56. Alberta Lindsey, "Vietnamese orphan nurtured by Baptists now serving others," *Baptist Standard*, March 22, 2000. <http://www.baptiststandard.com/2000/3_22/pages/vietnamese.html> Accessed November 1, 2006. "Kept in God's Hand ... Our Incredible Journey," *Buckner Bulletin*, July/August 1975. <http://www.pbase.com/kept_in_gods_hand/camranh1975&page=1> Accessed November 1, 2006.
57. *After Action Report*, Fort Chaffee, K-85, 86.
58. <http://www.uafortsmith.edu/CLH/InterviewWithDavidDehart?skin=text>

59. Report to the Congress, HEW Refugee Task Force, June 15, 1976, author's files.
60. Lewis, interview.
61. United States, Cong. House, *Refugees from Indochina*, 466–467.

Chapter 7

1. United States, Cong. House, *Refugees from Indochina*, Serial 43, 466–467.
2. United States, Cong. Senate, *Indochina Evacuations and Refugee Problems, Part IV*, 2.
3. Grant, 13.
4. United States, Cong. Senate, *Indochina Evacuations and Refugee Problems, Part IV*, 3.
5. Ibid., 2–3.
6. "Report to the Congress: HEW Refugee Task Force," September 20, 1976, 34.
7. Kelly, "Coping with America," 141.
8. United States, Comptroller General, *Domestic Resettlement*, 34.
9. Kelly, "Coping with America," 141.
10. *Monthly Labor Review*, Vol. 108, August 1985, 45.
11. United States, Comptroller General, *Domestic Resettlement*, 34.
12. Gim and Tybel, 15.
13. "Report to the Congress: HEW Refugee Task Force," March 15, 1976, 31. About 80,000 Indochinese refugees were also in other countries, mostly Thailand.
14. United States, Cong. Senate, *Indochina Evacuations and Refugee Problems, Part IV*, 22.
15. Statistics from "Report to the Congress: HEW Refugee Task Force," March 15, 1976.
16. Vo, 182.
17. Robert G. Kaiser, "On Parole," *The Washington Post*, May 1, 1977, 1.
18. Freeman, 11, quoting Ruben Rumbaut.
19. The story of the Le family is taken from a daughter's account. Phuong Le, "A Daughter's Journey: One Family's Passage from Vietnam," *Seattle Post Intelligencer*, March 6–9, 2000. <http://seattlepi.nwsource.com/adaughtersjourney/> Accessed November 3, 2006.
20. Gene Nguyen, "A Personal Look at Vietnamese in Arkansas." <http://asms.k12.ar.us/armem/nguyen/index.htm> December 14, 2006.
21. Kelley, *From Vietnam to America*, 201–202.
22. Ibid., 179.
23. Frances FitzGerald, "Punch in! Punch out! Eat quick!" *The New York Times*, December 28, 1975, 151.
24. Author's experiences.
25. Fitzgerald.
26. Molly Ivins, "Killing Sharpens Texas Feud on Vietnamese Fishing," *New York Times*, August 9, 1979, A-16. Vietnamese fishermen also had problems in California and Florida.
27. Maril, 210.

Notes—Chapter 8

28. Ivins.
29. <http://www.civilrightsmediation.org/interviews/Efrain_Martinez.shtml#D13801> March 23, 2006.
30. Ibid.
31. Maril, 233–234.
32. Ross Milloy, "Vietnam Fallout in a Texas Town," *The New York Times*, April 6, 1980, SM-10.
33. "Fishing Town in Texas tells the Klan to Stay Away," *The New York Times*, November 22, 1979, A-17.
34. "Vietnamese Find Ally in Texas: Time," *The New York Times*, September 29, 1986, A-12.
35. William K. Stevens, "Peace Returns to the Home of Shrimp Fishermen and Astronauts," *The New York Times*, June 27, 1981, A-6.
36. Thompson and Rosenblatt, interviews.
37. Quoted from Hein, 81.
38. Kue Chaw, interview. Comment to author by a neighbor of Kue Chaw. Also, articles by Sherman Spencer.
39. Stephen V. Roberts, "Laotian, After Years of Wars, Likes the Peace of Montana," *The New York Times*, April 2, 1978, 22. The article says that 5 or 6 of Vang Pao's wives were still in France and Thailand, but Mac Thompson believes they were in the United States.
40. *The Nation*, January 6, 7, and 8, 1981. Series written by Linda Kohl of the *St. Paul Dispatch*.
41. Bethan Jenkinson, "Hmong's New Lives in Caribbean." <http://news.bbc.co.uk/2/hi/asia-pacific/3498056.stm> December 1, 2006.
42. <www.girlscoutscv.org/for_friends/documents/Press0706_HmongFrGu.pdf> December 2, 2006.

Chapter 8

1. Thompson, interview.
2. United States, Cong. Senate, *Indochina Evacuation and Refugee Problems: Part IV*, 172–173. Actually, the government paroled 3,000 to 5,000 Lao. But 3,466 was the actual number of Lao who came to the United States.
3. Van-es-Beeck, 324.
4. Ibid., 324–25.
5. "Bureau of Refugee Services: History of Iowa Refugee Resettlement," <http://www.dhs.state.ia.us/refugee/bureau/history.asp> Accessed September 10, 2006.
6. Schill, 109.
7. Tucker, interview.
8. United States, Cong. House, *Refugees from Indochina*, Serial No.43, 511.
9. Yang Dao, Ph.D., "The Hmong Odyssey from Laos to America." <http://perso.organe.fr/laos/yangdao.htm> Accessed August 19, 2006.
10. United States, Cong. House, *Refugees from Indochina*, Serial 43, 538.
11. State Telegram 232910, September 30, 1975. For clarity's sake, I have changed the old name "Meo" to the more appropriate "Hmong" in this and other quoted material.
12. <http://www.fs.fed.us/fire/people/smokejumpers/missoula/History/General/daniels.htm> Accessed November 30, 2006.
13. Robbins, 386–87, from an interview published February 22, 1977, in the *Baltimore Sun*.
14. Personal communication from Mac Thompson.
15. United States, Cong. House, *Refugees from Indochina*, Serial 43, 510–511. A more precise definition of categories would soon be set up. See Table One.
16. Rosenblatt, interview.
17. Harris, 38.
18. United States, Cong. Senate, *Indochina Evacuation and Refugee Problems, Part IV*, 33.
19. Television News Archive, Vanderbilt University, "NBC News," May 14, 1975. <http://openweb.tvnews.vanderbilt.edu/1975-5/1975-05-14-NBC-4.html> Accessed August 16, 2006.
20. "The Situation in Asia," July 15, 1975, National Security Council Memorandum. <http://www.fordlibrarymuseum.gov/library/exhibits/vietnam/750715a.htm> Accessed August 24, 2006.
21. United States, Cong. House, *Refugees from Indochina*, Serial 43, 721.
22. United States, Cong. Senate, *The Aftermath of War*, 55.
23. Rosenblatt, personal communication.
24. Rosenblatt, interview.
25. Ibid.
26. United States, Cong. House, *Refugees from Indochina*, Serial 43, 507. Letter dated January 29, 1976, from INS Commissioner Chapman to Congressman Rodino. Author's files.
27. Lowman, interview.
28. United States, Cong. House, *Refugees from Indochina*, Serial 43, 518.
29. Ibid., 519–520.
30. Robinson, *Double Vision*, 30.
31. Pajaree, interview.
32. Pajaree and others, interview.
33. Romero, interview.
34. Author's experiences.
35. Rosenblatt and Thompson, interviews and personal correspondence.
36. Corcos letter, September 11, 2006, author's files.
37. Marie Ridder, "Inside Indochina, Helping Out," *The Washington Post*, January 21, 1979, F-1.
38. <http://www.kingsolomonsgate.com/JerryDaniels.htm> Accessed April 27, 2009.
39. Romero, interview.

40. Memo to Staff, "Internationalization Policy — Point System for Refugees with Bi-links or Poly-links to Third Countries," March 31, 1979, author's files.
41. Letter in author's files.
42 Quoted from Harris, 30.
43. Thai policy is discussed in Robinson, *Double Vision*, 5–7; and *Thailand: A First Asylum Country*, 5–32.
44. *Thailand: A First Asylum Country*, 35; Robinson, *Terms of Refuge*, 12, 14.
45. Robinson, 21.
46. *Thailand: A First Asylum Country*, 36.
47. Rosenblatt, interview.
48. United States, Cong. Senate, *The Aftermath of War*, 76–77.
49. Ibid., 77.
50. U.S. Government Memorandum, Minutes of meeting 4/13/76, author's files.
51. United States, Cong. House, *Refugees from Indochina*, Serial 43, 508.
52. Ibid., 524.
53. Ibid., 550.
54. Ibid., 591.
55. Ibid., 591.
56. "Expanded Parole Program," State Department Telegram 171536 from Washington to American Embassy Bangkok, July 12, 1976, author's files.
57. Loescher, 127.
58. Rosenblatt and Thompson, interviews.
59. Thompson, interview and personal correspondence.

Chapter 9

1. Rosenblatt and Lowman, interviews.
2. United States, Cong. House, *Refugees from Indochina: Current Problems and Prospects*, 18.
3. Lowman, interview; Cherne, 1–3.
4. United States, Cong. House, *Refugees from Indochina: Current Problems and Prospects*. Estimate interpolated from chart on page 22.
5. Cherne, 11–12.
6. Levine, 234–235. Several variants of this story exist.
7. Cherne, 6–10.
8. "Black Leaders Urge Admission of Indo-Chinese Refugees," *The New York Times*, March 19, 1978 (advertisement).
9. Cherne, 26–28.
10. Cherne, 16–17; Rosenblatt, interview; Smith, 120.
11. United States, Cong. House, *Indochinese Refugees: An Update*, 35–37.
12. United States, Cong. House, *Refugee Problems in Southeast Asia, 1981*, 37.
13. United States, Cong. House, *Indochinese Refugees: An Update*, 6.
14. Rosenblatt, interview.
15. <http://www.blogofdeath.com/archives/000880.html> Accessed September 5, 2006.
16. Author's recollections. See also Schill, 111–113.
17. Story as told by Mike Eiland.
18. Gerry Lamberty to author in conversation.

Chapter 10

1. Daniel Burstein, "On Cambodia: But, Yet," *The New York Times*, November 21, 1978, A-21.
2. See Sophal Ear for many variations on this theme. <http://jim.com/canon.htm>
3. Osborne, "Indochinese Refugees," 44.
4. Quoted from Loescher, 192–193.
5. "Here We Go Again," *US/Indochina Report*, April 30, 1976. Article signed "GP."
6. Baron and Paul, 201–206.
7. Sophal Ear. <http://jim.com/canon.htm> Accessed April 8, 2007.
8. Porter and Shawcross. <http://www.nybooks.com/articles/8106> Accessed August 27, 2006.
9. Ear.
10. The account of the hearing comes from United States, Cong. House, *Human Rights in Cambodia*.
11. Ibid., 8–9.
12. Ibid., 16–17.
13. United States, Cong. House, *Human Rights in Cambodia*, 19.
14. Ibid., 19–32.
15. Ibid., 32–33.
16. Ear, Chapter 4.
17. Porter and Shawcross.
18. Sharp, Chapter 3.
19. Ibid.
20. "Silence, Subterfuge and Surveillance," *Time*, January 8, 1979. <http://www.time.com/time/archive/preview/0,10987,919946,00.html> Accessed June 23, 2006.
21. Quoted from *Malcolm Caldwell's South-East Asia*. <http://www.diacritica.com/sobaka/dossier/caldwll.html> Accessed August 20, 2006.
22. Ear, Chapter IV.
23. "Pol Pot Remembered," BBC News. <http://news.bbc.co.uk/2/hi/programmes/from_our_own_correspondent/81048.stm> Accessed August 12, 2009.
24. "Silence, Subterfuge and Surveillance," *Time*, January 8, 1979. <http://www.time.com/time/archive/preview/0,10987,919946,00.html> Accessed June 23, 2006.
25. Becker, 426–427.
26. Ibid., 427–430.
27. United States, Cong. House, *Human Rights in Cambodia*, 27; Etcheson, 7.

28. Etcheson, 7.
29. Doyle and Maitland, 24.
30. Kiernan, *The Pol Pot Regime*, 456.
31. Kiernan, "Demography of Genocide in Southeast Asia."
32. Etcheson, 8.
33. Ibid., 11.

Chapter 11

1. "Toward the 'Ho Chi Minh Era,'" *Time*, May 26, 1975.
2. "The Slow Road to Socialism," *Time*, February 16, 1976.
3. <http://www.globalpolicy.org/security/membship/veto/vetosubj.htm> August 2, 2009.
4. "Dubious Battle," *Time*, December 6, 1976.
5. Doyle and Maitland, 25.
6. Nguyen Van Canh, 236–237.
7. United States, Cong. Senate, *The Aftermath of War*, draft copy, 3.
8. "Vietnam: The Cautious Conquerors of Saigon," *Time*, May 16, 1977. <http://www.time.com/time/printout/0,8816,918959,00.htm>
9. <http://www.aiipowmia.com/sea/nixonletter.htm> Quoted from *Department of State Bulletin*, 27 June 1977; Martini, 32–33.
10. Nguyen van Canh, 233.
11. Ibid., 232.
12. Ibid., 25.
13. Desbarats, "Repression in the Socialist Republic of Vietnam," January 10, 2007.
14. Doyle and Maitland, 25.
15. Desbarats, "Population Redistribution in the Socialist Republic of Vietnam."
16. Ibid.
17. *Chinese Aggression Against Vietnam*, 29.
18. Tucker, *Vietnam*, 198.
19. UNHCR, *State of the World's Refugees*, 82.
20. Tucker, *Encyclopedia*, 604.
21. Tucker, *Vietnam*, 193, 199; Institute of South East Asian Studies, 339.
22. Chanda, 22.
23. Duiker, 182.
24. <http://countrystudies.us/vietnam/61.htm> Accessed August 2, 2009.
25. Martini, 85–86.
26. *Time*, September 4, 1978. <http://www.time.com/time/printout/0,8816,912120,00,html> Accessed February 1, 2007.
27. Ablin and Hood, 358.
28. Duiker, 174.
29. Chanda, 350–353.
30. Ibid., 361.
31. Ibid., 360.
32. Duiker, 189.
33. <http://www.time.com/time/printout/0,8816,946300,00.html> Accessed January 28, 2007.
34. *People*, December 24, 1979. <http://www.people.com/people/archive/article/0,20075486,00.html> Accessed August 10, 2009.
35. "Joan Baez." <http://perso.wanadoo.fr/joan-baez/engagement/vietnam.html> Accessed July 12, 2007.
36. Doan Van Toai, "A Lament for Vietnam," *New York Times Magazine*, March 29, 1981.
37. <http://openweb.tvnews.vanderbilt.edu/1979-7/1979-07-18-CBS-17.html> Accessed January 28, 2007.
38. "The Truth About Vietnam," *The New York Times*, June 24, 1979.
39. Sagan and Denny, 6.
40. Ha, 28.
41. Hickey, 358–360.
42. Doyle and Maitland, 19; Robinson, *Terms of Refuge*, 103–104;<http://www.royalark.net/Laos/laos.htm> Accessed August 10, 2009.

Chapter 12

1. Grant, 116–117.
2. Story of *Southern Cross* from Grant, 116–121 and Wain, 17–20.
3. Miller, 183.
4. <http://archives.cbc.ca/society/immigration/topics/524-2709> Accessed February 24, 2009; Robinson, *Terms of Refuge*, 138.
5. Robinson, *Terms of Refuge*, 188.
6. Wain, 111.
7. Robinson, *Terms of Refuge*, 32
8. "Barring the Boat People," *Time*, December 4, 1978.
9. United States, Cong. House, *Refugees from Indochina: Current Problems and Prospects*, 5–7.
10. United States, Cong. House, *Piracy in the Gulf of Thailand*, 15–17.
11. Mac Thompson, personal correspondence.
12. Schill, 115.
13 Lowman, interview; Schill, 136.
14 Rosenblatt, interview.
15. The preceding story is drawn from Schill, 114–138.
16. Some estimate a higher population at this time. Wain, 265, for example, says 29,000 at the end of 1978. See also<http://www.thingsasian.com/stories-photos/2602>.
17. United States, Cong. House, *Refugees from Indochina. Current Problems and Prospects*, 9, 41.
18. Quoted from Mark Prutsalis of Refugees International after his visit to a Rwandan refugee camp in 1994.
19. United States, Cong. House, *Refugees from Indochina, Current Problems and Prospects*, 41.

20. Leo Cherne, "Hell Isle," *The New York Times*, February 3, 1979, 19.
21. "A Rocky Haven of Pulau Bidong," *Newsweek*, July 2, 1979, 47.
22 <http://pulaubidong.wordpress.com/> Accessed February 1, 2009.
23. Grant, 151.
24. Mike Connolly, "The Screeners: Men Who Play God," manuscript in author's files. Probably published in Gannett Newspapers.
25. <http://archives.cbc.ca/society/immigration/topics/524-2707/> Accessed April 8, 2009.
26. Henry Kamm, "38,000 Cram Biggest 'Boat People' Camp," *The New York Times*, July 17, 1979.
27. Robinson, *Terms of Refugee*, 50.

Chapter 13

1. "Special Study on Indochina Refugee Situation — July 1979," Folder 09, Box 33, Douglas Pike Collection. The Vietnam Archive, Texas Tech University, 17.
2. *Far Eastern Economic Review*, December 22, 1978, 12.
3. Strand and Jones, 31.
4. Lloyd Duong, "The Boat People: Imprints on History." <www.geocities.com/dangdthanh/html/galang/theboat.pdf>, 13. Accessed July 10, 2000.
5. *Far Eastern Economic Review*, June 23, 1978, 20.
6. "Joint Press statement of the special ASEAN Foreign Ministers Meeting on Indochinese Refugees," January 13, 1979, author's files.
7. "Special Study on Indochina Refugee Situation — July 1979, Folder 09, Box 33, Douglas Pike Collection. The Vietnam Archive, Texas Tech University, 6.
8. Grant, 150.
9. Ibid., 150.
10. Wain, 182.
11. "Malaysia Reports 13,000 Refugees Driven out to Sea," and "Asians Urge End to Refugee Flow," *The New York Times*, June 26, and June 29, 1979, 1; UNHCR, *State of the World's Refugees*, 83, 84.
12. "Special Study on Indochina Refugee Situation — July 1979," Folder 09, Box 33, Douglas Pike Collection. The Vietnam Archive, Texas Tech University, 17.
13. Comptroller General of the United States, B-19736, "Refugee Assistance Program Under the Fiscal Year 1980 Continuing Resolution." <http://archive.gao.gov/lglpapr2pdf7/111639.pdf> Accessed June 20, 2009.
14. *The New York Times*, August 8, 1979.
15. Morton, interview.
16. *Keesing's Contemporary Archives*, February 8, 1980, 3080.
17. "A Rescue Plan at Last," *Time*, July 30, 1979.
18. Comptroller General.
19. Loescher and Scanlan, 145–146; Wain, 225.
20. Personnel Evaluation Report for Rosenblatt, 1980, author's files.
21. "Statistical Update on Indochina Refugee Situation from the Indochina Refugee Action Center — Sept 24, 1980," Folder 13, Box 32, Douglas Pike Collection: Unit 03 — Refugees and Civilian Casualties, the Vietnam Archive, Texas Tech University.
22. "Refugee Reports," October 30, 1979.
23. Kumin, 107.
24. Ibid., 113.
25. Ibid., 117.
26. *Keesing's Contemporary Archives*, February 8, 1980, 30078.
27. Ibid., 30083.
28. <http://content.cdlib.org/xft/view?docId=hb3n7pm&doc.view=frames&chunk.id=ch02 &toc.depth=1&toc.id=ch02&brand=calisphere> Accessed June 23, 2009.
29. Ibid.
30. United States, Cong. House, *Reports on Refugee Aid*, 90.
31. Ibid., 92.
32. <http://www.historynet.com/joe-devlin-the-boat-peoples-priest.htm/5> Accessed September 25, 2006.
33. UNHCR, "The Adventures of Lien," *Refugees Magazine*, May 1983, 25–26.
34. The following story is from "One Man Against the Pirates," *Reader's Digest*, January 1986, 87–92 and<http://www.searescue.org/> Accessed June 10, 2009.
35. Robinson, *Terms of Refuge*, 61.
36. Probable in the author's opinion, that is.
37. Lloyd Thuong, "The Boat People: Imprints on History," 37. <www.geocities.com/dangdthanh/html/galang/theboat.pdf> Accessed July 10, 2009.
38. "A Tragedy Ignored," *Reader's Digest*, January 1986, 91.

Chapter 14

1. United States, Cong. House, *Human Rights in Cambodia*, July 26, 1977, 5.
2. Robinson, *Double Vision*, 167.
3. David W.P. Elliott in Ablin and Hood, 67.
4. Kamm, *Cambodia*, 160.
5. Pierpaoli, 113–115.
6. Abramowitz, interview.
7. Henry Kamm, "At Thai Camp, An Exile's Joy Turns to Grief" and "Cambodian Refugees Press Notes of Despair on U.S. Aides," *The New York Times*, June 14 and 15, 1979.

8. Rosenblatt, personal communication.
9. Thompson, personal correspondence.
10. Rosenblatt and Thompson, interviews; Thompson, correspondence.
11. Henry Kamm, "Refugee Tells of Comrades' Plight," *The New York Times*, June 25, 1979.
12. Memo from Steve S. (last name unknown) to Rosenblatt describing interview of survivor, June 24, 1981, author's files.
13. Interview with Ty Sopheap and An Tay by Susan Lenderking, September 7, 1979, and February 1980, author's files.
14. <http://www.quansuvn.net/index.php?topic-5972.220> Accessed May 15, 2009. English translation. Courtesy of Mike Eiland.
15. Shawcross, *Quality of Mercy*, 90–92.
16. Ibid., 90.
17. Henry Kamm, "Thais Readmit 1,000 Cambodians for Later Resettlement Elsewhere," *The New York Times*, July 11, 1979.
18. Karl Jackson, 333–334.
19. *The Nation* (Bangkok), June 13, 1979, quoted from Robinson, *Double Vision*, 57.
20. Robinson.
21. The story of Preah Vihear comes from Pierpaoli, 130–149; Rosenblatt, interview, Thompson, interview, and other sources as noted.
22. Pran's story is from Schanberg, 43–65.
23. Dith Pran, "Return to the Killing Fields," *The New York Times Magazine*, September 24, 1989, 53.
24. Schanberg, 53.
25. Ibid., 56.
26. Judy Kocher, interview. Copies of Pran's letters to *The Times* are in author's files.
27. Dith Pran, 30.
28. Letter in author's files.
29. Library of Congress, Country Study — Cambodia. <http://www.country-studies.com/cambodia/agriculture.html> Accessed February 11, 2009.

Chapter 15

1. Mason and Brown, 186.
2. Text of Hun Sen's letter is in Shawcross, *Quality of Mercy*, 437–438.
3. Stedman and Tanner, 33.
4. Ibid., 19.
5. Malloch Brown, interview.
6. Mason and Brown, 19–20.
7. John Collins Harvey, "Medical Relief Work Among Cambodian Refugees in Thailand." <http://www.pubmedcentral.nih.gov/articlerender.fcgi?artid=2279515> Accessed March 10, 2009.
8. Ann Grosvenor-Rosenblatt, interview; unpublished account of her experiences (in author's possession); and "The Early Days of Sa Kaeo" in Levy and Susott, 42–47.
9. Jackson, 335.

10. Then Mark Brown, now Baron Mark Malloch Brown.
11. <http://forcedmigration.ccnmtl.columbia.edu/book/export/html/184> Accessed February 1, 2009; Hans Nothdurft, "Organization of Sakaeo Refugee Center, October 1979–January 1980," 11–13, 37 in *Emergency Refugee Health Care*; Mason and Brown. Malloch Brown, interview.
12. Ann Rosenblatt, interview.
13. Malloch Brown, interview.
14. *Emergency Refugee Health Care*, 36.
15. *Time*, November 12, 1979, 45.
16. *Emergency Refugee Health Care*, 31. The preceding story of the founding of Sa Kaeo is primarily derived from interviews with Sheppie, Abramowitz, Susan Lenderking, and Ann Rosenblatt.
17. "Deathwatch: Cambodia," *Time*, November 12, 1979.
18. <www.supawangreen.in.th/eng-article/download/suffering.doc> Accessed February 20, 2009.
19. Ibid.
20. *Emergency Refugee Health Care*, 31.
21. *Time*, November 12, 1979, 49.
22. "Inside Indochina, Helping Out," *The Washington Post*, January 21, 1979. See also Schill, 111–112.
23. Rosalynn Carter in Levy and Susott, 56–60.
24. <http://www.oxfam.org.uk/resources/downloads/food_scarc_fam_app11.pdf> The math calculations are the author's.
25. "Indochinese Refugee Reports," November 29, 1979, 7.
26. Quoted from Shawcross, *The Quality of Mercy*, 178.
27. Abramowitz, interview, Shawcross, *The Quality of Mercy*, 171.
28. Undated memo (about November 6, 1979) titled "List of ICRC Shortcomings."
29. Morton, interview.
30. Nothdurft in *Emergency Refugee Health Care*, 13.
31. Abramowitz, interview.
32. Wain, 245; Malloch Brown, interview. Also known as Khao-i-Daeng and other variants.
33. *Emergency Refugee Health Care*, 15.
34. Eiland, personal correspondence.
35. Osborn, "Kampuchean Refugee Situation," 38.
36. Elizabeth Becker, "The Refugee Hilton," *The Washington Post*, February 1, 1981, C-1.
37. John Pilger, "America's Second War in Indochina," *New Standard*, August 1, 1980, 10.
38. Long, 45–46.
39. Robinson, *Double Vision*, 67, and Ivor Jackson, 337, give different dates for the Open Door policy.

40. Keesing's Contemporary Archives, January 23, 1981, 30770.
41. Morton, interview.
42. Ann Rosenblatt, interview.
43. UNESCO, 6.
44. Lenderking, interview.
45. Levy and Susott, 301–304.
46. Malloch Brown, interview.
47. Rosenblatt, interview.
48. Robinson, *Double Vision*, 76.
49. Ibid., 80.

Chapter 16

1. Robinson, *Double Vision*, 66, 109.
2. Robert Ashe, "Cross-Border Feeding," July 8, 1980, 3, memorandum in author's files.
3. Osborne, "Kampuchean Refugee Situation," 51.
4. Mason and Brown, 47–55; "Update: Kampuchea/Cambodia," April 1, 1980, Folder 27, Box 10, Douglas Pike Collection: Unit 15 — Cambodia, The Vietnam Archive, Texas Tech University; "Backgrounder: Current Status of Cambodian Refugees: A Staff Report," Republican Study Committee, n.d. (probably early 1980), author's files.
5. Gottesman, 89.
6. "After the Khmer new year, 1980," Folder 27, Box 10, Douglas Pike Collection: Unit 15 — Cambodia, The Vietnam Archive, Texas Tech University.
7. Robinson, *Double Vision*, 84.
8. <http://www.training.irri.org/courseware/online/plantingrice/PlantingRice.pdf> Accessed August 10, 2009; author's calculations.
9. Eiland, personal correspondence.
10. United States, Cong. House, *Tragedy in Indochina*, 187.
11. Another description of the land bridge is found at<http://www.geocities.com/thaiborder/?200916> Accessed June 20, 2009.
12. Draft Letter to the New Statesman from Morton Abramowitz (unpublished), author's files.
13. Eiland, personal correspondence.
14. Ibid.
15. See Shawcross, *The Quality of Mercy*, 100–103 and Mason and Brown, 178–184, for further discussion on this point.
16. Mason and Brown, 101.
17. Levy and Susott, 302–304.
18. Mason and Brown, 148; Shawcross, *The Quality of Mercy*, 183.
19. Robinson, *Double Vision*, 71.
20. "Mission Relationship to Khmer Relief Program," memo from Rosenblatt to Abramowitz, February 8, 1980, author's files.
21. Michael Haas, *Cambodia, Pol Pot, and the United States: the Faustian Pact*.
22. Quoted from Mason and Brown, 150.
23. United States, Cong. House, *1979: Tragedy in Indochina*, 156–157.
24. Ibid., 157.
25. Rosenblatt, interview.
26. Comment by Mark Malloch Brown, interview.
27. *Emergency Refugee Health Care*, 19, 22.
28. Robert Ashe, "Cross Border Feeding," July 8, 1980, memorandum in author's files.
29. Ibid.
30. Robinson, *Double Vision*, 155; Mason and Brown 155; *International Herald Tribune*, July 3, 1980.
31. Shawcross, *Quality of Mercy*, 283–284, 299–300.
32. Ibid., 372.
33. United States, Cong. House, *Tragedy in Indochina*, 72.
34. Shawcross, *Quality of Mercy*, 372.
35. United States, Cong. House, *Tragedy in Indochina*, 114.
36. <http://forcedmigration.ccnmtl.columbia.edu/book/export/html/25> Accessed March 25, 2009.
37. Gottesman, 85.
38. <http://forcedmigration.ccnmtl.columbia.edu/book/export/html/25> 4.
39. See Shawcross, *Quality of Mercy*, 155–168, for a fuller account of the negotiations between Cambodia and the international organizations.
40. Ibid., 365.
41. Gregory H. Stanton. <http://www.genocidewatch.org/aboutgenocide/stantoncambodianresurrection.htm> Accessed February 1, 2009.
42. Osborne, "Kampuchea," 17.
43. Keesing's Contemporary Archives, January 23, 1981, 30672–3.
44. Gottesman, 86.
45. *Washington Post*, November 18, 1979, C-1.
46. Shawcross, *Quality of Mercy*, 372–373.
47. Quoted from the *1980 World Refugee Survey*, United States Committee on Refugees, 29, author's files. Original source, *The Economist*, December 22, 1979.
48. United States, Cong. House, *Tragedy in Indochina*, 154.
49. Ibid., 154.
50. Ibid., 175–177.
51. Ibid., 185.
52. Ibid., 187.
53. Ibid., 187.
54. Ibid., 229.
55. Ibid., 181.
56. Ibid., 201, 202.
57. Ibid., 209–210.
58. Ibid., 226.
59. Shawcross, *The Quality of Mercy*, 366, 369.

60. Author's speculations.
61. <http://countrystudies.us/cambodia/40.htm> Accessed August 15, 2009. The estimate in this report is 6.3 million Cambodians in 1980. Given what we know now of KR killings, it may have been less.
62. Shawcross, *The Quality of Mercy*, 283–284, 295.
63. Robinson, *Double Vision*, 169.

Chapter 17

1. Paquette, interview.
2. The story of the Ha family is drawn from Kim Ha's book, *Stormy Escape*, except where otherwise noted.
3. Ha, 147.
4. Ibid., 159.
5. Eiland, personal correspondence.
6. United States, Cong. House, *Refugees from Indochina*, 9.
7. Eiland, personal correspondence.
8. Michael Fleming. <http://www.dutchgirl.com/foxpaws/essays/inamerica.html> Accessed March 9, 2009.
9. Ha, 231.
10. "Refugee Reports," November 13, 1979, 4, 5.
11. United States, Cong. House, *Refugees From Indochina: Current Problems and Prospects*, 26–27.
12. "Refugee Reports," November 19, 1979, 5.
13. Ha, 237.
14. Howell, interview.
15. Description of Ban Vinai from many sources, including interview with Charlene Day Howell and Torjesen, 70.
16. Torjesen, 74–75.
17. Thompson, interview; John Hail, "Dilemma for the Hmongs," *Focus Thailand*, December 1980, 21–23.
18. "Summary of Refugee Situation in Thailand: 31 July 1981," report by American Embassy Bangkok, author's files. Also, Mike Connolly, "Flight from Fear," author's files; probably also published in Gannett newspapers.
19. Torjesen, 63; Thompson, interview. Also called the Sokoto.
20. Paquette and Howell, interviews.
21. Mike Connolly, "Going to the U.S.— We Say Goodbye, Nothing Else," manuscript in author's files. Probably published by Gannett Newspapers.
22. Draft memorandum from Gary R. West to Mac Alan Thompson, July 11, 1981, author's files. Lionel Rosenblatt had reported on rumors of yellow rain as early as August 1978 according to Mac Thompson.
23. Many references, most accessible is <http://en.wikipedia.org/wiki/Yellow_rain>
24. <http://www.smokejumpers.com/smokejumper_magazine/item.php?articles_id=299&magazine_editions_id=19>
25. Long, 59.
26. Torjesen, 96.
27. Sherman, "The Hmong," 607.
28. Author's personal experiences.
29. Mason and Brown, 55.
30. Ibid., 45–46.
31. Ibid., 87–89.
32. *Khmer Emergency Health Care*, 75–84.
33. Paquette, interview.
34. Thompson, interview.

Chapter 18

1. "Issues Paper: The Refugee Situation in Thailand," American Embassy Bangkok, n.d., author's files.
2. Ferris, 136.
3. Indochina Refugee Action Center, "Statistical Update on Indochina Refugee Situation," September 24, 1980. "Summary of Refugees Situation in Thailand: 31 July 1981," author's files.
4. Levy and Susott, 355.
5. Eduardo Lachica, "Agencies in U.S. Dispute Indochinese Refugee Policies," *The Asian Wall Street Journal*, August 1, 1981.
6. Quoted from Loescher and Scanlan, 168.
7. Draft telegram from Songkhla to Washington, author's files.
8. Levy, 302.
9. Abramowitz, interview.
10. Bangkok telegram, 22129, May 7, 1981, author's files.
11. Lachica. Although the *Asian Wall Street Journal* article does not mention Abramowitz by name, it is clear that it is he the article refers to as the "bully."
12. Quoted from Tsamenyi from a statement by a UNHCR legal advisor, 369.
13. Ibid., 361.
14. Quoted from a draft memo from Leo Cherne to Secretary of State Alexander Haig, February 9, 1981, titled "The Indochinese Refugee Program and the Budget." It is unknown whether the memo was sent or not.
15. "Statement by Under Secretary of State for Political Affairs Walter J. Stoessel before the Judiciary Committee," draft, author's files.
16. "Refugee Reports," December 28, 1984, 9.
17. Levy, 301.
18. Citizens Commission on Indochinese Refugees, "The Indochinese Refugee Crisis Today: Statement and Recommendations," 3, author's files.
19. Rosenblatt, interview.
20. "Table V: Report to the Congress: Proposed Refugee Admissions and Allocations for

FY 1982," U.S. Department of State, author's files.

21. Statistics derived from a chart titled "Indochinese Refugee Resettlement to the United States and Other Nations: July 1979 to July 1982," author's files.

22. Schill, oral history and interview. Recollections of this incident differ. I have relied mostly on Schill's written description. Also Lowman interview.

23. Rosenblatt, interview.

24. George Warner is named by Shawcross, 289–290, Mason and Brown, 103, and *The New York Times* on September 25 and November 21, 1980, and *The Washington Post* on September 24, 1980. See Pierpaoli, 162–175, for her account of dealings with Warner.

25. News reports say that Kurt paid Warner $9,000 on this occasion; Yvette's book says $45,000.

26. *Washington Post*, September 24, 1980, 1.

27. Shawcross, 290.

28. Author's talk with Pierpaoli in 1997.

29. Author's recollections.

30. Author's recollections.

31. Schill, oral history; Kue Chaw interview.

32. "Hmong Voices in Montana," Missoula Museum of the Arts. <www.hndlink.org/Daniels.htm> Accessed December 31, 2007.

33. For example, a draft memorandum by Leo Cherne titled "Indochina Refugees: The Challenge Ahead," March 24, 1981, author's files.

34. "Refugee Reports," January 28, 1983, 3.

35. For one summary of the ongoing dispute see Astri Suhrke, "A New Look at America's Refugee Policy," *Indochina Issues*, Center for International Policy, September 1980, author's files.

36. "Refugee Reports," January 28, 1983.

37. Thompson, interview; Eiland, correspondence; and "Refugee Reports," January 28, 1983.

38. Rosenblatt, personal communication.

39. <http://www.montagnards.org/army.cfm?sect=muster> Accessed August 1, 2009.

40. Thayer, 16–22.

41. Quoted from Power, 121. Rosenblatt proudly displayed a copy of this fax on his office wall for years, but it was misplaced. Also, Rosenblatt, interview and correspondence.

42. Text of Abramowitz speech, October 31, 1980, author's files.

43. Rosenblatt, interview.

44. "The Long Term: Preserving Asylum with a Smaller Resettlement Off-Take," State Department Memorandum, June 23, 1981, author's files.

BIBLIOGRAPHY

Note: Internet sources are given in the endnotes, but only very important internet sources are listed in the bibliography. Many unpublished documents are sourced only in endnotes and are identified as being in the author's possession. Articles from popular magazines and newspapers are sourced in the endnotes; important articles from professional journals are listed in the bibliography.

Interviews, Correspondence, and Sources of Documents

Abramowitz, Mort and Sheppie
Aderholt, Harry C. "Heinie"
Calabia, Dawn
Corcos, Albert
Culpepper, Patty
Eckes, Jim
Eiland, Michael
Enders, Arthur "Skip"
Herr, Paul (Pao)
Howell, Charlene Day
Jenkin, G. R.
Kamol Prachuabmoh
Kocher, Rich and Judy
Kue Chaw
Lenderking, Susan
Lewis, David
Lowman, Shepard
Malloch Brown, Mark
McBride, Joe
McManaway, Clay
Mlo (pseudonym)
Morton, Sue
Nguyen Thi Hue
Pajaree Sritham (Tim)
Pranai Suvanrath
Paquette, Paul
Quinn, Kenneth
Rogers, Ron
Romero, Berta
Rosenblatt, Lionel and Ann
Sanam Kajormklam
Schill, James
Secord, Richard
Shepard, George
Solarz, Stephen
Songsit Charuparn
Taft, Julia V.
Thompson, MacAlan
Tomsen, Peter
Tran Dinh Tru
Tucker, John
Wannida Mekvishai
Wisner, Frank

Books, Articles, and Documents

Ablin, David A., and Marlowe Hood. *The Cambodian Agony.* Armonk, NY: M.E. Sharpe, 1987.
After Action Report. Fort Chaffee. (Unbound collection of documents).
Allegra, Donald T., Phillip Nieburg, and Magnus Grabe. *Emergency Refugee Health Care—A Chronicle of the Khmer Refugee-Assistance Operation.* Public Health Service, Centers for Disease Control, 1984.
American Friends Service Committee. "Camp Experiences of Indochinese Refugees in the United States." Summer 1975. Unpublished.

Appy, Christian G. *Patriots: The Vietnam War Remembered from All Sides*. London: Penguin, 2003.
Barnes, Thomas J. "Of All the 36 Alternatives: Indochinese Resettlement in America." Senior Seminar in Foreign Policy, Department of State, 1977.
Barron, John, and Anthony Paul. *Murder of a Gentle Land: The Untold Story of Communist Genocide in Cambodia*. New York: Reader's Digest Press, 1977.
Becker, Elizabeth. *When the War Was Over: Cambodia and the Khmer Rouge Revolution*. New York: Public Affairs Books, 1998.
Belgrad, Eric A., and Nita Nachmias. *The Politics of International Aid Operations*. Westport, CT: Greenwood Publishing, 1997.
Bizot, Francois. *The Gate*. New York: Alfred A. Knopf, 2003.
Butler, David. *The Fall of Saigon*. New York: Simon & Schuster, 1985.
Carter, Alan. "Last Days in Vietnam." <http://www.clemson.edu/caah/history/FacultyPages/EdMoise/end.html> Note: item not found on internet in 2009. Copy in author's files.
Chan, Sucheng, ed. *Hmong Means Free: Life in Laos and America*. Philadelphia: Temple University Press, 1994.
_____. *The Vietnamese Americans 1.5 Generation*. Philadelphia: Temple University Press, 2006.
Chanda, Nayan. *Brother Enemy: The War After the War*. San Diego: Harcourt Brace, 1986.
Chen, King C. *China's War with Vietnam, 1979*. Stanford: Hoover Institution Press, 1987.
Cherne, Leo. *A Personal Recollection*, International Rescue Committee: Citizens Commission on Indochinese Refugees: February–March 1978. Unpublished manuscript.
Chinese Aggression Against Vietnam: The Root of the Problem. Hanoi: Foreign Languages Publishing House, 1979.
Crossan, John Dominic. *The Historical Jesus: The Life of a Mediterranean Jewish Peasant*. San Francisco: Harper, 1991.
Deac, Wilfred P. *The Road to the Killing Fields: The Cambodian War of 1970–1975*. College Station: Texas A&M University Press, 1997.
Desbarats, J. "Population Redistribution in the Socialist Republic of Vietnam." *Population and Development Review*, Vol. 13, No. 1, 43–76, 1987.
Desbarats, Jacqueline. "Repression in the Socialist Republic of Vietnam: Executions and Population Relocations." <http://www.jim.com/repression.htm> Accessed January 20, 2007.
Doyle, Edward, and Terrence Maitland. *The Vietnam Experience: The Aftermath: 1975–1985*. Boston: Boston Publishing, 1985.
Duiker, William J. *Vietnam Since the Fall of Saigon*. Athens: Ohio University Center for International Studies, 1989.
Ear, Sophal. "The Khmer Rouge Cannon 1975–1979: The Standard Total Academic View on Cambodia." <http://jim.com/canon.htm> Accessed July 14, 2009.
Elman, Richard, and Maggie Black. *The Children and the Nations: The Story of UNICEF*. Salt Lake City: Peregrine Smith Books, 1988.
Emergency Refugee Health-Care — A Chronicle of Experience in the Khmer Assistance Operation 1979–1980. U.S. Department of Health and Human Services, Centers for Disease Control, n.d.
Engelmann, Larry. *Tears Before the Rain: An Oral History of the Fall of South Vietnam*. New York: Oxford University Press, 1990.
"Environmental Impact Assessment: Vietnamese Evacuation and Refugee Program." May 30, 1975. Draft in author's files.
Etcheson, Craig. "The Number" — Quantifying Crimes Against Humanity in Cambodia." <http://www.mekong.net/cambodia/toll.htm> Accessed August 3, 2009.
Faderman, Lillian. *I Begin My Life All Over: The Hmong and the American Immigrant Experience*. Boston: Beacon Press, 1999.
Ferris, Elizabeth G., ed. *Refugees and World Politics*. New York: Praeger, 1985.
Freeman, James M. *Hearts of Sorrow: Vietnamese-American Lives*. Stanford: Stanford University Press, 1989.

Gallagher, Dennis. "The Evolution of the International Refugee System." Washington, D.C.: Refugee Policy Group, June 1988. Paper written for the Conference on International Migration.
Gim, Wever, and Tybel Litwin. "Indochinese Refugees in America: Profiles of Five Communities." Executive Seminar in National and International Affairs, Department of State, 1979–1980.
Gottesman, Evan. *Cambodia after the Khmer Rouge*. New Haven: Yale University Press, 2003.
Grant, Bruce. *The Boat People: An "Age" Investigation*. Harmondsworth, UK: Penguin, 1979.
Ha, Kim. *Stormy Escape: A Vietnamese Woman's Account of Her 1980 Flight through Cambodia to Thailand*. Jefferson, NC: McFarland, 1997.
Haas, Michael. *Cambodia, Pol Pot, and the United States: The Faustian Pact*. New York: Praeger, 1991.
Halberstadt, Hans. *Green Berets: Unconventional Warriors*. Novato, CA: Presidio, 1988.
Hamilton-Merritt, Jane. *Tragic Mountains: The Hmong, the Americans, and the Secret Wars for Laos, 1942–1992*. Bloomington: Indiana University Press, 1993.
Harris, David W. "The Indochinese Refugee Problem in Thailand: A Political Analysis." Dissertation, first draft. George Washington University, 1992.
Hein, Jeremy. *From Vietnam, Laos, and Cambodia: A Refugee Experience in the United States*. New York: Twayne, 1995.
Henderson, Charles. *Goodnight Saigon*. New York: Berkley Publishing, 2005.
Hickey, Gerald C. *Window on a War*. Lubbock: Texas Tech University Press, 2002.
Indiantown Gap. Refugee Resettlement Center. Operation New Arrivals. After Action Report. Collection of documents.
Institute of Southeast Asian Studies. *Southeast Asian Affairs*. 1980.
Isaacs, Arnold R. *Without Honor*. Baltimore: Johns Hopkins University Press, 1983.
Jackson, Ivor C. *The Refugee Concept in Group Situations*. Boston: Martinus Nijhoff, 1979.
Jackson, Karl D. *Cambodia: 1975–1978, Rendezvous with Death*. Princeton: Princeton University Press, 1989.
Jacques, Leslie. *The Mark: A War Correspondent's Memoir of Vietnam and Cambodia*. New York: Four Walls Eight Windows, 1995.
Kamm, Henry. *Cambodia: Report from a Stricken Land*. New York: Arcade, 1998.
Kelly, Gail P. "Coping with America. Refugees from Vietnam, Cambodia, and Laos in the 1970s and 1980s." *Annals of the American Academy of Political and Social Science*, Vol. 487, September 1986, 138–149.
Kelly, Gail Paradise. *From Vietnam to America: A Chronicle of the Vietnamese Immigration to the United States*. Boulder, CO: Westview, 1977.
Kiernan, Ben. "The Demography of Genocide in Southeast Asia." *Critical Asian Studies*, Vol. 35, No. 4, 2003, 585–597.
_____. *The Pol Pot Regime: Race, Power, and Genocide in Cambodia Under the Khmer Rouge, 1975–1979*. New Haven: Yale University Press, 2002.
Kirk, Donald. *Wider War: The Struggle for Cambodia, Thailand and Laos*. New York. Praeger, 1971.
Kissinger, Henry. *Ending the Vietnam War: A History of America's Involvement in and Extrication from the Vietnam War*. New York: Simon & Schuster, 2003.
Kumin, Judith. "Orderly Departure from Vietnam: Cold War Anomaly or Humanitarian Innovation." *Refugee Survey Quarterly*, Vol. 1, No. 27, 2008, 104–117.
Lavalle, Lt. Col. A.J.C. *Last Flight from Saigon*. USAF Southeast Asia Monograph Series, Vol. IV, Monograph, 1978.
Le Carré, John. "The Constant Muse." *The New Yorker*, December 25, 2000, and January 1, 2001, 66–74.
Lehmann, Wolfgang J. "Last Days in Vietnam." <http://www.clemson.edu/caah/history/FacultyPages/EdMoise/end.html> Note: Item not found on internet in 2009. Copy in author's files.
Levine, Daniel. *Bayard Rustin and the Civil Rights Movement*. New Brunswick, NJ: Rutgers University Press, 2000.

Levy, Barry S., and Daniel C. Susott, eds. *Responding to the Cambodian Refugee Crisis*. Millwood, NY: Associated Faculty Press, 1986.
Loescher, Gil. *The UNHCR and World Politics: A Perilous Path*. Oxford: Oxford University Press, 2002.
_____, and John A. Scanlan. *Calculated Kindness: Refugees and America's Half-Open Door, 1945 to the Present*. New York: Free Press, 1986.
Long, Lynellyn D. *Ban Vinai: The Refugee Camp*. New York: Columbia University Press, 1993.
Mackie, Richard. *Operation Newlife: The Untold Story*. Concord, CA: Solution, 1998.
Maguire, Peter. *Facing Death in Cambodia*. New York: Columbia University Press, 2005.
Maril, Robert Lee. *The Bay Shrimpers of Texas*. Lawrence: University Press of Kansas, 1995.
Martini, Edwin A. *Invisible Enemies: The American War on Vietnam, 1975–1980*. Amherst: University of Massachusetts Press, 2007.
Mason, Linda, and Roger Brown. *Rice, Rivalry, and Politics: Managing Cambodian Relief*. Notre Dame: University of Notre Dame Press, 1983.
Mee, Her. "The Art of Giving," in *Gender: Multicultural Perspectives*, edited by Judith T. Gonzalez-Calvo, 192–195. Dubuque: Kendall-Hunt, 1993.
Miller, Robert Hopkins. *Vietnam and Beyond: A Diplomat's Cold War Education*. Lubbock: Texas Tech University Press, 2002.
Moos, Felix, and C.S. Morrison. "The Vietnamese Refugees at Our Doorstep: Political Ambiguity and Successful Improvisation," *Policy Studies Review*, Vol. I, No. 1, August 1981, 28–47.
Morrison, C.S., and Felix Moos. "Halfway to Nowhere: Vietnamese Refugees on Guam," in *Involuntary Migration and Resettlement*, edited by Art Hansen and Anthony Oliver-Smith. Boulder, CO: Westview, 1982.
Morrison, Gayle L. *Sky Is Falling: An Oral History of the CIA's Evacuation of the Hmong from Laos*. Jefferson, NC: McFarland, 1999.
Mote, Sue Murphy. *Hmong and American: Stories of Transition to a Strange Land*. Jefferson, NC: McFarland, 2004.
Nguyen Van Canh. *Vietnam Under Communism, 1975–1982*. Stanford, CA: Hoover Institution Press, 1983.
Osborne, Milton. "The Indochinese Refugees: Cause and Effects." *International Affairs*, Vol. 56, No. 1, January 1980, 37–53.
_____. "The Kampuchean Refugee Situation: A Survey and Commentary." Manuscript dated April 23, 1980. Author's files.
Parker, James E., Jr. *Covert Ops: The CIA's Secret War in Laos*. New York: St. Martin's Paperbacks, 1997.
Pierpaoli, Yvette. *Mother to a Thousand Children*. (Published as *La Femme Aux Milles Enfants*. Paris: Robert Laffont, 1992). Unpublished English translation.
Pilger, John. "America's Second War in Indochina." *New Statesman*, August 1, 1980, 10–15.
Podhoretz, Norman. *Why We Were in Vietnam*. New York: Simon & Schuster, 1982.
Ponchaud, Francois. *Cambodia: Year Zero*. New York: Henry Holt, 1978.
Porter, Gareth, and William Shawcross. "An Exchange on Cambodia." *New York Review of Books*. July 20, 1978. <http://www.nybooks.com/articles/8106> Accessed August 27, 2006.
Power, Samantha. *Chasing the Flame: One Man's Fight to Save the World*. London: Penguin, 2008.
Proudfoot, Robert. *Even the Birds Don't Sound the Same Here: The Laotian Refugees' Search for Heart in American Culture*. New York: Peter Lang, 1990.
Quincy, Keith. *Harvesting Pa Chay's Wheat: The Hmong and America's Secret War in Laos*. Spokane: Eastern Washington University Press, 2000.
Quinn, Kenneth Michael. "The Origins and Development of Radical Cambodian Communism." Diss. University of Maryland, 1982.
"Refugee Reports." A biweekly report published by the Information Exchange Project of the American Public Welfare Association, 1979–1981.
Reporting Vietnam, Part Two, American Journalism 1969–1975. New York: Literary Classics of the United States, 1998.

Robbins, Christopher. *The Ravens: Pilots of the Secret War of Laos.* Bangkok: Asia Books, 2000.
Robinson, W. Courtland. *Double Vision: A History of Cambodian Refugees in Thailand.* Bangkok: Asian Research Center for Migration, 1996.
_____. *Terms of Refuge: The Indochinese Exodus and the International Response.* London: Zed Books, 1998.
Salemink, Oscar. *The Ethnography of Vietnam's Central Highlanders.* Honolulu: University of Hawaii Press, 2003.
Santoli, Al. *To Bear Any Burden.* New York: E.P. Dutton, 1985.
Schanberg, Sydney H. *The Death and Life of Dith Pran.* New York: Viking Adult, 1985.
Schill, James. *Reflections on Indochina, July 1996.* Folder 01, Box 01, James Schill Collection, the Vietnam Archive, Texas Tech University.
Scott, Joanna. *Indochina's Refugees.* Jefferson, NC: McFarland, 1989.
Sharp, Bruce. "Averaging Wrong Answers: Noam Chomsky and the Cambodian Controversy." <http://www.mekong.net/cambodia/chomsky.htm> Accessed August 1, 2009.
Shawcross, William. *The Quality of Mercy.* New York: Simon & Schuster, 1984.
_____. *Sideshow.* New York: Simon & Schuster, 1979.
Sherman, Spencer. "The Hmong." *National Geographic,* October 1988, 586–610.
_____. "The Hmong's Blue Ridge Refuge." <http://www.aliciaatterson.org/APF0901/Sherman/Sherman/html> Accessed July 18, 2009.
Short, Philip. *Pol Pot: Anatomy of a Nightmare.* New York: Henry Holt, 2004.
Smith, Andrew F. *Rescuing the World: The Life and Times of Leo Cherne.* Albany: State University of New York Press, 2002.
Snepp, Frank. *Decent Interval.* New York: Random House, 1977.
"Statistical Update on Indochina Refugee Situation from the Indochinese Refugee Action Center, 24 September 1980." Folder 13, Box 32, Douglas Pike Collection: Unit 03 Refugees and Civilian Casualties, the Vietnam Archive, Texas Tech University.
Stedman, John Stephen, and Fred Tanner, eds. *Refugee Manipulation: War, Politics, and the Abuse of Human Suffering.* Washington, D.C.: Brookings Institution, 2003.
Strand, Paul J., and Woodrow Jones, Jr. *Indochinese Refugees in America: Problems of Adaptation and Assimilation.* Durham: Duke University Press, 1985.
Summers, Col. Harry G., Jr. "America's Bitter End in Vietnam." *Vietnam Magazine.* <http://history.net.com/vn/blthebitterend/index.html>
_____. "Last Days in Vietnam." <http://www.clemson.edu/caah/history/FacultyPages/EdMoise/end.html> Note: Item not found on internet in 2009. Author's files.
Sutter, Valerie O'Connor. *The Indochinese Refugee Dilemma.* Baton Rouge: Louisiana State University Press, 1990.
Taft, Julia. "Oral Histories of State Department Officials," Box 1, Folder 80, Special Collections Division, Georgetown University Library.
Thailand: A First Asylum Country for Indochinese Refugees. Bangkok: Institute of Asian Studies, Chulalongkorn University, 1988.
Thayer, Nate. "The Forgotten Army." *Far Eastern Economic Review.* September 10, 1992, 16–22.
Tomsen, Peter. "Vietnam Diary." Unpublished.
Torjesen, Hakon, Karen Olness, and Erick Torjesen. *The Gift of the Refugees.* Eden Prairie, MN: The Garden, 1981.
Tran Dinh Tru, and To Hong Duc. *My Mistep and Mishap Under the Cyclops.* 2002. Unpublished manuscript.
Tsamenyi, B. Martin. "The 'Boat People': Are They Refugees." *Human Rights Quarterly,* August 1983, 348–373.
Tucker, Spencer, ed. *Encyclopedia of the Vietnam War.* Santa Barbara: ABC-CLIO, 1998.
_____. *Vietnam.* Lexington: University Press of Kentucky, 1999.
UNESCO. "Management of Education Systems in Zones of Conflict-Relief Operations." UNRDVO Principal Regional Office, Bangkok. n.d.
United Nations High Commissioner for Refugees. *The State of the World's Refugees: Fifty Years of Humanitarian Action.* Oxford: Oxford University Press, 2000.

United States. Comptroller General. *Domestic Resettlement of Indochinese Refugees — Struggle for Self Reliance.* May 10, 1977.
_____. _____. *The Indochinese Exodus: A Humanitarian Dilemma.* April 24, 1979.
_____. _____. *Indochinese Refugees: Protection, Care, and Processing Can Be Improved.* August 19, 1980.
_____. Congress. House. *1979 — Tragedy in Indochina: War, Refugees, and Famine.* 96th Congress, 1st Session. Washington, D.C.: GPO, 1980.
_____. _____. _____. *Human Rights in Cambodia.* 95th Congress, 1st Session. Washington, D.C.: GPO, 1977.
_____. _____. _____. *Indochinese Refugees: An Update.* 95th Congress, 1st Session, Washington, D.C.: GPO, 1978.
_____. _____. _____. *Piracy in the Gulf of Thailand: A Crisis for the International Community.* 97th Congress, 2nd Session. Washington, D.C.: GPO, 1982.
_____. _____. _____. *Refugee Crisis in Indochina, 1978.* 95th Congress, 2nd Session. Washington, D.C.: GPO, 1978.
_____. _____. _____. *Refugee Problems in Southeast Asia, 1981: A Staff Report.* 97th Congress, 2nd Session. Washington, D.C.: GPO, 1982.
_____. _____. _____. *Refugees from Indochina: Current Problems and Prospects.* 96th Congress, 1st Session. Washington, D.C.: GPO, April 30, 1979.
_____. _____. _____. *Refugees from Indochina: Serial No. 43.* 94th Congress, 1st and 2nd Sessions. Washington, D.C.: GPO, 1976.
_____. _____. _____. *Report to the Congress. U.S. Provides Safe Haven for Indochinese Refugees.* June 16, 1976.
_____. _____. _____. *Reports on Refugee AID: UN High Commissioner for Refugees, Refugees in Somalia, Refugees in Pakistan, Bataan Refugee Processing Center: Report of Staff Study Missions to the Committee on Foreign Affairs.* 97th Congress, 1st Session. Washington, D.C.: GPO, 1981.
_____. _____. _____. *The Vietnam-Cambodia Emergency, 1975. Part III — Vietnam Evacuation: Testimony of Ambassador Graham A. Martin.* 94th Congress, 2nd Session. Washington, D.C.: GPO, 1976.
_____. _____. Senate. *The Aftermath of War: Humanitarian Problems of Southeast Asia.* 94th Congress, 2nd Session, May 17, 1976. Narrative copy.
_____. _____. _____. *Indochina Evacuation and Refugee Problems, Part IV.* 94th Congress, 1st Session. Washington, D.C.: GPO, 1975.
_____. _____. _____. *Refugee Problems in Southeast Asia, 1981: A Staff Report.* 97th Congress, 2nd Session. Washington, D.C.: GPO, 1982.
_____. _____. _____. *Refugee Resettlement.* 97th Congress, 1st Session. Washington, D.C.: GPO, 1982.
_____. Department of Defense. Army. *Operations New Life/New Arrivals: US Army Support to the Indochinese Refugee Program, 1 April 1975 –1 June 1976. Indiantown Gap Refugee Resettlement Center: Operation New Arrivals: After Action Report.*
Van-es-Beeck, Bernard J. "Refugees from Laos, 1975 –1979," in *Contemporary Laos,* edited by Martin Stuart-Fox, 324 –334. St. Lucia: University of Queensland Press, 1982.
Vo, Nghia M. *The Vietnamese Boat People, 1954 and 1975 –1992.* Jefferson, NC: McFarland, 2006.
Wain, Barry. *The Refused: the Agony of the Indochina Refugees.* New York: Simon & Schuster, 1981.
Warner, Roger. *Backfire: The CIA's Secret War in Laos and Its Link to the War in Vietnam.* New York: Simon & Schuster, 1995. (Also published as *Shooting at the Moon.*)
Willenson, Kim. *The Bad War: An Oral History of the Vietnam War.* New York: New American Library, 1987.

INDEX

Numbers in **_bold italics_** indicate pages with photographs.

Abramowitz, Morton 154, 174, 182, 194, **_195_**, 203, 204, 205, 206, 213, 236, 239, 246, 263
Abramowitz, Sheppie 187, 193, 263
Aderholt, Heinie 49, 55–56, 57, 263
Afghan refugees 230
AFL/CIO 124
Agency for International Development (USAID or AID) 19, 29, 48, 51, 53, 81, 82, 103, 105, 110, 118, 153–154, 156, 239–240
Ahern, John 125, 126
Air America 9, 51, 105
Air Force, U.S. 47, 51, 52, 62, 63, 65
Amar, Francis 176
Amarillo, Texas 197
American Council for Nationality Services (ACNS) 155
American Council of Voluntary Agencies (ACVA) 127
American Friends Service Committee (AFSC) 66, 75–76, 213, 236
Amnesty International 147
An Ngo 157
Anambas Islands 155
Andelman, David 58
Andersen AFB 62, 63
Angkor (Wat) 32, 144, 175, 241
Aplin, Billy Joe 98
Aranyaprathet, Thailand 171, 174, 184, 186, 196, 197, 200, 204
Arlington, Virginia 96
ASEAN 145, 162–163
Ashe, Robert 184, 200, 201, 203, 207, 221
Australia 122, 150, 158, 159, 174, 217

Baez, Joan 146–147
Ban Me Thout 7
Ban Sangae 200
Ban Vinai 60–61, 226–230
Bangkok, Thailand 29, 36, 46, 52, 55, 126, 127, 128, 129, 151, 173, 174, 175, 177, 180, 197, 206, 210, 211, 225, 228, 229, 235, 238, 239, 240, 241, 242; refugee office 103–119
Bangladesh 216
Baptists 88, 94
"bar girls" 91–92, 93
Barber, Martin 236, 237
Barron, John 40; Congressional hearing 131–133
Battambang, Cambodia 41
Beaumont, Texas 87
Becker, Elizabeth 136, 137
Berrigan, Daniel 146
Berta, Cesare 117
Bidong Island 156–160
Bird Air 55, 56, 58
"Boat People" 122, 126, 150–170, 234, 237
Bordallo, Ricardo (Ricky) 63
Border Camps (Cambodian) 200–226, 231
Borton, Nan 127
Boyce, Harold 158
Bradley, Ed 135
Broken Bow, Oklahoma 85
Brown, Edmund G. (Jerry) 62, 85, 95
Brown, Mark Malloch see Malloch Brown, Mark
Bu Tith 110
Buckner Children's Home 88–89
Buell, Pop 49–51, 52, 53, 103, 105
Buffalo, New York 95
Bullington, Jim 6
Burlington, Vermont 158

Calabia, Dawn 263
Caldwell, Malcolm 131, 136–137, 144
Calhoun, Olnie 78
California 85, 95, 96
Cam Ranh Bay 8, 9, 88
Cambodia 1, 2, 3, 7, 13, 62, 103, 116, 148, 181, 219, 220; border camps 200–226, 231, 240; fall to Khmer Rouge 32–46; famine 182–187, 209–216; holocaust 130–138, 179, 237,

269

241; land bridge 200–209; Vietnamese rule 143–145
Cambodian refugees 35, 45–46, 52, 82, 93, 107, 114, 130–134, 165, 166, 234, 235, 243; border camps 200–226, 231; push back 171–178; Thai camps 182–199
Canada 93, 122, 217 ; boat people 150–151, 158–159, 160
CARE 231
Carr, Mike 111
Carter, Alan 2, 30–31, 82
Carter, Jimmy 126, 140, 145, 163, 175, 209
Carter, Rosalynn 191, *192*
Casey, William 123, 124
CAT IV 155
Catholic Relief Services (CRS) 177
Central Intelligence Agency (CIA) 2, 9, 34, 49, 51, 53, 54, 58, 83, 105, 108, 115, 123, 127, 147, 161, 163, 242
Chaffee, Fort 94, 95, 96; resettlement 78–90
Chamy Thor 59–60
Chanda, Nayan 143, 145, 148
Chandler, David 132, 134, 135
Chapman, Leonard F. 77
Chavez, Cesar 146
Cherne, Leo 122–123, 125–126, 130, 157, 212, 236, 237
Childress, Dick 245
China 2, 3, 37, 120, 130, 142–143, 144–146, 150, 158, 161–162, 165, 172, 173, 206, 235
Cholon 142
Chonburi, Thailand 224
Christian Outreach 184
Church of Latter Day Saints 80
Church World Services (CWS) 80, 213
Citizens Commission on Indochinese Refugees 123–126, 237
Colby, William 61
Congress, U.S. 10–11, 14, 38, 44, 69, 91, 108, 109, 116–117, 125–126, 128–129, 140–141, 144, 152, 209, 218, 223, 235, 236, 238, 244; Cambodia hearing 212–214; Solarz hearing 132–135
Connolly, Mike 158–159
Connors, Jimmy 13
Continental Air Services 34, 45, 52, 56, 105
Continental Airlines 17
Continental Oil Company 154
Convoy of Tears 8
Cope, John 88–89
Corcos, Albert 113, 117, 127, 263
Crisfield, Arthur 104
Crowley, John 175, 191, 198
CSM, CSB 233
Culpepper, Patty 111, 263
Cushing, Henry "Hank" 110, 154, 238, 239

Danang (Da Nang) 8, 9, 55
Daniels, Jerry 47, *50*, 51, 53, 54, 60, 105, 106, 108, 111–114, 117, 127, 154, 230, 246; death 241–243; evacuation of Long Tieng 55–58

Davidson 94
Day, Charlene 196, 226, 263
Dean, John Gunther 36
Dega *see* Montagnard
Dehart, David 89
Deng Xiaoping 145
Department of Health, Education, and Welfare 76, 80
Department of State 2, 3, 11, 13, 21, 52, 67, 75, 77, 82, 84, 106, 107, 109–110, 118, 126–128, 156, 158, 164, 165, 206, 214, 235, 236, 237, 246; refugee office 120–121, 154, 238, 239, 245
Derian, Patricia M. 121
Desbarats, Jacqueline 141
DeVecchi, Robert 80, 123, 127
Devlin, Joe 167
Dith Pran 44; escape 178–180, 181
Doctors Without Borders 184
"Dodge City" 18, 22
Drago, Ron 127
Dudman, Richard 136
Duong Cong Son (Sonnie) 20

Eagleburger, Lawrence 11
Eckes, Jim 17, 19, 45, 263
Edwards, Ellis 20, 85
Eiland, Mike 204, 243–244, 246, 263
Eilberg, Joshua 116–117, 125–126, 128–129
Elgin Air Force Base 78, 86, 90
Embassy, American (Bangkok) 103, 104, 105, 109, 112, 184, 193, 198, 225, 240, 241, 242
Embassy, American (Saigon) 6, 7, 9, 12, 16–17, 140; evacuation 21–27
Embassy, American (Vientiane) 36–37, 55
Embassy, French (Phnom Penh) 37, 44–45
Enders, Arthur "Skip" 263
Espanola, New Mexico 114
Estes, Barbara 97
Etcheson, Craig 138

Family reunification 87–88, 218
Fayetteville, Arkansas 89
FBI 118, 127, 240
Feldman, Sam 106
Fenwick, Millicent 38, 213, 214
Finley, Lowell 147
Finney, John 123
Fish, Hamilton 11
Fisher, Gene 98
Fishermen 91–92, 96–99
Fitzgerald, Frances 97
Food distribution 230–233
Food for the Hungry 190
Ford, Betty 79
Ford, Gerald 5, 11, 31, 70, 79, 87; speech 14–15
Fort Smith, Arkansas 95
France 2, 32, 93, 102, 104, 122, 140, 158, 159, 174, 214, 217, 235, 240
Francis, Albert 8, 9, 82

French Guiana 101-102
Furrer, Kurt 33, 36, 45, 173, 203, 239-240

Gardener, Norm 52
Geneva, Switzerland 161, 163, 169
Go Dau 219
Golden Palace, Bangkok 112
Grace, Dennis 245
Grannis, Oklahoma 85
Green, Supawan 190-191
Green Berets see Special Forces, U.S.
Greensboro, North Carolina 246
Guam 62-71, 77, 78, 80, 91, 105
Guldam, Georgia 225

Ha, Kim and family 148, 218-226
Habib, Phillip C. 11, 106
Hackworth, Col. David 8
Hai Hong 151, 159
Haig, Alexander 229
Hamilton, Ian 151
Hamilton-Merritt, Jane 61
Hannan, Phillip M. 87
Hannibal, Missouri 168
Hartling, Poul 234
Hartmann, Robert 14
Hatfield, Mark 245
Heng Samrin 183, 207, 209
Hermann, David 81
Herr, Paul (Pao) 263
Herrington, Stuart 26
Hickey, Gerald 30
Hickory, North Carolina 100
Hildebrand, George 132
Hmong 2, 148-149, 241, 242; "secret army" 47-61
Hmong refugees 52-53, 59-61, 115, 123, 148, 167, 184, 218, 241-243; Ban Vinai 226-230; polygamy 112-113; resettlement 99-102, 106, 228-229; in Thailand 103-109, 226-230
Ho Chi Minh 10, 74, 224
Ho Chi Minh City see Saigon
Hoa 142-143, 152, 158
Hoang Van Cuong 26
Hoff, Matt 55-56
"Hog" see Daniels, Jerry
Holbrooke, Richard 120, 128, 140, 154, **192**, 213
Holtzman, Elizabeth 129
Hong Kong 122, 155, 160, 226, 234, 235
Howell, Charlene Day see Day, Charlene
Huddleston, Walter 235, 236, 237
Hue (city) 8
Hun Sen 183
Huu (driver) 17, 18

Immigration and Naturalization Service (INS) 75, 82, 106, 111, 118, 154, 158-159, 217, 225, 233, 235, 238, 246; "reign of terror" 243-245

Indiantown Gap, Fort 77-90
Indochina 1-3, 62, 103, 115, 139, 149, 160, 207, 237, 245, 246; see also Cambodia; Laos; Vietnam
Indochinese refugees 2, 52, 68, 75, 79, 110, 112, 116, 117, 122, 124, 126, 128, 159, 230, 234, 235, 238, 243, 244; criteria for admission 76; numbers 1, 163, 235, 236, 237, 244, 246; in the United States 91-102
Indonesia 122, 123, 165, 235, 246; boat people 150-156, 160, 162
Interagency Task Force (IATF) 11, 64, 69, 75, 79, 80, 82, 83, 90, 92, 107
Intergovernmental Committee on European Migration (ICEM) 10, 111, 112, 117, 127
International Committee of the Red Cross (ICRC) 176, 183, 184, 197, 206, 207, 209-214, 221, 222, 223, 224, 240
International Rescue Committee (IRC) 80, 122, 126, 128, 184, 185, 222
International Voluntary Service (IVS) 49, 105

Jacobson, Col George D. 12
Jacques, Leslie 36
Japan 93, 166
Jenkin, G.R. 54, 263
Jenkins, Ron 94
Johnstone, Craig 13, 14, 15, 16-19, 31, 63-64, 77
Joint Volunteer Agency (JVA) 112, 126-128, 154-156, 158, 180, 196, 217, 225, 227, 233, 243-244, 245, 246
Jonesboro, Arkansas 84
Jordan, Vernon 75
Judge, Darwin 22

K-Mix-II 232
Kamm, Henry 32, 44, 121, 177
Kamol Prachuabmoh 263
Kampong Som 211
Kampuchean Emergency Group (KEG) 204-207
Kamput 197, 243-244
Kann, Peter 58
Kean, James 27
Kelly, Gail 84, 95
Kennedy, Edward M. 76
Khao I Dang 194-199, 200, 234
Khien Theeravit 171
Khmer, Khmer Republic, Kampuchea see Cambodia
Khmer Rouge 2, 7, 53, 74, 77, 107, 110, 114, 115, 116, 162, 171, 172, 178, 180, 181, 182, 183, 184, 188, 194, 196, 198, 199, 204, 206, 207, 210, 216, 219, 220, 245, 246; holocaust 130-138; take over Cambodia 32-46
Khmer Serei 171, 172, 194, 216, 220
Kiernan, Ben 135, 138
Killing Fields 44, 178
Kim Ha see Ha, Kim

Kingsport, Tennessee 85
Kinlen Dermot 147
Kirk, Donald 33, 43, 44
Kissinger, Henry 7, 10, 14, 45, 64, 69, 70, 107, 140
Klein, Wells 155
Knotts, Jack 58
Ko Kra 168–169
Kocher, Judy 114, 180–181, 196, 263
Kocher, Rich 114, 174, 180, 263
Kompong Som 34
Kong Sileah 201
Kontum 7
Kouba, Dave 58
Krakor 133
Kriangsak, Prime Minister 187
Ku Klux Klan 98–99
Kuala Lumpur, Malaysia 150
Kue Chaw 56–57, 60, 100–101, 263
Kuntsler, William 147

Lafayette, Louisiana 87
Lair, Bill 49, 115
Land Bridge 201–209, 210, 213, 214, 215, 216, 221
Lao refugees 52, 103, 116, 121, 123, 154, 166, 226–227, 228, 234, 235; *see also* Hmong refugees
Lao Theung 48
Laos 1, 3, 7, 34, 62, 103, 143, 148–149, 233, 242; population 3; takeover by communists 47–59
Le Carré, John 241
Lee Kwan Yew 162
Lenderking, Bill 188
Lenderking, Susan 187–189, **190**, 263
Le Van Me family 94–95
Leviton, Carol 114
Lewis, Anthony 47
Lewis, David 81, 85, 87, 90, 263
Loei Province 113
Lon Nol 33, 35, 37, 44, 176
Long Boret 37
Long Tieng 53, **54**, 59, 100; evacuation 55–58
Lowman, Hiep 21
Lowman, Shep 109–110, 112, 121–123, 125–127, 154–156, 166, 239, 263; Saigon evacuation 21–23
Lu Phuoc 152
Luang Prabang 48
"lunch group 6, 11, 43
Lutheran Immigration and Refugee Service (LIRS) 80, 82, 85

Macau 235
Mackie, Richard 62–63, 66
Madam Lulu's 51–52, 59
Mak Mun 200, 204, 207, 231
Malaysia 122, 123, 165, 235, 246; boat people 150–151, 155–160, 162

Malloch Brown, Mark 184, 187, 193, 194, 196, 198
Manila 29, 91, 151
Mao Moua 101
Mao Zedong 42
Marathon Oil Company 155
Mariel, Robert Lee 98
Marines, U.S. 7, 9, 36, 81; Saigon evacuation 22–27, 28
Marshalltown, Iowa 22
Martin, Graham 6, 10, 14, 21, 25
Martinez, Efrain 97–99
Maxwell, Sally 111
Mazzoli, Congressman 129
McBride, Joe 17, 23–25, 263
McGovern, George 62
McGrory, Mary 212
McMahon, Charles Jr. 22
McManaway, Clay 11, 263
Mekong River and delta 13, 34, 35, 48, 59, 60, 86, 103, 123, 144, 228
Meo *see* Hmong
Michener, James 123
Mien 103, **232**
Military, U.S. 2, 14, 47–48, 63, 78; *see also* Air Force, U.S.; Marines, U.S., Navy, U.S.
Minneapolis, Minnesota 99
Minnesota 99, 102
Missoula, Montana 61, 101, 105, 241, 242
Mlo (pseud) 263
Mondale, Walter 164, 182
Mondulkiri 245
Montagnards 5, 8, 11–12, 29–30, 48, 49, 78, 141, 148; rescue 245–246
Montana 47, 61, 105
Moorefield, Ken 18, 23, 26
Morrison, George S. 63, 64, 77
Morrison, Jim 63
Morton, Sue 46, 163, 196, 239, 263
Mote, Sue Murphy 59
Mott, Russell 9
Moua Sue **50**
Mullin, Scott 151

Nader, Ralph 62
Nam Lik 59
Nam Pong 106
Nan Province 233
Navy, U.S. 8, 9, 27–29, 63, 86, 91
Negroponte, John 34
New Economic Zones 141–142, 219
New Orleans, Louisiana 14, 86, 87
Nguyen, Gene 95
Nguyen Thi Hue 16, 79, 263
Nguyen Van Nam 98–99
Nguyen Van Sau 98
Nguyen Xuan Ha 88
Nha Trang 9, 71
Nixon, Richard 7, 33, 140
Noel, Missouri 95

Non Governmental Organizations *see* Voluntary Agencies
Nong Chan 201, 202, 203, 207, 221, 222
Nong Khai 103, 123, 226, 227, 228
Nong Pru 200
Nong Samet 200, 204
North Vietnam 3, 140–141; victory of 5–31
North Vietnamese Army (NVA) 5, 7, 8, 12, 13, 14, 16, 22, 27, 33–34, 37, 53, 54, 56, 57, 61, 74, 88, 144
Northwest Nine (NW 9) 222, 223, 224
Nothdurft, Hans 193
Nung 103

Oakley, Bob 154
Obledo, Mario 85
Oferdorfer, Dan 8
Oklahoma City, Oklahoma 85
Olness, Karen 227
Opium 47, 52
Orderly Departure Program 165, 235
Oregon State University 181
OXFAM 209–214, 236

Pajaree Sritham (Tim) 111, 263
Pakse, Laos 105
Pan American Airlines 16, 19, 20
Panat Nikhom 224
Paquette, Paul 228, 232, 233, 263
"Para" 220–222
Paris Peace Accord 7, 34, 53, 140
Pathet Lao 7, 47, 48, 53, 54, 56, 57, 58, 59, 60, 148
Paul, Anthony 40, 131–133
Peace Corps 49, 111, 113, 114, 127, 154
Pendleton, Camp 78, 86, 90, 156
Phan Hien 140
Philadelphia 99, 100
Philippines 14, 16, 20, 22, 29, 52, 63, 91, 122, 145, 160, 235; Refugee Processing Centers 165–167
Phnom Penh 46, 133, 136, 137, 145, 176, 181, 183, 195, 207, 209–211, 215, 245; fall to Khmer Rouge 32–41
Phoenix program 13
Phon Hong 59
Phuoc Binh 5, 7
Pierpaoli, Manou 32–33, 173, 174
Pierpaoli, Olivier 35, 173
Pierpaoli, Yvette 45, 68, 203, 216, **241**; in Phnom Penh 32–35; Preah Vihear 173–177; Warner scandal 239–240
Pirates 152, 159, 167–170
Plain of Jars 47
Pleiku 7
Pol Pot 136, 137, 138, 207, 213
Ponchaud, François 38, 39, 43, 131, 134
Poole, Peter 132, 134
Port Arthur, Texas 96
Port Isabel, Texas 97
Porter, Gareth 130–136

"pot hunters" 197
Poteet, Joy 111
Pranai Suanrath 263
Preah Vihear 171–178, 182
Pride, Dan 113
Prisoners of War (POWs) 7, 140, 141
Provisional Revolutionary Government of South Vietnam 7, 66, 67, 139

Quakers 123; *see also* American Friends Service Committee
Quinn, Ken 5, 10, 43, 44, 77–78, 79, 263

Raleigh, North Carolina 245
Rangsit Transit Center 225
Ray, Robert 104
Red Crescent Society 157
Red Cross 82, 88, 184, 196; *see also* International Committee of the Red Cross
"Re-education" 72–74, 140, 141–142, 148–149
Refouler 68
Refugee Convention 67–68, 172, 173
Refugee Processing Centers (RFC) 165–166
Refugee resettlement, U.S. 75–90, 109, 127, 164, 211, 234, 236–238, 244
Refugees International 13, 163, 196, 239, 240
"REMF" 51, 56
"Les Rendevous des Amis" *see* Madame Lulu
Resettlement 68–69; 75–90, 106, 110, 126, 217, 235–238, 246–247
Rich, Allen 56
Robinson, Court 178
Rockoff, Al 39, 44, 178
Rogers, Arkansas 95
Rogers, Ron 19, 27–29, 263
Romero, Berta 35, 60, 111, 114, **124**, 154, 196, 263
Roque, Levi 184, 188, 190
Rose, Jerry 64
Rosenblatt, Ann Grosvenor 184, **185**, 186–187, 189, 191, 206, 263
Rosenblatt, Lionel 1, 5, 14, 15, 21, 33, 36, 43, 45, 50, 68, 70, 71, 77, 101, 109–110, 125, 126, 129, 152, 182, 184, 185, 191, **192**, 194, **195**, 197, 201, 203, 208, 228, 229, 237, 238–**241**, 245, 246, 263; bio 13, 30–31; on Guam 63–64; KEG 204–207; Montagnards 245–246; Preah Vihear 173–177; in Saigon 16–19; in Thailand 107–108, 111–118, 153–154, 164; in Washington 5–6, 106, 120–121
Rosslyn, Virginia 120
Round, Roswell 55
Ruebensall, Rich 204
Rustin, Bayard 123, **124**, 125, 126

Sa Kaeo 187–198, 200, 209, 214, 232, 234
Sadruddin Aga Khan 116
Sage, Bill 127
Saigon (Ho Chi Minh City) 2, 5–15, 36, 37, 55, 62, 64, 66, 67, 69, 74, 77, 82, 91, 96, 122,

140, 142, 145, 148, 150, 197, 219, 223, 246; evacuation 16–31
Sampson, W. J. 135
San Diego, California 92
San Jose, California 95
Sanam Kajormklam 263
Savannakhet, Laos 105
Schanberg, Sydney 44, 178, 181
Schill, Jim 53, 58, 238, 241, 263; boat people 153–156
Schweitzer, Ted 168–169
Scowcroft, Brent 70
Seabees 65
Seabrook, Texas 98
Seadrift, Texas 97, 98
Secord, Richard 263
Sedalia, Missouri 94
Shapp, Milton 77
Sharp, Bruce 135
Shawcross, William 132, 215
Shepard, George 263
Siem Reap 179–180
Sihanouk, Norodom 33, 37, 201, 207
Simpkins, Billy 94
Singapore 19, 88, 150, 154, 155, 162, 235
Sisowath Sirik Matak 37, 44, 45
"Sky" 53, 54, 56
Smith, William French 244
Snepp, Frank 10, 25–26
So Ko Tou 228
Solarz, Stephen 46, 263; Congressional hearing 132–135
Songkhla, Thailand 168, 236
Songsit Charuparn 263
Sophal Ear 131
South Vietnam 3, 63, 66, 71, 74, 92, 139, 140, 141; defeat of 5–31
Southern Cross 150–151, 159
Souvanna Phouma 54
Soviet Union 139, 143, 144, 148–149, 183, 204, 215, 229
Special Forces, U.S. 12, 94, 243
Sponsors 80, 84
"Standard Total Academic View on Cambodia" (STAV) 131, 132, 137
Stanfield, James 99
Stoessel, Walter J. 236
Strouse, Les 52, 56
Stutzman, Homer 119
Styron, William 146
Summers, Harry 21, 26–27
Swain, Jon 44, 178
Sweden 140

Taft, Julia 64, 69, 70, 107, 263; resettlement 75–90
Tan Son Nhut (airport) 14, 18, 22
Tanebaum, Marc 123
Tap Prik 200
Texas 96–97; fishermen 97–99
Thai Dam 103–104, 105

Thailand 22, 29, 48, 59, 99, 100, 121, 122, 123, 144, 145, 219, 246; boat people 152–154, 157, 160, 162, 210, 213, 214, 219, 234, 246; Cambodian border 46, 182–199; land bridge 200–209; new refugees 103–119; piracy 167–169; push back 171–178; refugee camps 60–61, 126, 221–233; refugee policy 171–173, 187; refugee population 152, 218, 234, 235
Thang 88, 89
Theroux, Paul 51
Thieu, President Nguyen Van 7, 11
Thomas, John 10
Thomas, Norman 74
Thompson, Larry 141
Thompson, MacAlan 3, 99, **104**, 105, 111, 113, 114, 117, 153, 154, 175, 204, 227, 242, 243–244, 263; fired 118–119; in Udorn 103–108
Tokyo, Japan 163
Tomsen, Peter 30, 263
Ton Thai Dinh 96
Topping, Al 19–20
Touneh Han Tho 29–30
Towey, Jim 245
Tran Dinh Tru 67–73, 273
Tran van Khoat, Peter 86–87, 96–97
Tron Ngoc Ann 21
Truong Nhu Trang 139–140
Tuan Ti Tran 159–160
Tucker, John 105, 106, 108, 111, 127, 154, 241, 263
Tulane University 14
Tung An 151
Tuong Tin 69–71, 73
Twining, Charles 46, 206

U-Tapao airbase 22
Udorn, Thailand 55, 57, 103, 104, 106, 108, 113, 118
Unaccompanied Minors (UAMs) 88–89, 244
United Nations 108, 139, 157, 169, 170, 171, 183, 191, 200, 205, 206, 212, 217, 231, 246
United Nations Children's Fund (UNICEF) 183, 184, 198, 206, 207, 209–211, 221, 231
United Nations High Commissioner for Refugees (UNHCR) 45, 111, 112, 116, 117, 124, 128, 130, 175, 177, 184, 187, 213, 216, 227, 234, 243; boat people 150–157 160–170, 191, 206, 236, 237; repatriation 67–69; 71, 73, 197–199, 207, 208
United States 1, 2, 6, 7, 33, 37–38, 44, 48, 53, 62, 70, 71, 132, 140, 141, 144, 145, 150, 163, 165, 173, 179, 182, 184, 193, 205–207, 212, 213, 217, 221, 227, 233, 236; refugees in 91–101; resettlement 75–90, 164, 211, 234, 236–238, 244; *see also* Washington, D.C.
USAID *see* Agency for International Development
United States Catholic Conference (USCC) 80, 81–82, 84, 89

Index

United States Information Service (USIS) 23, 30–31

Vang Meng 227–228
Vang Pao 48, 51, 53–55, 59–61, 101, 105, 148, 227, 229, 241; bio, 49; evacuation 57–58
Van Saren 200, 202
Vieira de Miello, Sergio 245–246
Vientiane, Laos 48, 51, 52, 54, 55, 59, 103, 105, 110, 226
Viet Cong *see* Provincial Revolutionary Government.
Vietnam 1, 2, 5–31, 33, 55, 61, 73, 75, 80, 81, 83, 85, 88, 103, 116, 138, 148, 149, 194, 213, 218–219, 222, 246; boat people 112, 150–165, 234; communist rule 139–146; on Guam 62–74; letter to 146–147; occupation of Cambodia 171, 179–183, 206–212, 214–216; war with China 145–146; war with KR 143–145, 171
Vietnam War 1, 2, 5–15, 33, 63, 146, 206, 212, 213, 229, 246, 247
Vietnamese refugees 5, 8, 52, 122, 234, 235; boat people 150–170; evacuation 16–30; Guam 63–66; land 217–226; numbers 6, 11, 14, 29, 65; repatriation 67–71; resettlement 75–90; in the United States 91–99
Voluntary Agencies (VOLAGs) 80–84, 108, 127–128, 171, 183, 191, 205, 209, 210, 211, 214, 221, 227, 230
Vung Tau 71, 86

Wake Island 65
Wannida Mekvishai 263
Warner, George 239–240
Warsaw, Missouri 94–95
Washington, D.C. 13, 43, 61, 96, 107, 109, 119, 155, 240; *see also* Congress, U.S.; Department of State
Wat Ko 174
Watts, Charlie 85
Watts, Clyde 20, 85
Weber, Phillip 75
Weinglass, Leonard 147
West, Gary 229
Wharton, Chris 114
"White Rose" 51–52, 58
Whitehouse, Charles 105, 107, 117
Wichita, Kansas 85
Williams, Richard 62
Wisner, Frank 5, 6, 67, 78, 80, 263
Woburn, Massachusetts 22
World Food Program 183, 206
World Vision 36, 184, 230
Wright, Lacey 10

Xuan Loc 14
Xuwicha Hiranprueck (Noi) 263

Yang Dao 106, 110
Yao 103
"Yellow Rain" 229–230

www.ingramcontent.com/pod-product-compliance
Ingram Content Group UK Ltd.
Pitfield, Milton Keynes, MK11 3LW, UK
UKHW041930140426
5217IPUK00014B/399